# An Illustrated Guide to
# SHARK ETIQUETTE

**Other Books by Jim Toomey**

*Sherman's Lagoon: Ate That, What's Next?*

*Poodle: The Other White Meat*

# An Illustrated Guide to Shark Etiquette

The Third Sherman's Lagoon Collection

by Jim Toomey

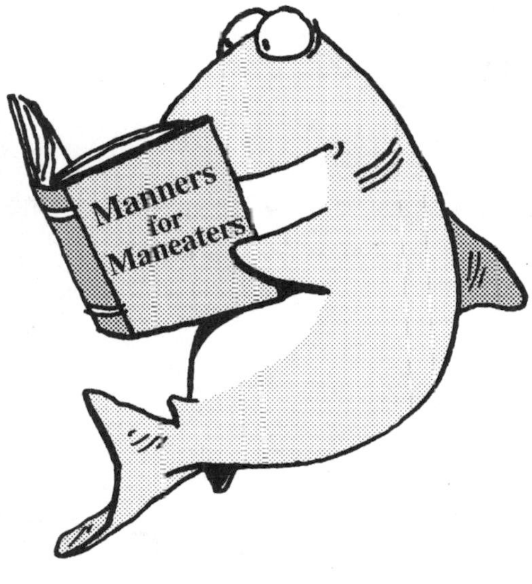
Manners for Maneaters

Andrews McMeel Publishing

Kansas City

**Sherman's Lagoon** is distributed internationally by King Features Syndicate, Inc. For information, write King Features Syndicate, Inc., 235 East 45th Street, New York, New York 10017.

00 01 02 03 04  BAH  10 9 8 7 6 5 4 3 2 1

ISBN: 0-7407-1247-0

Library of Congress Catalog Card Number: 00-103484

**Sherman's Lagoon** may be viewed on the Internet at:
www.slagoon.com

──────── **ATTENTION: SCHOOLS AND BUSINESSES** ────────

Andrews McMeel books are available at quantity discounts with bulk purchase for educational, business, or sales promotional use. For information, please write to: Special Sales Department, Andrews McMeel Publishing, 4520 Main Street, Kansas City, Missouri 64111.

**To Johnny**

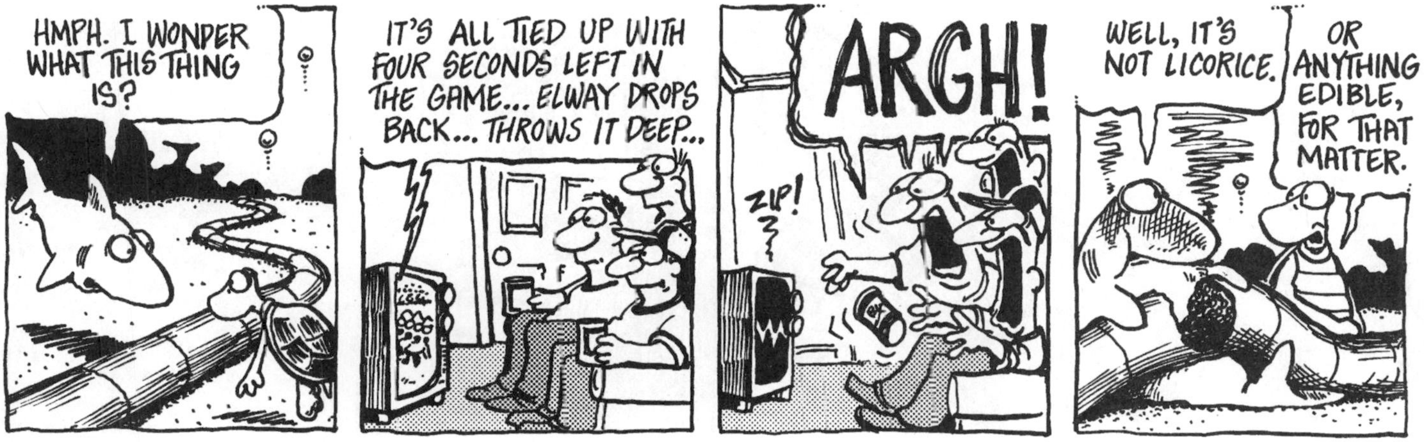
HMPH. I WONDER WHAT THIS THING IS?
IT'S ALL TIED UP WITH FOUR SECONDS LEFT IN THE GAME... ELWAY DROPS BACK... THROWS IT DEEP...
ARGH!
ZIP!
WELL, IT'S NOT LICORICE.
OR ANYTHING EDIBLE, FOR THAT MATTER.

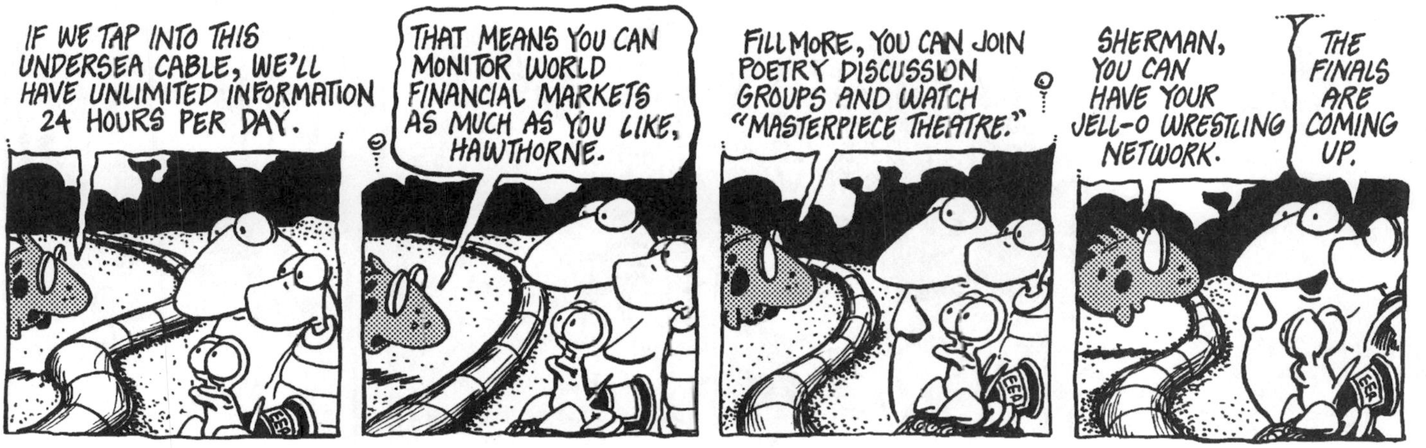
IF WE TAP INTO THIS UNDERSEA CABLE, WE'LL HAVE UNLIMITED INFORMATION 24 HOURS PER DAY.
THAT MEANS YOU CAN MONITOR WORLD FINANCIAL MARKETS AS MUCH AS YOU LIKE, HAWTHORNE.
FILLMORE, YOU CAN JOIN POETRY DISCUSSION GROUPS AND WATCH "MASTERPIECE THEATRE."
SHERMAN, YOU CAN HAVE YOUR JELL-O WRESTLING NETWORK.
THE FINALS ARE COMING UP.

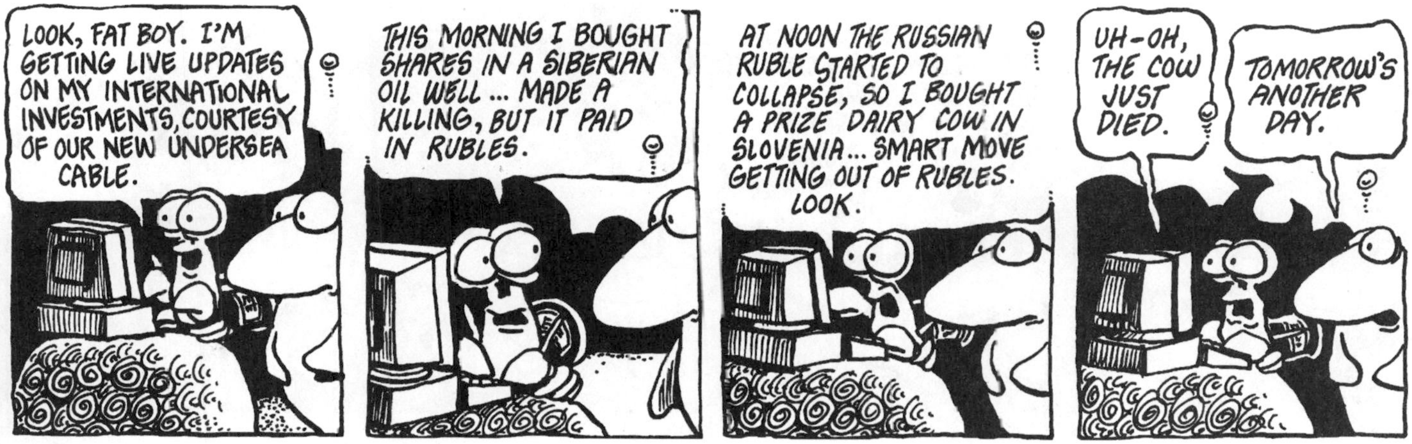
LOOK, FAT BOY. I'M GETTING LIVE UPDATES ON MY INTERNATIONAL INVESTMENTS, COURTESY OF OUR NEW UNDERSEA CABLE.
THIS MORNING I BOUGHT SHARES IN A SIBERIAN OIL WELL ... MADE A KILLING, BUT IT PAID IN RUBLES.
AT NOON THE RUSSIAN RUBLE STARTED TO COLLAPSE, SO I BOUGHT A PRIZE DAIRY COW IN SLOVENIA... SMART MOVE GETTING OUT OF RUBLES. LOOK.
UH-OH, THE COW JUST DIED.
TOMORROW'S ANOTHER DAY.

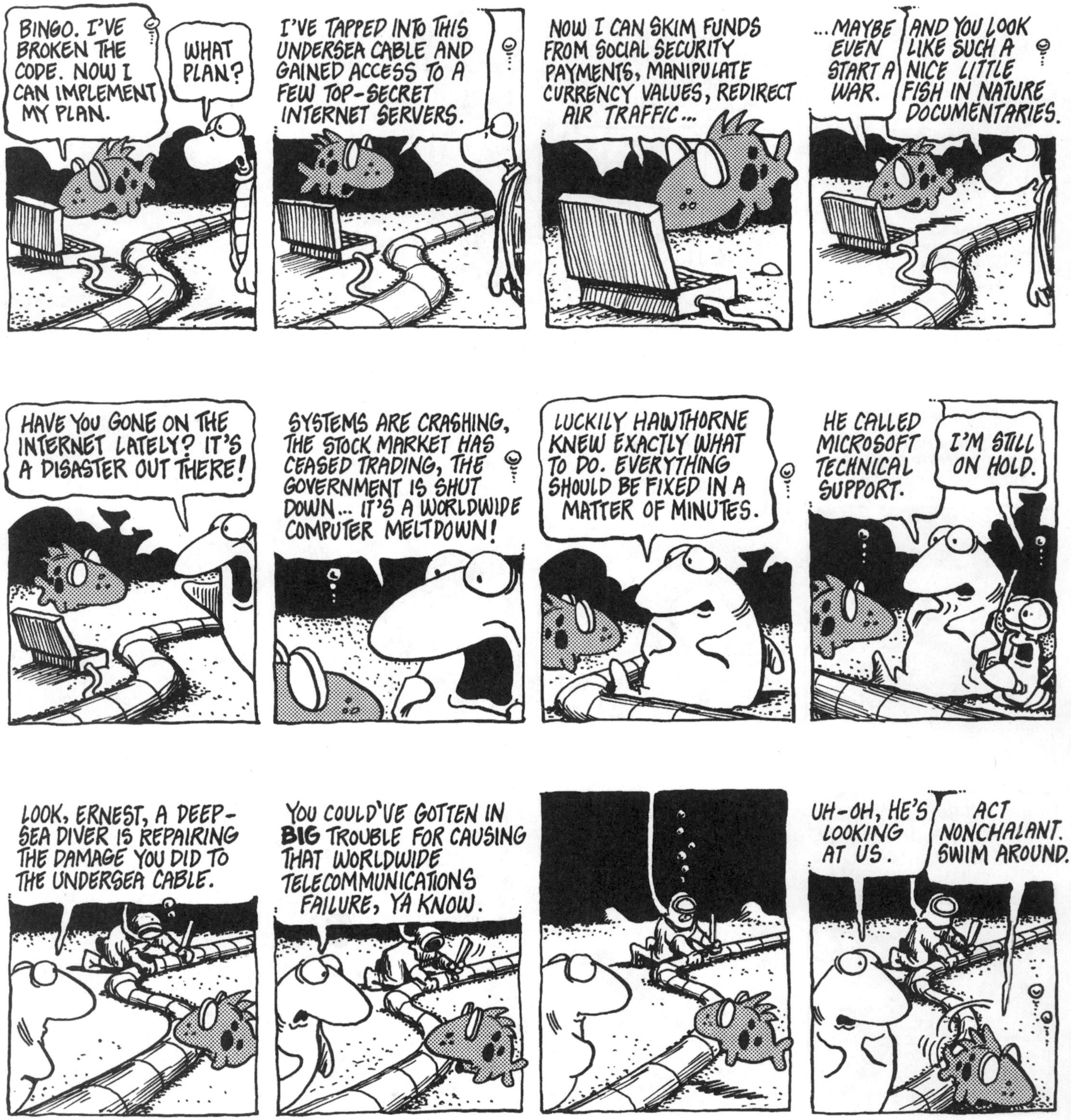
BINGO. I'VE BROKEN THE CODE. NOW I CAN IMPLEMENT MY PLAN.
WHAT PLAN?
I'VE TAPPED INTO THIS UNDERSEA CABLE AND GAINED ACCESS TO A FEW TOP-SECRET INTERNET SERVERS.
NOW I CAN SKIM FUNDS FROM SOCIAL SECURITY PAYMENTS, MANIPULATE CURRENCY VALUES, REDIRECT AIR TRAFFIC...
...MAYBE EVEN START A WAR.
AND YOU LOOK LIKE SUCH A NICE LITTLE FISH IN NATURE DOCUMENTARIES.
HAVE YOU GONE ON THE INTERNET LATELY? IT'S A DISASTER OUT THERE!
SYSTEMS ARE CRASHING, THE STOCK MARKET HAS CEASED TRADING, THE GOVERNMENT IS SHUT DOWN... IT'S A WORLDWIDE COMPUTER MELTDOWN!
LUCKILY HAWTHORNE KNEW EXACTLY WHAT TO DO. EVERYTHING SHOULD BE FIXED IN A MATTER OF MINUTES.
HE CALLED MICROSOFT TECHNICAL SUPPORT.
I'M STILL ON HOLD.
LOOK, ERNEST, A DEEP-SEA DIVER IS REPAIRING THE DAMAGE YOU DID TO THE UNDERSEA CABLE.
YOU COULD'VE GOTTEN IN BIG TROUBLE FOR CAUSING THAT WORLDWIDE TELECOMMUNICATIONS FAILURE, YA KNOW.
UH-OH, HE'S LOOKING AT US.
ACT NONCHALANT. SWIM AROUND.

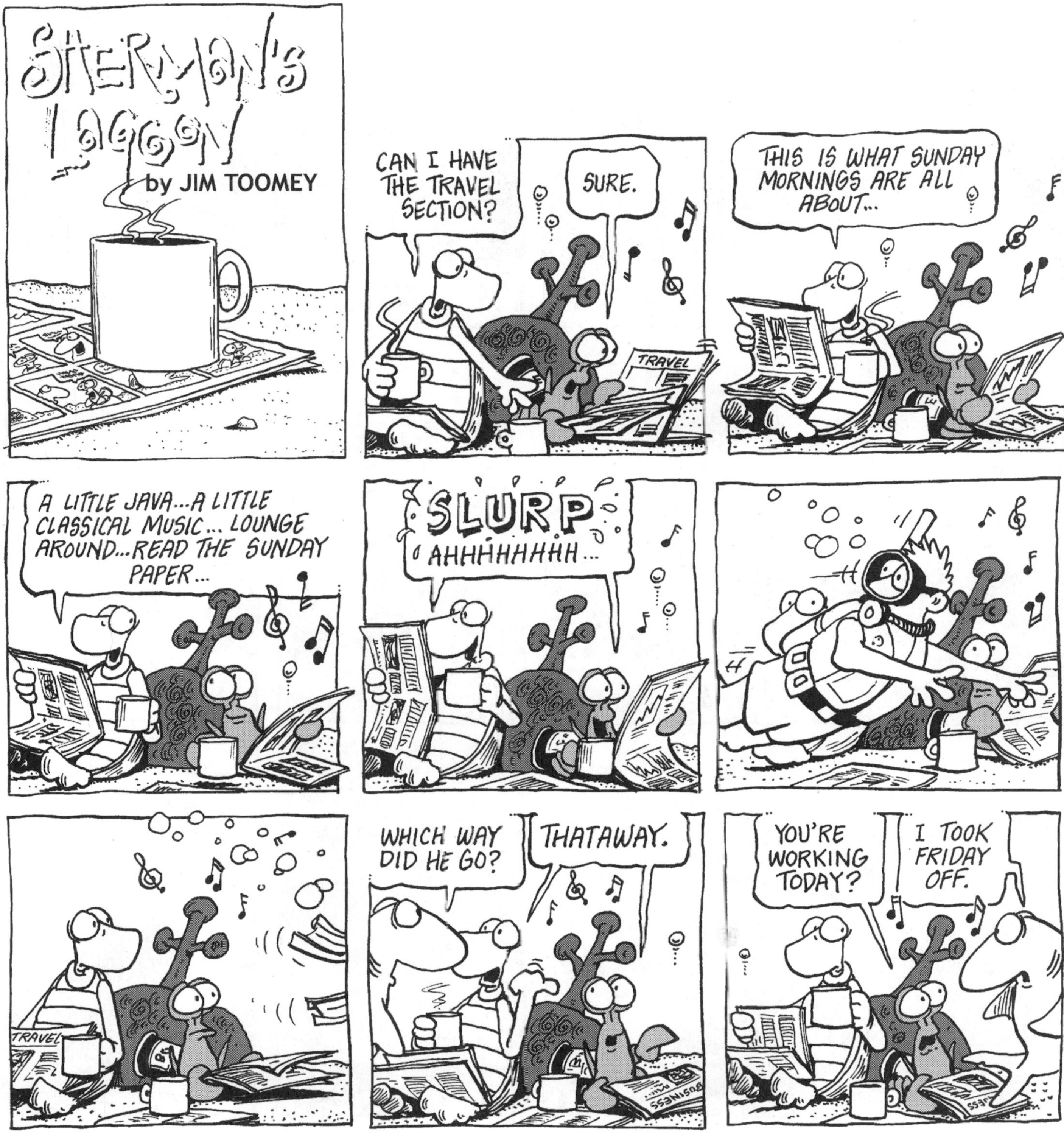
SHERMAN'S LAGOON
by JIM TOOMEY
CAN I HAVE THE TRAVEL SECTION?
SURE.
TRAVEL
THIS IS WHAT SUNDAY MORNINGS ARE ALL ABOUT...
A LITTLE JAVA...A LITTLE CLASSICAL MUSIC... LOUNGE AROUND...READ THE SUNDAY PAPER...
SLURP
AHHHHHHHH...
TRAVEL
WHICH WAY DID HE GO?
THATAWAY.
BUSINESS
YOU'RE WORKING TODAY?
I TOOK FRIDAY OFF.

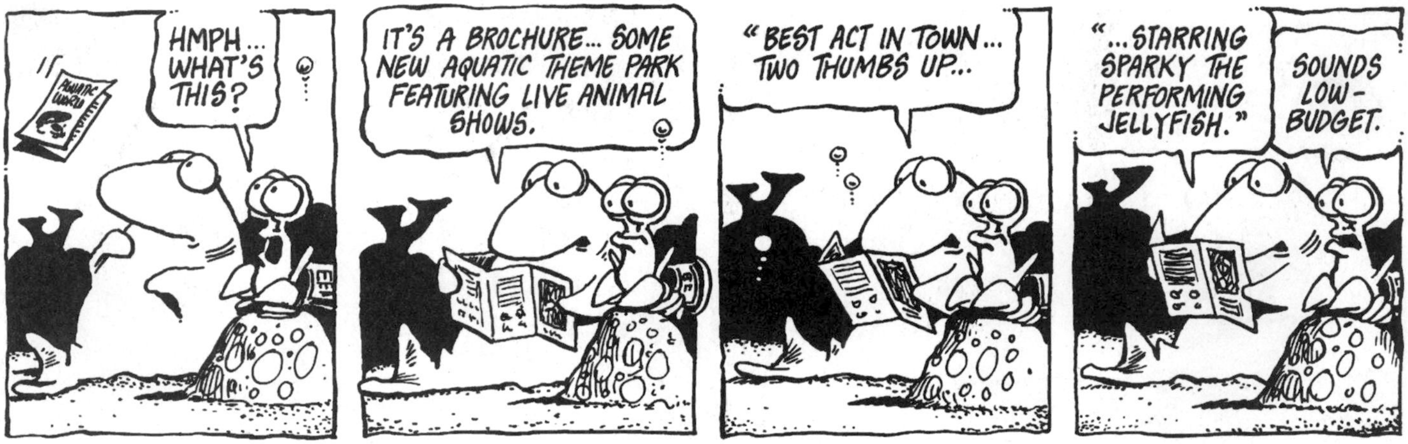
HMPH... WHAT'S THIS?
IT'S A BROCHURE... SOME NEW AQUATIC THEME PARK FEATURING LIVE ANIMAL SHOWS.
"BEST ACT IN TOWN... TWO THUMBS UP...
"...STARRING SPARKY THE PERFORMING JELLYFISH."
SOUNDS LOW-BUDGET.

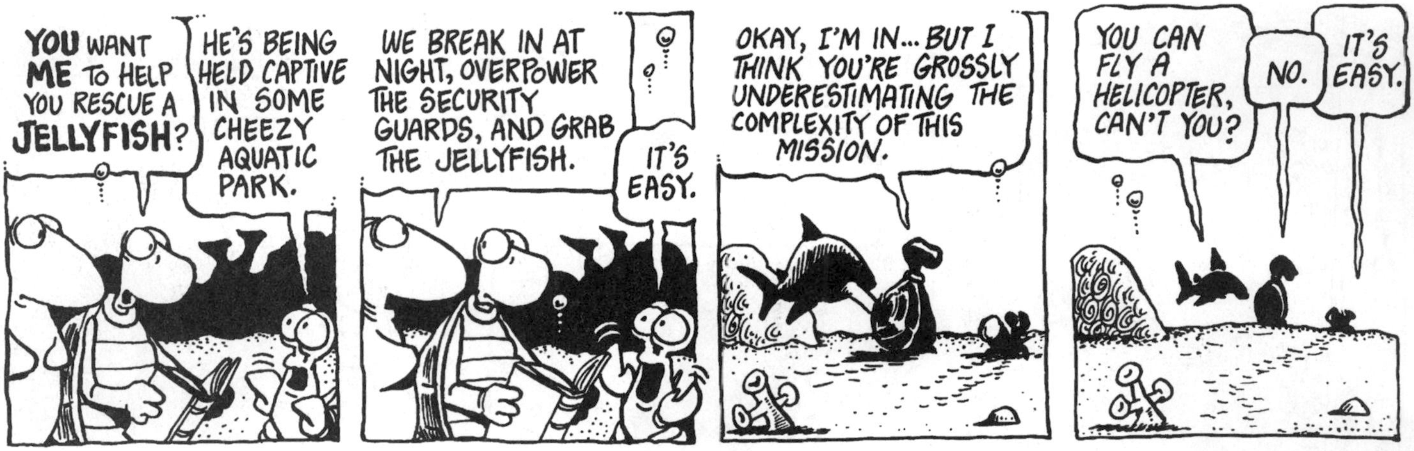
YOU WANT ME TO HELP YOU RESCUE A JELLYFISH?
HE'S BEING HELD CAPTIVE IN SOME CHEEZY AQUATIC PARK.
WE BREAK IN AT NIGHT, OVERPOWER THE SECURITY GUARDS, AND GRAB THE JELLYFISH.
IT'S EASY.
OKAY, I'M IN... BUT I THINK YOU'RE GROSSLY UNDERESTIMATING THE COMPLEXITY OF THIS MISSION.
YOU CAN FLY A HELICOPTER, CAN'T YOU?
NO.
IT'S EASY.

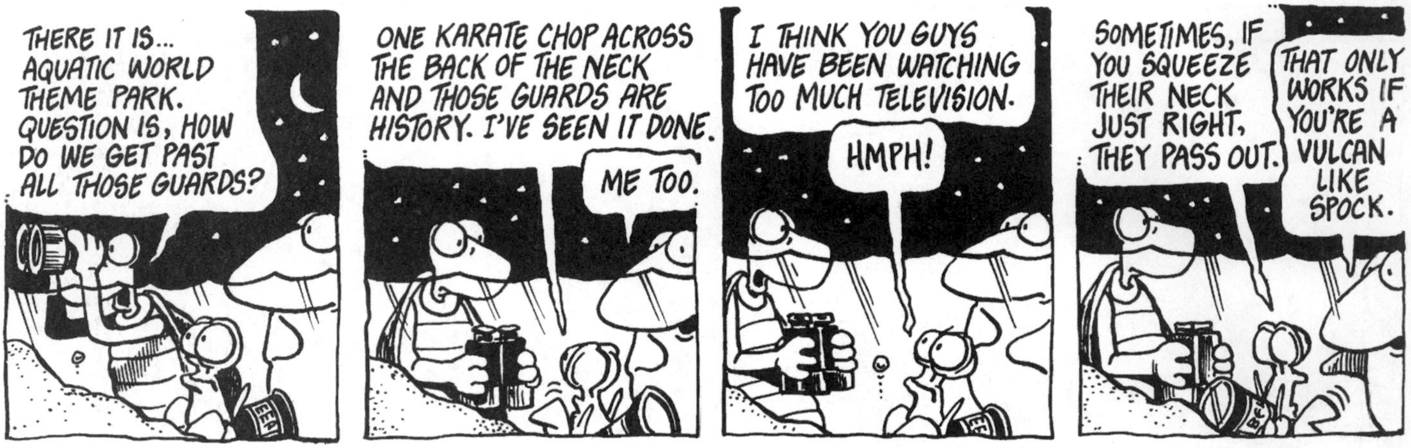
THERE IT IS... AQUATIC WORLD THEME PARK. QUESTION IS, HOW DO WE GET PAST ALL THOSE GUARDS?
ONE KARATE CHOP ACROSS THE BACK OF THE NECK AND THOSE GUARDS ARE HISTORY. I'VE SEEN IT DONE.
ME TOO.
I THINK YOU GUYS HAVE BEEN WATCHING TOO MUCH TELEVISION.
HMPH!
SOMETIMES, IF YOU SQUEEZE THEIR NECK JUST RIGHT, THEY PASS OUT.
THAT ONLY WORKS IF YOU'RE A VULCAN LIKE SPOCK.

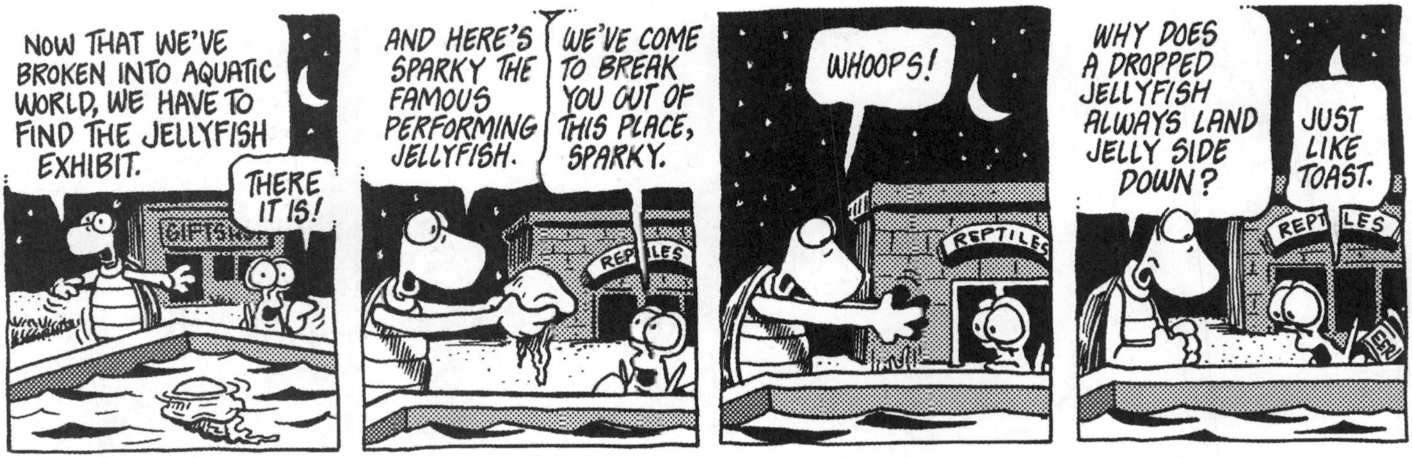
NOW THAT WE'VE BROKEN INTO AQUATIC WORLD, WE HAVE TO FIND THE JELLYFISH EXHIBIT.
THERE IT IS!
AND HERE'S SPARKY THE FAMOUS PERFORMING JELLYFISH.
WE'VE COME TO BREAK YOU OUT OF THIS PLACE, SPARKY.
REPTILES
WHOOPS!
REPTILES
WHY DOES A DROPPED JELLYFISH ALWAYS LAND JELLY SIDE DOWN?
JUST LIKE TOAST.

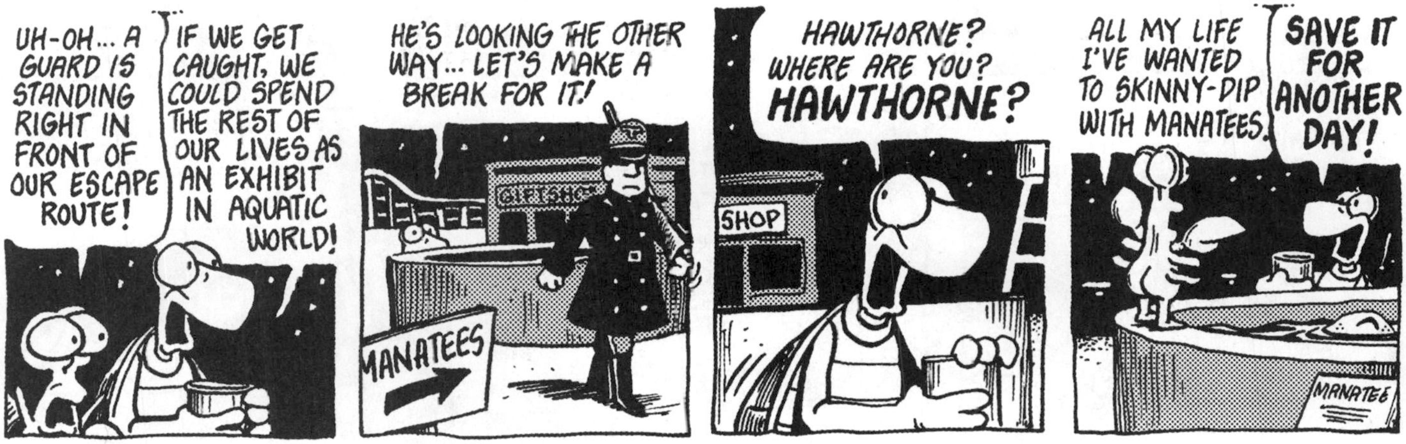
UH-OH... A GUARD IS STANDING RIGHT IN FRONT OF OUR ESCAPE ROUTE!
IF WE GET CAUGHT, WE COULD SPEND THE REST OF OUR LIVES AS AN EXHIBIT IN AQUATIC WORLD!
HE'S LOOKING THE OTHER WAY... LET'S MAKE A BREAK FOR IT!
MANATEES
HAWTHORNE? WHERE ARE YOU? HAWTHORNE?
SHOP
ALL MY LIFE I'VE WANTED TO SKINNY-DIP WITH MANATEES.
SAVE IT FOR ANOTHER DAY!
MANATEE

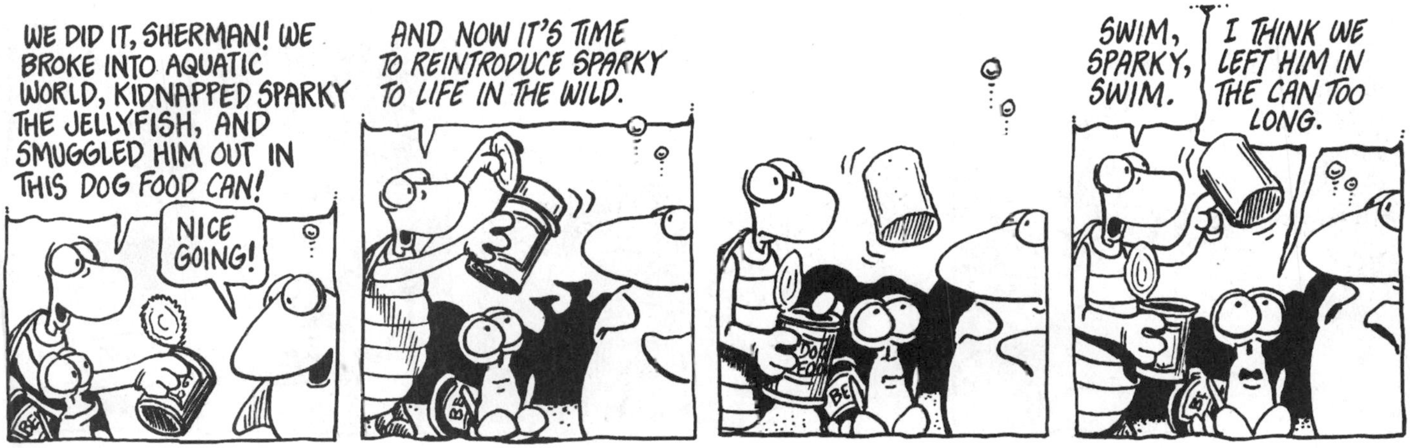
WE DID IT, SHERMAN! WE BROKE INTO AQUATIC WORLD, KIDNAPPED SPARKY THE JELLYFISH, AND SMUGGLED HIM OUT IN THIS DOG FOOD CAN!
NICE GOING!
AND NOW IT'S TIME TO REINTRODUCE SPARKY TO LIFE IN THE WILD.
SWIM, SPARKY, SWIM.
I THINK WE LEFT HIM IN THE CAN TOO LONG.

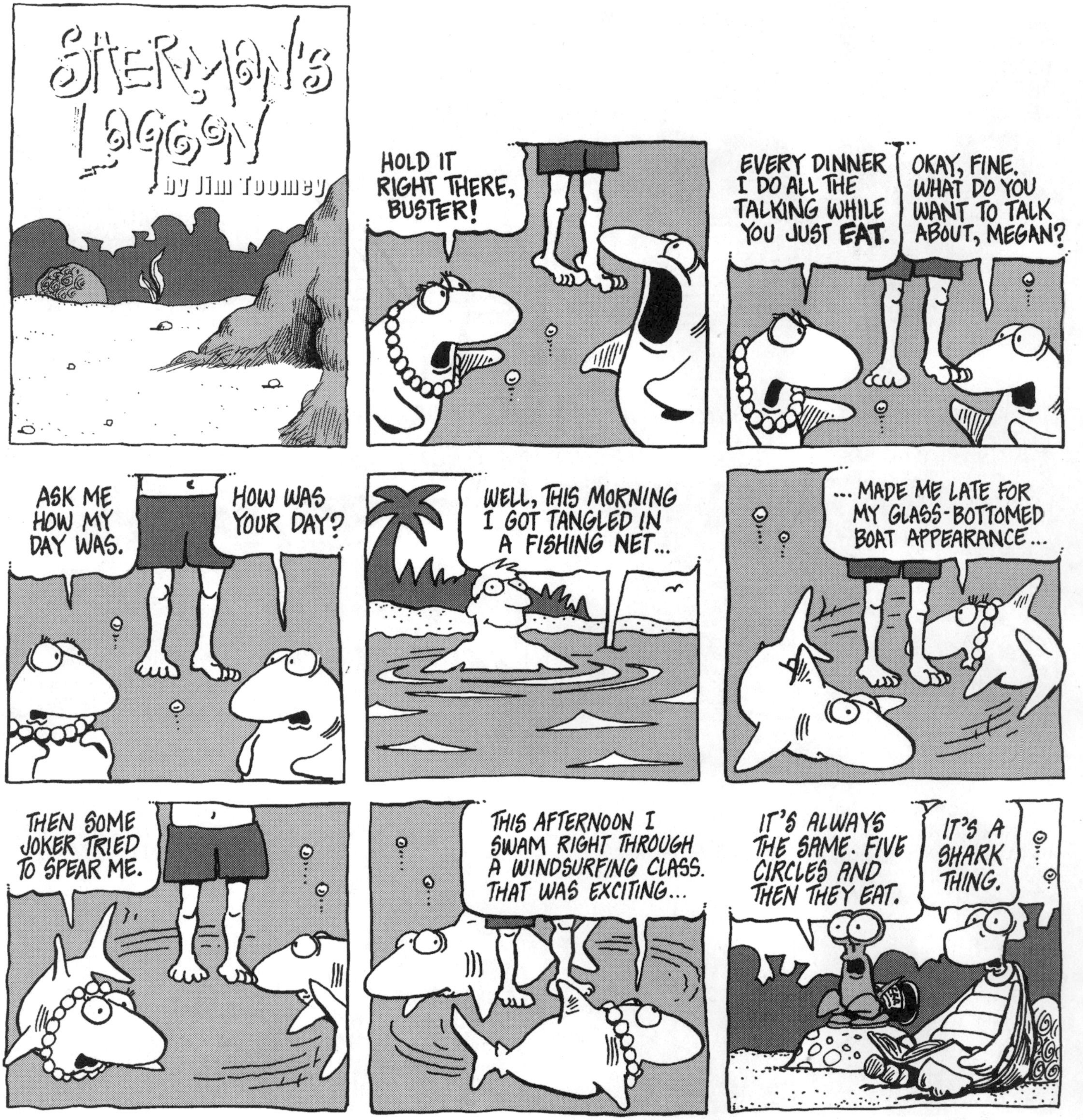
SHERMAN'S LAGOON
by Jim Toomey
HOLD IT RIGHT THERE, BUSTER!
EVERY DINNER I DO ALL THE TALKING WHILE YOU JUST EAT.
OKAY, FINE. WHAT DO YOU WANT TO TALK ABOUT, MEGAN?
ASK ME HOW MY DAY WAS.
HOW WAS YOUR DAY?
WELL, THIS MORNING I GOT TANGLED IN A FISHING NET...
... MADE ME LATE FOR MY GLASS-BOTTOMED BOAT APPEARANCE...
THEN SOME JOKER TRIED TO SPEAR ME.
THIS AFTERNOON I SWAM RIGHT THROUGH A WINDSURFING CLASS. THAT WAS EXCITING...
IT'S ALWAYS THE SAME. FIVE CIRCLES AND THEN THEY EAT.
IT'S A SHARK THING.

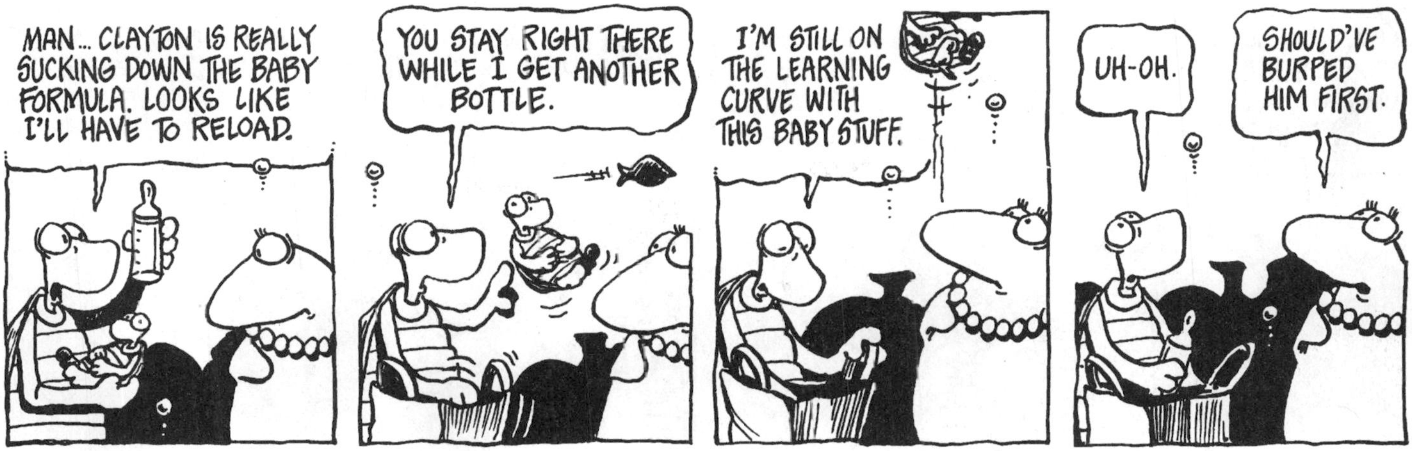
MAN... CLAYTON IS REALLY SUCKING DOWN THE BABY FORMULA. LOOKS LIKE I'LL HAVE TO RELOAD.
YOU STAY RIGHT THERE WHILE I GET ANOTHER BOTTLE.
I'M STILL ON THE LEARNING CURVE WITH THIS BABY STUFF.
UH-OH.
SHOULD'VE BURPED HIM FIRST.

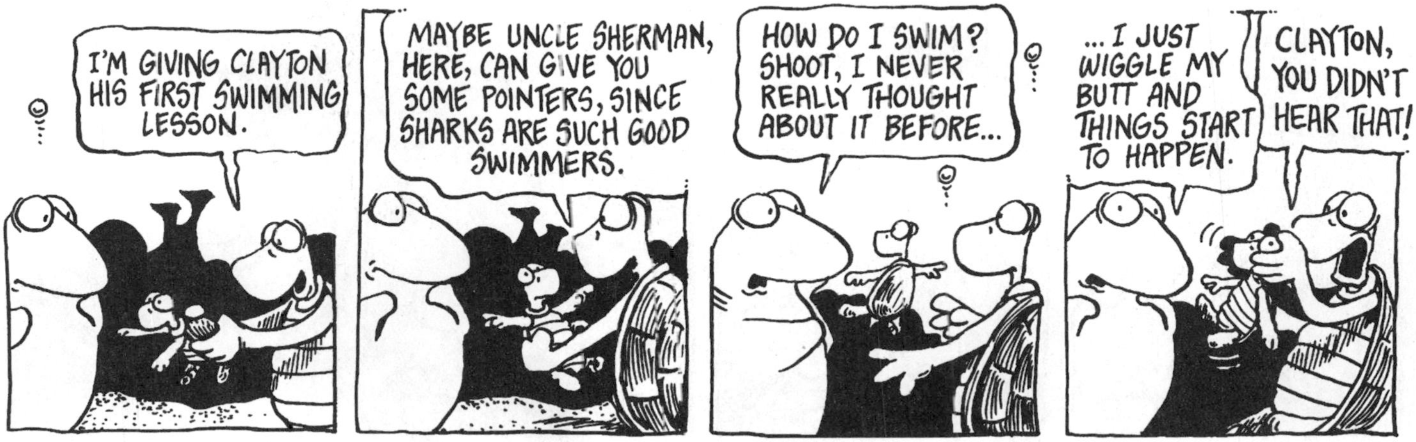
I'M GIVING CLAYTON HIS FIRST SWIMMING LESSON.
MAYBE UNCLE SHERMAN, HERE, CAN GIVE YOU SOME POINTERS, SINCE SHARKS ARE SUCH GOOD SWIMMERS.
HOW DO I SWIM? SHOOT, I NEVER REALLY THOUGHT ABOUT IT BEFORE...
... I JUST WIGGLE MY BUTT AND THINGS START TO HAPPEN.
CLAYTON, YOU DIDN'T HEAR THAT!

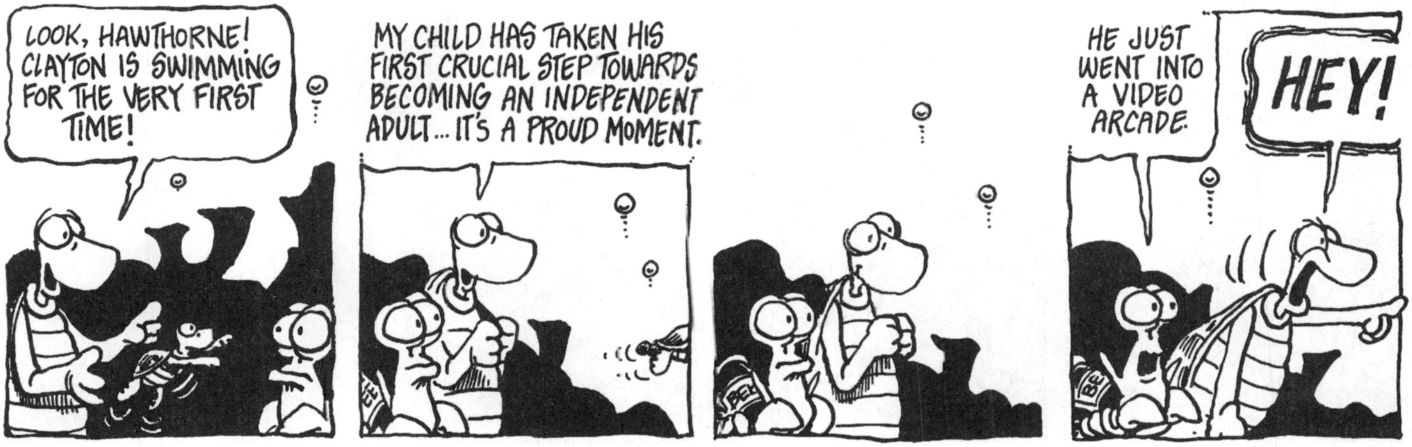
LOOK, HAWTHORNE! CLAYTON IS SWIMMING FOR THE VERY FIRST TIME!
MY CHILD HAS TAKEN HIS FIRST CRUCIAL STEP TOWARDS BECOMING AN INDEPENDENT ADULT... IT'S A PROUD MOMENT.
HE JUST WENT INTO A VIDEO ARCADE.
HEY!

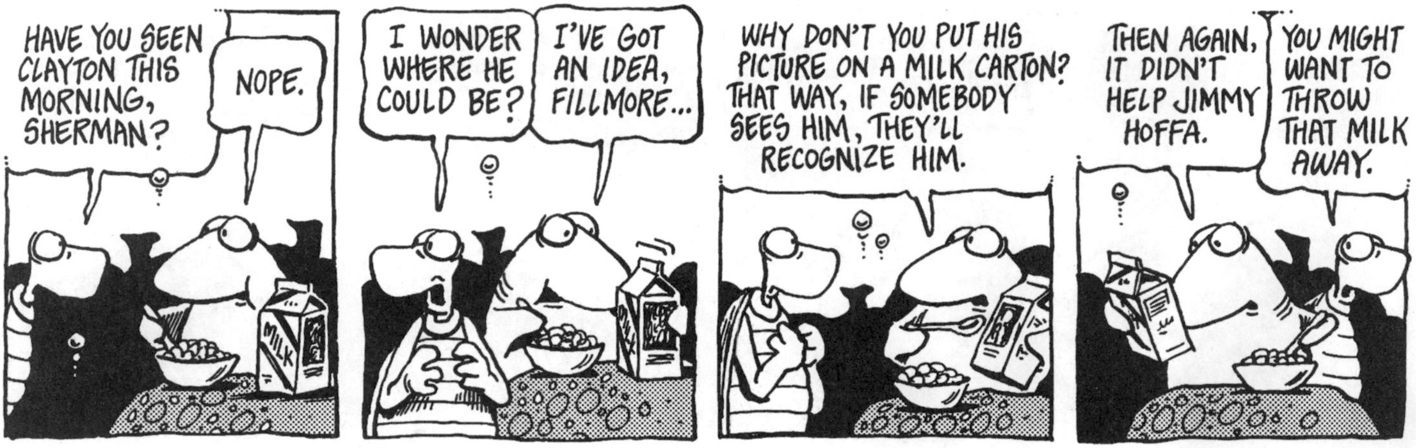
HAVE YOU SEEN CLAYTON THIS MORNING, SHERMAN?
NOPE.
MILK
I WONDER WHERE HE COULD BE?
I'VE GOT AN IDEA, FILLMORE...
WHY DON'T YOU PUT HIS PICTURE ON A MILK CARTON? THAT WAY, IF SOMEBODY SEES HIM, THEY'LL RECOGNIZE HIM.
THEN AGAIN, IT DIDN'T HELP JIMMY HOFFA.
YOU MIGHT WANT TO THROW THAT MILK AWAY.

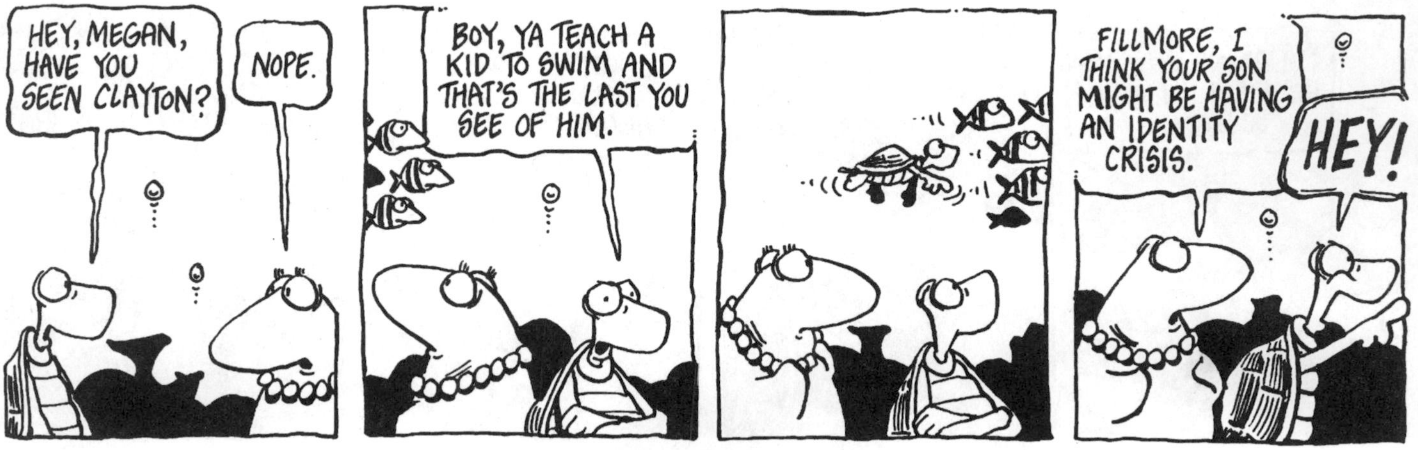
HEY, MEGAN, HAVE YOU SEEN CLAYTON?
NOPE.
BOY, YA TEACH A KID TO SWIM AND THAT'S THE LAST YOU SEE OF HIM.
FILLMORE, I THINK YOUR SON MIGHT BE HAVING AN IDENTITY CRISIS.
HEY!

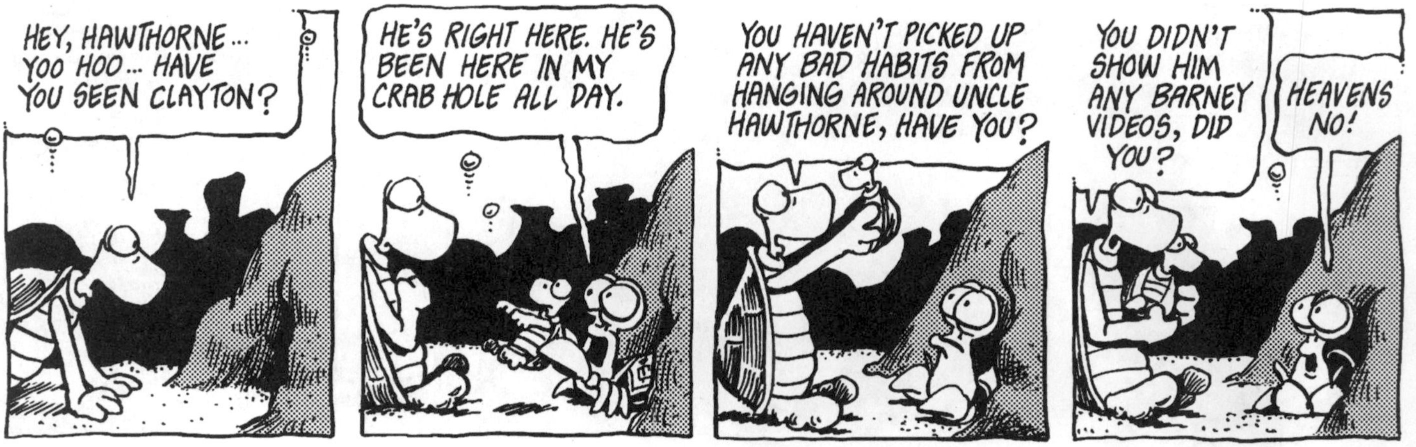
HEY, HAWTHORNE... YOO HOO... HAVE YOU SEEN CLAYTON?
HE'S RIGHT HERE. HE'S BEEN HERE IN MY CRAB HOLE ALL DAY.
YOU HAVEN'T PICKED UP ANY BAD HABITS FROM HANGING AROUND UNCLE HAWTHORNE, HAVE YOU?
YOU DIDN'T SHOW HIM ANY BARNEY VIDEOS, DID YOU?
HEAVENS NO!

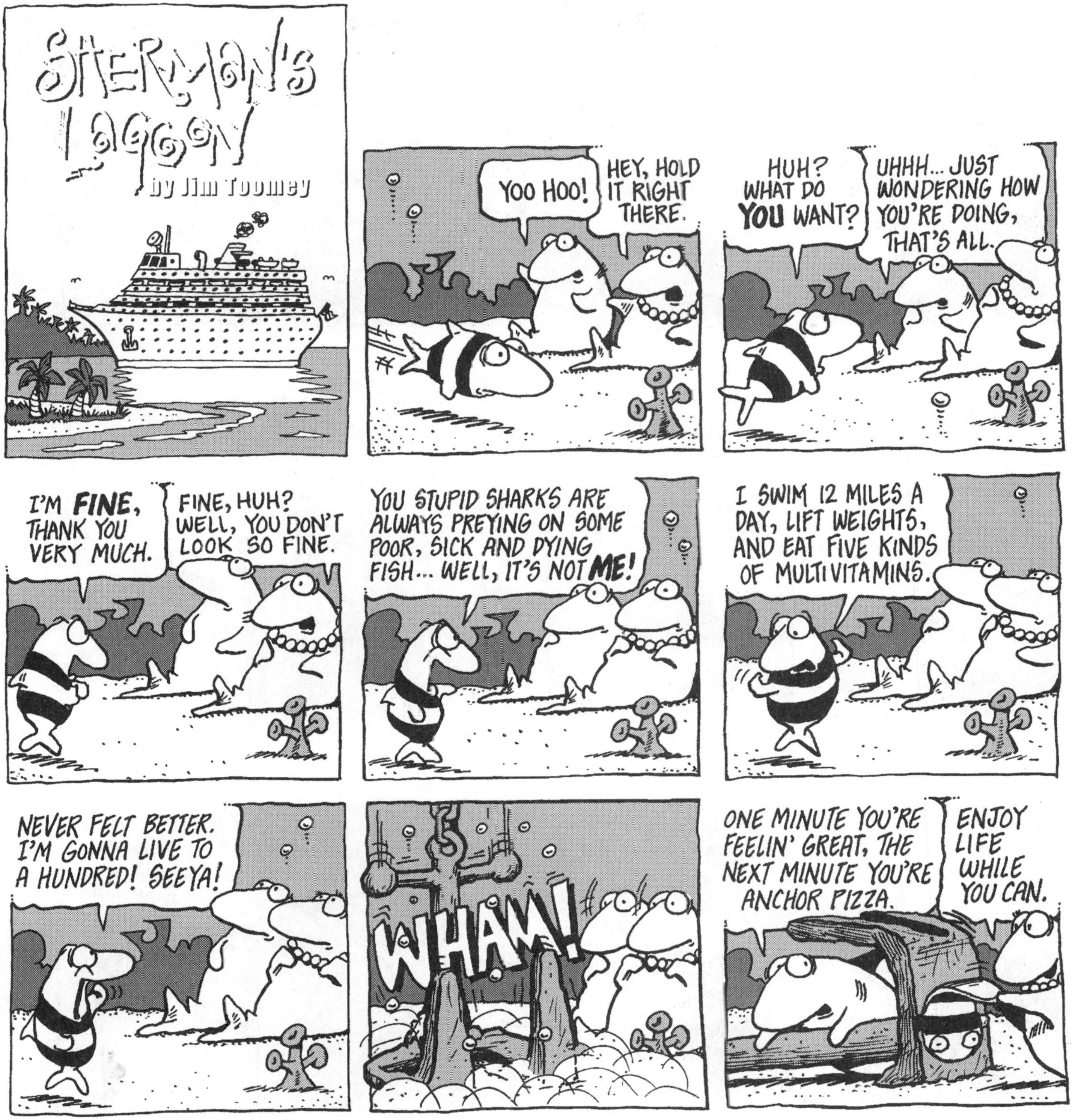
SHERMAN'S LAGOON
by Jim Toomey
YOO HOO!
HEY, HOLD IT RIGHT THERE.
HUH? WHAT DO YOU WANT?
UHHH... JUST WONDERING HOW YOU'RE DOING, THAT'S ALL.
I'M FINE, THANK YOU VERY MUCH.
FINE, HUH? WELL, YOU DON'T LOOK SO FINE.
YOU STUPID SHARKS ARE ALWAYS PREYING ON SOME POOR, SICK AND DYING FISH... WELL, IT'S NOT ME!
I SWIM 12 MILES A DAY, LIFT WEIGHTS, AND EAT FIVE KINDS OF MULTIVITAMINS.
NEVER FELT BETTER. I'M GONNA LIVE TO A HUNDRED! SEEYA!
WHAM!
ONE MINUTE YOU'RE FEELIN' GREAT, THE NEXT MINUTE YOU'RE ANCHOR PIZZA.
ENJOY LIFE WHILE YOU CAN.

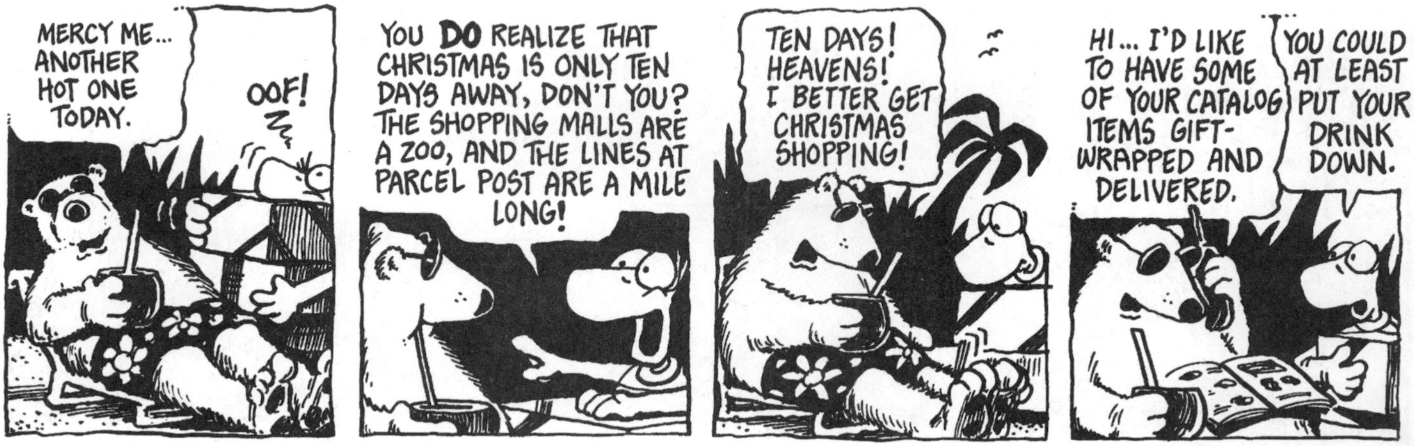
MERCY ME... ANOTHER HOT ONE TODAY.
OOF!
YOU **DO** REALIZE THAT CHRISTMAS IS ONLY TEN DAYS AWAY, DON'T YOU? THE SHOPPING MALLS ARE A ZOO, AND THE LINES AT PARCEL POST ARE A MILE LONG!
TEN DAYS! HEAVENS! I BETTER GET CHRISTMAS SHOPPING!
HI... I'D LIKE TO HAVE SOME OF YOUR CATALOG ITEMS GIFT-WRAPPED AND DELIVERED.
YOU COULD AT LEAST PUT YOUR DRINK DOWN.

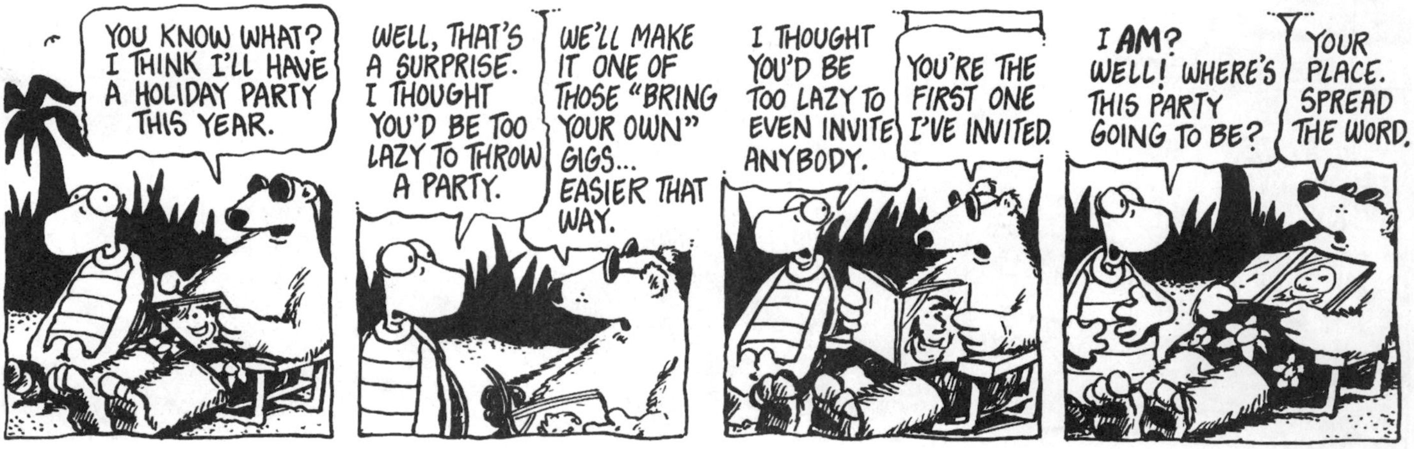
YOU KNOW WHAT? I THINK I'LL HAVE A HOLIDAY PARTY THIS YEAR.
WELL, THAT'S A SURPRISE. I THOUGHT YOU'D BE TOO LAZY TO THROW A PARTY.
WE'LL MAKE IT ONE OF THOSE "BRING YOUR OWN" GIGS... EASIER THAT WAY.
I THOUGHT YOU'D BE TOO LAZY TO EVEN INVITE ANYBODY.
YOU'RE THE FIRST ONE I'VE INVITED.
I **AM**? WELL! WHERE'S THIS PARTY GOING TO BE?
YOUR PLACE. SPREAD THE WORD.

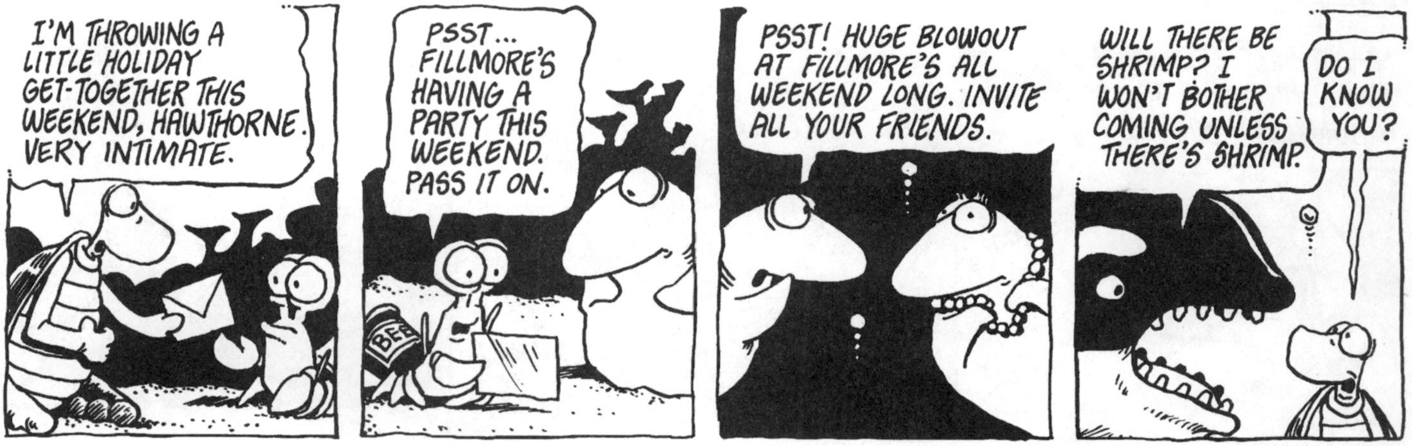
I'M THROWING A LITTLE HOLIDAY GET-TOGETHER THIS WEEKEND, HAWTHORNE. VERY INTIMATE.
PSST... FILLMORE'S HAVING A PARTY THIS WEEKEND. PASS IT ON.
PSST! HUGE BLOWOUT AT FILLMORE'S ALL WEEKEND LONG. INVITE ALL YOUR FRIENDS.
WILL THERE BE SHRIMP? I WON'T BOTHER COMING UNLESS THERE'S SHRIMP.
DO I KNOW YOU?

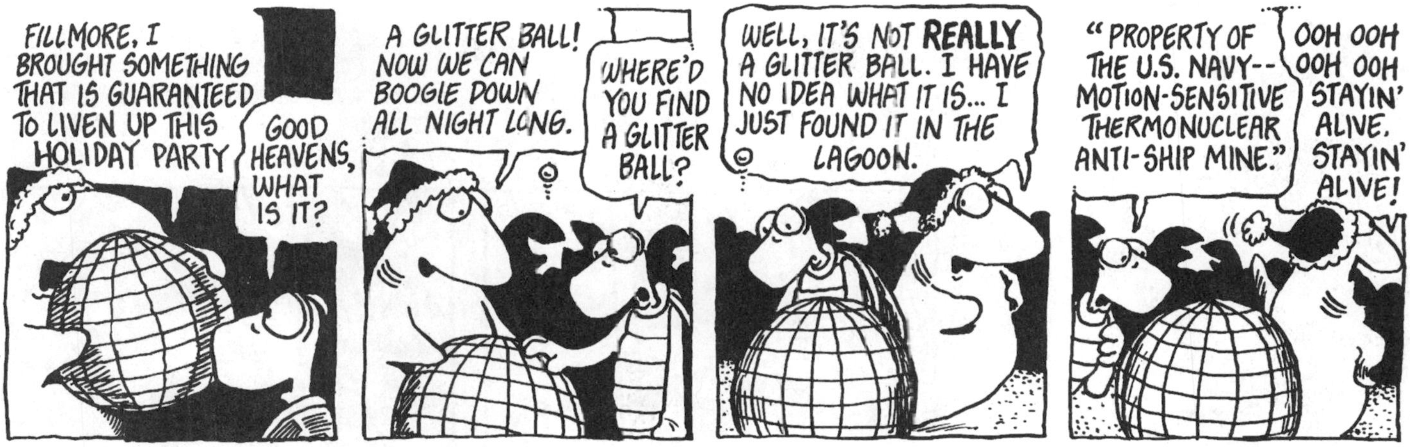
FILLMORE, I BROUGHT SOMETHING THAT IS GUARANTEED TO LIVEN UP THIS HOLIDAY PARTY
GOOD HEAVENS, WHAT IS IT?
A GLITTER BALL! NOW WE CAN BOOGIE DOWN ALL NIGHT LONG.
WHERE'D YOU FIND A GLITTER BALL?
WELL, IT'S NOT **REALLY** A GLITTER BALL. I HAVE NO IDEA WHAT IT IS... I JUST FOUND IT IN THE LAGOON.
"PROPERTY OF THE U.S. NAVY-- MOTION-SENSITIVE THERMONUCLEAR ANTI-SHIP MINE."
OOH OOH OOH OOH STAYIN' ALIVE. STAYIN' ALIVE!

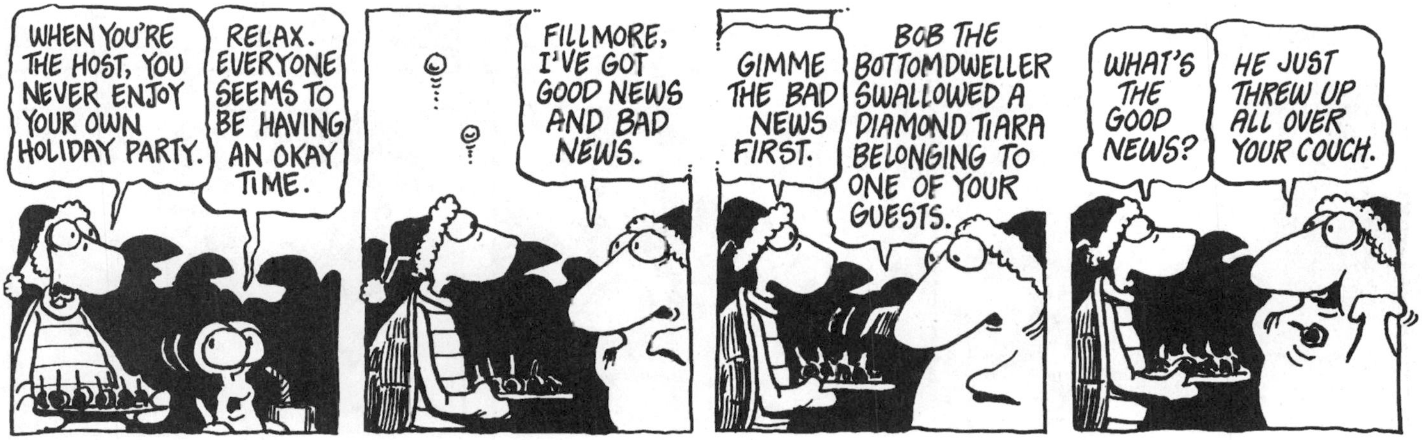
WHEN YOU'RE THE HOST, YOU NEVER ENJOY YOUR OWN HOLIDAY PARTY.
RELAX. EVERYONE SEEMS TO BE HAVING AN OKAY TIME.
FILLMORE, I'VE GOT GOOD NEWS AND BAD NEWS.
GIMME THE BAD NEWS FIRST.
BOB THE BOTTOMDWELLER SWALLOWED A DIAMOND TIARA BELONGING TO ONE OF YOUR GUESTS.
WHAT'S THE GOOD NEWS?
HE JUST THREW UP ALL OVER YOUR COUCH.

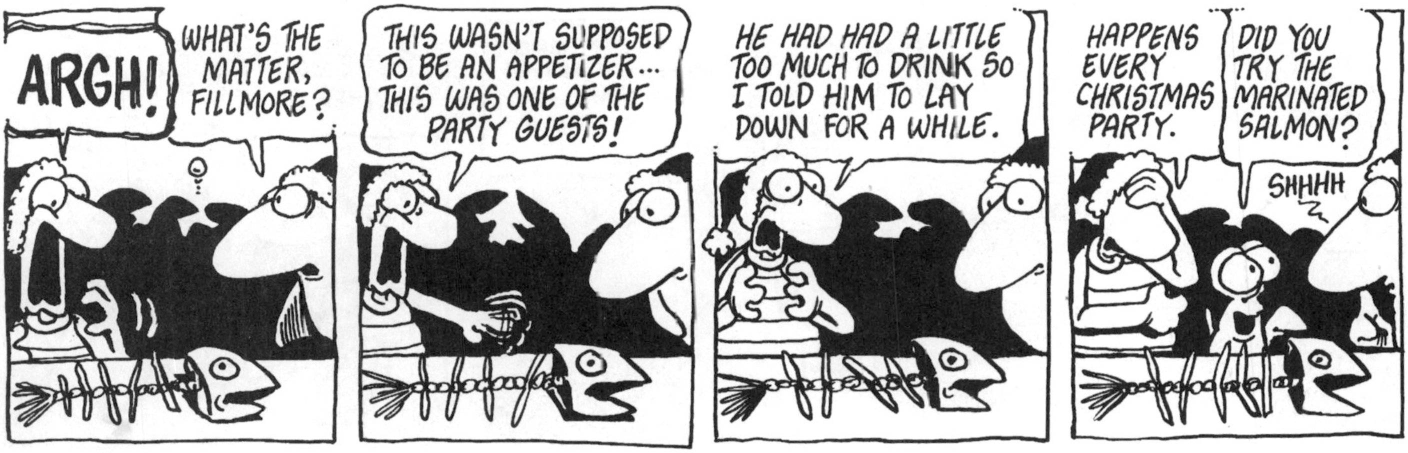
ARGH!
WHAT'S THE MATTER, FILLMORE?
THIS WASN'T SUPPOSED TO BE AN APPETIZER... THIS WAS ONE OF THE PARTY GUESTS!
HE HAD HAD A LITTLE TOO MUCH TO DRINK SO I TOLD HIM TO LAY DOWN FOR A WHILE.
HAPPENS EVERY CHRISTMAS PARTY.
DID YOU TRY THE MARINATED SALMON?
SHHHH

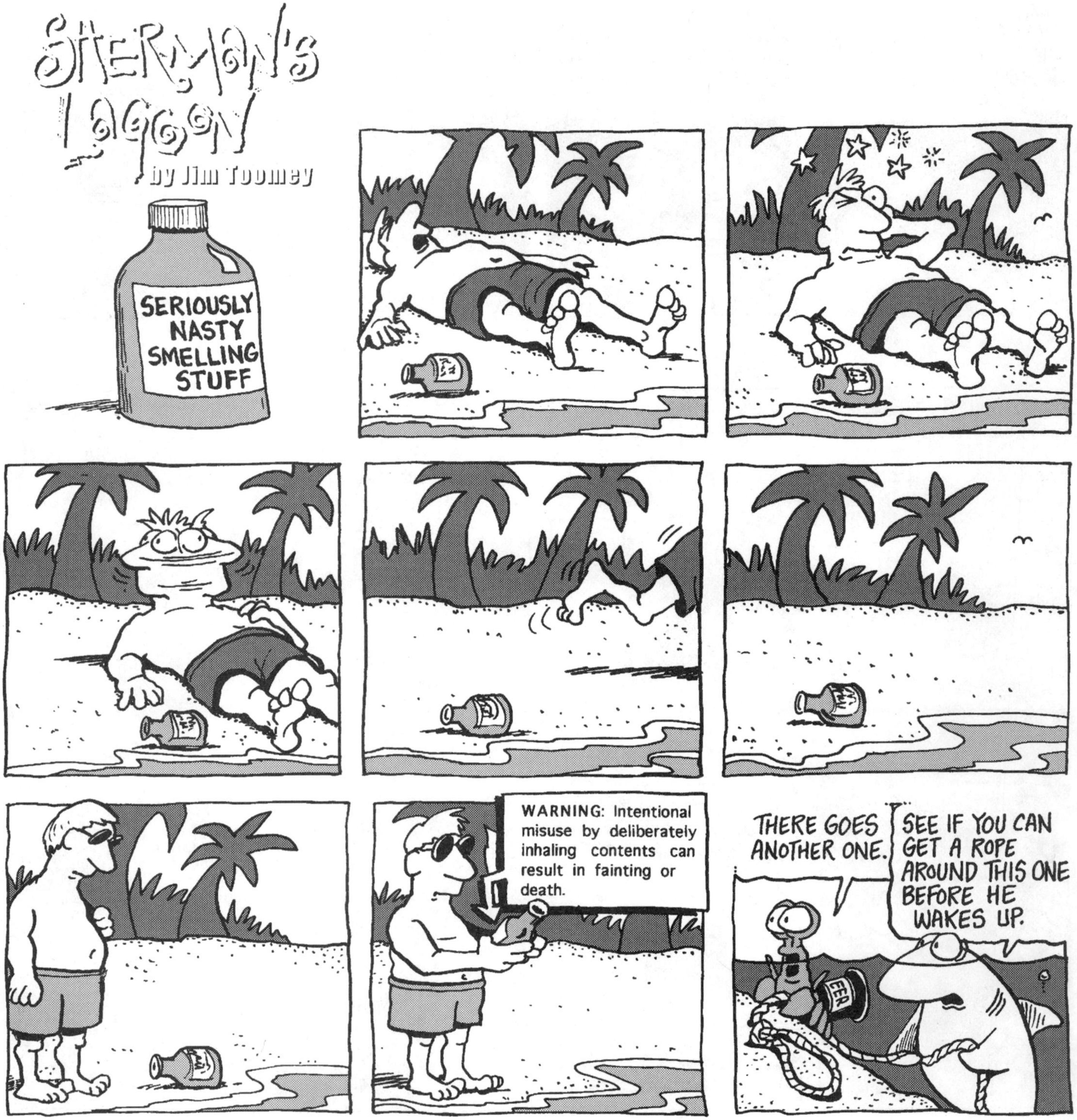
SHERMAN'S LAGOON
by Jim Toomey
SERIOUSLY NASTY SMELLING STUFF
WARNING: Intentional misuse by deliberately inhaling contents can result in fainting or death.
THERE GOES ANOTHER ONE.
SEE IF YOU CAN GET A ROPE AROUND THIS ONE BEFORE HE WAKES UP.

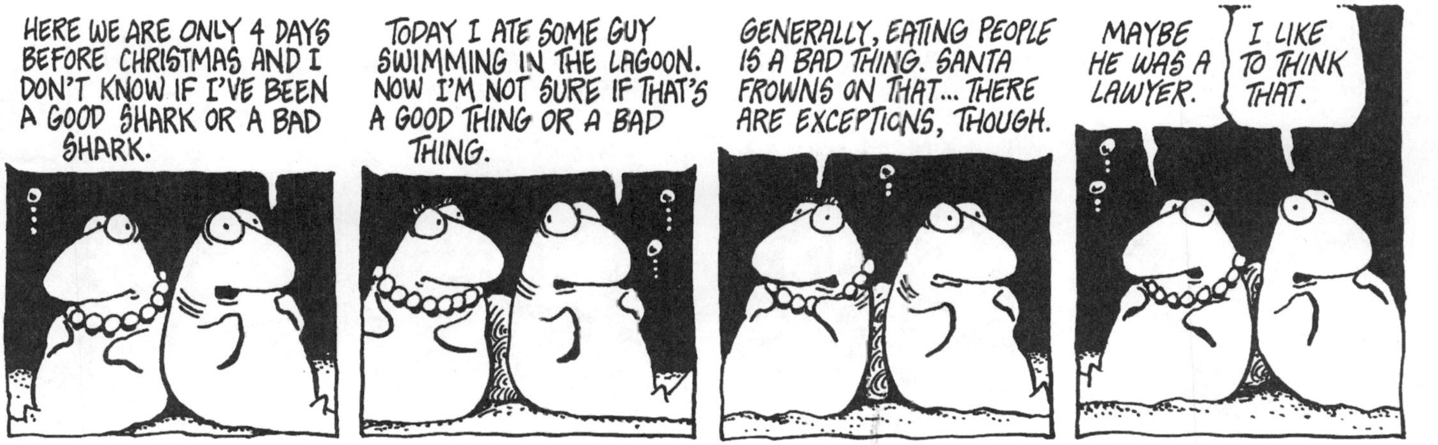
HERE WE ARE ONLY 4 DAYS BEFORE CHRISTMAS AND I DON'T KNOW IF I'VE BEEN A GOOD SHARK OR A BAD SHARK.
TODAY I ATE SOME GUY SWIMMING IN THE LAGOON. NOW I'M NOT SURE IF THAT'S A GOOD THING OR A BAD THING.
GENERALLY, EATING PEOPLE IS A BAD THING. SANTA FROWNS ON THAT... THERE ARE EXCEPTIONS, THOUGH.
MAYBE HE WAS A LAWYER.
I LIKE TO THINK THAT.

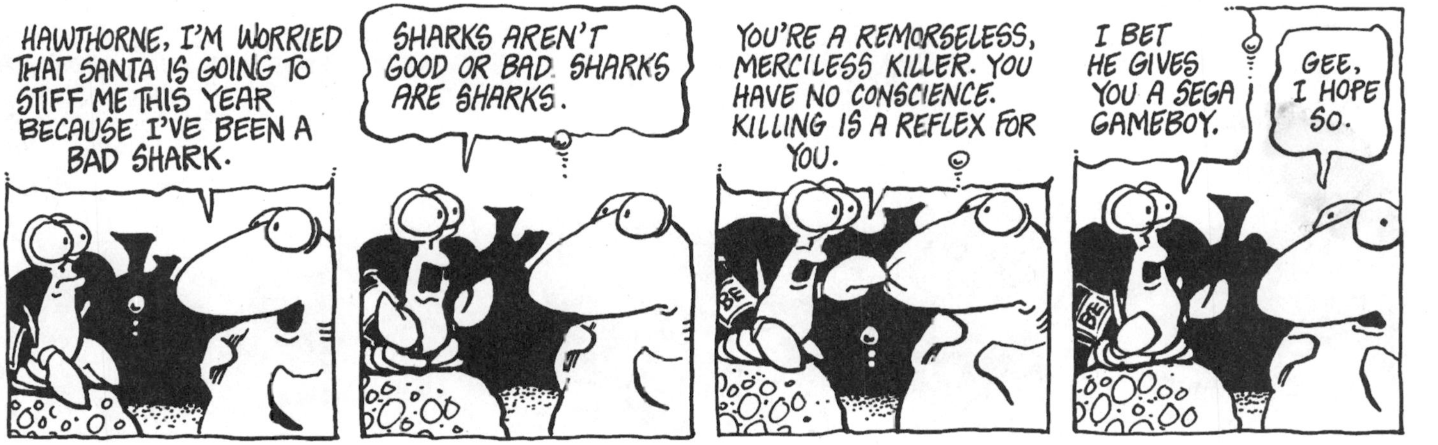
HAWTHORNE, I'M WORRIED THAT SANTA IS GOING TO STIFF ME THIS YEAR BECAUSE I'VE BEEN A BAD SHARK.
SHARKS AREN'T GOOD OR BAD. SHARKS ARE SHARKS.
YOU'RE A REMORSELESS, MERCILESS KILLER. YOU HAVE NO CONSCIENCE. KILLING IS A REFLEX FOR YOU.
I BET HE GIVES YOU A SEGA GAMEBOY.
GEE, I HOPE SO.

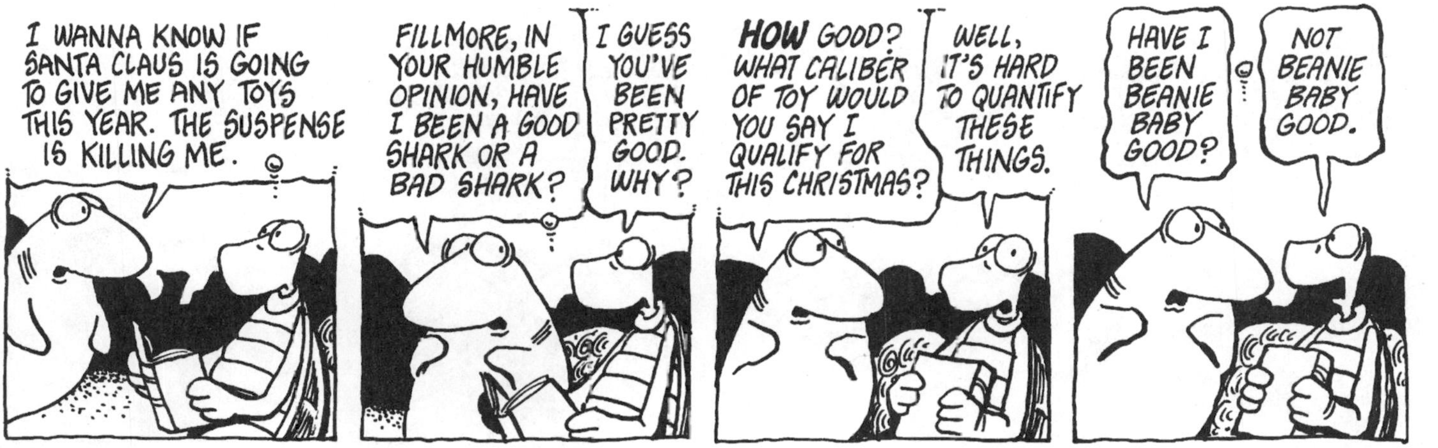
I WANNA KNOW IF SANTA CLAUS IS GOING TO GIVE ME ANY TOYS THIS YEAR. THE SUSPENSE IS KILLING ME.
FILLMORE, IN YOUR HUMBLE OPINION, HAVE I BEEN A GOOD SHARK OR A BAD SHARK?
I GUESS YOU'VE BEEN PRETTY GOOD. WHY?
HOW GOOD? WHAT CALIBER OF TOY WOULD YOU SAY I QUALIFY FOR THIS CHRISTMAS?
WELL, IT'S HARD TO QUANTIFY THESE THINGS.
HAVE I BEEN BEANIE BABY GOOD?
NOT BEANIE BABY GOOD.

**Panel 1:** SHERM, WHY ARE YOU COLLECTING LITTER ON CHRISTMAS EVE?

**Panel 2:** I'M TRYING TO GET ONE LAST GOOD DEED IN SO SANTA WILL BRING ME MORE TOYS. / TOO LATE. SANTA ALREADY CLOSED HIS BOOKS FOR '98.

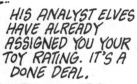

**Panel 3:** HIS ANALYST ELVES HAVE ALREADY ASSIGNED YOU YOUR TOY RATING. IT'S A DONE DEAL.

**Panel 4:** SO, I'M BEING CONSCIENTIOUS AND WELL-INTENTIONED FOR NO APPARENT REASON? / GIVE IT UP, MAN. IT'S CHRISTMAS.

**Panel 5:** LOOKS LIKE SOMEBODY TOOK A BITE OUT OF THE CHRISTMAS COOKIE I LEFT OUT LAST NIGHT.

**Panel 6:** IT'S PROOF THAT SANTA HIMSELF PASSED THIS WAY NOT LONG AGO.

**Panel 7:** (no dialogue)

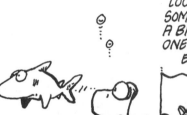 

**Panel 8:** LOOKS LIKE SOMEBODY TOOK A BITE OUT OF ONE OF SANTA'S ELVES. / PROOF THAT SHERMAN PASSED THIS WAY NOT LONG AGO.

**Panel 9:** SANTA STIFFED ME AGAIN. NOT A SINGLE PRESENT. / IT MIGHT HAVE SOMETHING TO DO WITH THE FACT THAT YOU **ATE** ONE OF HIS ELVES.

**Panel 10:** THAT'S BAD FORM.

**Panel 11:** I'VE ALWAYS WANTED TO EAT AN ELF. NOW I HAVE. / WELL, YOU SHOULDN'T GO AROUND EATING **SANTA'S** ELVES.

**Panel 12:** LITTLE-KNOWN FACT: ELVES TASTE LIKE CHICKEN. / HOW'D YOU PREPARE IT?

20

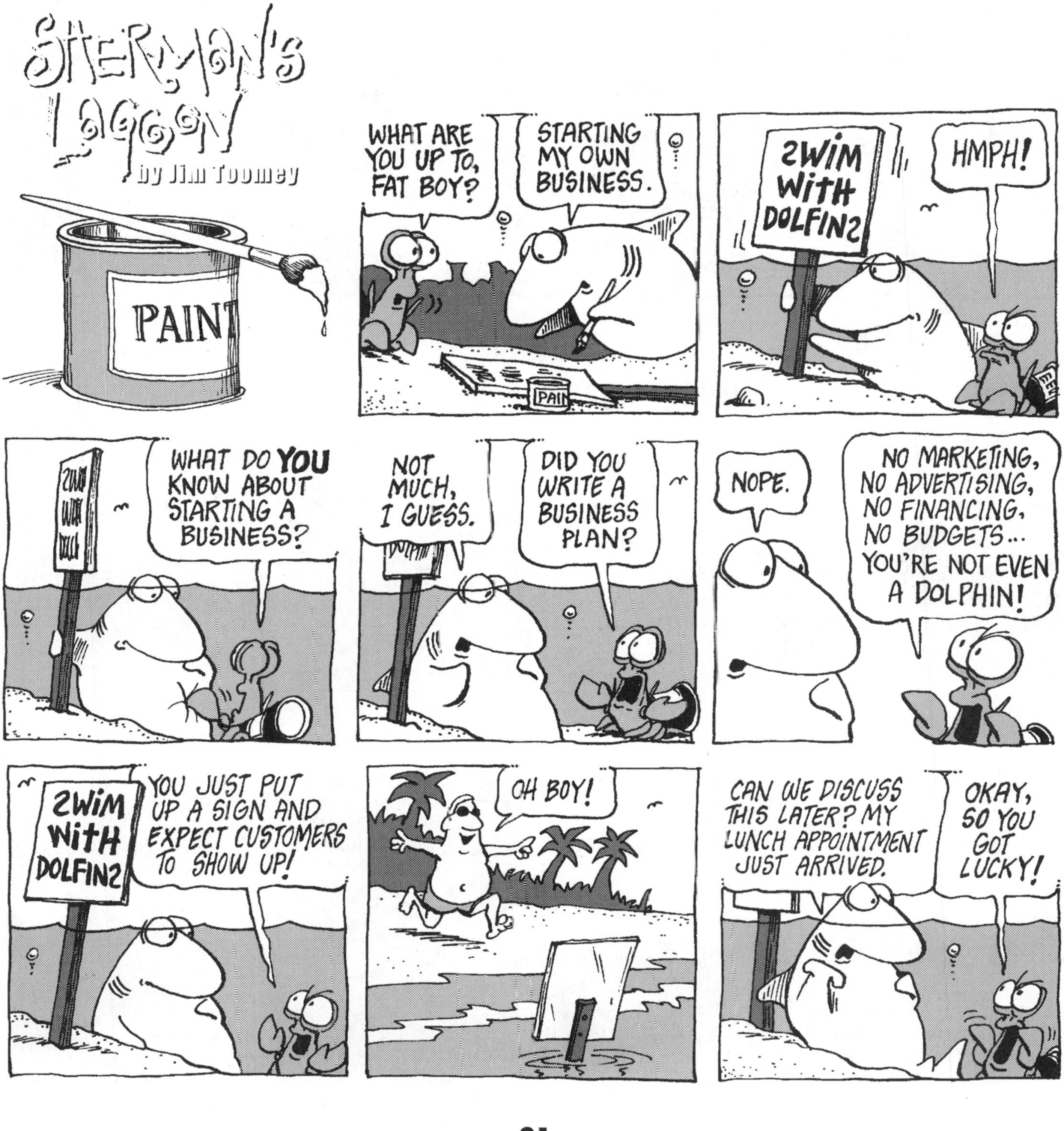
SHERMAN'S LAGOON
by Jim Toomey
PAINT
WHAT ARE YOU UP TO, FAT BOY?
STARTING MY OWN BUSINESS.
PAIN
SWIM WITH DOLFINS
HMPH!
WHAT DO YOU KNOW ABOUT STARTING A BUSINESS?
NOT MUCH, I GUESS.
DID YOU WRITE A BUSINESS PLAN?
NOPE.
NO MARKETING, NO ADVERTISING, NO FINANCING, NO BUDGETS... YOU'RE NOT EVEN A DOLPHIN!
SWIM WITH DOLFINS
YOU JUST PUT UP A SIGN AND EXPECT CUSTOMERS TO SHOW UP!
OH BOY!
CAN WE DISCUSS THIS LATER? MY LUNCH APPOINTMENT JUST ARRIVED.
OKAY, SO YOU GOT LUCKY!

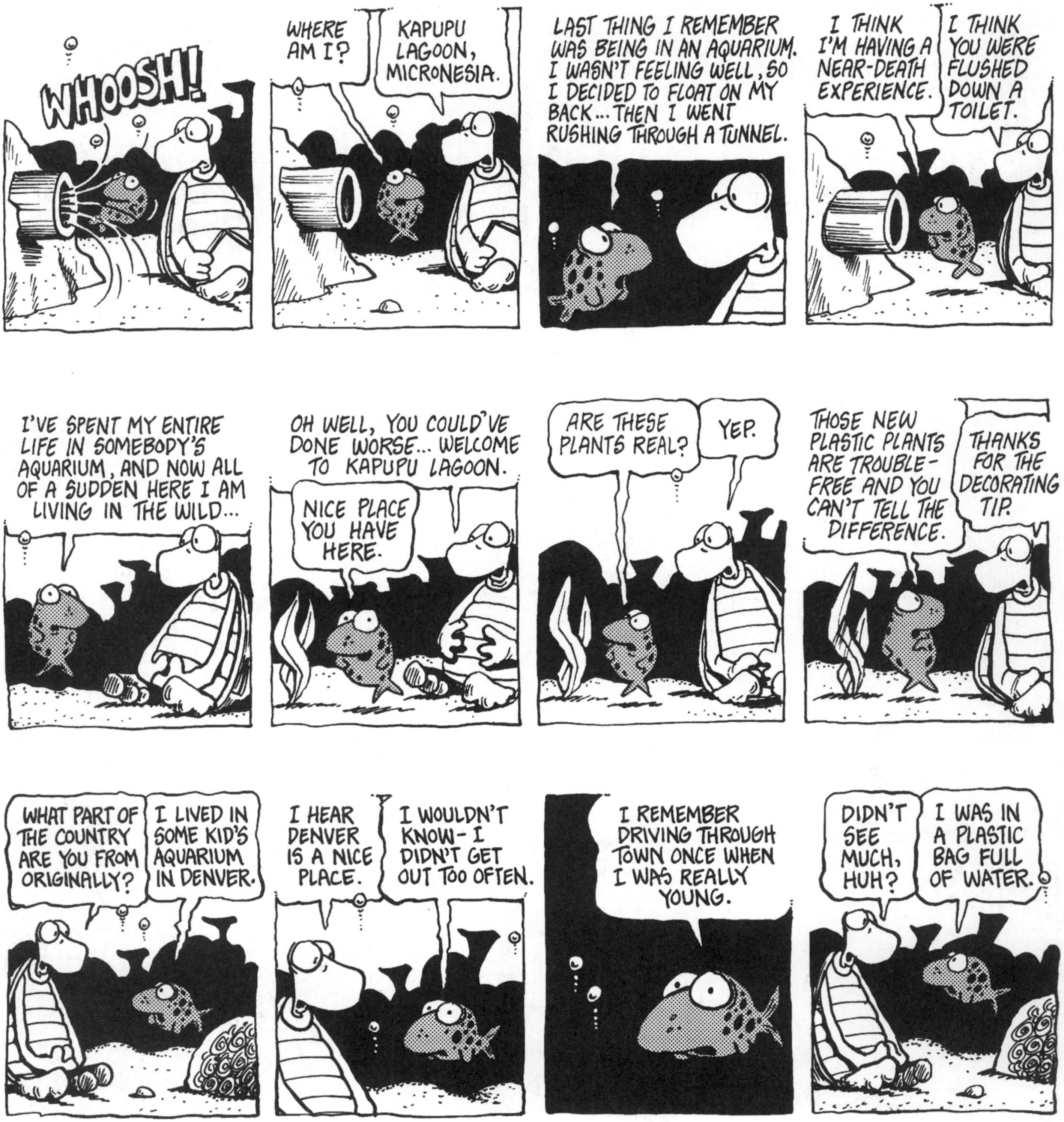
WHOOSH!
WHERE AM I?
KAPUPU LAGOON, MICRONESIA.
LAST THING I REMEMBER WAS BEING IN AN AQUARIUM. I WASN'T FEELING WELL, SO I DECIDED TO FLOAT ON MY BACK... THEN I WENT RUSHING THROUGH A TUNNEL.
I THINK I'M HAVING A NEAR-DEATH EXPERIENCE.
I THINK YOU WERE FLUSHED DOWN A TOILET.
I'VE SPENT MY ENTIRE LIFE IN SOMEBODY'S AQUARIUM, AND NOW ALL OF A SUDDEN HERE I AM LIVING IN THE WILD...
OH WELL, YOU COULD'VE DONE WORSE... WELCOME TO KAPUPU LAGOON.
NICE PLACE YOU HAVE HERE.
ARE THESE PLANTS REAL?
YEP.
THOSE NEW PLASTIC PLANTS ARE TROUBLE-FREE AND YOU CAN'T TELL THE DIFFERENCE.
THANKS FOR THE DECORATING TIP.
WHAT PART OF THE COUNTRY ARE YOU FROM ORIGINALLY?
I LIVED IN SOME KID'S AQUARIUM IN DENVER.
I HEAR DENVER IS A NICE PLACE.
I WOULDN'T KNOW- I DIDN'T GET OUT TOO OFTEN.
I REMEMBER DRIVING THROUGH TOWN ONCE WHEN I WAS REALLY YOUNG.
DIDN'T SEE MUCH, HUH?
I WAS IN A PLASTIC BAG FULL OF WATER.

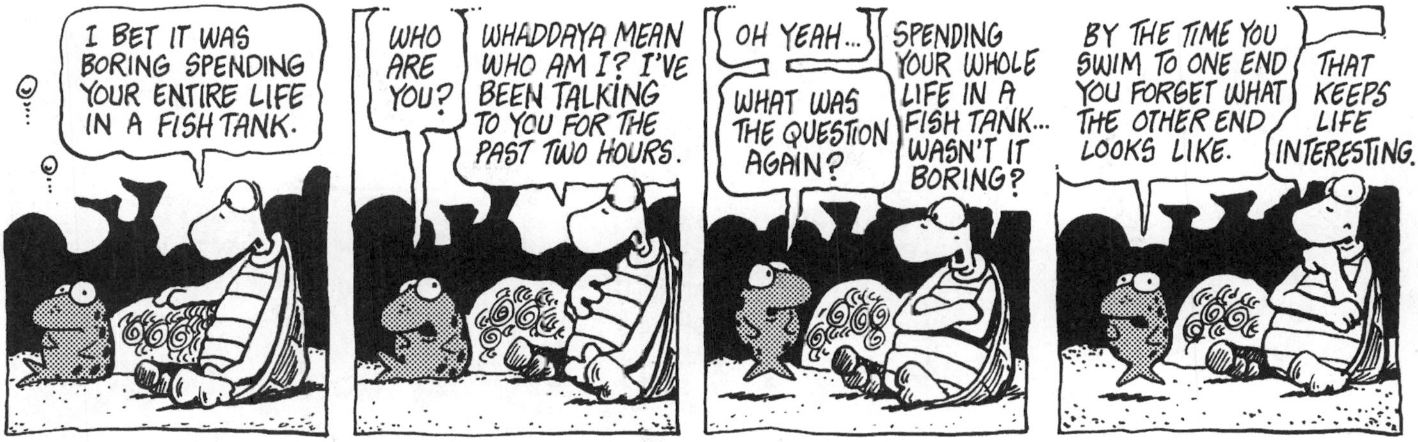
I BET IT WAS BORING SPENDING YOUR ENTIRE LIFE IN A FISH TANK.
WHO ARE YOU?
WHADDAYA MEAN WHO AM I? I'VE BEEN TALKING TO YOU FOR THE PAST TWO HOURS.
OH YEAH...
WHAT WAS THE QUESTION AGAIN?
SPENDING YOUR WHOLE LIFE IN A FISH TANK... WASN'T IT BORING?
BY THE TIME YOU SWIM TO ONE END YOU FORGET WHAT THE OTHER END LOOKS LIKE.
THAT KEEPS LIFE INTERESTING.

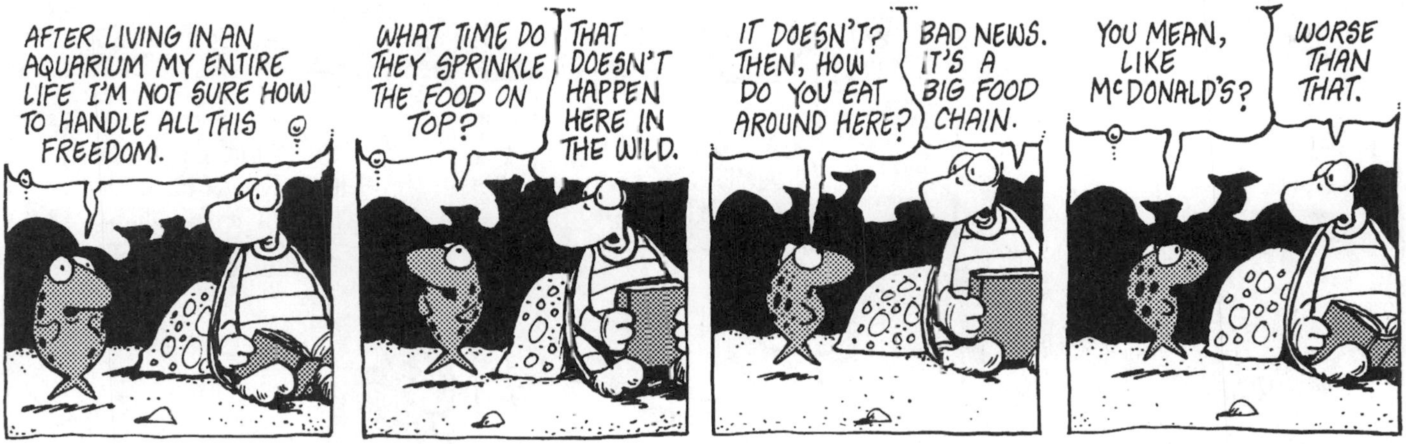
AFTER LIVING IN AN AQUARIUM MY ENTIRE LIFE I'M NOT SURE HOW TO HANDLE ALL THIS FREEDOM.
WHAT TIME DO THEY SPRINKLE THE FOOD ON TOP?
THAT DOESN'T HAPPEN HERE IN THE WILD.
IT DOESN'T? THEN, HOW DO YOU EAT AROUND HERE?
BAD NEWS. IT'S A BIG FOOD CHAIN.
YOU MEAN, LIKE McDONALD'S?
WORSE THAN THAT.

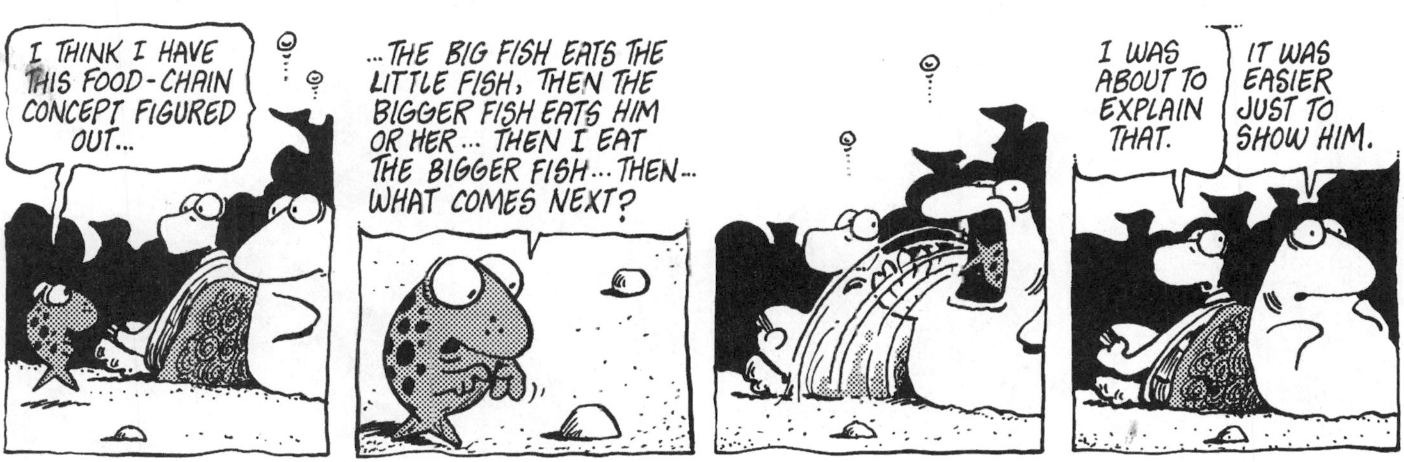
I THINK I HAVE THIS FOOD-CHAIN CONCEPT FIGURED OUT...
...THE BIG FISH EATS THE LITTLE FISH, THEN THE BIGGER FISH EATS HIM OR HER... THEN I EAT THE BIGGER FISH... THEN... WHAT COMES NEXT?
I WAS ABOUT TO EXPLAIN THAT.
IT WAS EASIER JUST TO SHOW HIM.

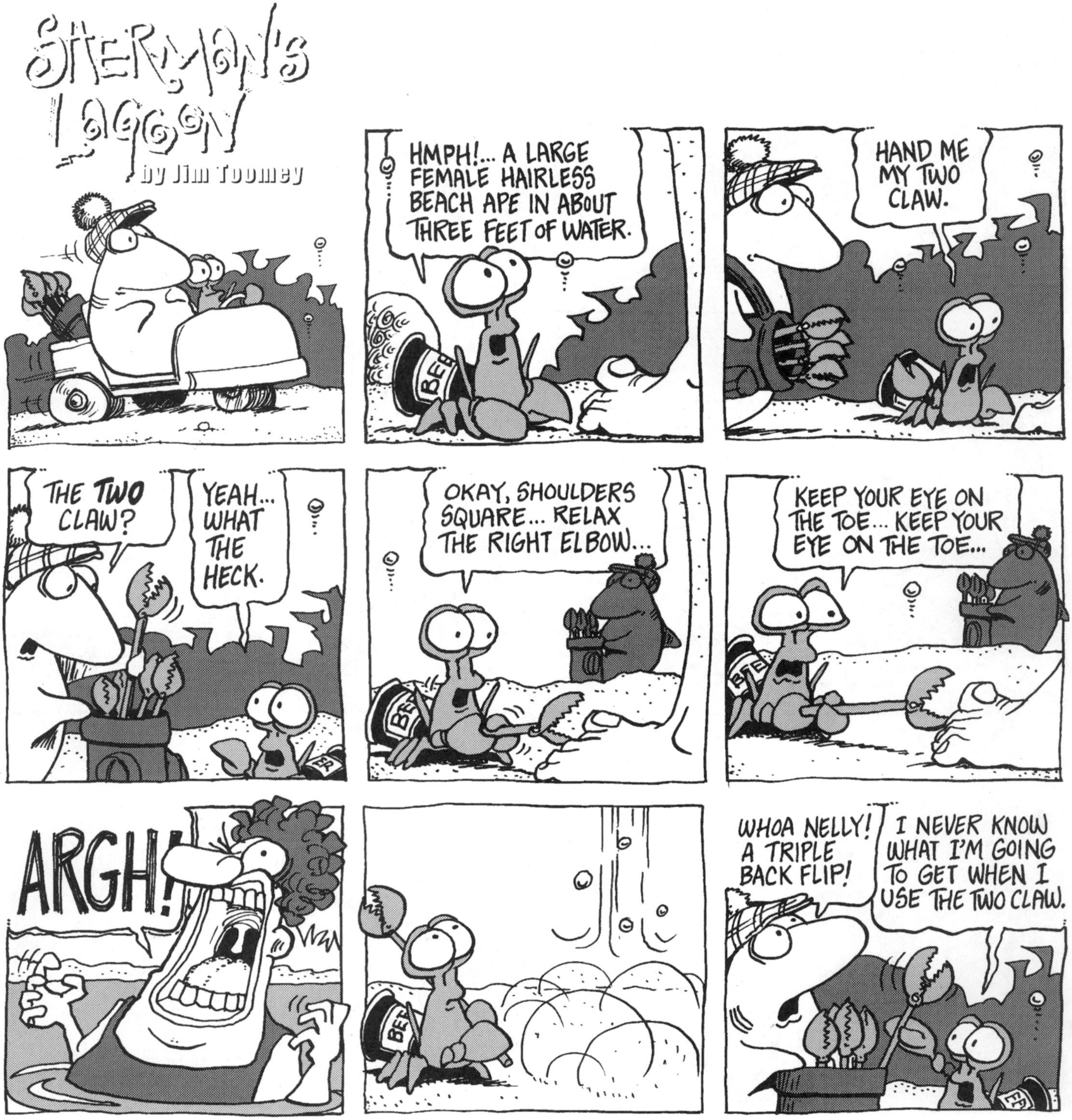
SHERMAN'S LAGOON
by Jim Toomey
HMPH!... A LARGE FEMALE HAIRLESS BEACH APE IN ABOUT THREE FEET OF WATER.
HAND ME MY TWO CLAW.
THE **TWO** CLAW?
YEAH... WHAT THE HECK.
OKAY, SHOULDERS SQUARE... RELAX THE RIGHT ELBOW...
KEEP YOUR EYE ON THE TOE... KEEP YOUR EYE ON THE TOE...
ARGH!
WHOA NELLY! A TRIPLE BACK FLIP!
I NEVER KNOW WHAT I'M GOING TO GET WHEN I USE THE TWO CLAW.

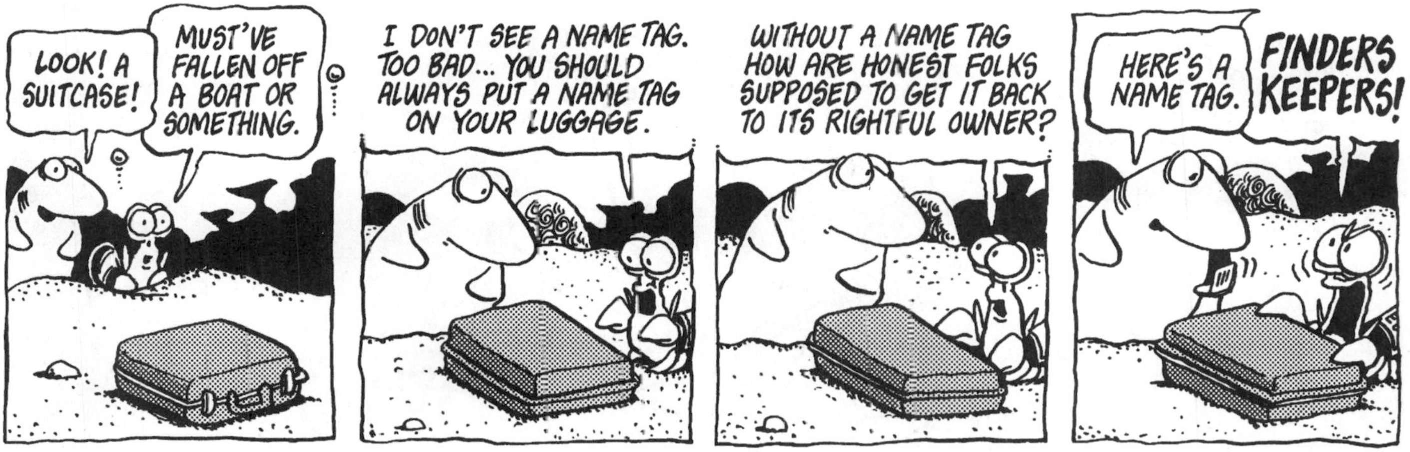
LOOK! A SUITCASE!
MUST'VE FALLEN OFF A BOAT OR SOMETHING.
I DON'T SEE A NAME TAG. TOO BAD... YOU SHOULD ALWAYS PUT A NAME TAG ON YOUR LUGGAGE.
WITHOUT A NAME TAG HOW ARE HONEST FOLKS SUPPOSED TO GET IT BACK TO ITS RIGHTFUL OWNER?
HERE'S A NAME TAG.
FINDERS KEEPERS!

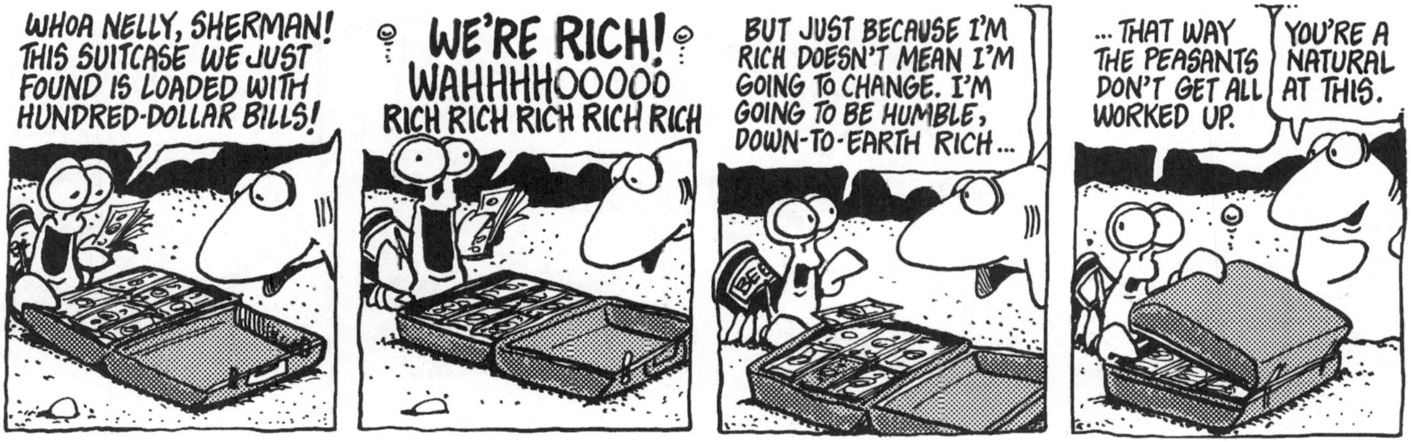
WHOA NELLY, SHERMAN! THIS SUITCASE WE JUST FOUND IS LOADED WITH HUNDRED-DOLLAR BILLS!
WE'RE RICH! WAHHHHOOOOO RICH RICH RICH RICH RICH
BUT JUST BECAUSE I'M RICH DOESN'T MEAN I'M GOING TO CHANGE. I'M GOING TO BE HUMBLE, DOWN-TO-EARTH RICH...
...THAT WAY THE PEASANTS DON'T GET ALL WORKED UP.
YOU'RE A NATURAL AT THIS.

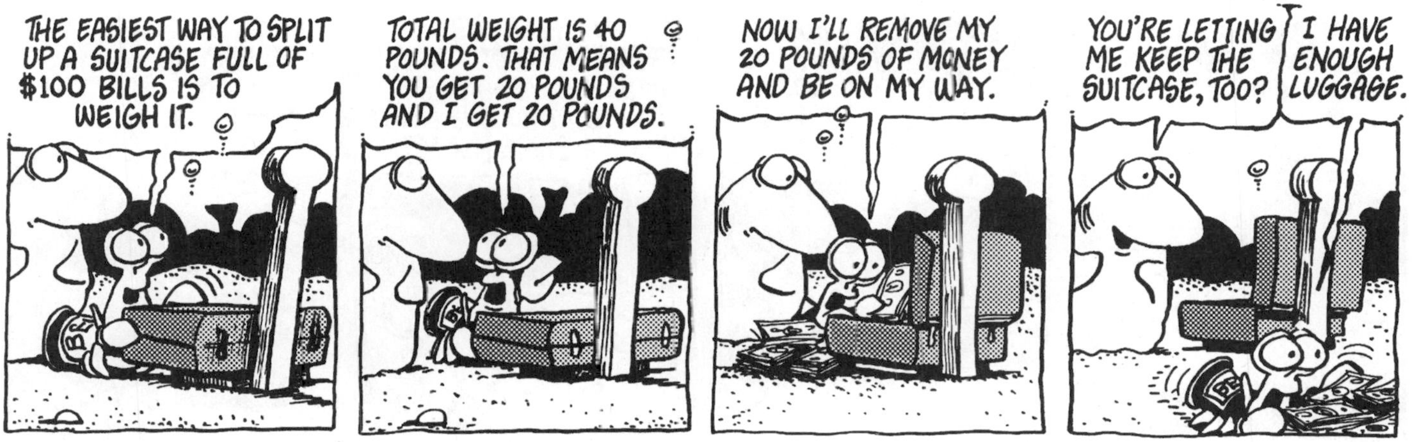
THE EASIEST WAY TO SPLIT UP A SUITCASE FULL OF $100 BILLS IS TO WEIGH IT.
TOTAL WEIGHT IS 40 POUNDS. THAT MEANS YOU GET 20 POUNDS AND I GET 20 POUNDS.
NOW I'LL REMOVE MY 20 POUNDS OF MONEY AND BE ON MY WAY.
YOU'RE LETTING ME KEEP THE SUITCASE, TOO?
I HAVE ENOUGH LUGGAGE.

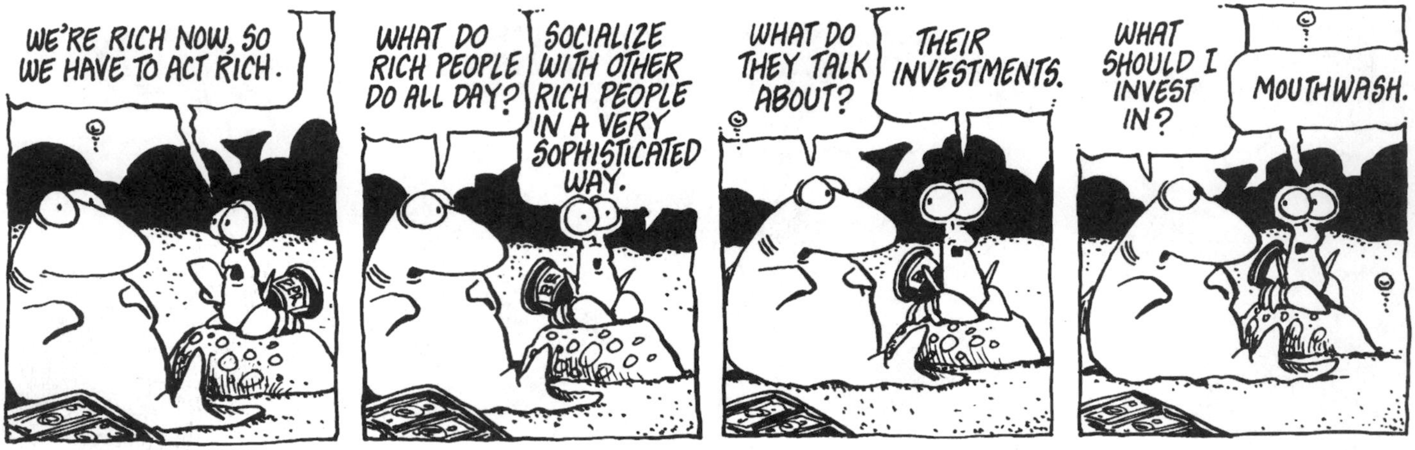
WE'RE RICH NOW, SO WE HAVE TO ACT RICH.
WHAT DO RICH PEOPLE DO ALL DAY?
SOCIALIZE WITH OTHER RICH PEOPLE IN A VERY SOPHISTICATED WAY.
WHAT DO THEY TALK ABOUT?
THEIR INVESTMENTS.
WHAT SHOULD I INVEST IN?
MOUTHWASH.

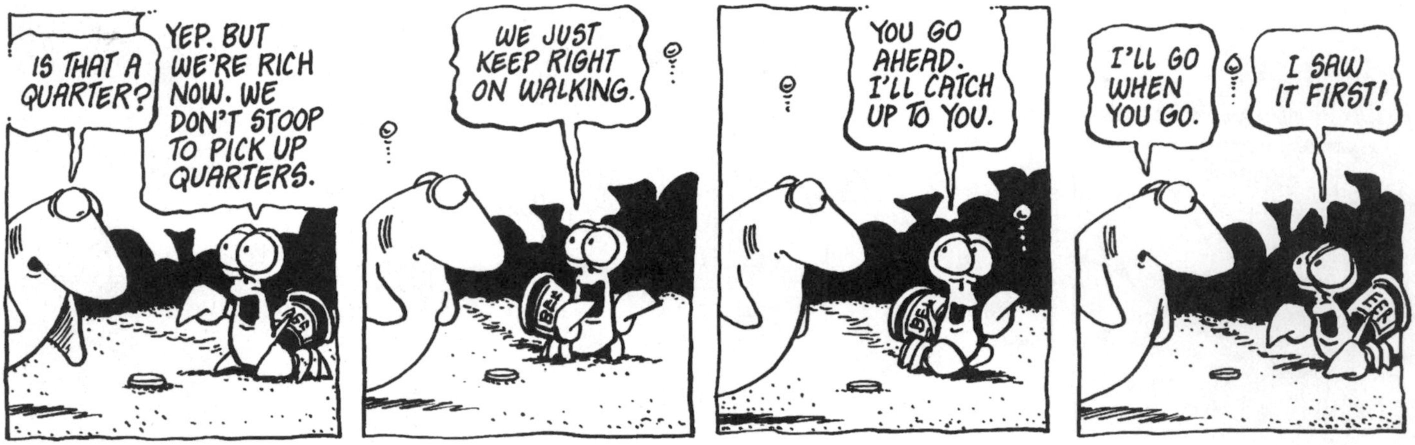
IS THAT A QUARTER?
YEP. BUT WE'RE RICH NOW. WE DON'T STOOP TO PICK UP QUARTERS.
WE JUST KEEP RIGHT ON WALKING.
YOU GO AHEAD. I'LL CATCH UP TO YOU.
I'LL GO WHEN YOU GO.
I SAW IT FIRST!

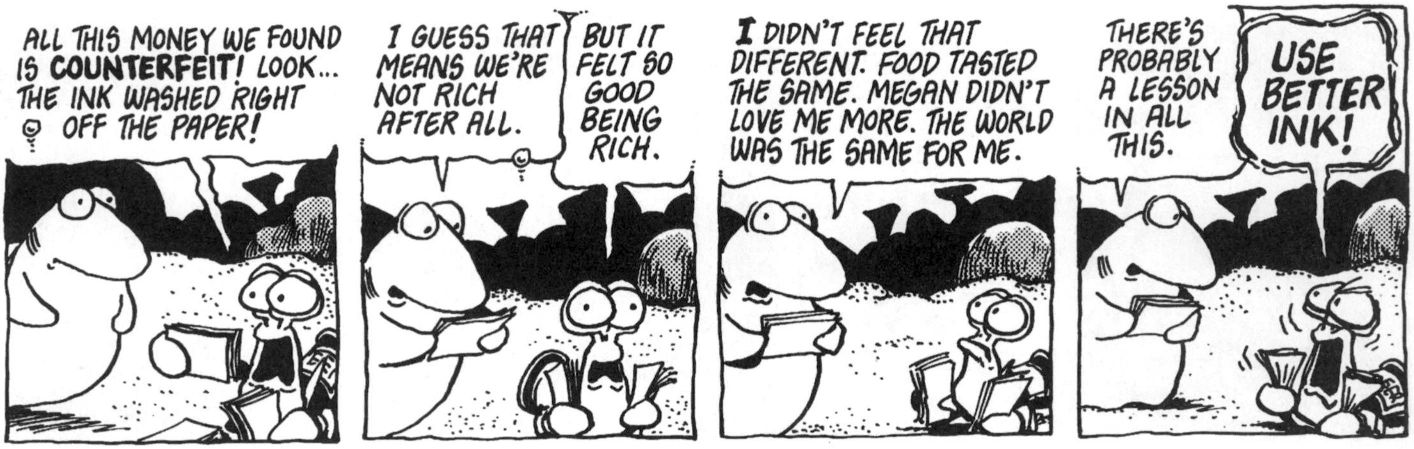
ALL THIS MONEY WE FOUND IS COUNTERFEIT! LOOK... THE INK WASHED RIGHT OFF THE PAPER!
I GUESS THAT MEANS WE'RE NOT RICH AFTER ALL.
BUT IT FELT SO GOOD BEING RICH.
I DIDN'T FEEL THAT DIFFERENT. FOOD TASTED THE SAME. MEGAN DIDN'T LOVE ME MORE. THE WORLD WAS THE SAME FOR ME.
THERE'S PROBABLY A LESSON IN ALL THIS.
USE BETTER INK!

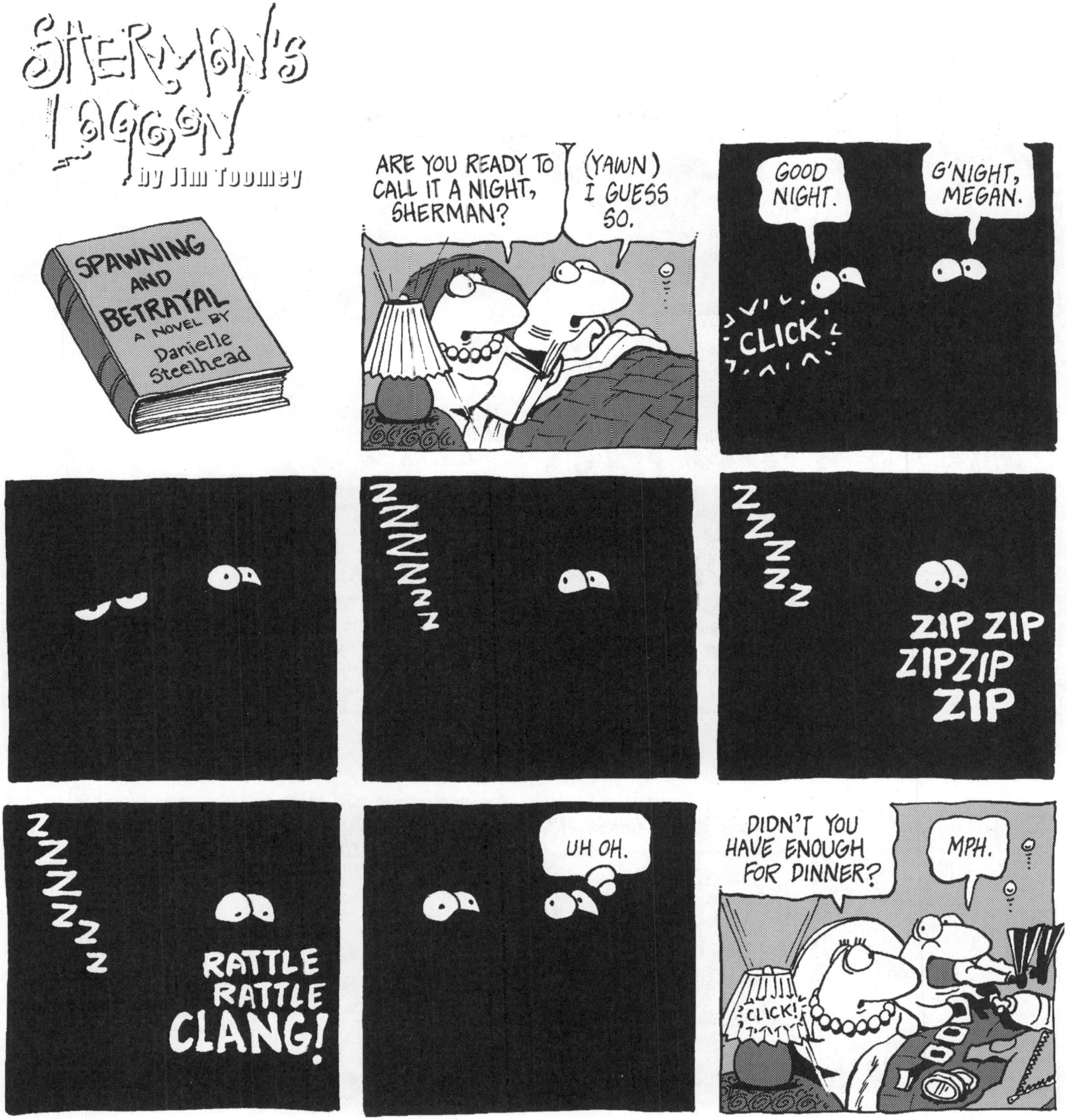
SHERMAN'S LAGOON
by Jim Toomey
SPAWNING AND BETRAYAL
A NOVEL BY
Danielle Steelhead
ARE YOU READY TO CALL IT A NIGHT, SHERMAN?
(YAWN) I GUESS SO.
GOOD NIGHT.
G'NIGHT, MEGAN.
CLICK
ZZZZZZZ
ZZZZZ
ZIP ZIP
ZIPZIP
ZIP
ZZZZZZ
RATTLE
RATTLE
CLANG!
UH OH.
DIDN'T YOU HAVE ENOUGH FOR DINNER?
MPH.
CLICK!

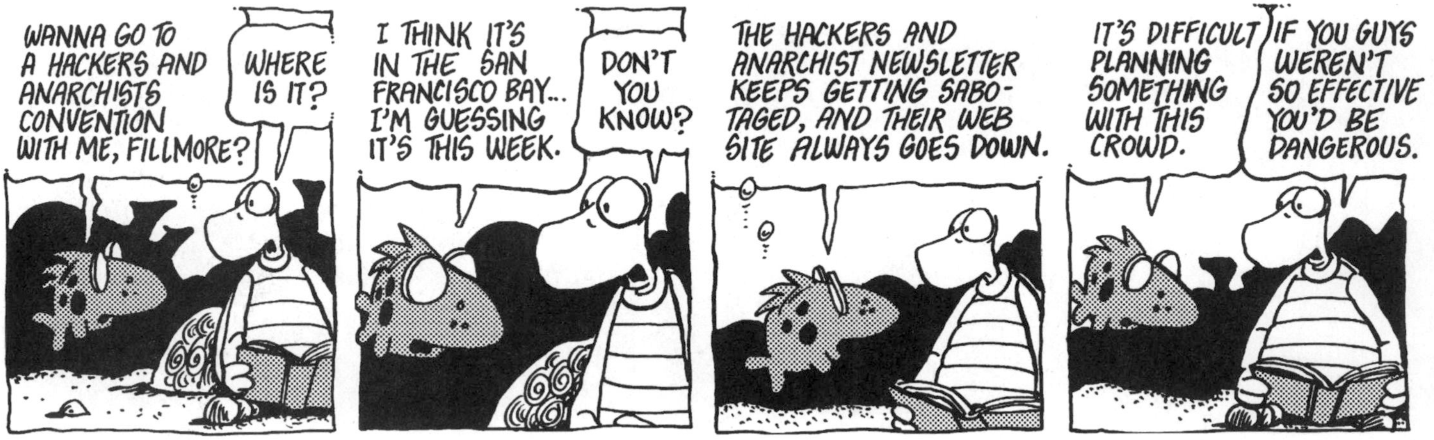
WANNA GO TO A HACKERS AND ANARCHISTS CONVENTION WITH ME, FILLMORE?
WHERE IS IT?
I THINK IT'S IN THE SAN FRANCISCO BAY... I'M GUESSING IT'S THIS WEEK.
DON'T YOU KNOW?
THE HACKERS AND ANARCHIST NEWSLETTER KEEPS GETTING SABOTAGED, AND THEIR WEB SITE ALWAYS GOES DOWN.
IT'S DIFFICULT PLANNING SOMETHING WITH THIS CROWD.
IF YOU GUYS WEREN'T SO EFFECTIVE YOU'D BE DANGEROUS.

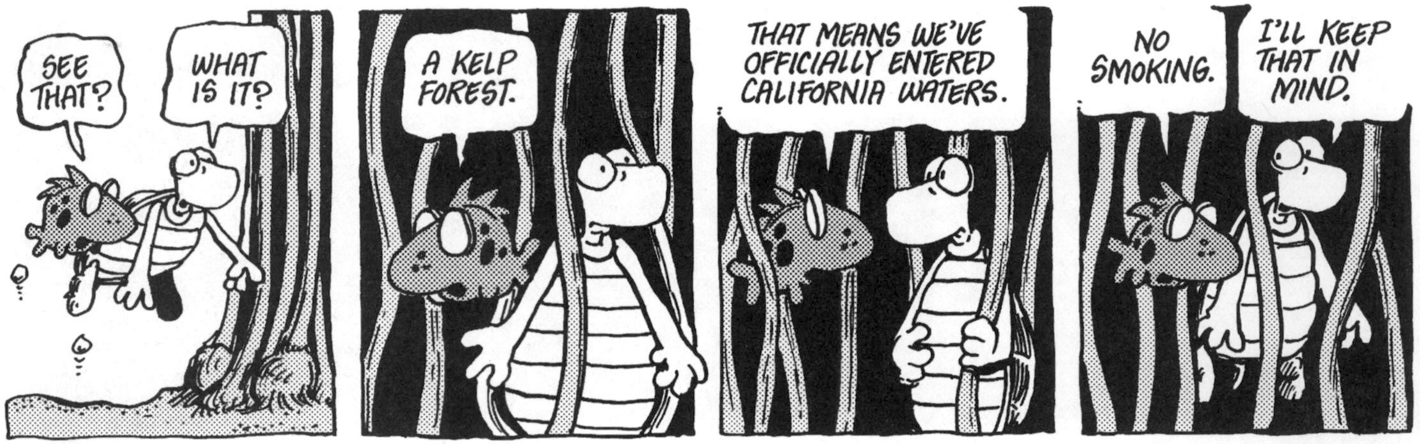
SEE THAT?
WHAT IS IT?
A KELP FOREST.
THAT MEANS WE'VE OFFICIALLY ENTERED CALIFORNIA WATERS.
NO SMOKING.
I'LL KEEP THAT IN MIND.

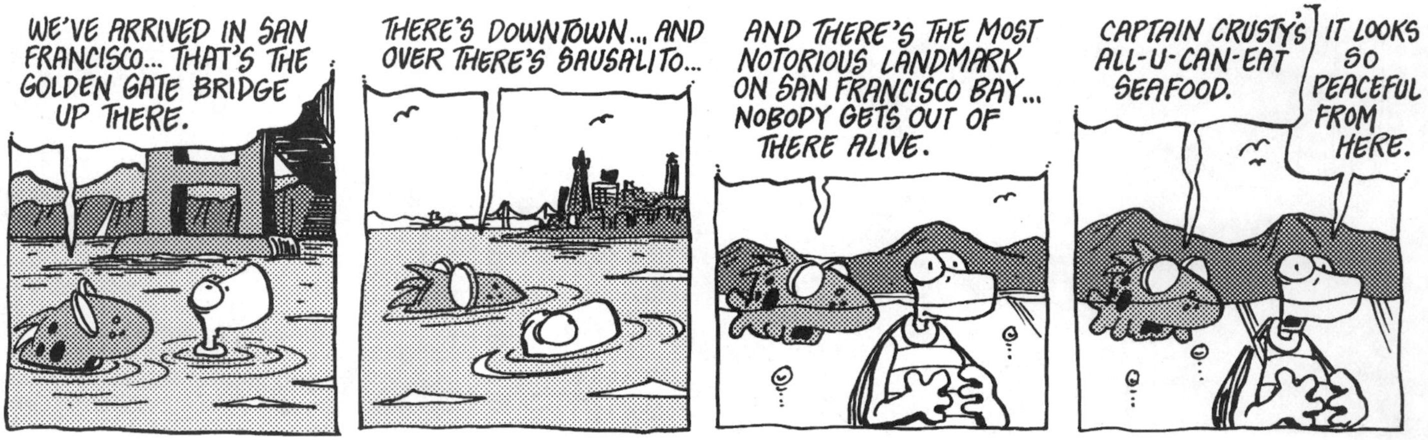
WE'VE ARRIVED IN SAN FRANCISCO... THAT'S THE GOLDEN GATE BRIDGE UP THERE.
THERE'S DOWNTOWN... AND OVER THERE'S SAUSALITO...
AND THERE'S THE MOST NOTORIOUS LANDMARK ON SAN FRANCISCO BAY... NOBODY GETS OUT OF THERE ALIVE.
CAPTAIN CRUSTY'S ALL-U-CAN-EAT SEAFOOD.
IT LOOKS SO PEACEFUL FROM HERE.

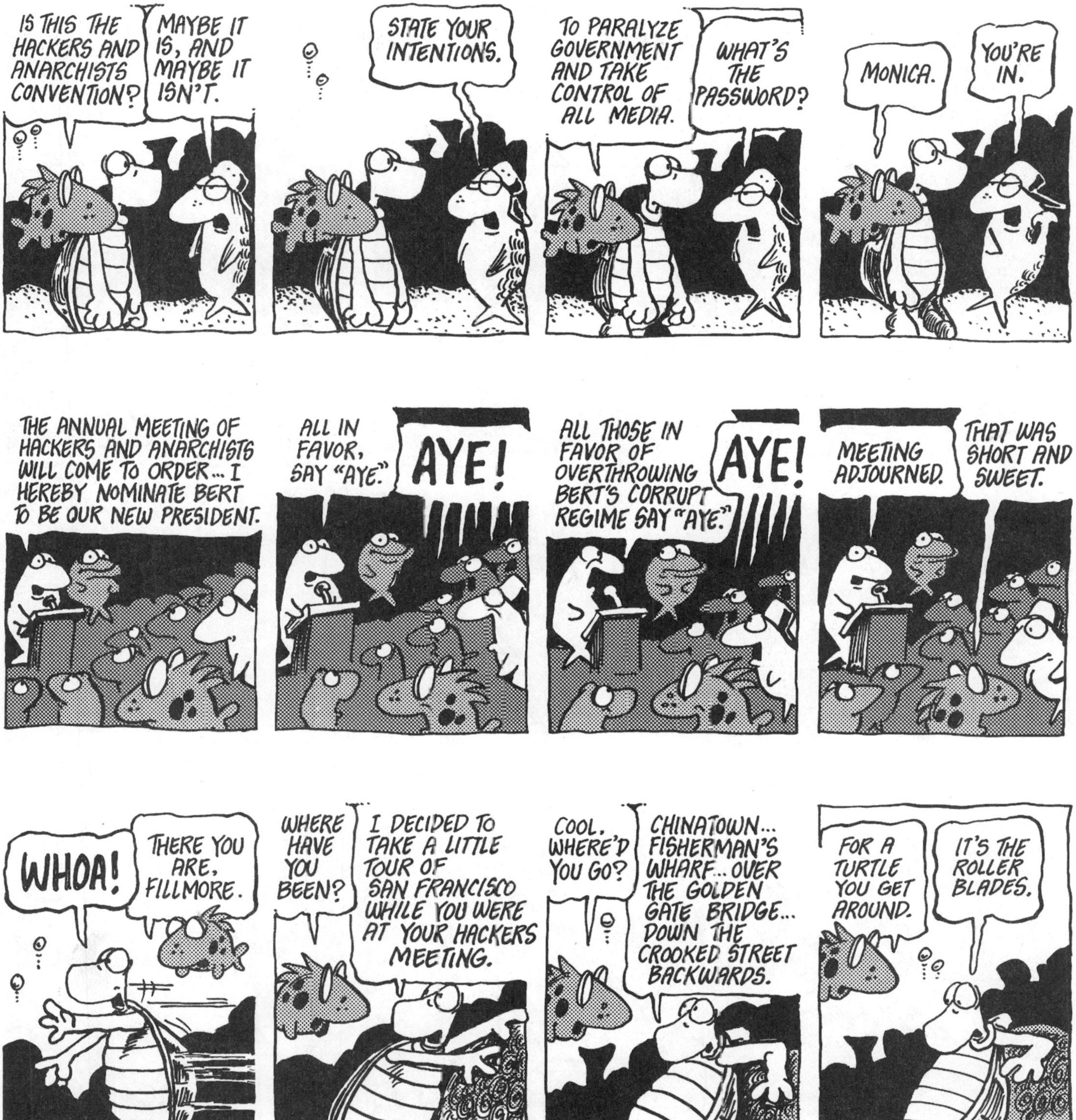
IS THIS THE HACKERS AND ANARCHISTS CONVENTION?
MAYBE IT IS, AND MAYBE IT ISN'T.
STATE YOUR INTENTIONS.
TO PARALYZE GOVERNMENT AND TAKE CONTROL OF ALL MEDIA.
WHAT'S THE PASSWORD?
MONICA.
YOU'RE IN.
THE ANNUAL MEETING OF HACKERS AND ANARCHISTS WILL COME TO ORDER... I HEREBY NOMINATE BERT TO BE OUR NEW PRESIDENT.
ALL IN FAVOR, SAY "AYE."
AYE!
ALL THOSE IN FAVOR OF OVERTHROWING BERT'S CORRUPT REGIME SAY "AYE."
AYE!
MEETING ADJOURNED.
THAT WAS SHORT AND SWEET.
WHOA!
THERE YOU ARE, FILLMORE.
WHERE HAVE YOU BEEN?
I DECIDED TO TAKE A LITTLE TOUR OF SAN FRANCISCO WHILE YOU WERE AT YOUR HACKERS MEETING.
COOL. WHERE'D YOU GO?
CHINATOWN... FISHERMAN'S WHARF... OVER THE GOLDEN GATE BRIDGE... DOWN THE CROOKED STREET BACKWARDS.
FOR A TURTLE YOU GET AROUND.
IT'S THE ROLLER BLADES.

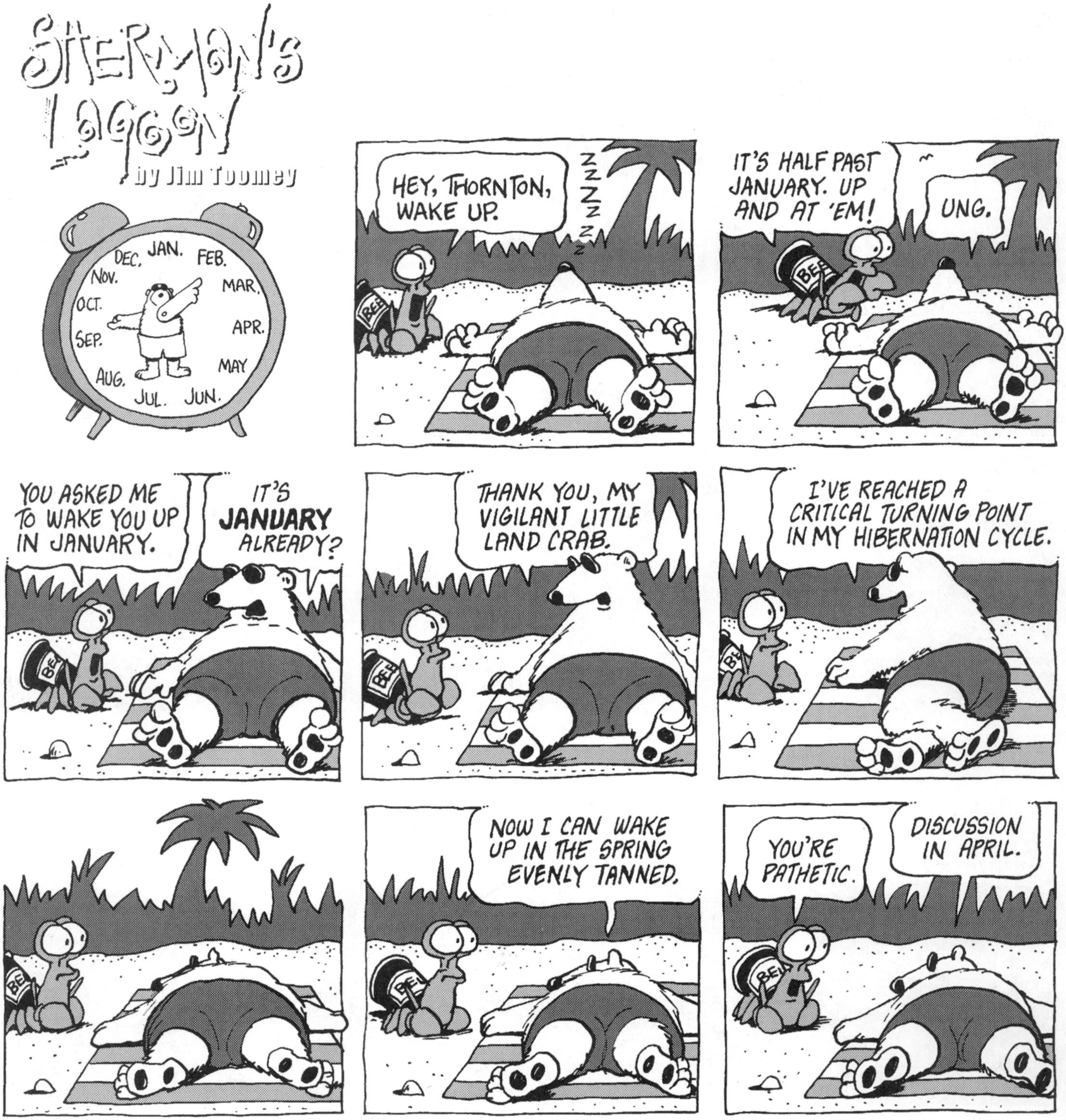
SHERMAN'S LAGOON
by Jim Toomey
DEC. JAN. FEB.
NOV. MAR.
OCT.
SEP. APR.
AUG. MAY
JUL. JUN.
HEY, THORNTON, WAKE UP.
Z Z Z Z Z Z
IT'S HALF PAST JANUARY. UP AND AT 'EM!
UNG.
YOU ASKED ME TO WAKE YOU UP IN JANUARY.
IT'S **JANUARY** ALREADY?
THANK YOU, MY VIGILANT LITTLE LAND CRAB.
I'VE REACHED A CRITICAL TURNING POINT IN MY HIBERNATION CYCLE.
NOW I CAN WAKE UP IN THE SPRING EVENLY TANNED.
YOU'RE PATHETIC.
DISCUSSION IN APRIL.

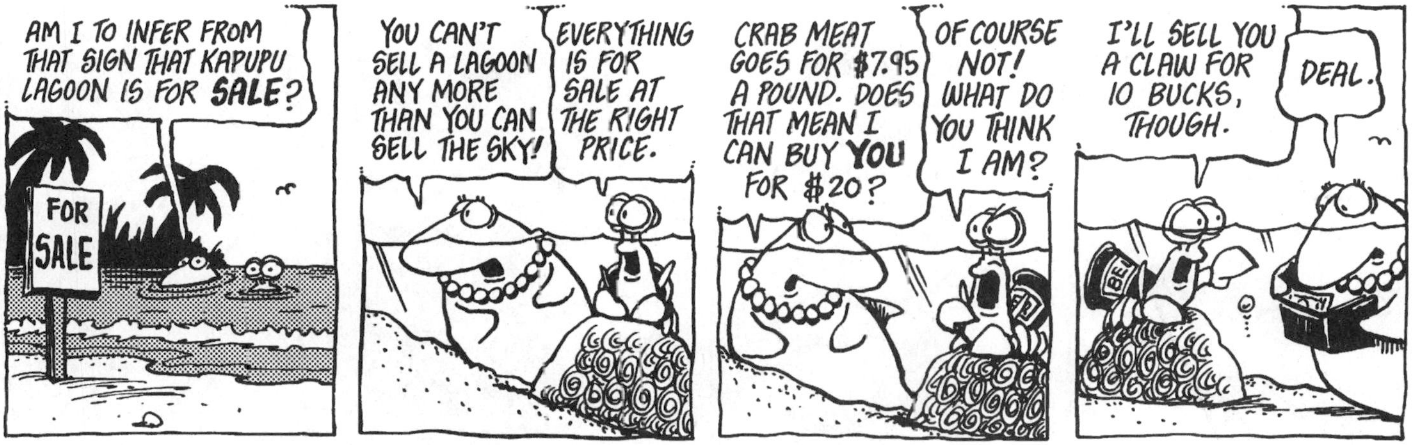
AM I TO INFER FROM THAT SIGN THAT KAPUPU LAGOON IS FOR **SALE**?
FOR SALE
YOU CAN'T SELL A LAGOON ANY MORE THAN YOU CAN SELL THE SKY!
EVERYTHING IS FOR SALE AT THE RIGHT PRICE.
CRAB MEAT GOES FOR $7.95 A POUND. DOES THAT MEAN I CAN BUY **YOU** FOR $20?
OF COURSE NOT! WHAT DO YOU THINK I AM?
I'LL SELL YOU A CLAW FOR 10 BUCKS, THOUGH.
DEAL.

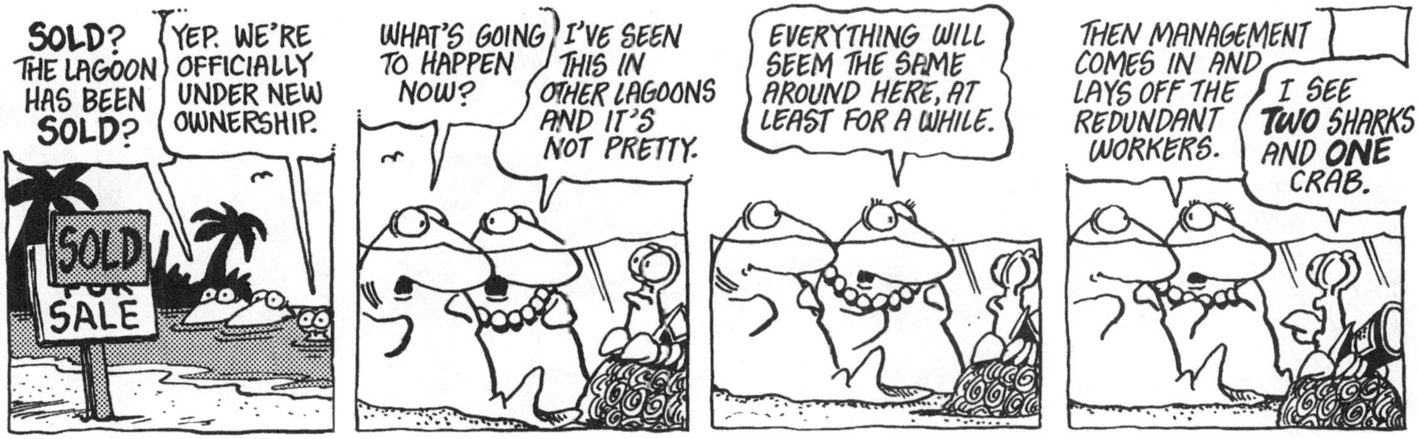
**SOLD**? THE LAGOON HAS BEEN **SOLD**?
YEP. WE'RE OFFICIALLY UNDER NEW OWNERSHIP.
SOLD
SALE
WHAT'S GOING TO HAPPEN NOW?
I'VE SEEN THIS IN OTHER LAGOONS AND IT'S NOT PRETTY.
EVERYTHING WILL SEEM THE SAME AROUND HERE, AT LEAST FOR A WHILE.
THEN MANAGEMENT COMES IN AND LAYS OFF THE REDUNDANT WORKERS.
I SEE **TWO** SHARKS AND **ONE** CRAB.

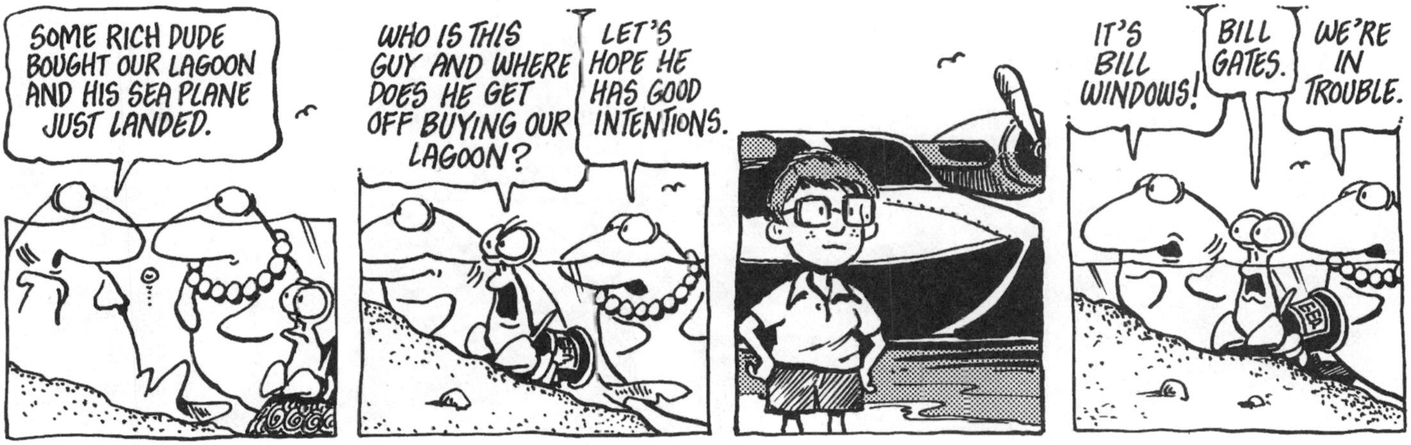
SOME RICH DUDE BOUGHT OUR LAGOON AND HIS SEA PLANE JUST LANDED.
WHO IS THIS GUY AND WHERE DOES HE GET OFF BUYING OUR LAGOON?
LET'S HOPE HE HAS GOOD INTENTIONS.
IT'S BILL WINDOWS!
BILL GATES.
WE'RE IN TROUBLE.

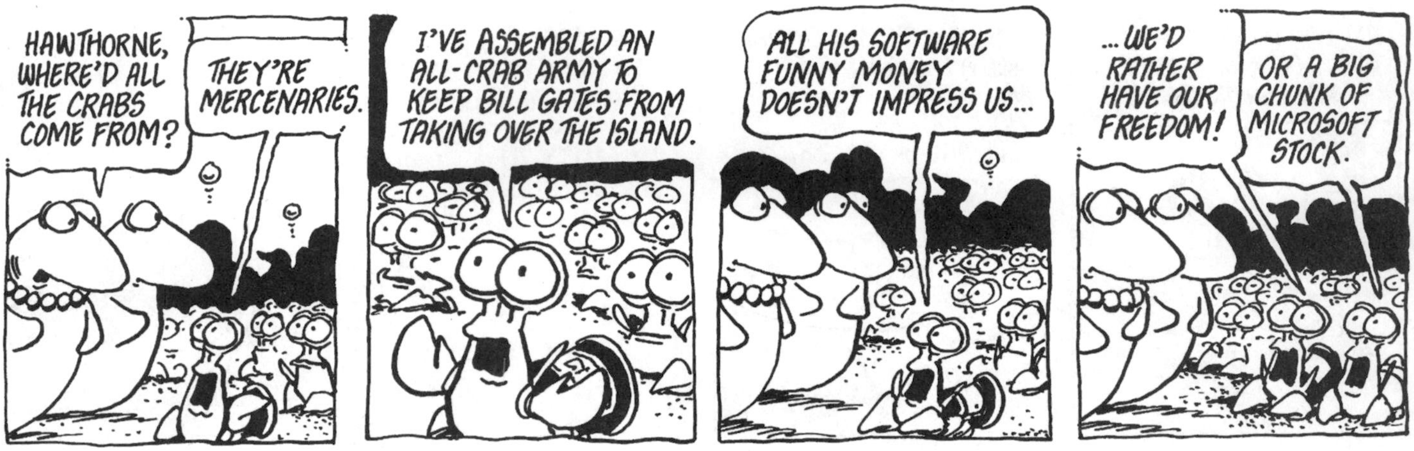
HAWTHORNE, WHERE'D ALL THE CRABS COME FROM?
THEY'RE MERCENARIES.
I'VE ASSEMBLED AN ALL-CRAB ARMY TO KEEP BILL GATES FROM TAKING OVER THE ISLAND.
ALL HIS SOFTWARE FUNNY MONEY DOESN'T IMPRESS US...
...WE'D RATHER HAVE OUR FREEDOM!
OR A BIG CHUNK OF MICROSOFT STOCK.

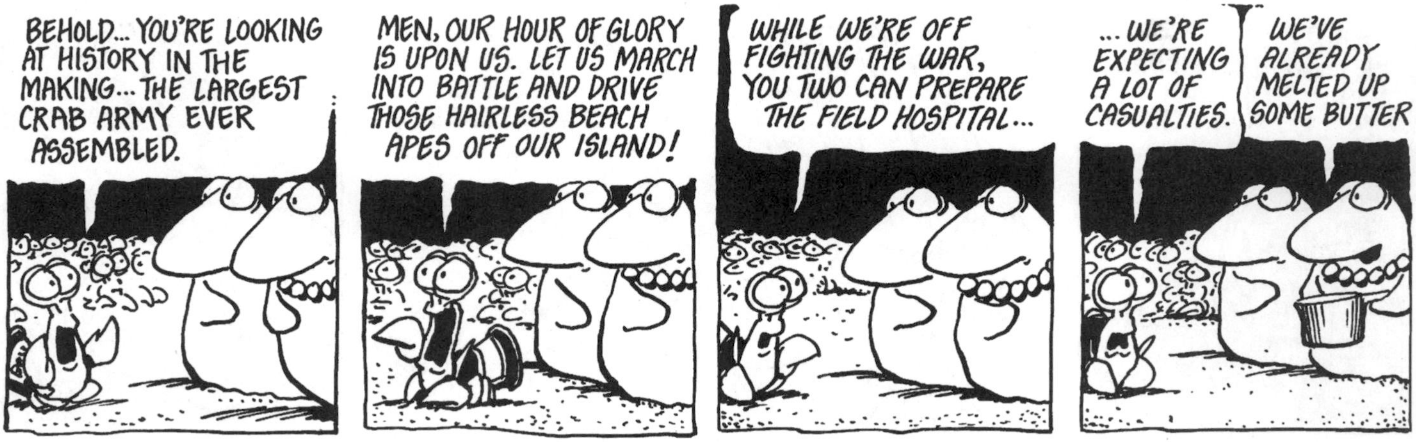
BEHOLD... YOU'RE LOOKING AT HISTORY IN THE MAKING... THE LARGEST CRAB ARMY EVER ASSEMBLED.
MEN, OUR HOUR OF GLORY IS UPON US. LET US MARCH INTO BATTLE AND DRIVE THOSE HAIRLESS BEACH APES OFF OUR ISLAND!
WHILE WE'RE OFF FIGHTING THE WAR, YOU TWO CAN PREPARE THE FIELD HOSPITAL...
...WE'RE EXPECTING A LOT OF CASUALTIES.
WE'VE ALREADY MELTED UP SOME BUTTER

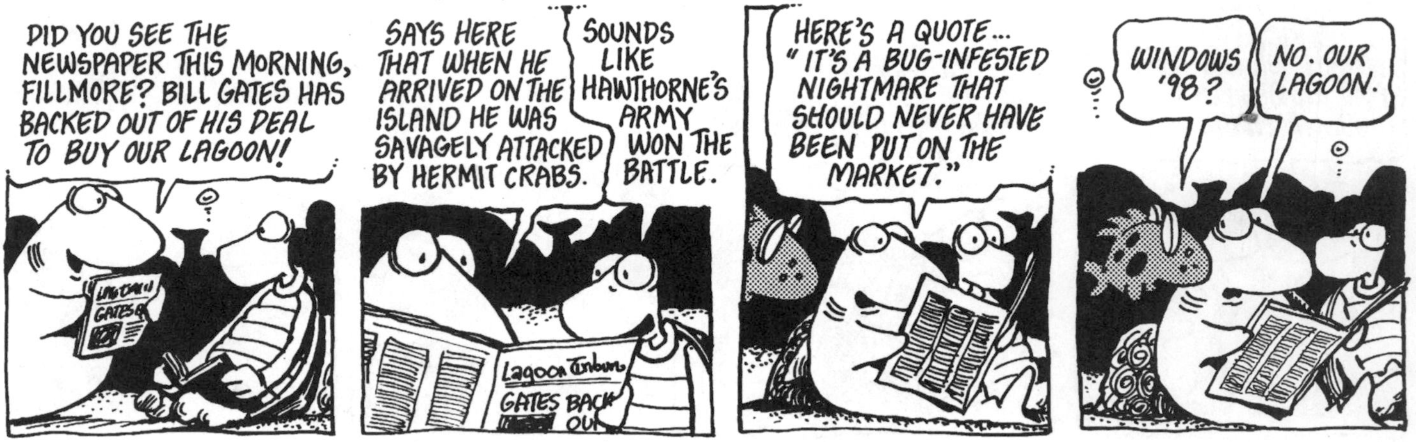
DID YOU SEE THE NEWSPAPER THIS MORNING, FILLMORE? BILL GATES HAS BACKED OUT OF HIS DEAL TO BUY OUR LAGOON!
SAYS HERE THAT WHEN HE ARRIVED ON THE ISLAND HE WAS SAVAGELY ATTACKED BY HERMIT CRABS.
SOUNDS LIKE HAWTHORNE'S ARMY WON THE BATTLE.
HERE'S A QUOTE... "IT'S A BUG-INFESTED NIGHTMARE THAT SHOULD NEVER HAVE BEEN PUT ON THE MARKET."
WINDOWS '98?
NO. OUR LAGOON.

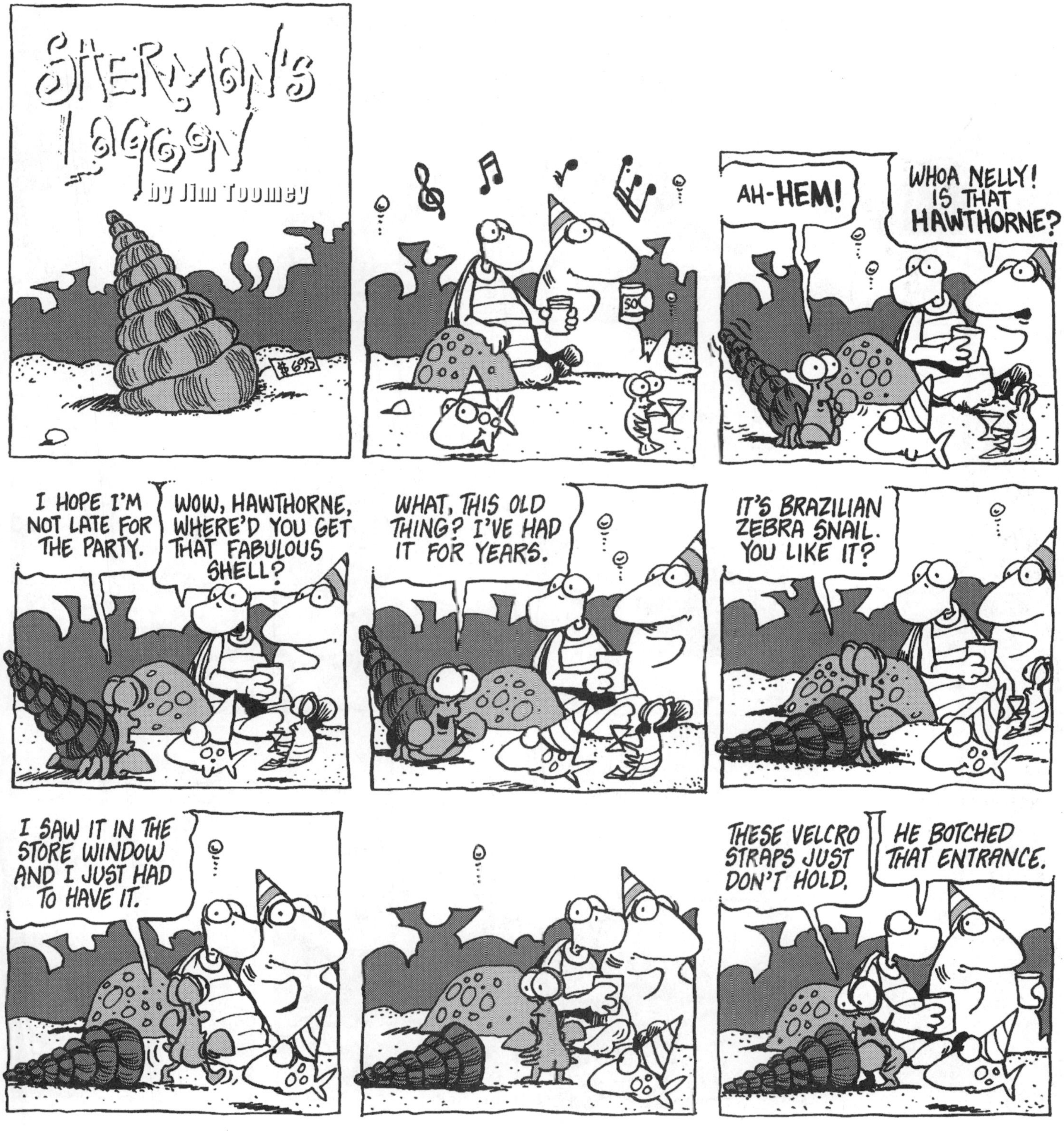
Sherman's Lagoon
by Jim Toomey
$69.95
AH-HEM!
WHOA NELLY! IS THAT HAWTHORNE?
I HOPE I'M NOT LATE FOR THE PARTY.
WOW, HAWTHORNE, WHERE'D YOU GET THAT FABULOUS SHELL?
WHAT, THIS OLD THING? I'VE HAD IT FOR YEARS.
IT'S BRAZILIAN ZEBRA SNAIL. YOU LIKE IT?
I SAW IT IN THE STORE WINDOW AND I JUST HAD TO HAVE IT.
THESE VELCRO STRAPS JUST DON'T HOLD.
HE BOTCHED THAT ENTRANCE.

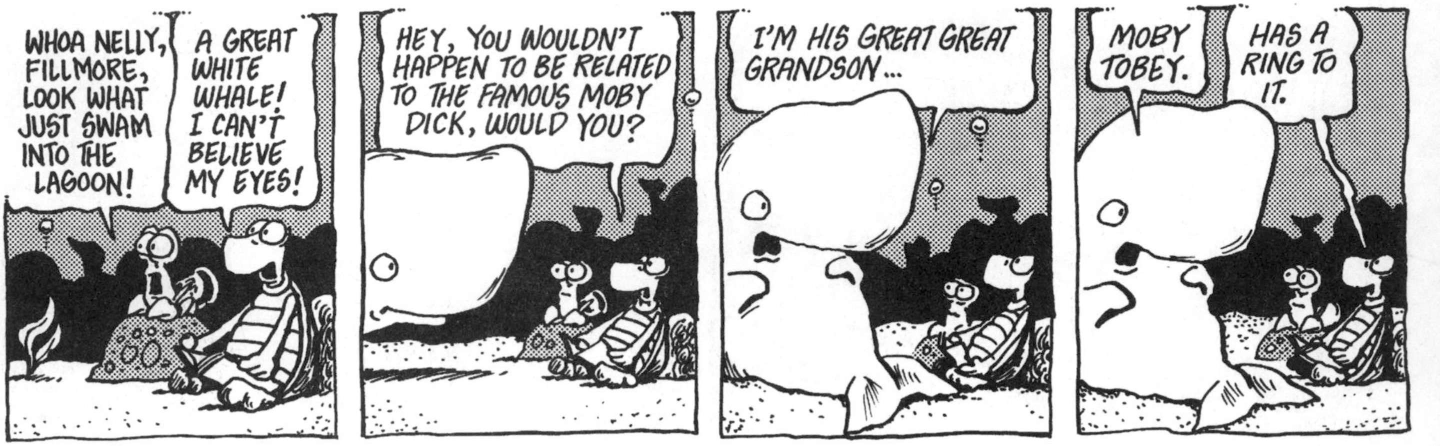
WHOA NELLY, FILLMORE, LOOK WHAT JUST SWAM INTO THE LAGOON!
A GREAT WHITE WHALE! I CAN'T BELIEVE MY EYES!
HEY, YOU WOULDN'T HAPPEN TO BE RELATED TO THE FAMOUS MOBY DICK, WOULD YOU?
I'M HIS GREAT GREAT GRANDSON...
MOBY TOBEY.
HAS A RING TO IT.

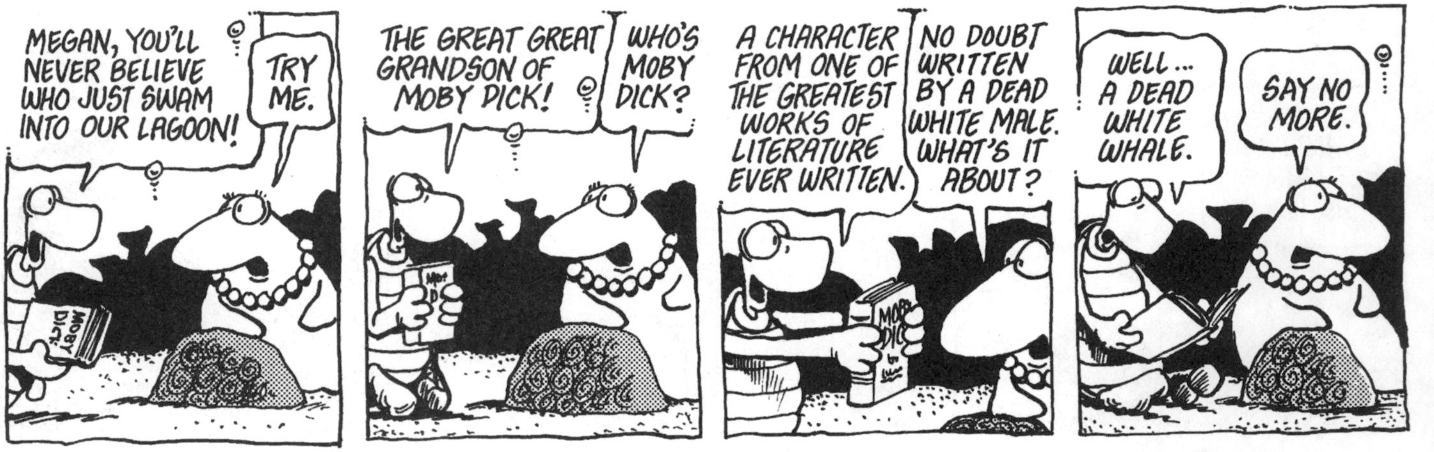
MEGAN, YOU'LL NEVER BELIEVE WHO JUST SWAM INTO OUR LAGOON!
TRY ME.
THE GREAT GREAT GRANDSON OF MOBY DICK!
WHO'S MOBY DICK?
A CHARACTER FROM ONE OF THE GREATEST WORKS OF LITERATURE EVER WRITTEN.
NO DOUBT WRITTEN BY A DEAD WHITE MALE. WHAT'S IT ABOUT?
WELL ... A DEAD WHITE WHALE.
SAY NO MORE.

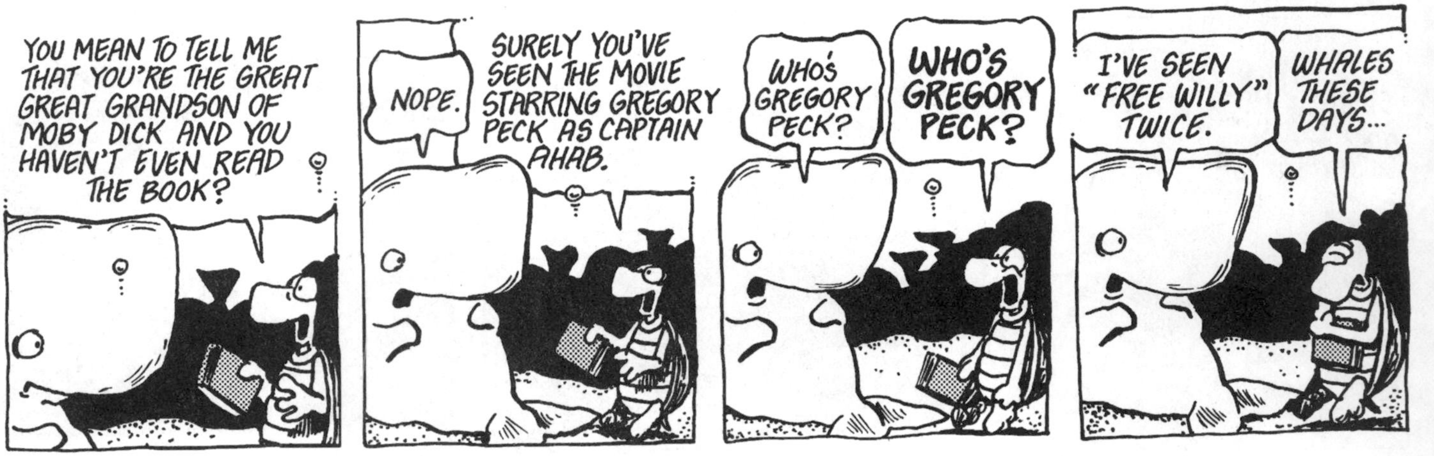
YOU MEAN TO TELL ME THAT YOU'RE THE GREAT GREAT GRANDSON OF MOBY DICK AND YOU HAVEN'T EVEN READ THE BOOK?
NOPE.
SURELY YOU'VE SEEN THE MOVIE STARRING GREGORY PECK AS CAPTAIN AHAB.
WHO'S GREGORY PECK?
WHO'S GREGORY PECK?
I'VE SEEN "FREE WILLY" TWICE.
WHALES THESE DAYS...

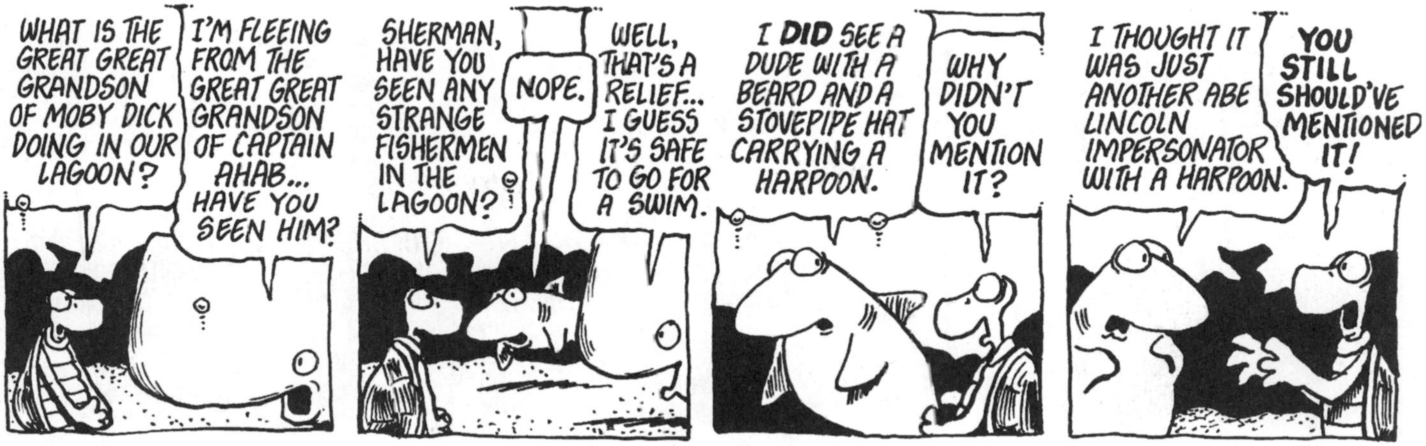
WHAT IS THE GREAT GREAT GRANDSON OF MOBY DICK DOING IN OUR LAGOON?
I'M FLEEING FROM THE GREAT GREAT GRANDSON OF CAPTAIN AHAB... HAVE YOU SEEN HIM?
SHERMAN, HAVE YOU SEEN ANY STRANGE FISHERMEN IN THE LAGOON?
NOPE.
WELL, THAT'S A RELIEF... I GUESS IT'S SAFE TO GO FOR A SWIM.
I DID SEE A DUDE WITH A BEARD AND A STOVEPIPE HAT CARRYING A HARPOON.
WHY DIDN'T YOU MENTION IT?
I THOUGHT IT WAS JUST ANOTHER ABE LINCOLN IMPERSONATOR WITH A HARPOON.
YOU STILL SHOULD'VE MENTIONED IT!

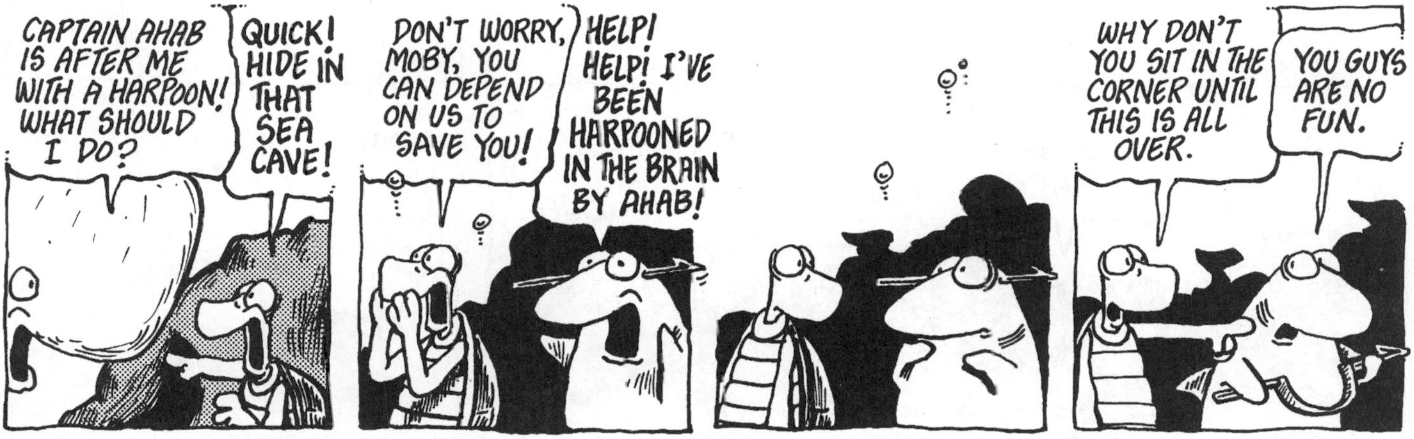
CAPTAIN AHAB IS AFTER ME WITH A HARPOON! WHAT SHOULD I DO?
QUICK! HIDE IN THAT SEA CAVE!
DON'T WORRY, MOBY, YOU CAN DEPEND ON US TO SAVE YOU!
HELP! HELP! I'VE BEEN HARPOONED IN THE BRAIN BY AHAB!
WHY DON'T YOU SIT IN THE CORNER UNTIL THIS IS ALL OVER.
YOU GUYS ARE NO FUN.

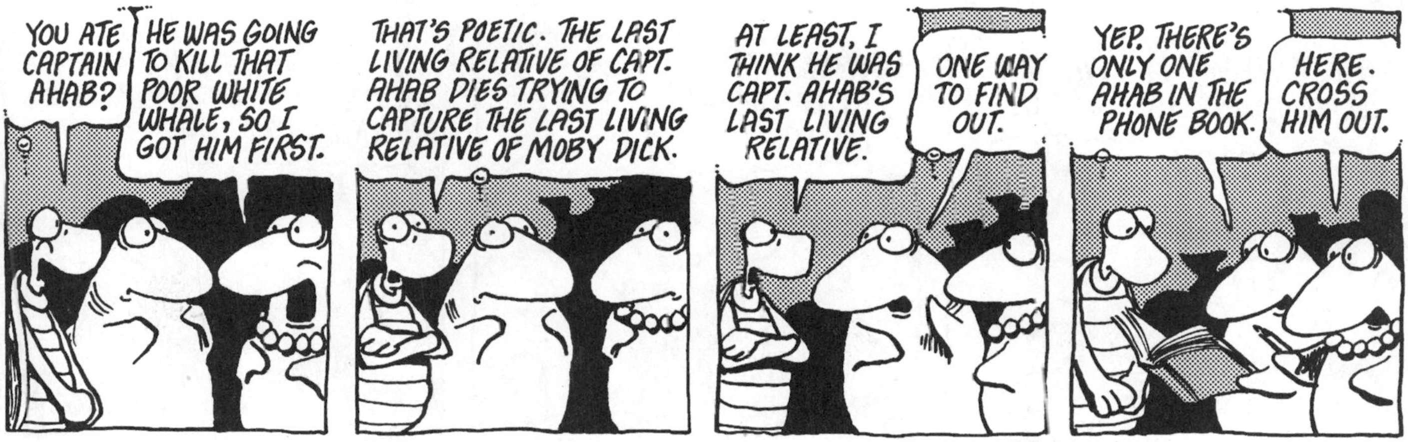
YOU ATE CAPTAIN AHAB?
HE WAS GOING TO KILL THAT POOR WHITE WHALE, SO I GOT HIM FIRST.
THAT'S POETIC. THE LAST LIVING RELATIVE OF CAPT. AHAB DIES TRYING TO CAPTURE THE LAST LIVING RELATIVE OF MOBY DICK.
AT LEAST, I THINK HE WAS CAPT. AHAB'S LAST LIVING RELATIVE.
ONE WAY TO FIND OUT.
YEP. THERE'S ONLY ONE AHAB IN THE PHONE BOOK.
HERE. CROSS HIM OUT.

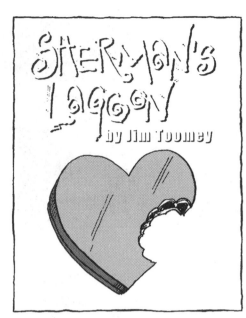

**SHERMAN'S LAGOON**
by Jim Toomey

WHAT DID YOU GET FOR YOUR SWEETHEART THIS VALENTINE'S DAY?

A DOZEN LONG STEM ROSES.

PUT THEM OVER THERE. WHAT ELSE?

GOLD CHAINS AND PRECIOUS STONES.

BORE ME. WHAT ELSE?

ASSORTED CHOCOLATES.

COME TO MAMA. WHAT ELSE?

GODIVA DARK CHOCOLATES.

MPHT! WHAT ELSE?

CHOCOLATE-COVERED CARAMEL PEANUT CLUSTERS.

MPHT...MMM... WHAT ELSE?

...A SILK SCARF.

GRRR..MPTH.. ARPH! OOMPH! MPHT...

I DON'T THINK IT'S SAFE TO BE IN THE WATER RIGHT NOW.

I'M GOING UP ON THE BEACH.

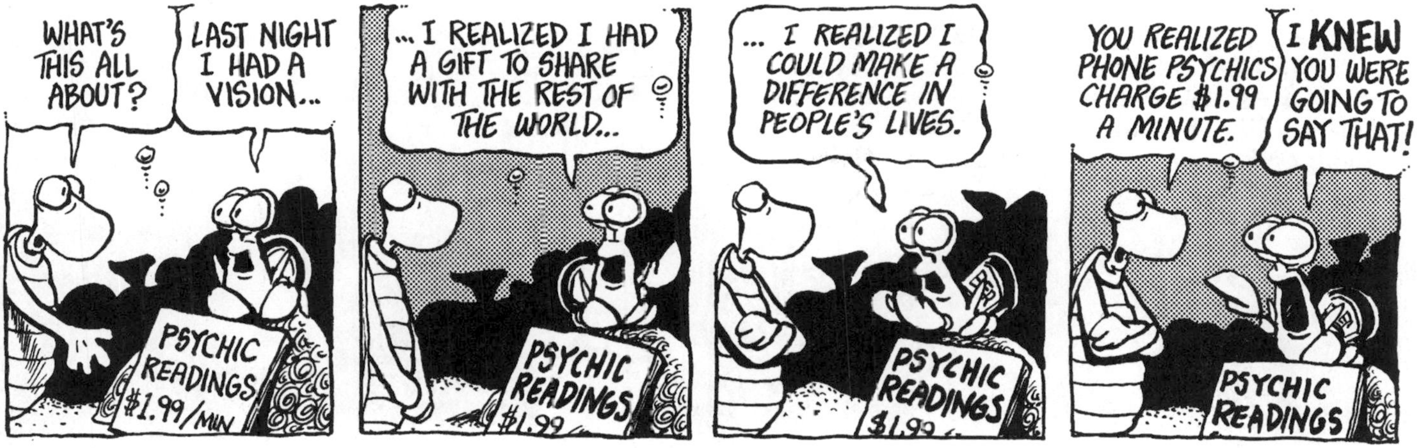
WHAT'S THIS ALL ABOUT?
LAST NIGHT I HAD A VISION...
PSYCHIC READINGS $1.99/MIN
... I REALIZED I HAD A GIFT TO SHARE WITH THE REST OF THE WORLD...
PSYCHIC READINGS
... I REALIZED I COULD MAKE A DIFFERENCE IN PEOPLE'S LIVES.
PSYCHIC READINGS
YOU REALIZED PHONE PSYCHICS CHARGE $1.99 A MINUTE.
I **KNEW** YOU WERE GOING TO SAY THAT!
PSYCHIC READINGS

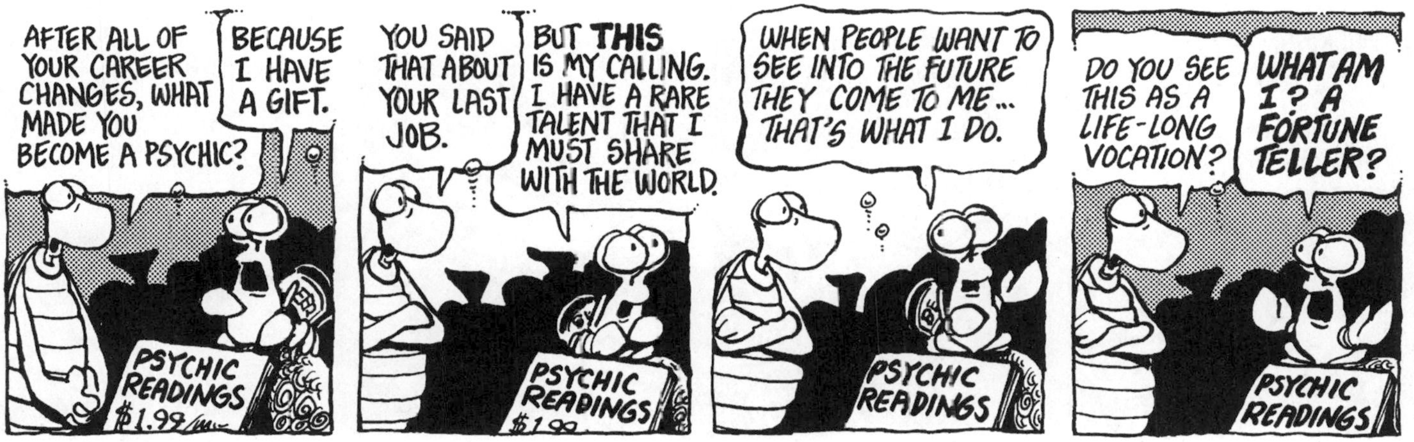
AFTER ALL OF YOUR CAREER CHANGES, WHAT MADE YOU BECOME A PSYCHIC?
BECAUSE I HAVE A GIFT.
PSYCHIC READINGS
YOU SAID THAT ABOUT YOUR LAST JOB.
BUT **THIS** IS MY CALLING. I HAVE A RARE TALENT THAT I MUST SHARE WITH THE WORLD.
PSYCHIC READINGS
WHEN PEOPLE WANT TO SEE INTO THE FUTURE THEY COME TO ME... THAT'S WHAT I DO.
PSYCHIC READINGS
DO YOU SEE THIS AS A LIFE-LONG VOCATION?
**WHAT AM I? A FORTUNE TELLER?**
PSYCHIC READINGS

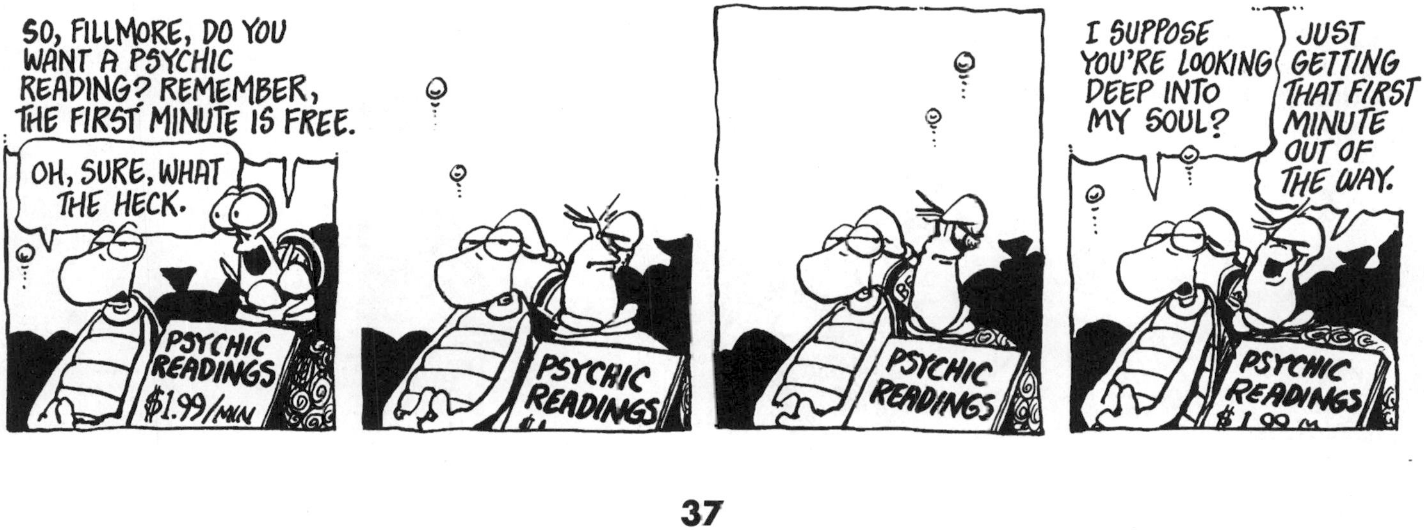
SO, FILLMORE, DO YOU WANT A PSYCHIC READING? REMEMBER, THE FIRST MINUTE IS FREE.
OH, SURE, WHAT THE HECK.
PSYCHIC READINGS $1.99/MIN
PSYCHIC READINGS
PSYCHIC READINGS
I SUPPOSE YOU'RE LOOKING DEEP INTO MY SOUL?
JUST GETTING THAT FIRST MINUTE OUT OF THE WAY.
PSYCHIC READINGS

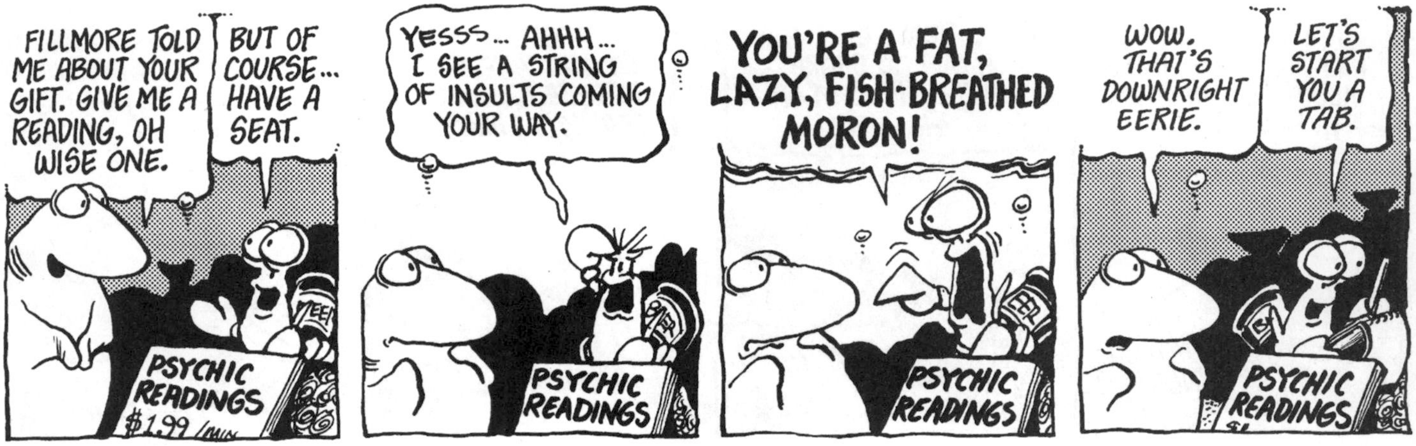
FILLMORE TOLD ME ABOUT YOUR GIFT. GIVE ME A READING, OH WISE ONE.
BUT OF COURSE... HAVE A SEAT.
PSYCHIC READINGS
YESSS... AHHH... I SEE A STRING OF INSULTS COMING YOUR WAY.
PSYCHIC READINGS
YOU'RE A FAT, LAZY, FISH-BREATHED MORON!
PSYCHIC READINGS
WOW. THAT'S DOWNRIGHT EERIE.
LET'S START YOU A TAB.
PSYCHIC READINGS

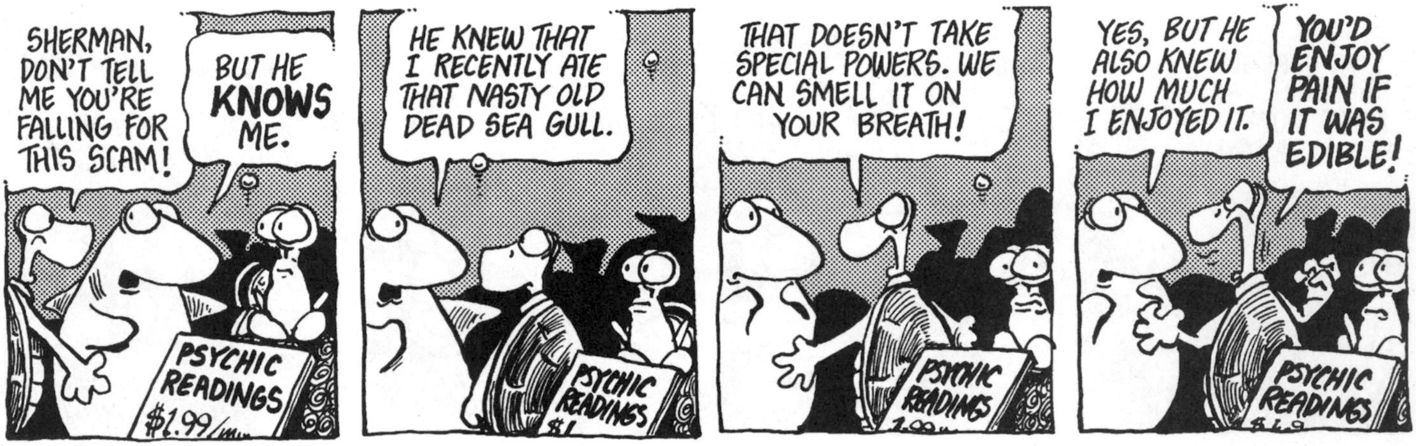
SHERMAN, DON'T TELL ME YOU'RE FALLING FOR THIS SCAM!
BUT HE **KNOWS** ME.
PSYCHIC READINGS
HE KNEW THAT I RECENTLY ATE THAT NASTY OLD DEAD SEA GULL.
PSYCHIC READINGS
THAT DOESN'T TAKE SPECIAL POWERS. WE CAN SMELL IT ON YOUR BREATH!
PSYCHIC READINGS
YES, BUT HE ALSO KNEW HOW MUCH I ENJOYED IT.
YOU'D ENJOY PAIN IF IT WAS EDIBLE!
PSYCHIC READINGS

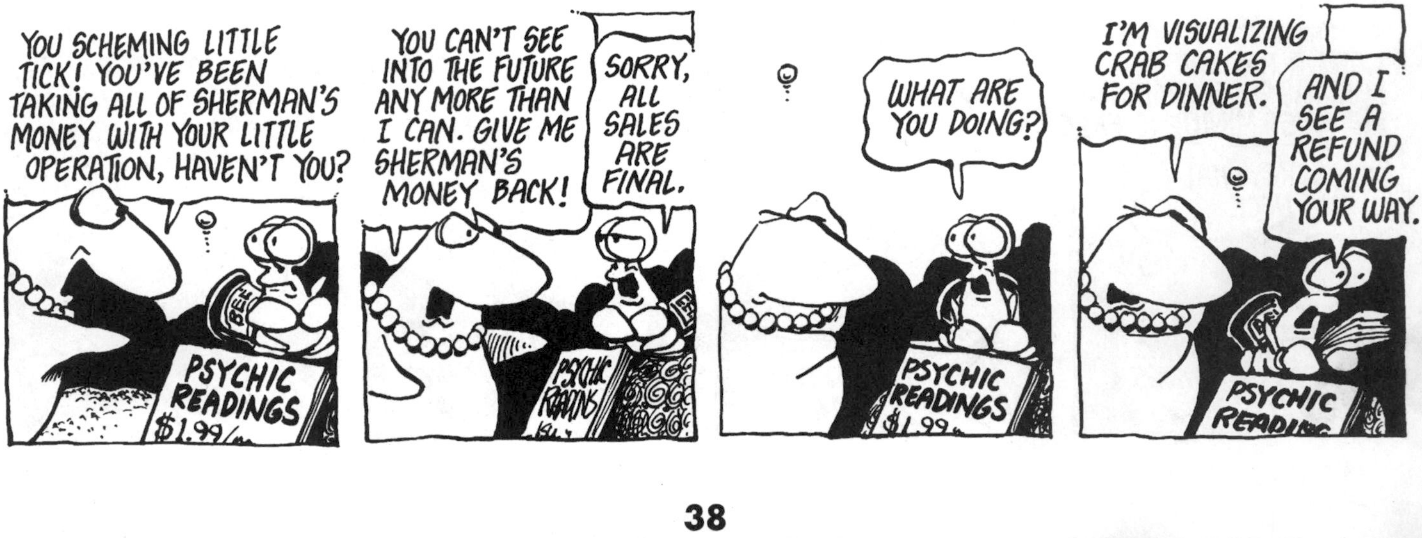
YOU SCHEMING LITTLE TICK! YOU'VE BEEN TAKING ALL OF SHERMAN'S MONEY WITH YOUR LITTLE OPERATION, HAVEN'T YOU?
PSYCHIC READINGS
YOU CAN'T SEE INTO THE FUTURE ANY MORE THAN I CAN. GIVE ME SHERMAN'S MONEY BACK!
SORRY, ALL SALES ARE FINAL.
WHAT ARE YOU DOING?
PSYCHIC READINGS
I'M VISUALIZING CRAB CAKES FOR DINNER.
AND I SEE A REFUND COMING YOUR WAY.

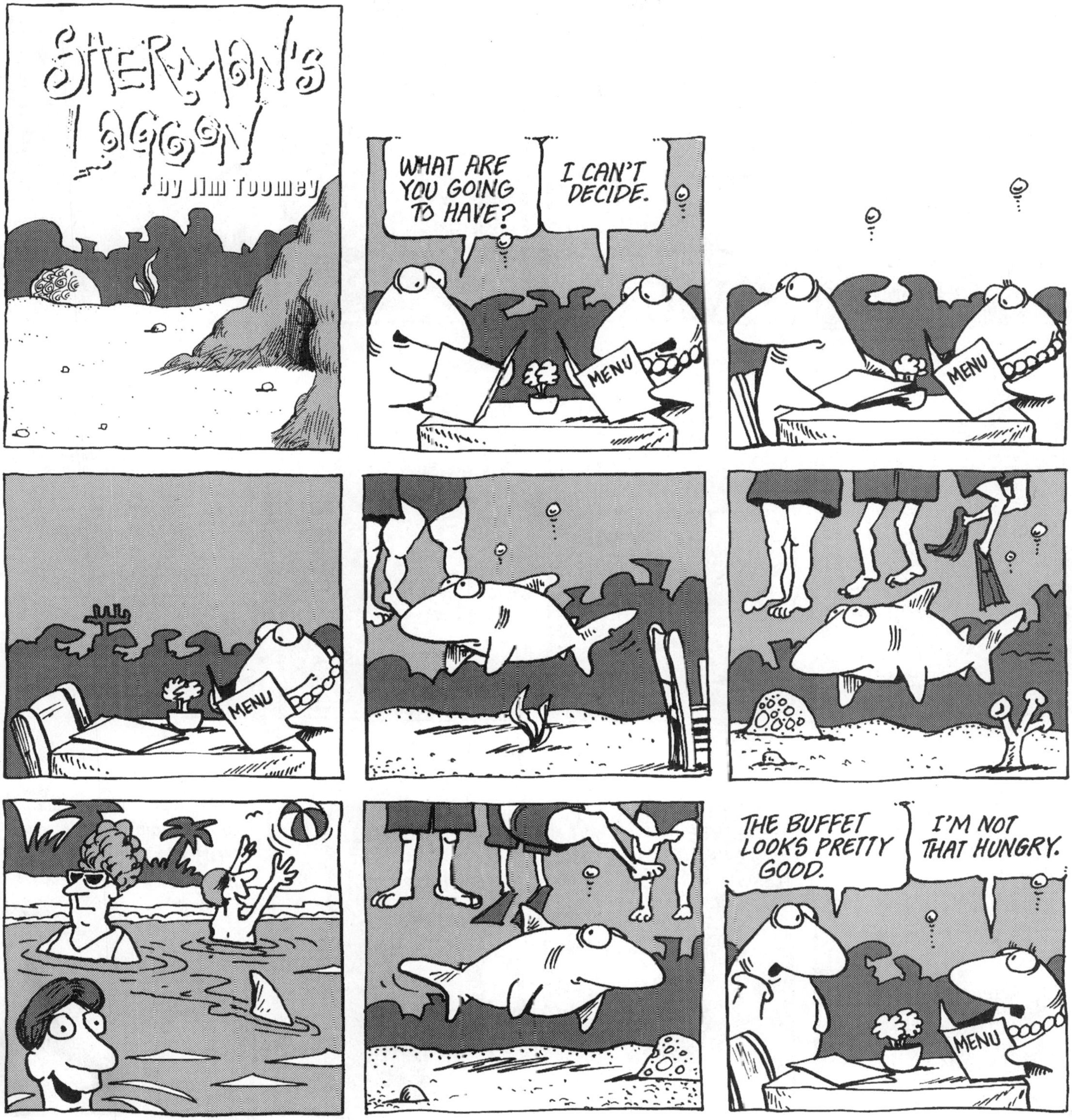
SHERMAN'S LAGOON
by Jim Toomey
WHAT ARE YOU GOING TO HAVE?
I CAN'T DECIDE.
MENU
MENU
MENU
THE BUFFET LOOKS PRETTY GOOD.
I'M NOT THAT HUNGRY.
MENU

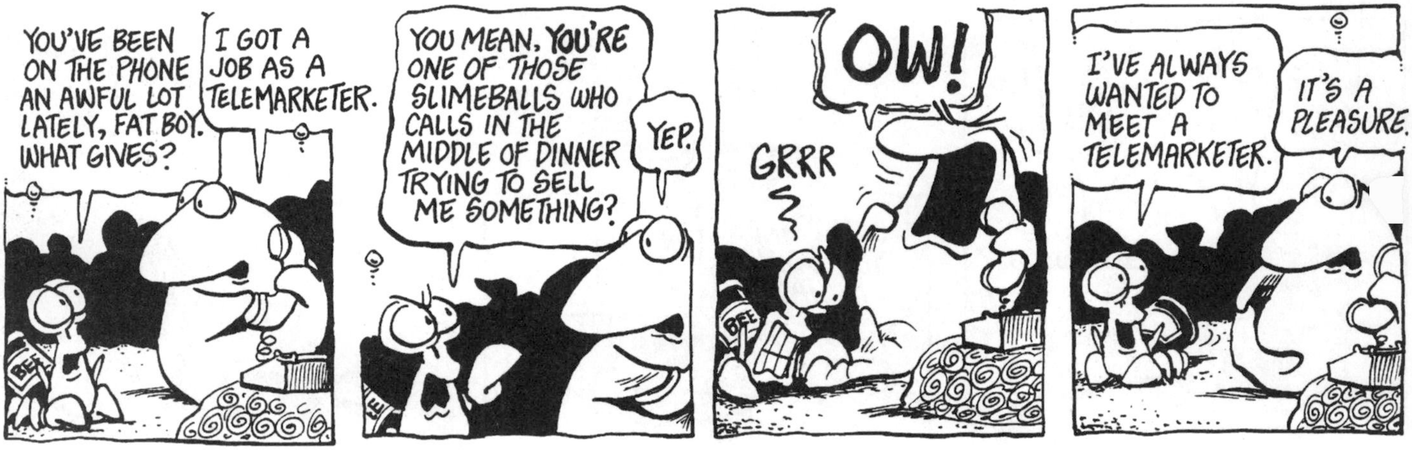
YOU'VE BEEN ON THE PHONE AN AWFUL LOT LATELY, FAT BOY. WHAT GIVES?
I GOT A JOB AS A TELEMARKETER.
YOU MEAN, YOU'RE ONE OF THOSE SLIMEBALLS WHO CALLS IN THE MIDDLE OF DINNER TRYING TO SELL ME SOMETHING?
YEP.
OW!
GRRR
I'VE ALWAYS WANTED TO MEET A TELEMARKETER.
IT'S A PLEASURE.

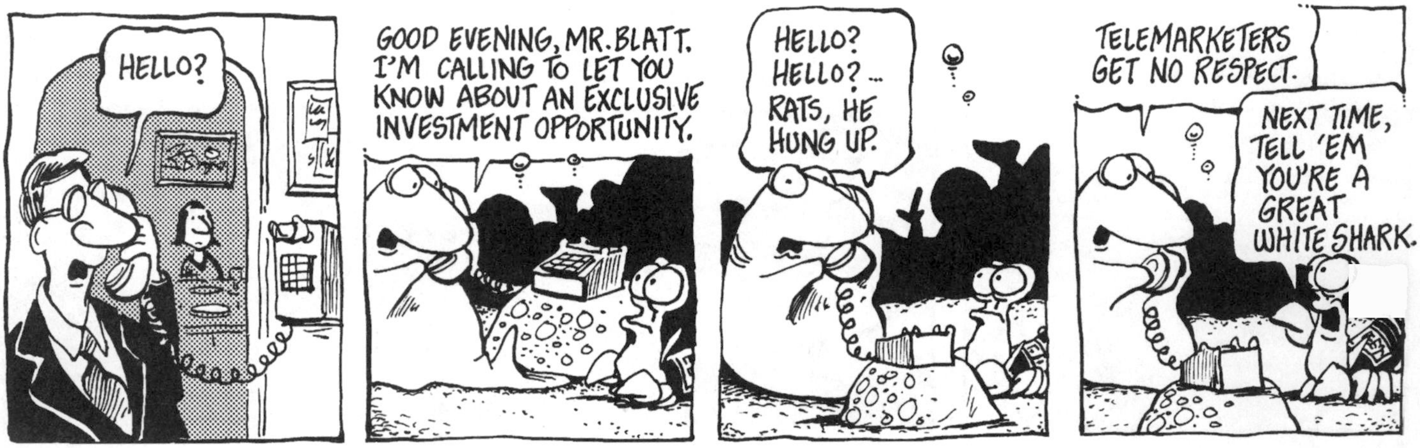
HELLO?
GOOD EVENING, MR. BLATT. I'M CALLING TO LET YOU KNOW ABOUT AN EXCLUSIVE INVESTMENT OPPORTUNITY.
HELLO? HELLO? ... RATS, HE HUNG UP.
TELEMARKETERS GET NO RESPECT.
NEXT TIME, TELL 'EM YOU'RE A GREAT WHITE SHARK.

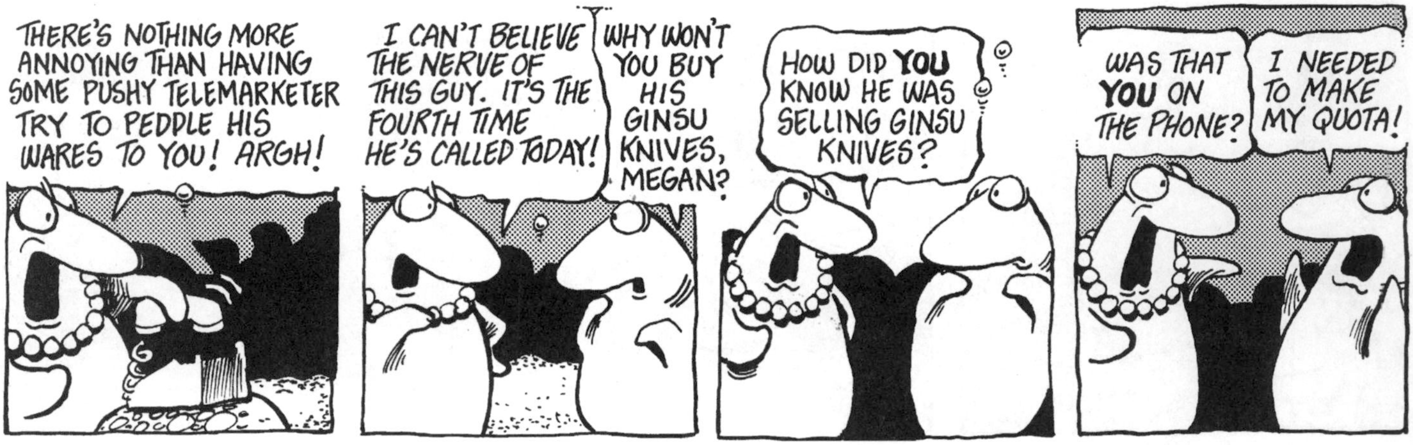
THERE'S NOTHING MORE ANNOYING THAN HAVING SOME PUSHY TELEMARKETER TRY TO PEDDLE HIS WARES TO YOU! ARGH!
I CAN'T BELIEVE THE NERVE OF THIS GUY. IT'S THE FOURTH TIME HE'S CALLED TODAY!
WHY WON'T YOU BUY HIS GINSU KNIVES, MEGAN?
HOW DID YOU KNOW HE WAS SELLING GINSU KNIVES?
WAS THAT YOU ON THE PHONE?
I NEEDED TO MAKE MY QUOTA!

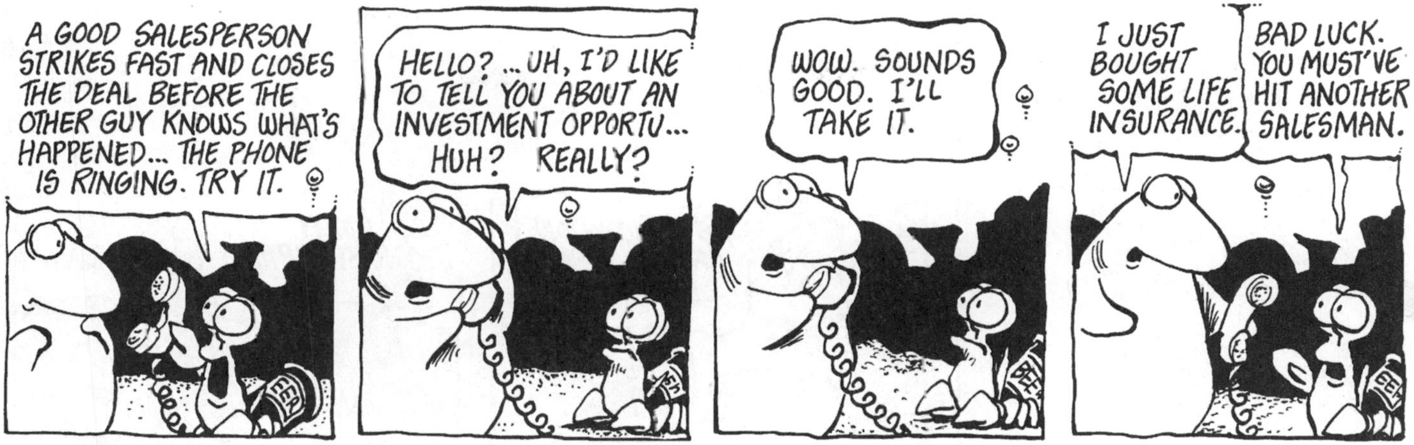
A GOOD SALESPERSON STRIKES FAST AND CLOSES THE DEAL BEFORE THE OTHER GUY KNOWS WHAT'S HAPPENED... THE PHONE IS RINGING. TRY IT.
HELLO? ...UH, I'D LIKE TO TELL YOU ABOUT AN INVESTMENT OPPORTU... HUH? REALLY?
WOW. SOUNDS GOOD. I'LL TAKE IT.
I JUST BOUGHT SOME LIFE INSURANCE.
BAD LUCK. YOU MUST'VE HIT ANOTHER SALESMAN.

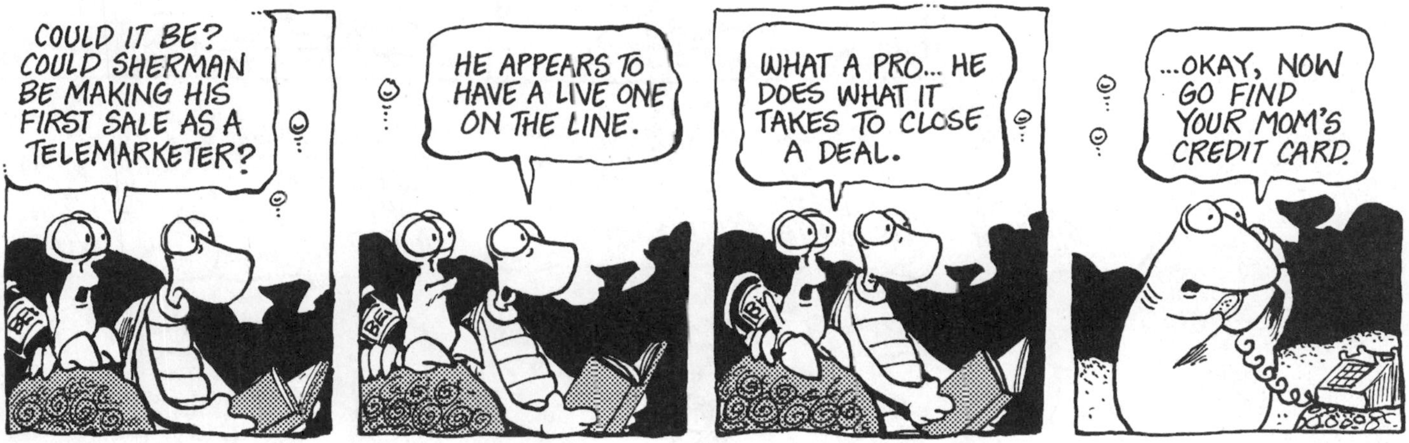
COULD IT BE? COULD SHERMAN BE MAKING HIS FIRST SALE AS A TELEMARKETER?
HE APPEARS TO HAVE A LIVE ONE ON THE LINE.
WHAT A PRO... HE DOES WHAT IT TAKES TO CLOSE A DEAL.
...OKAY, NOW GO FIND YOUR MOM'S CREDIT CARD.

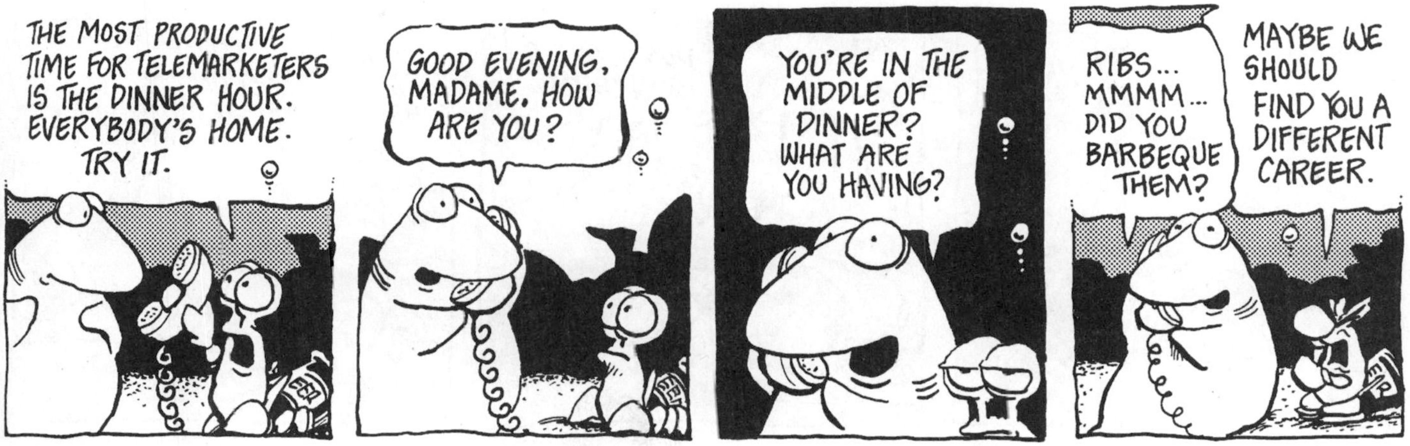
THE MOST PRODUCTIVE TIME FOR TELEMARKETERS IS THE DINNER HOUR. EVERYBODY'S HOME. TRY IT.
GOOD EVENING, MADAME. HOW ARE YOU?
YOU'RE IN THE MIDDLE OF DINNER? WHAT ARE YOU HAVING?
RIBS... MMMM... DID YOU BARBEQUE THEM?
MAYBE WE SHOULD FIND YOU A DIFFERENT CAREER.

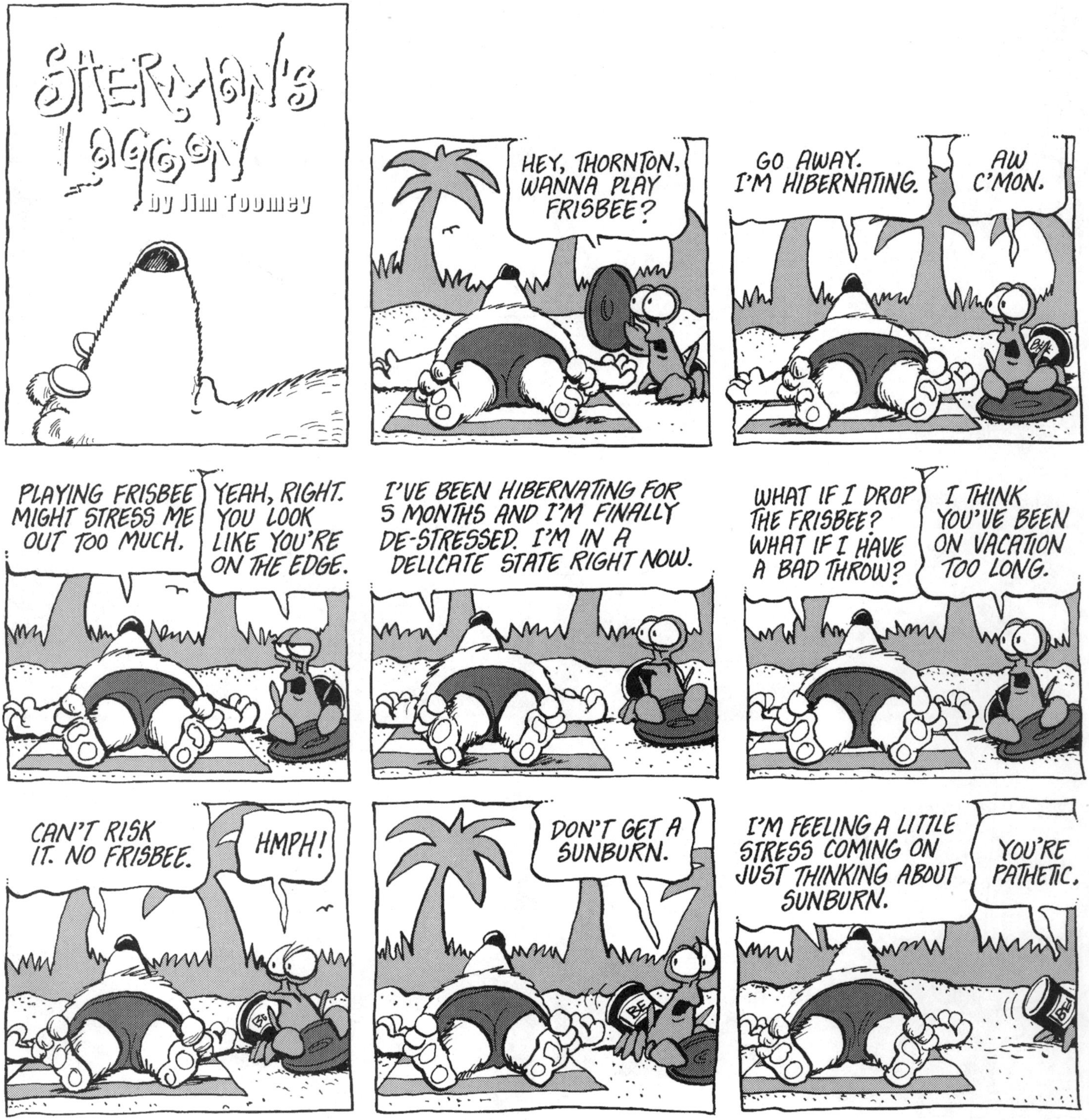
Sherman's Lagoon
by Jim Toomey
HEY, THORNTON, WANNA PLAY FRISBEE?
GO AWAY. I'M HIBERNATING.
AW C'MON.
PLAYING FRISBEE MIGHT STRESS ME OUT TOO MUCH.
YEAH, RIGHT. YOU LOOK LIKE YOU'RE ON THE EDGE.
I'VE BEEN HIBERNATING FOR 5 MONTHS AND I'M FINALLY DE-STRESSED. I'M IN A DELICATE STATE RIGHT NOW.
WHAT IF I DROP THE FRISBEE? WHAT IF I HAVE A BAD THROW?
I THINK YOU'VE BEEN ON VACATION TOO LONG.
CAN'T RISK IT. NO FRISBEE.
HMPH!
DON'T GET A SUNBURN.
I'M FEELING A LITTLE STRESS COMING ON JUST THINKING ABOUT SUNBURN.
YOU'RE PATHETIC.

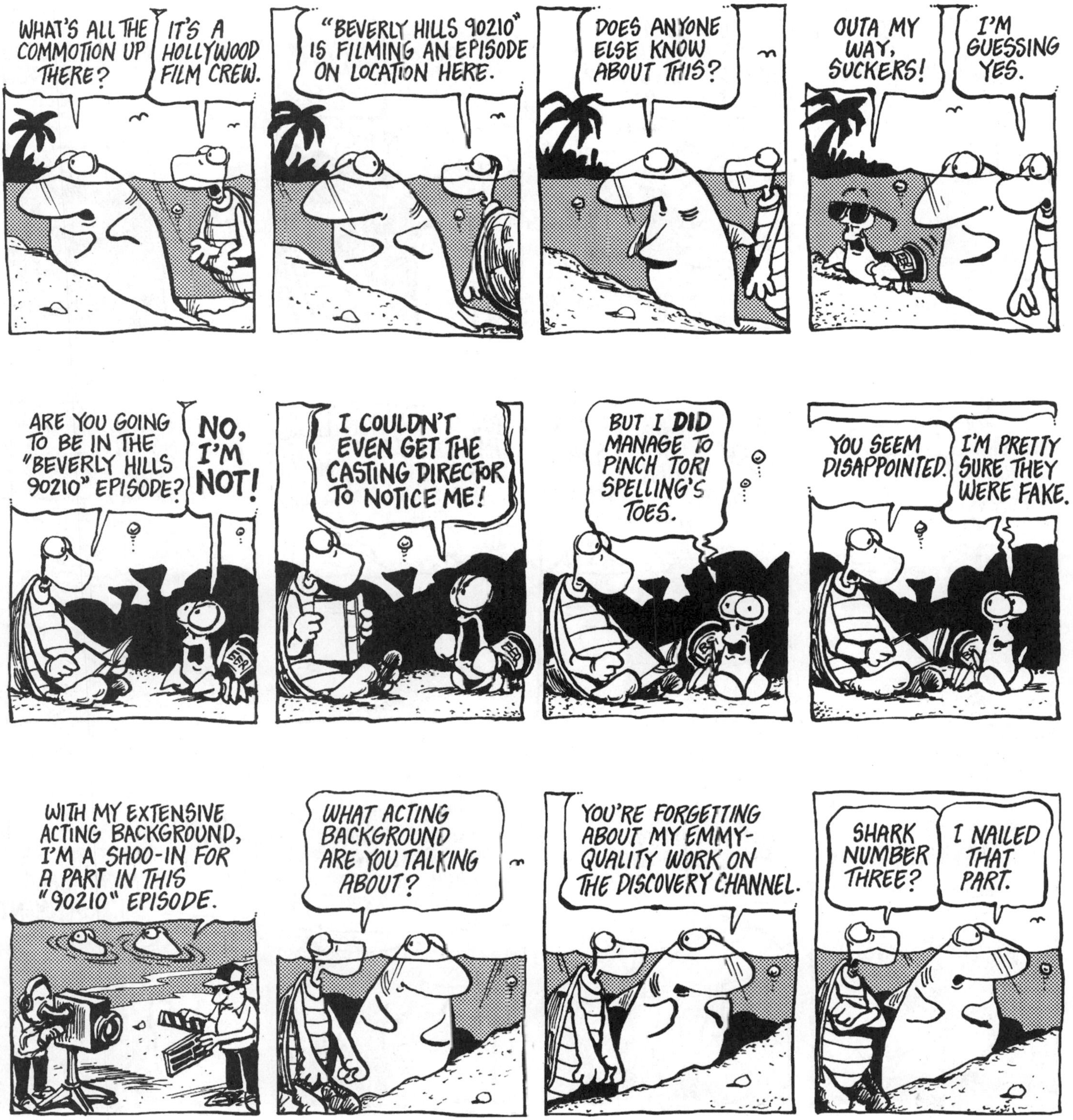
WHAT'S ALL THE COMMOTION UP THERE?
IT'S A HOLLYWOOD FILM CREW.
"BEVERLY HILLS 90210" IS FILMING AN EPISODE ON LOCATION HERE.
DOES ANYONE ELSE KNOW ABOUT THIS?
OUTA MY WAY, SUCKERS!
I'M GUESSING YES.
ARE YOU GOING TO BE IN THE "BEVERLY HILLS 90210" EPISODE?
NO, I'M NOT!
I COULDN'T EVEN GET THE CASTING DIRECTOR TO NOTICE ME!
BUT I DID MANAGE TO PINCH TORI SPELLING'S TOES.
YOU SEEM DISAPPOINTED.
I'M PRETTY SURE THEY WERE FAKE.
WITH MY EXTENSIVE ACTING BACKGROUND, I'M A SHOO-IN FOR A PART IN THIS "90210" EPISODE.
WHAT ACTING BACKGROUND ARE YOU TALKING ABOUT?
YOU'RE FORGETTING ABOUT MY EMMY-QUALITY WORK ON THE DISCOVERY CHANNEL.
SHARK NUMBER THREE?
I NAILED THAT PART.

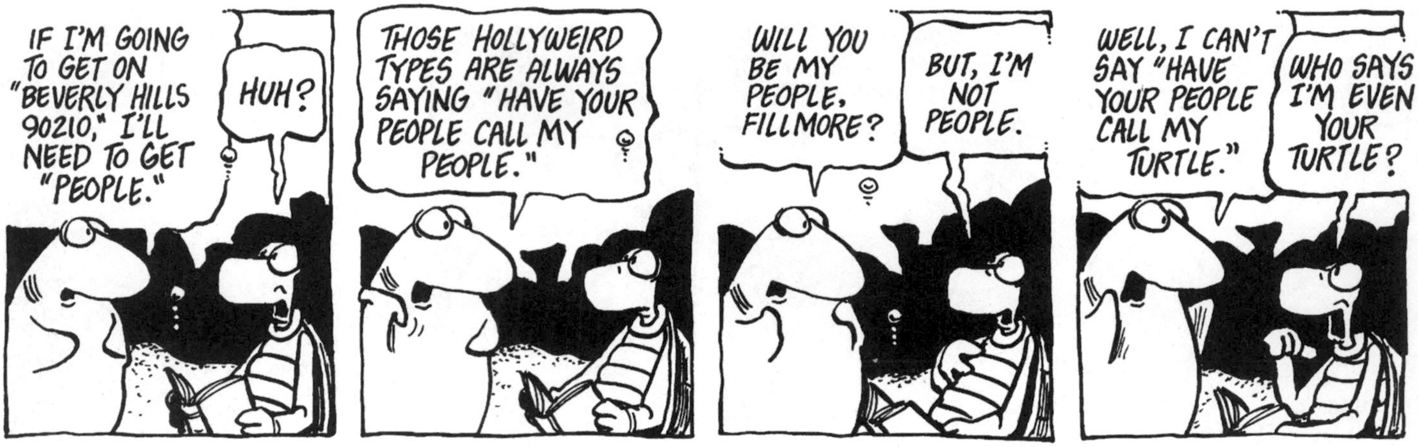
IF I'M GOING TO GET ON "BEVERLY HILLS 90210," I'LL NEED TO GET "PEOPLE."
HUH?
THOSE HOLLYWEIRD TYPES ARE ALWAYS SAYING "HAVE YOUR PEOPLE CALL MY PEOPLE."
WILL YOU BE MY PEOPLE, FILLMORE?
BUT, I'M NOT PEOPLE.
WELL, I CAN'T SAY "HAVE YOUR PEOPLE CALL MY TURTLE."
WHO SAYS I'M EVEN YOUR TURTLE?

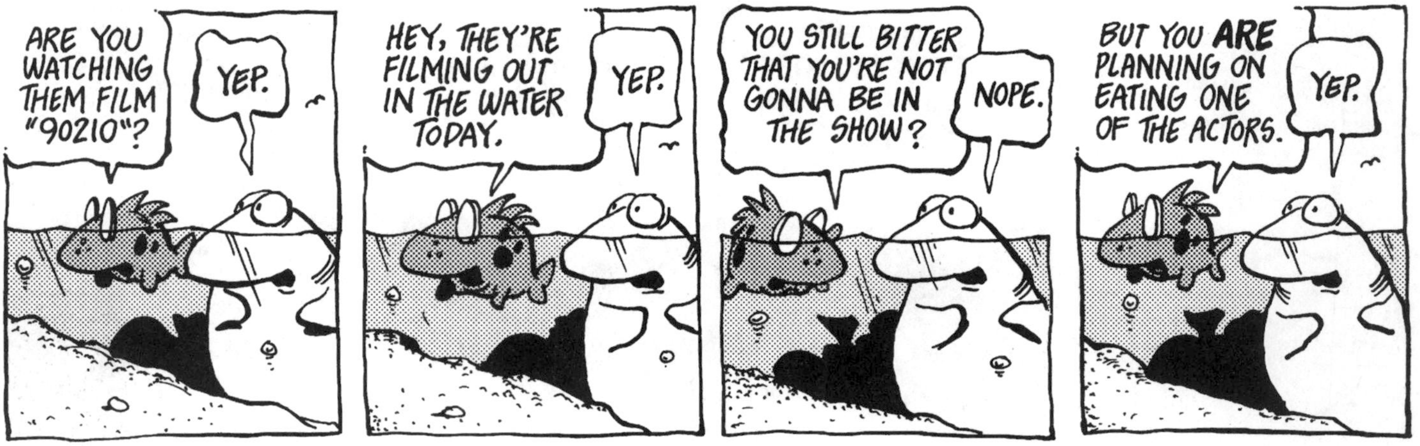
ARE YOU WATCHING THEM FILM "90210"?
YEP.
HEY, THEY'RE FILMING OUT IN THE WATER TODAY.
YEP.
YOU STILL BITTER THAT YOU'RE NOT GONNA BE IN THE SHOW?
NOPE.
BUT YOU ARE PLANNING ON EATING ONE OF THE ACTORS.
YEP.

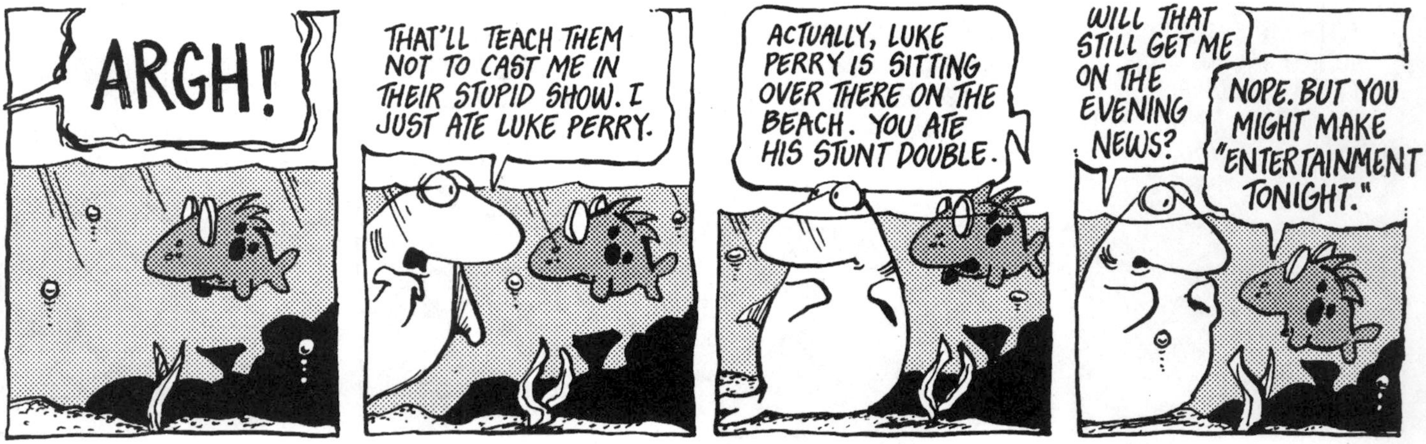
ARGH!
THAT'LL TEACH THEM NOT TO CAST ME IN THEIR STUPID SHOW. I JUST ATE LUKE PERRY.
ACTUALLY, LUKE PERRY IS SITTING OVER THERE ON THE BEACH. YOU ATE HIS STUNT DOUBLE.
WILL THAT STILL GET ME ON THE EVENING NEWS?
NOPE. BUT YOU MIGHT MAKE "ENTERTAINMENT TONIGHT."

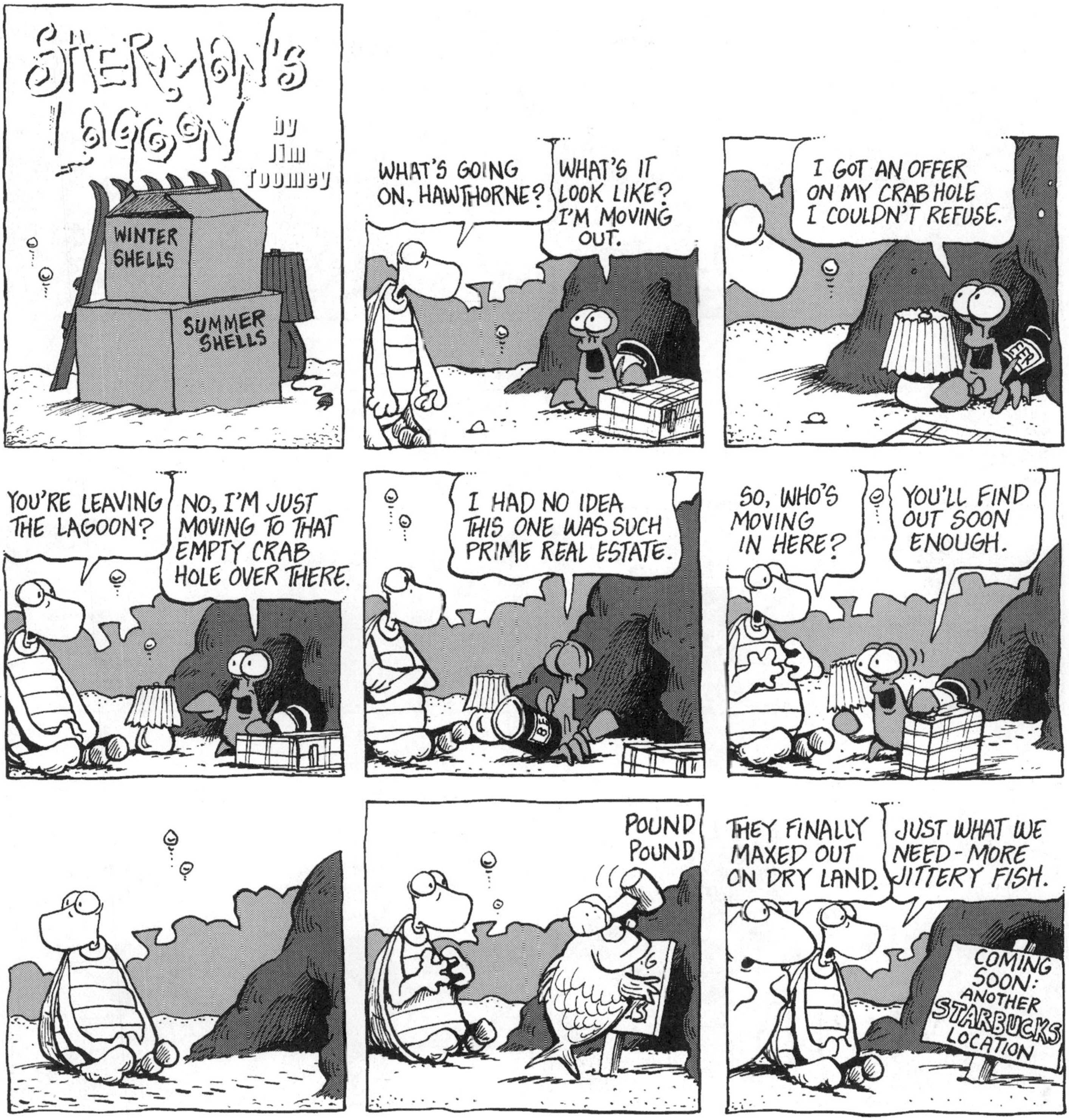
SHERMAN'S LAGOON
by Jim Toomey
WINTER SHELLS
SUMMER SHELLS
WHAT'S GOING ON, HAWTHORNE?
WHAT'S IT LOOK LIKE? I'M MOVING OUT.
I GOT AN OFFER ON MY CRAB HOLE I COULDN'T REFUSE.
YOU'RE LEAVING THE LAGOON?
NO, I'M JUST MOVING TO THAT EMPTY CRAB HOLE OVER THERE.
I HAD NO IDEA THIS ONE WAS SUCH PRIME REAL ESTATE.
SO, WHO'S MOVING IN HERE?
YOU'LL FIND OUT SOON ENOUGH.
POUND POUND
THEY FINALLY MAXED OUT ON DRY LAND.
JUST WHAT WE NEED-MORE JITTERY FISH.
COMING SOON: ANOTHER STARBUCKS LOCATION

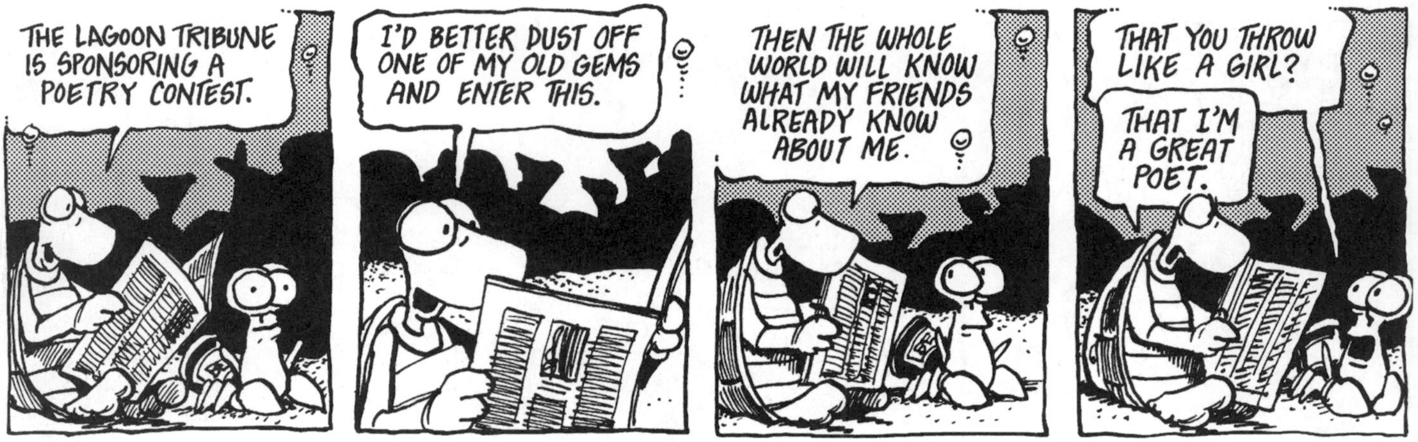
THE LAGOON TRIBUNE IS SPONSORING A POETRY CONTEST.
I'D BETTER DUST OFF ONE OF MY OLD GEMS AND ENTER THIS.
THEN THE WHOLE WORLD WILL KNOW WHAT MY FRIENDS ALREADY KNOW ABOUT ME.
THAT I'M A GREAT POET.
THAT YOU THROW LIKE A GIRL?

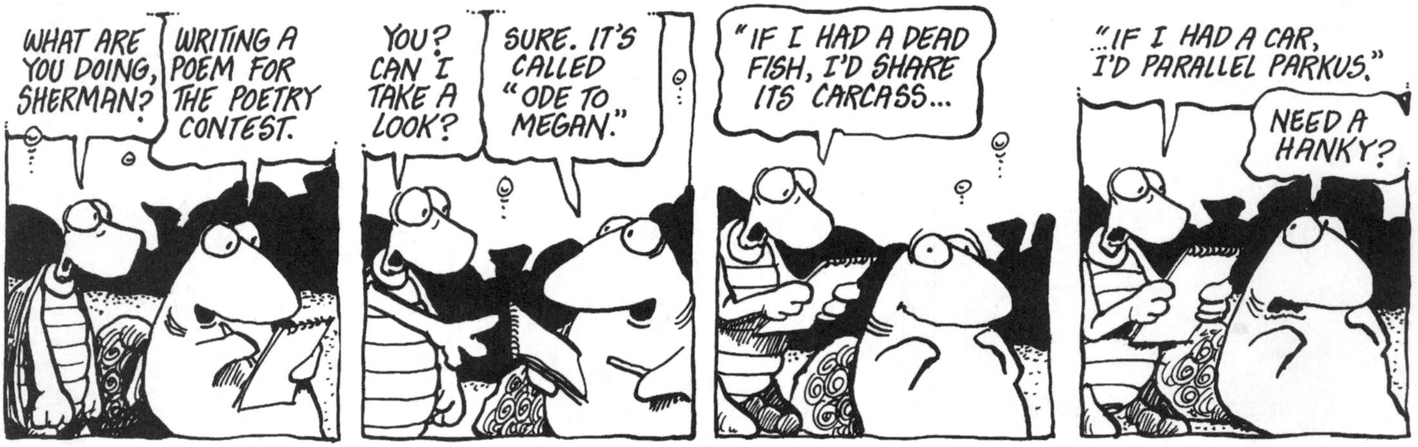
WHAT ARE YOU DOING, SHERMAN?
WRITING A POEM FOR THE POETRY CONTEST.
YOU? CAN I TAKE A LOOK?
SURE. IT'S CALLED "ODE TO MEGAN."
"IF I HAD A DEAD FISH, I'D SHARE ITS CARCASS...
..IF I HAD A CAR, I'D PARALLEL PARKUS."
NEED A HANKY?

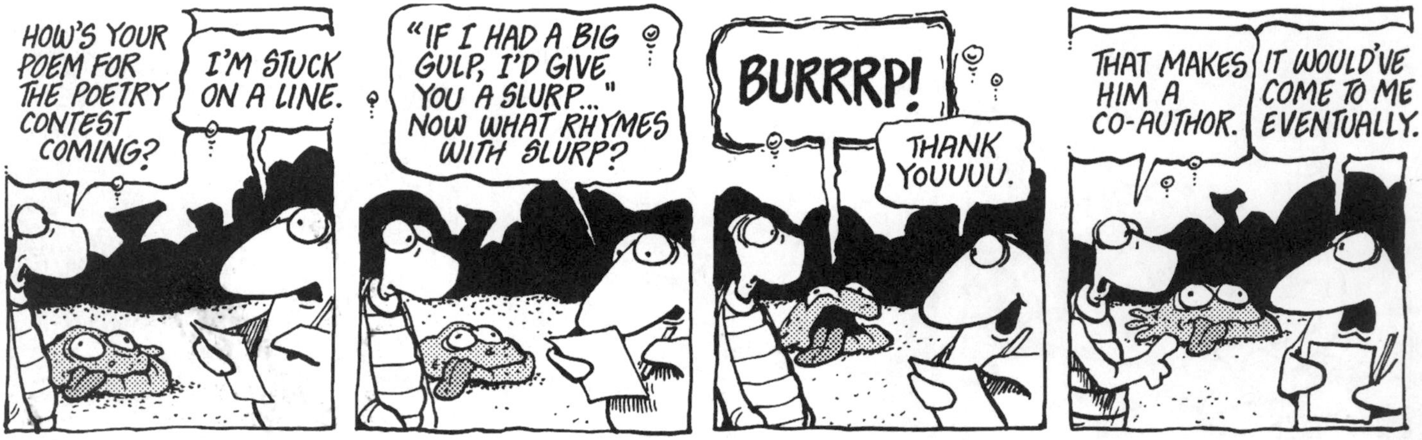
HOW'S YOUR POEM FOR THE POETRY CONTEST COMING?
I'M STUCK ON A LINE.
"IF I HAD A BIG GULP, I'D GIVE YOU A SLURP..." NOW WHAT RHYMES WITH SLURP?
BURRRP!
THANK YOUUUU.
THAT MAKES HIM A CO-AUTHOR.
IT WOULD'VE COME TO ME EVENTUALLY.

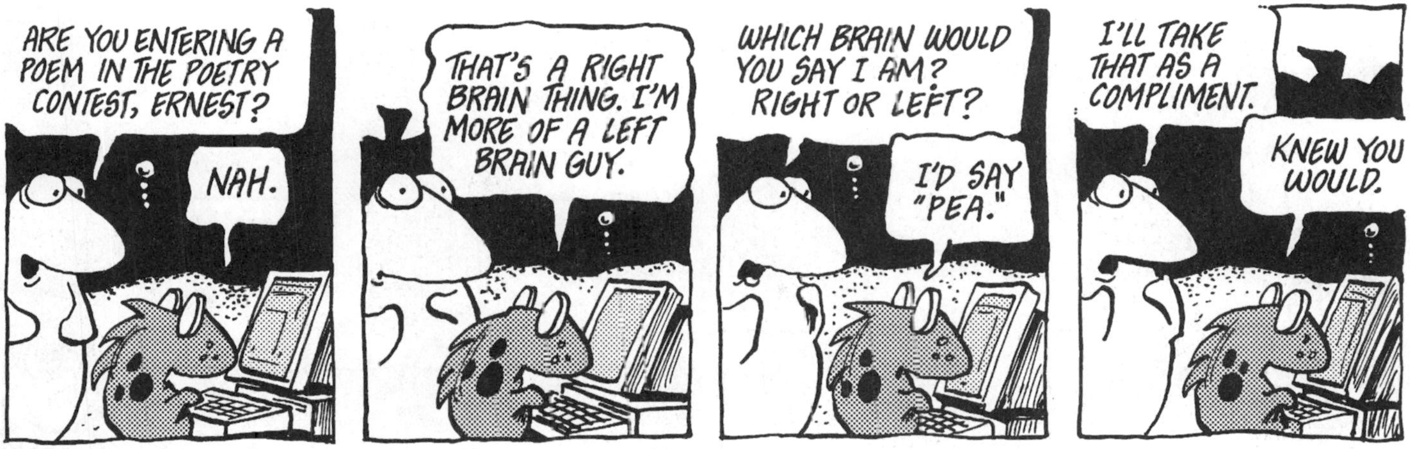
ARE YOU ENTERING A POEM IN THE POETRY CONTEST, ERNEST?
NAH.
THAT'S A RIGHT BRAIN THING. I'M MORE OF A LEFT BRAIN GUY.
WHICH BRAIN WOULD YOU SAY I AM? RIGHT OR LEFT?
I'D SAY "PEA."
I'LL TAKE THAT AS A COMPLIMENT.
KNEW YOU WOULD.

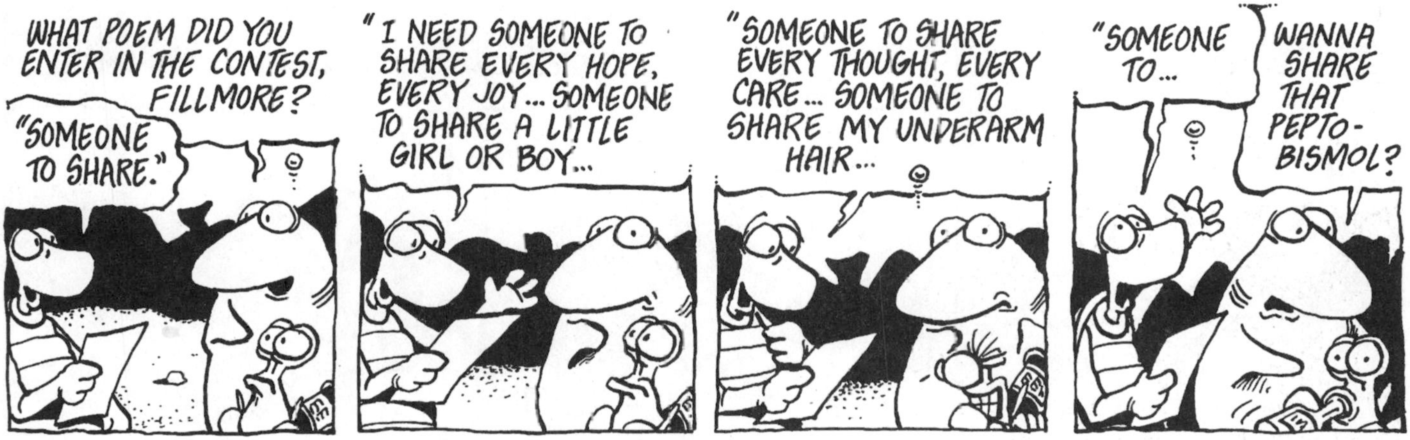
WHAT POEM DID YOU ENTER IN THE CONTEST, FILLMORE?
"SOMEONE TO SHARE."
"I NEED SOMEONE TO SHARE EVERY HOPE, EVERY JOY... SOMEONE TO SHARE A LITTLE GIRL OR BOY...
"SOMEONE TO SHARE EVERY THOUGHT, EVERY CARE... SOMEONE TO SHARE MY UNDERARM HAIR...
"SOMEONE TO...
WANNA SHARE THAT PEPTO-BISMOL?

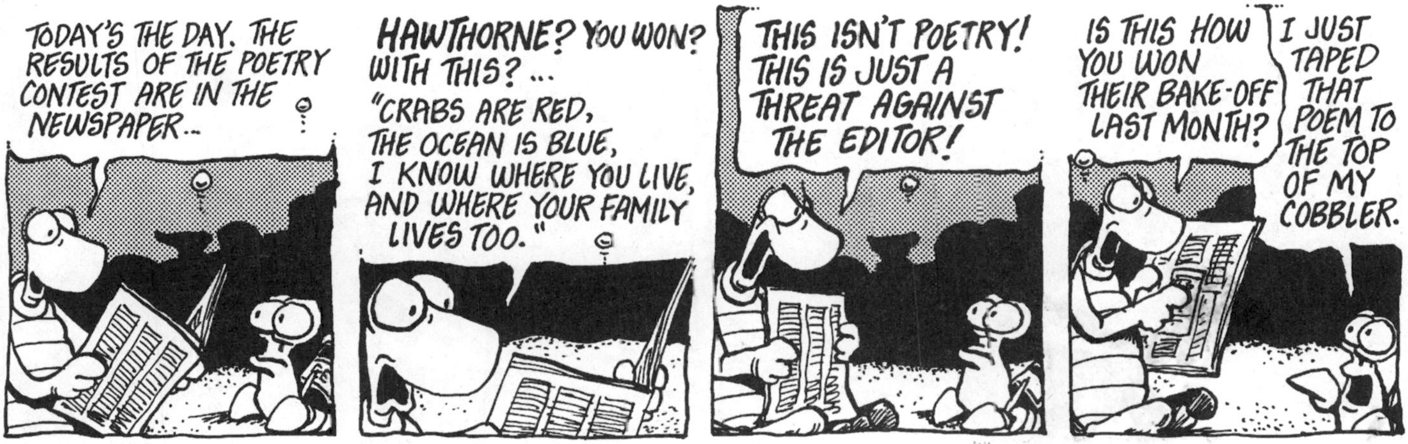
TODAY'S THE DAY. THE RESULTS OF THE POETRY CONTEST ARE IN THE NEWSPAPER...
HAWTHORNE? YOU WON? WITH THIS?... "CRABS ARE RED, THE OCEAN IS BLUE, I KNOW WHERE YOU LIVE, AND WHERE YOUR FAMILY LIVES TOO."
THIS ISN'T POETRY! THIS IS JUST A THREAT AGAINST THE EDITOR!
IS THIS HOW YOU WON THEIR BAKE-OFF LAST MONTH?
I JUST TAPED THAT POEM TO THE TOP OF MY COBBLER.

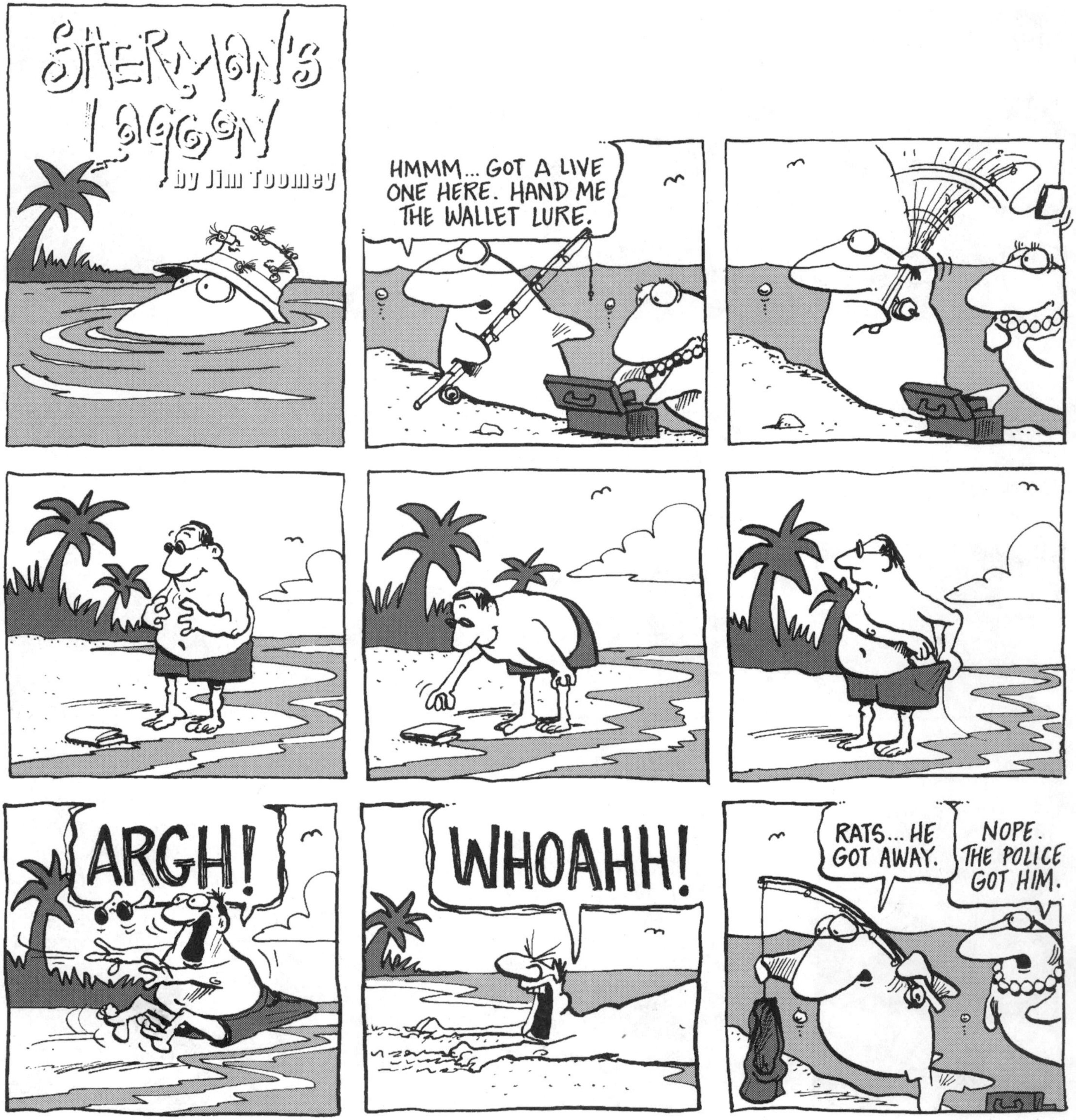
SHERMAN'S LAGOON
by Jim Toomey
HMMM... GOT A LIVE ONE HERE. HAND ME THE WALLET LURE.
ARGH!
WHOAHH!
RATS... HE GOT AWAY.
NOPE. THE POLICE GOT HIM.

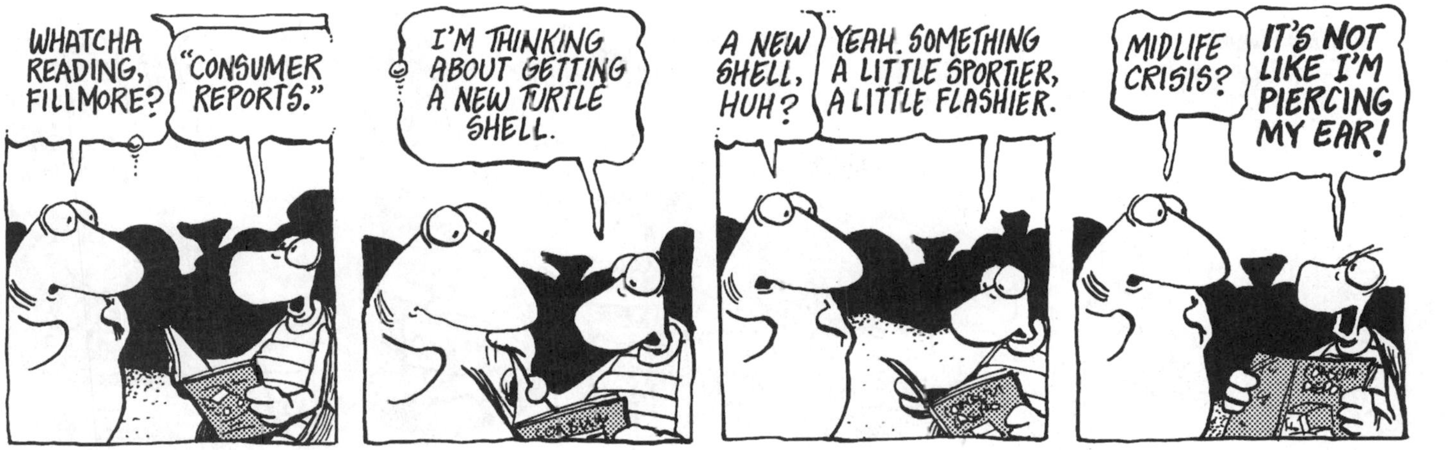
WHATCHA READING, FILLMORE?
"CONSUMER REPORTS."
I'M THINKING ABOUT GETTING A NEW TURTLE SHELL.
A NEW SHELL, HUH?
YEAH. SOMETHING A LITTLE SPORTIER, A LITTLE FLASHIER.
MIDLIFE CRISIS?
IT'S NOT LIKE I'M PIERCING MY EAR!

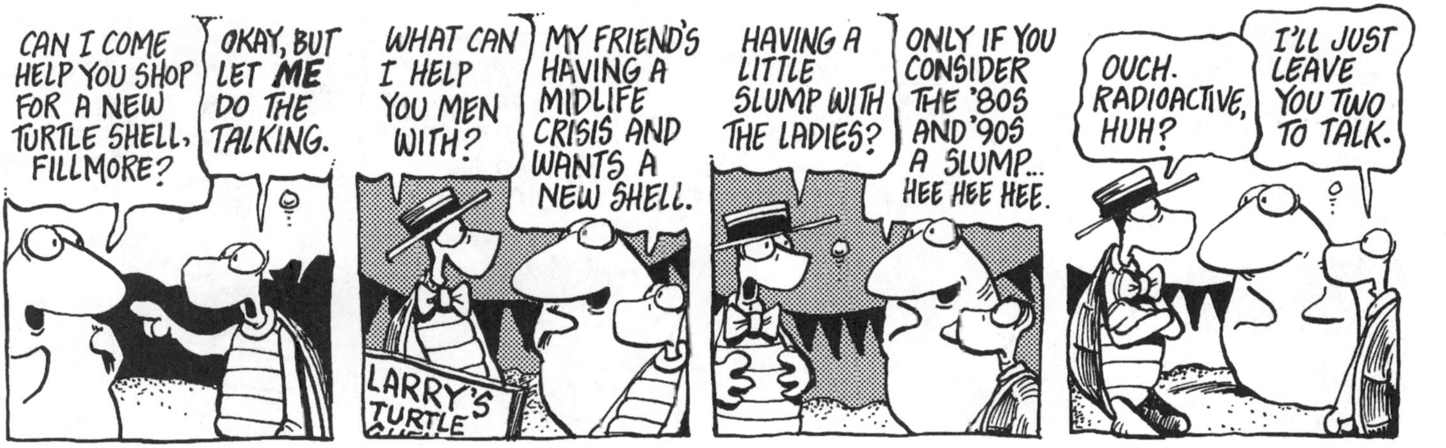
CAN I COME HELP YOU SHOP FOR A NEW TURTLE SHELL, FILLMORE?
OKAY, BUT LET **ME** DO THE TALKING.
WHAT CAN I HELP YOU MEN WITH?
MY FRIEND'S HAVING A MIDLIFE CRISIS AND WANTS A NEW SHELL.
LARRY'S TURTLE
HAVING A LITTLE SLUMP WITH THE LADIES?
ONLY IF YOU CONSIDER THE '80S AND '90S A SLUMP... HEE HEE HEE.
OUCH. RADIOACTIVE, HUH?
I'LL JUST LEAVE YOU TWO TO TALK.

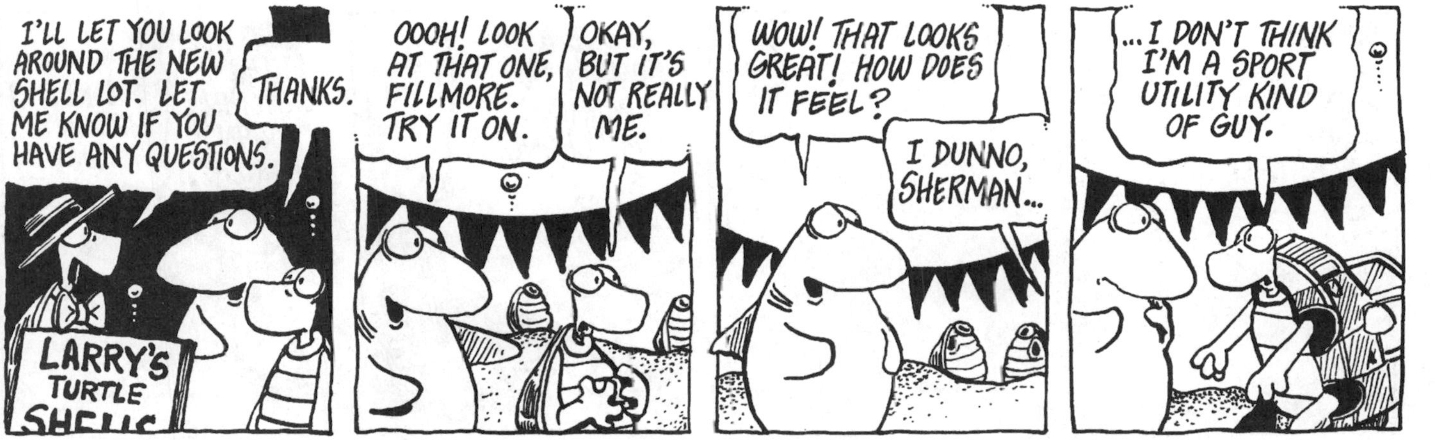
I'LL LET YOU LOOK AROUND THE NEW SHELL LOT. LET ME KNOW IF YOU HAVE ANY QUESTIONS.
THANKS.
LARRY'S TURTLE
OOOH! LOOK AT THAT ONE, FILLMORE. TRY IT ON.
OKAY, BUT IT'S NOT REALLY ME.
WOW! THAT LOOKS GREAT! HOW DOES IT FEEL?
I DUNNO, SHERMAN...
...I DON'T THINK I'M A SPORT UTILITY KIND OF GUY.

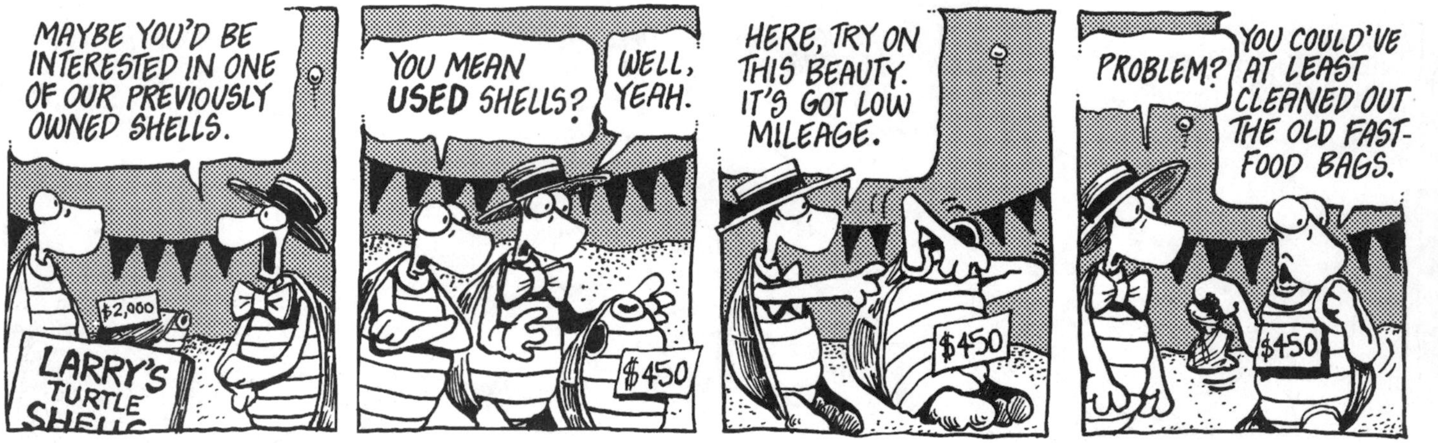
MAYBE YOU'D BE INTERESTED IN ONE OF OUR PREVIOUSLY OWNED SHELLS.
$2,000
LARRY'S TURTLE
YOU MEAN **USED** SHELLS?
WELL, YEAH.
$450
HERE, TRY ON THIS BEAUTY. IT'S GOT LOW MILEAGE.
$450
PROBLEM?
YOU COULD'VE AT LEAST CLEANED OUT THE OLD FAST-FOOD BAGS.
$450

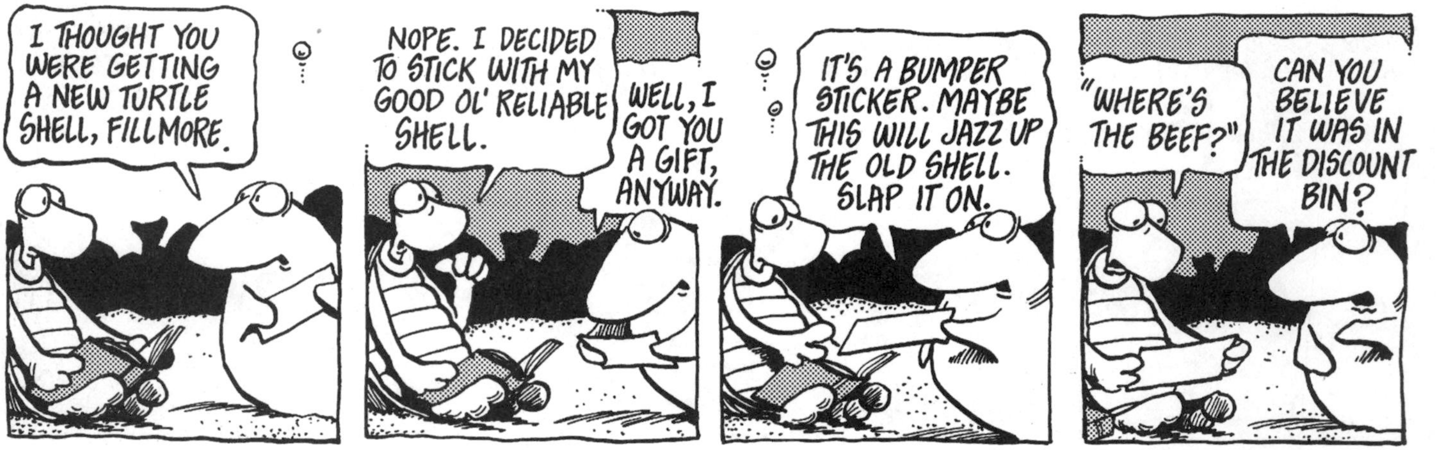
I THOUGHT YOU WERE GETTING A NEW TURTLE SHELL, FILLMORE.
NOPE. I DECIDED TO STICK WITH MY GOOD OL' RELIABLE SHELL.
WELL, I GOT YOU A GIFT, ANYWAY.
IT'S A BUMPER STICKER. MAYBE THIS WILL JAZZ UP THE OLD SHELL. SLAP IT ON.
"WHERE'S THE BEEF?"
CAN YOU BELIEVE IT WAS IN THE DISCOUNT BIN?

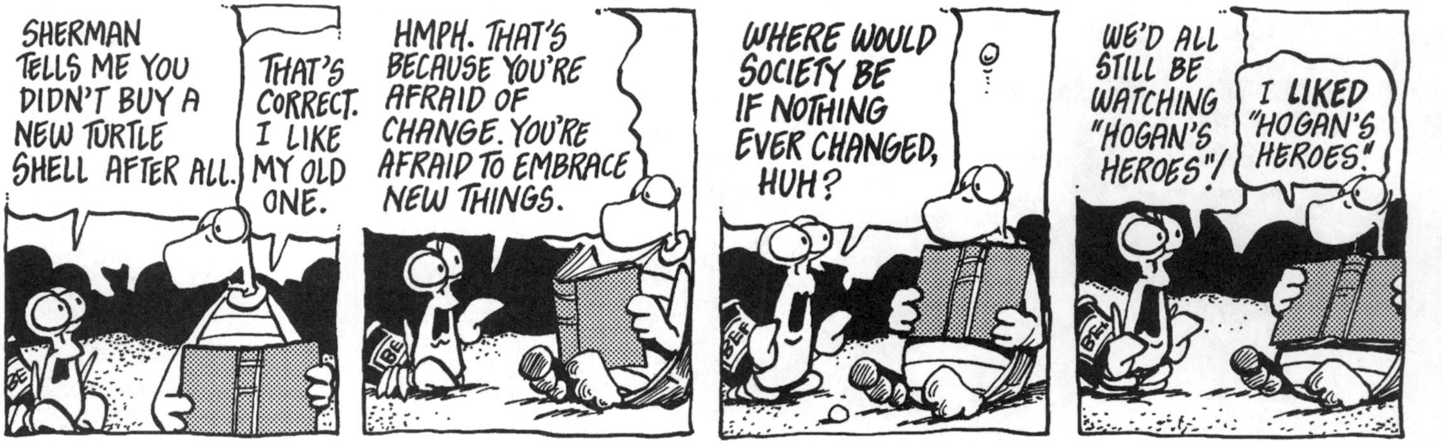
SHERMAN TELLS ME YOU DIDN'T BUY A NEW TURTLE SHELL AFTER ALL.
THAT'S CORRECT. I LIKE MY OLD ONE.
HMPH. THAT'S BECAUSE YOU'RE AFRAID OF CHANGE. YOU'RE AFRAID TO EMBRACE NEW THINGS.
WHERE WOULD SOCIETY BE IF NOTHING EVER CHANGED, HUH?
WE'D ALL STILL BE WATCHING "HOGAN'S HEROES"!
I **LIKED** "HOGAN'S HEROES."

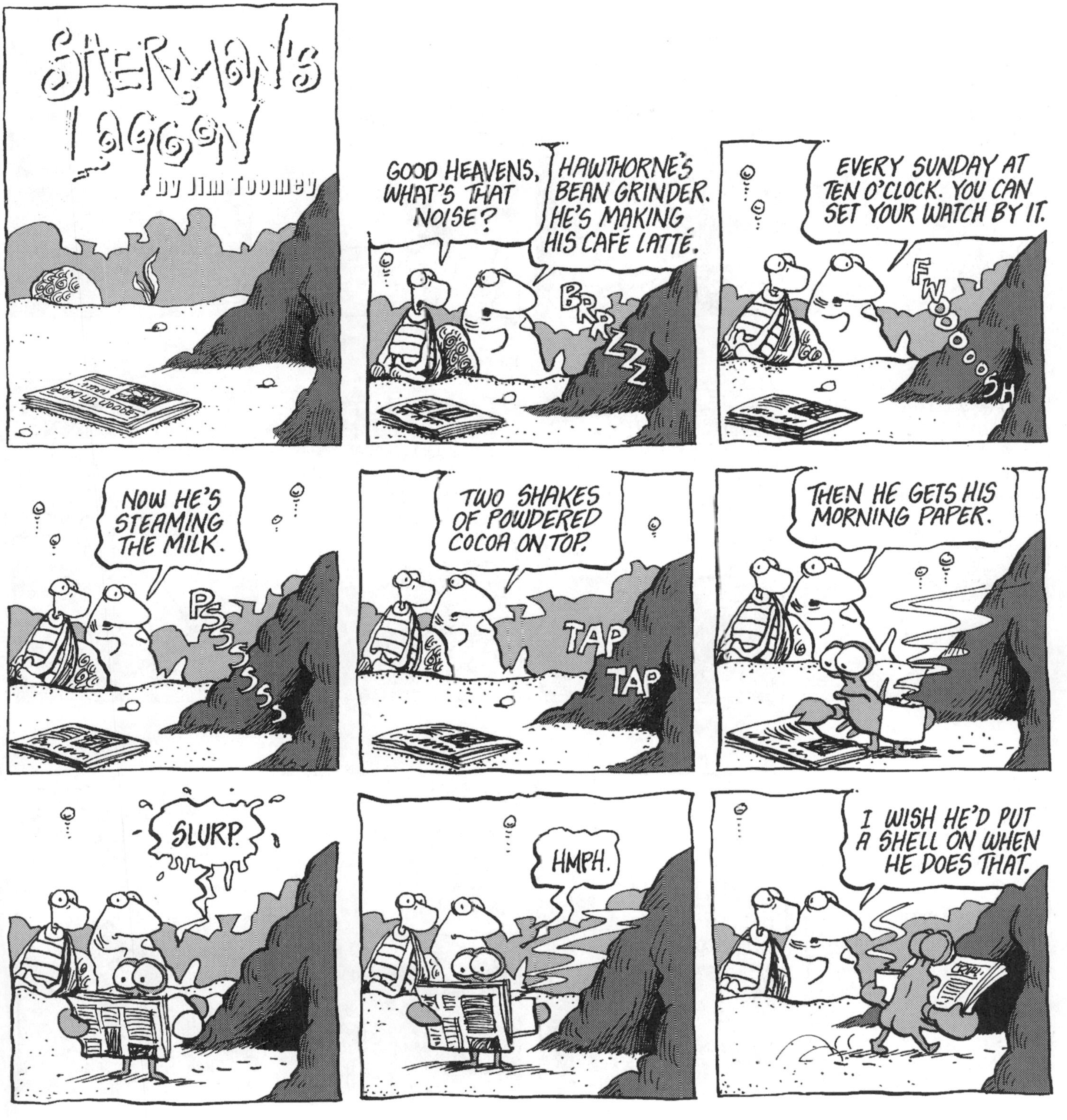
SHERMAN'S LAGOON
by Jim Toomey
GOOD HEAVENS, WHAT'S THAT NOISE?
HAWTHORNE'S BEAN GRINDER. HE'S MAKING HIS CAFÉ LATTÉ.
BRRRZZZ
EVERY SUNDAY AT TEN O'CLOCK. YOU CAN SET YOUR WATCH BY IT.
FWOOOOOSH
NOW HE'S STEAMING THE MILK.
PSSSSSSS
TWO SHAKES OF POWDERED COCOA ON TOP.
TAP
TAP
THEN HE GETS HIS MORNING PAPER.
SLURP.
HMPH.
I WISH HE'D PUT A SHELL ON WHEN HE DOES THAT.

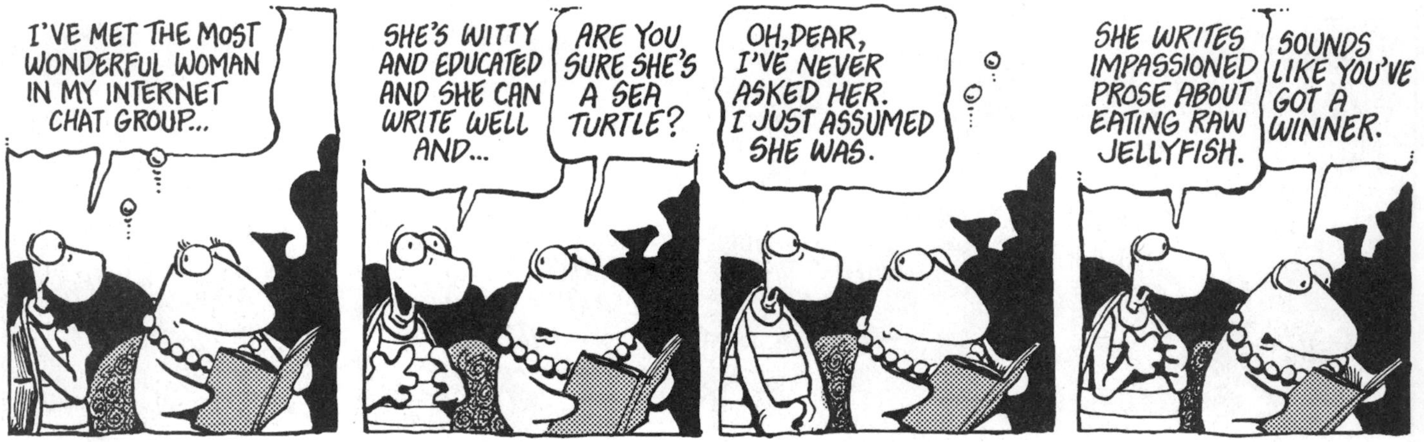
I'VE MET THE MOST WONDERFUL WOMAN IN MY INTERNET CHAT GROUP...
SHE'S WITTY AND EDUCATED AND SHE CAN WRITE WELL AND...
ARE YOU SURE SHE'S A SEA TURTLE?
OH, DEAR, I'VE NEVER ASKED HER. I JUST ASSUMED SHE WAS.
SHE WRITES IMPASSIONED PROSE ABOUT EATING RAW JELLYFISH.
SOUNDS LIKE YOU'VE GOT A WINNER.

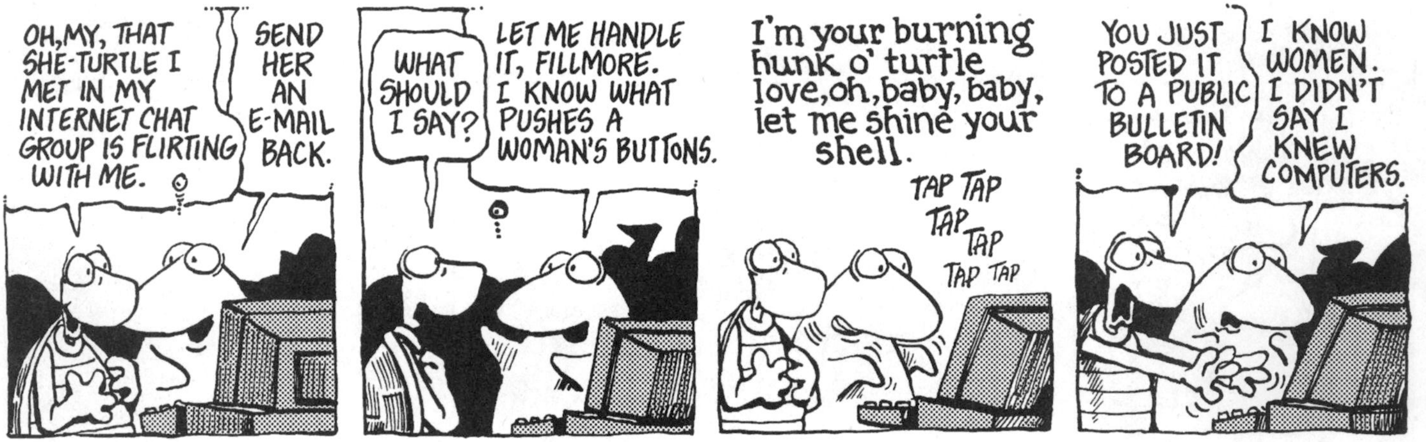
OH, MY, THAT SHE-TURTLE I MET IN MY INTERNET CHAT GROUP IS FLIRTING WITH ME.
SEND HER AN E-MAIL BACK.
WHAT SHOULD I SAY?
LET ME HANDLE IT, FILLMORE. I KNOW WHAT PUSHES A WOMAN'S BUTTONS.
I'm your burning hunk o' turtle love, oh, baby, baby, let me shine your shell.
TAP TAP TAP TAP TAP TAP
YOU JUST POSTED IT TO A PUBLIC BULLETIN BOARD!
I KNOW WOMEN. I DIDN'T SAY I KNEW COMPUTERS.

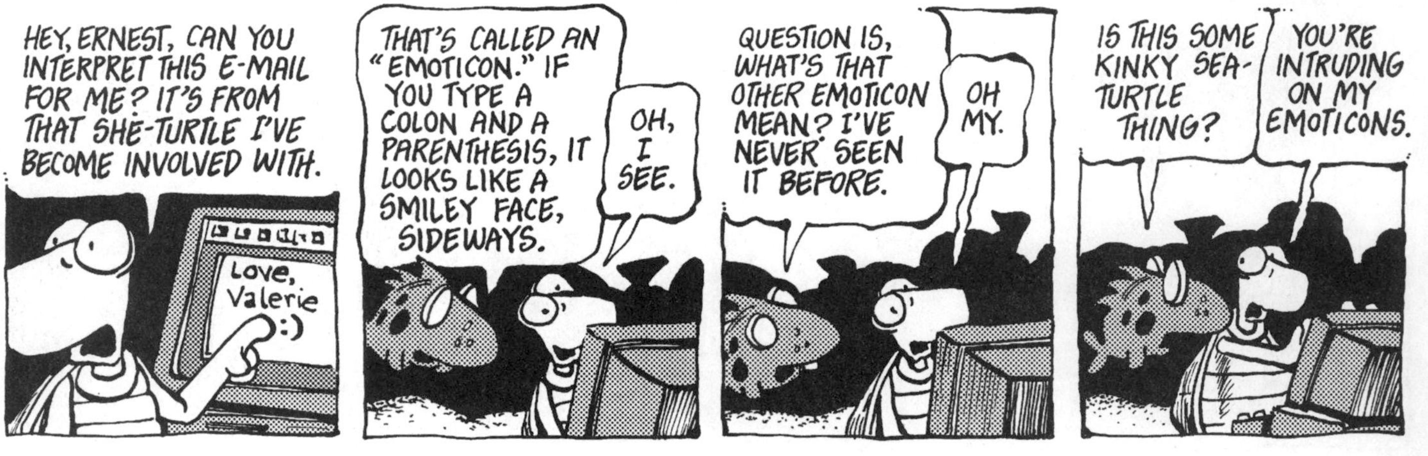
HEY, ERNEST, CAN YOU INTERPRET THIS E-MAIL FOR ME? IT'S FROM THAT SHE-TURTLE I'VE BECOME INVOLVED WITH.
Love, Valerie :)
THAT'S CALLED AN "EMOTICON." IF YOU TYPE A COLON AND A PARENTHESIS, IT LOOKS LIKE A SMILEY FACE, SIDEWAYS.
OH, I SEE.
QUESTION IS, WHAT'S THAT OTHER EMOTICON MEAN? I'VE NEVER SEEN IT BEFORE.
OH MY.
IS THIS SOME KINKY SEA-TURTLE THING?
YOU'RE INTRUDING ON MY EMOTICONS.

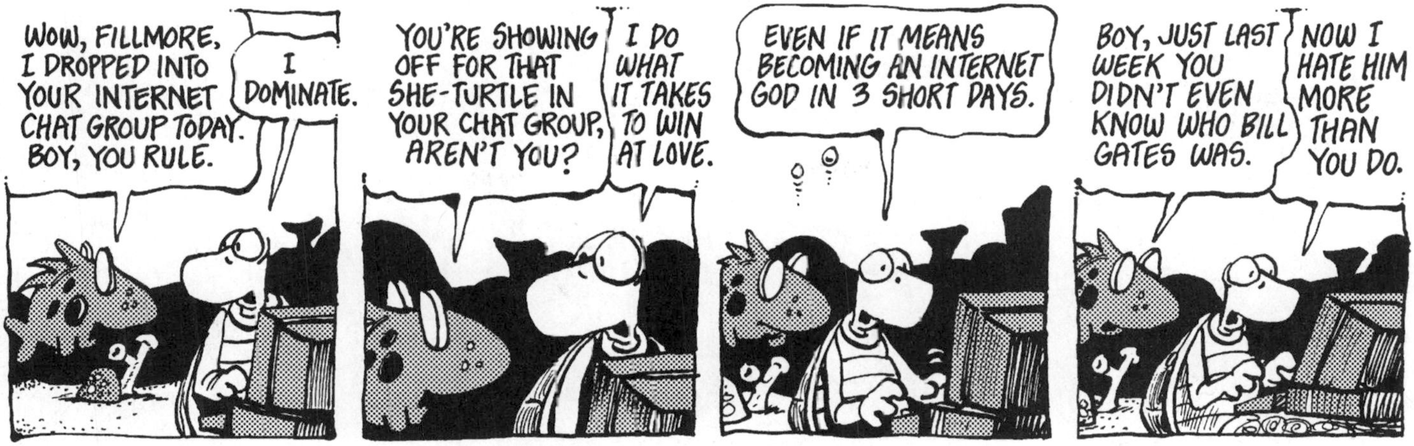
WOW, FILLMORE, I DROPPED INTO YOUR INTERNET CHAT GROUP TODAY. BOY, YOU RULE.
I DOMINATE.
YOU'RE SHOWING OFF FOR THAT SHE-TURTLE IN YOUR CHAT GROUP, AREN'T YOU?
I DO WHAT IT TAKES TO WIN AT LOVE.
EVEN IF IT MEANS BECOMING AN INTERNET GOD IN 3 SHORT DAYS.
BOY, JUST LAST WEEK YOU DIDN'T EVEN KNOW WHO BILL GATES WAS.
NOW I HATE HIM MORE THAN YOU DO.

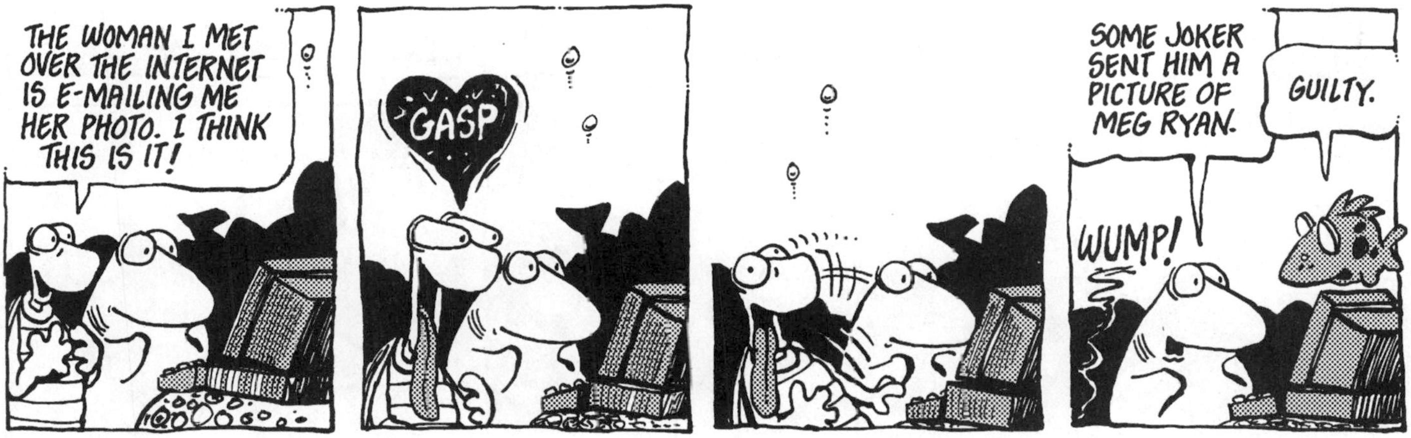
THE WOMAN I MET OVER THE INTERNET IS E-MAILING ME HER PHOTO. I THINK THIS IS IT!
GASP
SOME JOKER SENT HIM A PICTURE OF MEG RYAN.
GUILTY.
WUMP!

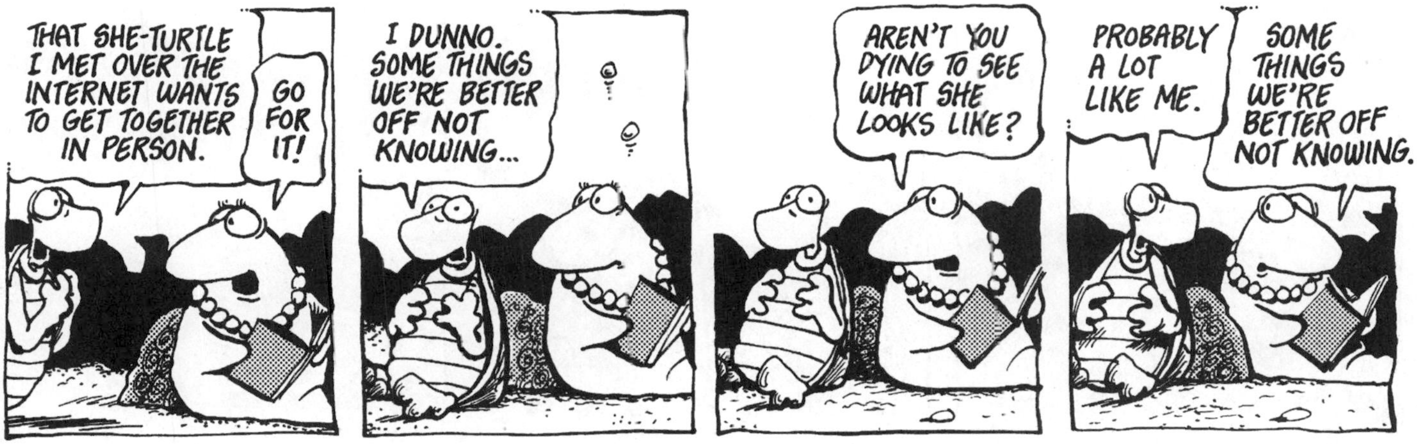
THAT SHE-TURTLE I MET OVER THE INTERNET WANTS TO GET TOGETHER IN PERSON.
GO FOR IT!
I DUNNO. SOME THINGS WE'RE BETTER OFF NOT KNOWING...
AREN'T YOU DYING TO SEE WHAT SHE LOOKS LIKE?
PROBABLY A LOT LIKE ME.
SOME THINGS WE'RE BETTER OFF NOT KNOWING.

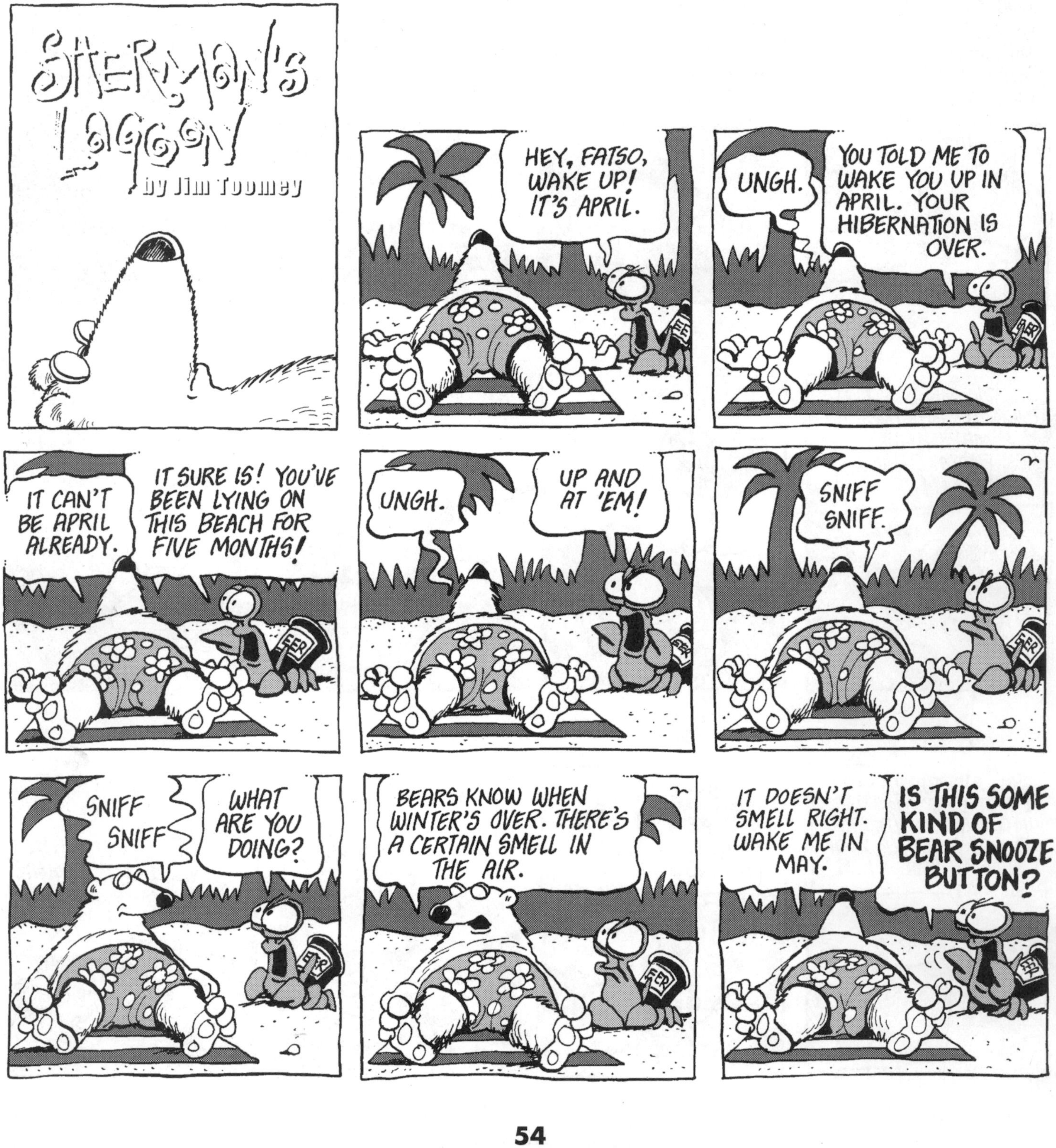
SHERMAN'S LAGOON
by Jim Toomey
HEY, FATSO, WAKE UP! IT'S APRIL.
UNGH.
YOU TOLD ME TO WAKE YOU UP IN APRIL. YOUR HIBERNATION IS OVER.
IT CAN'T BE APRIL ALREADY.
IT SURE IS! YOU'VE BEEN LYING ON THIS BEACH FOR FIVE MONTHS!
UNGH.
UP AND AT 'EM!
SNIFF SNIFF.
SNIFF SNIFF
WHAT ARE YOU DOING?
BEARS KNOW WHEN WINTER'S OVER. THERE'S A CERTAIN SMELL IN THE AIR.
IT DOESN'T SMELL RIGHT. WAKE ME IN MAY.
IS THIS SOME KIND OF BEAR SNOOZE BUTTON?

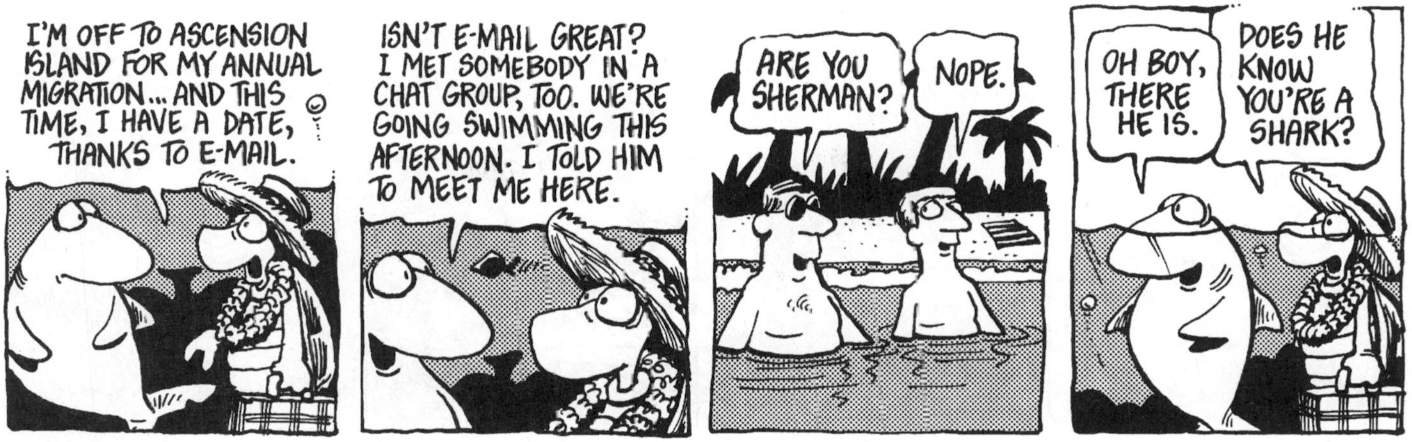
I'M OFF TO ASCENSION ISLAND FOR MY ANNUAL MIGRATION... AND THIS TIME, I HAVE A DATE, THANKS TO E-MAIL.
ISN'T E-MAIL GREAT? I MET SOMEBODY IN A CHAT GROUP, TOO. WE'RE GOING SWIMMING THIS AFTERNOON. I TOLD HIM TO MEET ME HERE.
ARE YOU SHERMAN?
NOPE.
OH BOY, THERE HE IS.
DOES HE KNOW YOU'RE A SHARK?

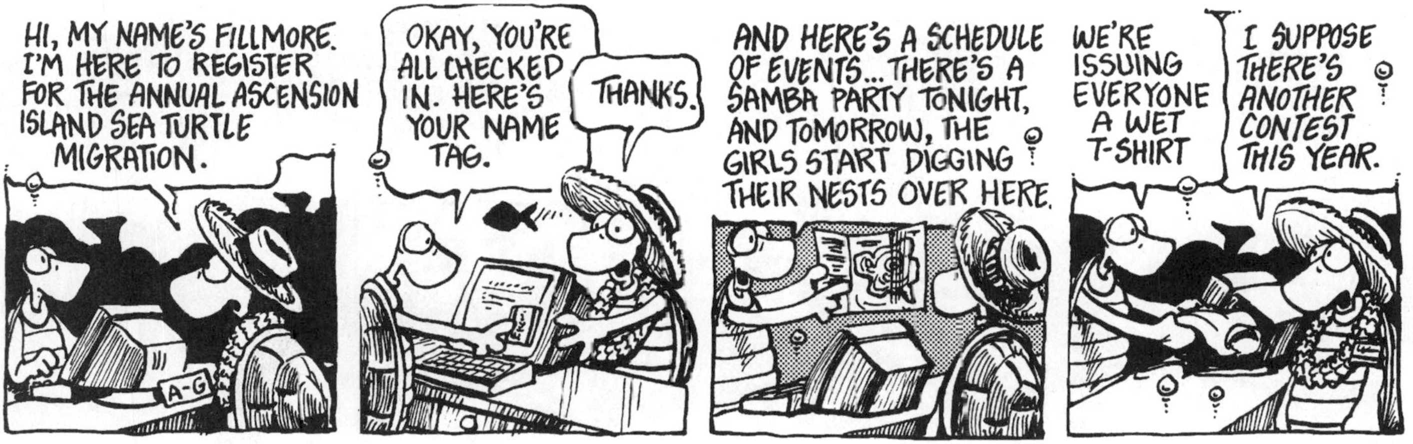
HI, MY NAME'S FILLMORE. I'M HERE TO REGISTER FOR THE ANNUAL ASCENSION ISLAND SEA TURTLE MIGRATION.
A-G
OKAY, YOU'RE ALL CHECKED IN. HERE'S YOUR NAME TAG.
THANKS.
AND HERE'S A SCHEDULE OF EVENTS... THERE'S A SAMBA PARTY TONIGHT, AND TOMORROW, THE GIRLS START DIGGING THEIR NESTS OVER HERE.
WE'RE ISSUING EVERYONE A WET T-SHIRT
I SUPPOSE THERE'S ANOTHER CONTEST THIS YEAR.

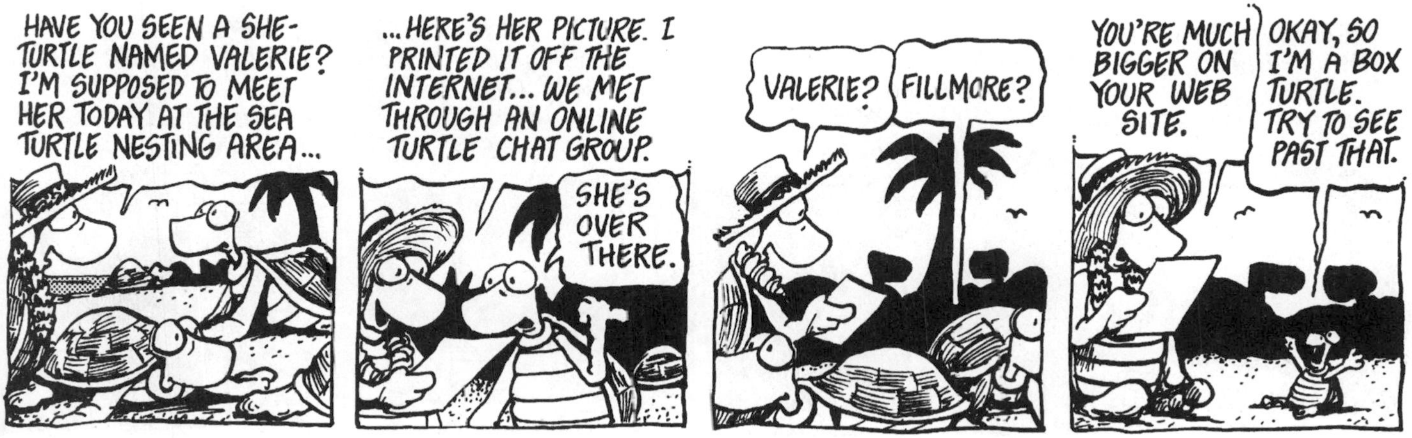
HAVE YOU SEEN A SHE-TURTLE NAMED VALERIE? I'M SUPPOSED TO MEET HER TODAY AT THE SEA TURTLE NESTING AREA...
...HERE'S HER PICTURE. I PRINTED IT OFF THE INTERNET... WE MET THROUGH AN ONLINE TURTLE CHAT GROUP.
SHE'S OVER THERE.
VALERIE?
FILLMORE?
YOU'RE MUCH BIGGER ON YOUR WEB SITE.
OKAY, SO I'M A BOX TURTLE. TRY TO SEE PAST THAT.

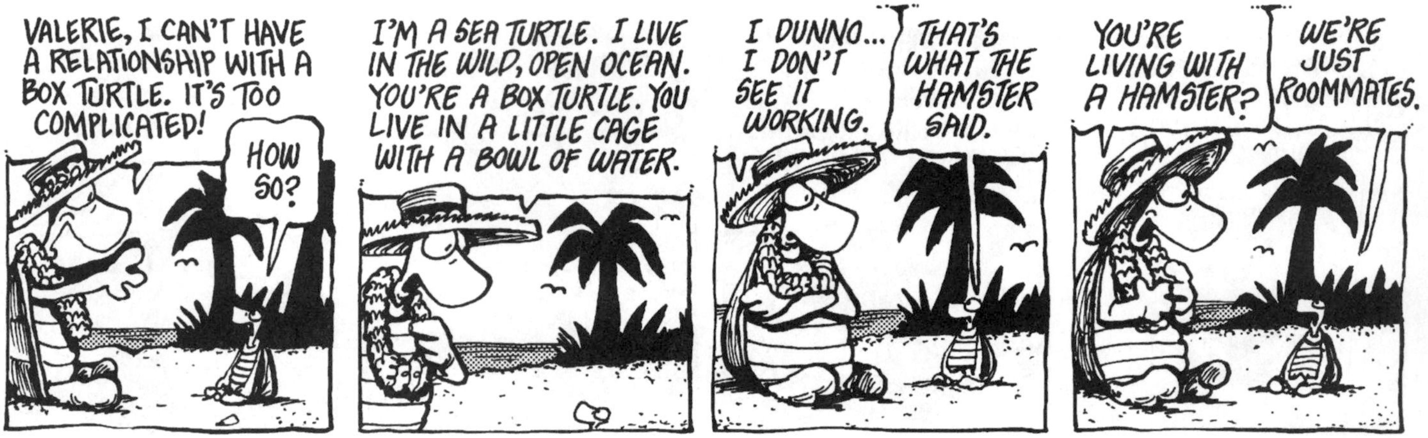
VALERIE, I CAN'T HAVE A RELATIONSHIP WITH A BOX TURTLE. IT'S TOO COMPLICATED!
HOW SO?
I'M A SEA TURTLE. I LIVE IN THE WILD, OPEN OCEAN. YOU'RE A BOX TURTLE. YOU LIVE IN A LITTLE CAGE WITH A BOWL OF WATER.
I DUNNO... I DON'T SEE IT WORKING.
THAT'S WHAT THE HAMSTER SAID.
YOU'RE LIVING WITH A HAMSTER?
WE'RE JUST ROOMMATES.

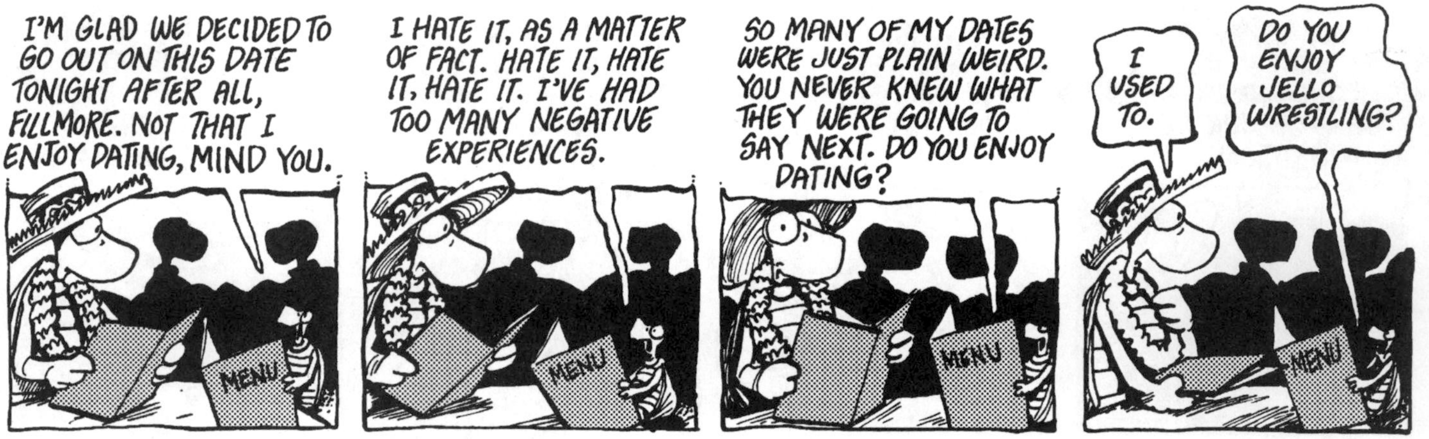
I'M GLAD WE DECIDED TO GO OUT ON THIS DATE TONIGHT AFTER ALL, FILLMORE. NOT THAT I ENJOY DATING, MIND YOU.
MENU
I HATE IT, AS A MATTER OF FACT. HATE IT, HATE IT, HATE IT. I'VE HAD TOO MANY NEGATIVE EXPERIENCES.
MENU
SO MANY OF MY DATES WERE JUST PLAIN WEIRD. YOU NEVER KNEW WHAT THEY WERE GOING TO SAY NEXT. DO YOU ENJOY DATING?
MENU
I USED TO.
DO YOU ENJOY JELLO WRESTLING?
MENU

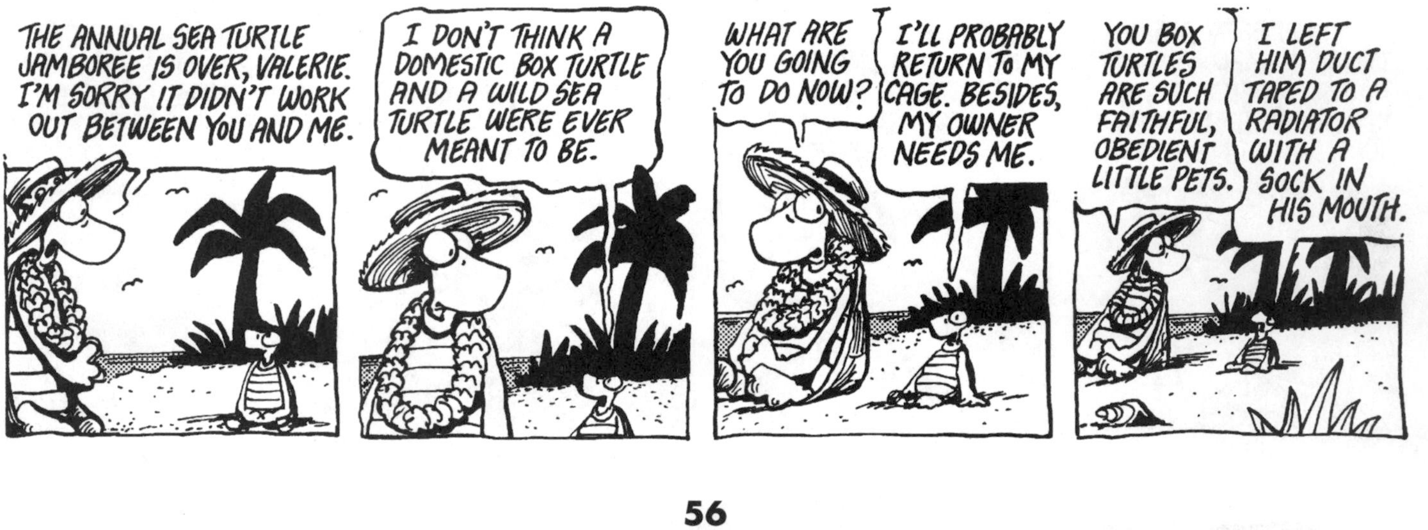
THE ANNUAL SEA TURTLE JAMBOREE IS OVER, VALERIE. I'M SORRY IT DIDN'T WORK OUT BETWEEN YOU AND ME.
I DON'T THINK A DOMESTIC BOX TURTLE AND A WILD SEA TURTLE WERE EVER MEANT TO BE.
WHAT ARE YOU GOING TO DO NOW?
I'LL PROBABLY RETURN TO MY CAGE. BESIDES, MY OWNER NEEDS ME.
YOU BOX TURTLES ARE SUCH FAITHFUL, OBEDIENT LITTLE PETS.
I LEFT HIM DUCT TAPED TO A RADIATOR WITH A SOCK IN HIS MOUTH.

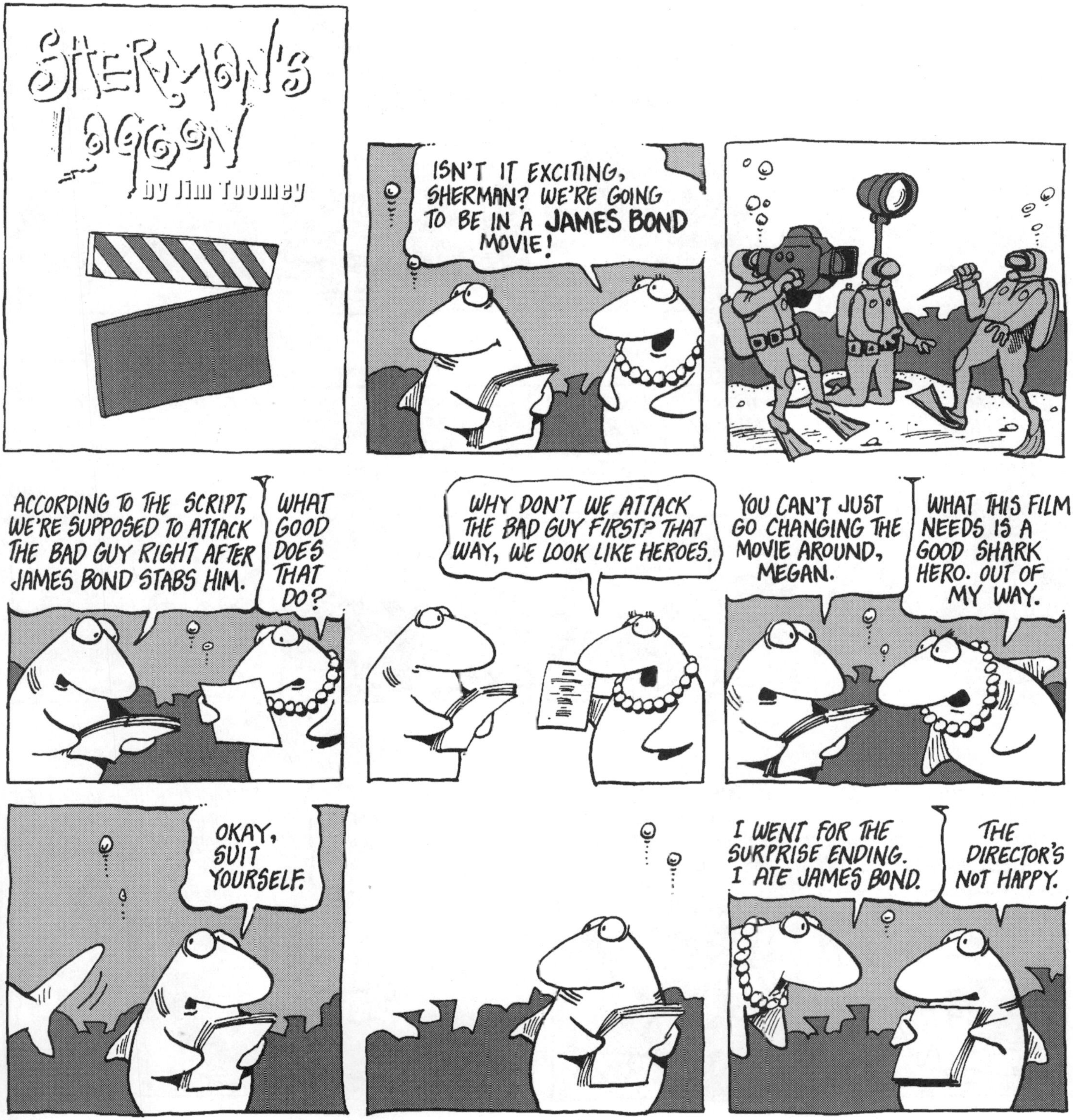
SHERMAN'S LAGOON
by Jim Toomey
ISN'T IT EXCITING, SHERMAN? WE'RE GOING TO BE IN A JAMES BOND MOVIE!
ACCORDING TO THE SCRIPT, WE'RE SUPPOSED TO ATTACK THE BAD GUY RIGHT AFTER JAMES BOND STABS HIM.
WHAT GOOD DOES THAT DO?
WHY DON'T WE ATTACK THE BAD GUY FIRST? THAT WAY, WE LOOK LIKE HEROES.
YOU CAN'T JUST GO CHANGING THE MOVIE AROUND, MEGAN.
WHAT THIS FILM NEEDS IS A GOOD SHARK HERO. OUT OF MY WAY.
OKAY, SUIT YOURSELF.
I WENT FOR THE SURPRISE ENDING. I ATE JAMES BOND.
THE DIRECTOR'S NOT HAPPY.

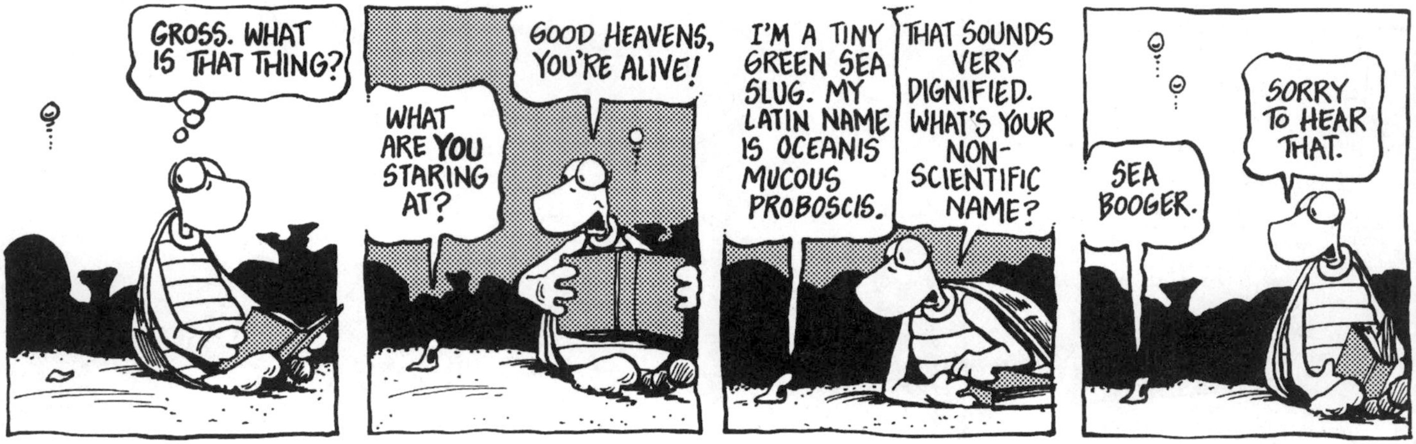
GROSS. WHAT IS THAT THING?
WHAT ARE YOU STARING AT?
GOOD HEAVENS, YOU'RE ALIVE!
I'M A TINY GREEN SEA SLUG. MY LATIN NAME IS OCEANIS MUCOUS PROBOSCIS.
THAT SOUNDS VERY DIGNIFIED. WHAT'S YOUR NON-SCIENTIFIC NAME?
SEA BOOGER.
SORRY TO HEAR THAT.

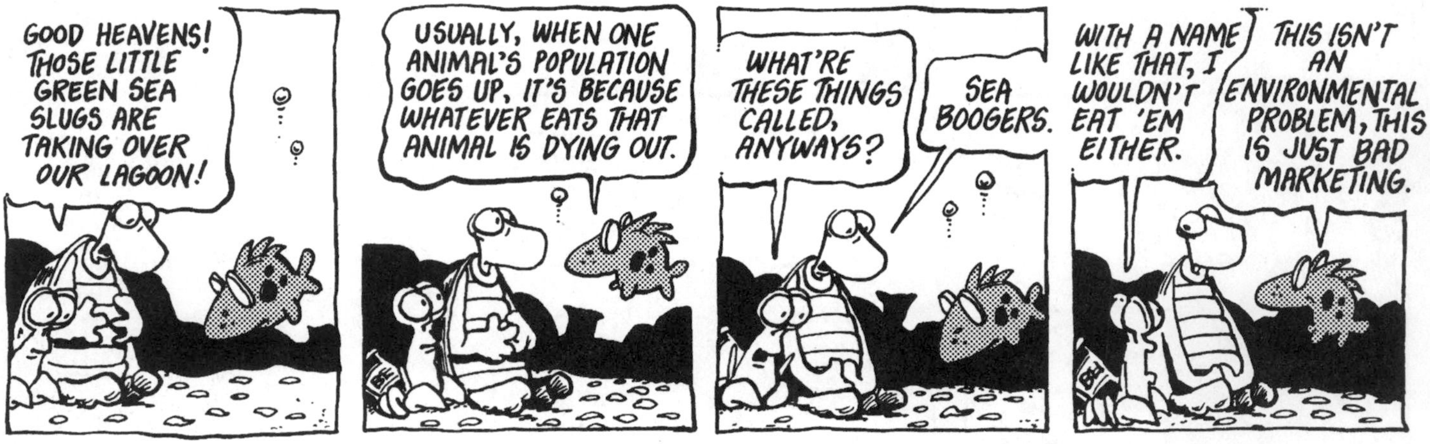
GOOD HEAVENS! THOSE LITTLE GREEN SEA SLUGS ARE TAKING OVER OUR LAGOON!
USUALLY, WHEN ONE ANIMAL'S POPULATION GOES UP, IT'S BECAUSE WHATEVER EATS THAT ANIMAL IS DYING OUT.
WHAT'RE THESE THINGS CALLED, ANYWAYS?
SEA BOOGERS.
WITH A NAME LIKE THAT, I WOULDN'T EAT 'EM EITHER.
THIS ISN'T AN ENVIRONMENTAL PROBLEM, THIS IS JUST BAD MARKETING.

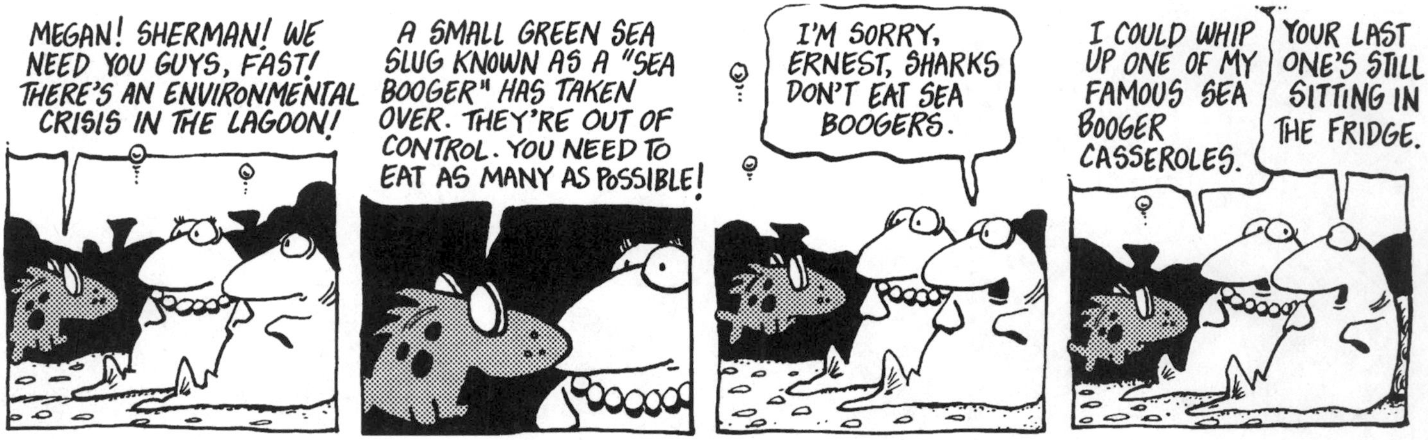
MEGAN! SHERMAN! WE NEED YOU GUYS, FAST! THERE'S AN ENVIRONMENTAL CRISIS IN THE LAGOON!
A SMALL GREEN SEA SLUG KNOWN AS A "SEA BOOGER" HAS TAKEN OVER. THEY'RE OUT OF CONTROL. YOU NEED TO EAT AS MANY AS POSSIBLE!
I'M SORRY, ERNEST, SHARKS DON'T EAT SEA BOOGERS.
I COULD WHIP UP ONE OF MY FAMOUS SEA BOOGER CASSEROLES.
YOUR LAST ONE'S STILL SITTING IN THE FRIDGE.

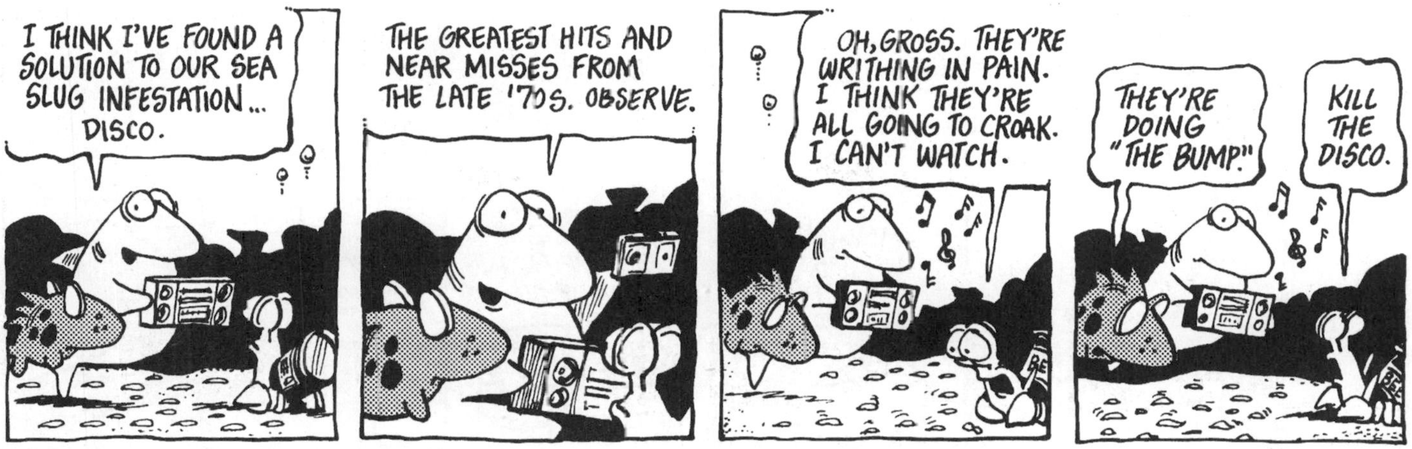
I THINK I'VE FOUND A SOLUTION TO OUR SEA SLUG INFESTATION... DISCO.
THE GREATEST HITS AND NEAR MISSES FROM THE LATE '70S. OBSERVE.
OH, GROSS. THEY'RE WRITHING IN PAIN. I THINK THEY'RE ALL GOING TO CROAK. I CAN'T WATCH.
THEY'RE DOING "THE BUMP."
KILL THE DISCO.

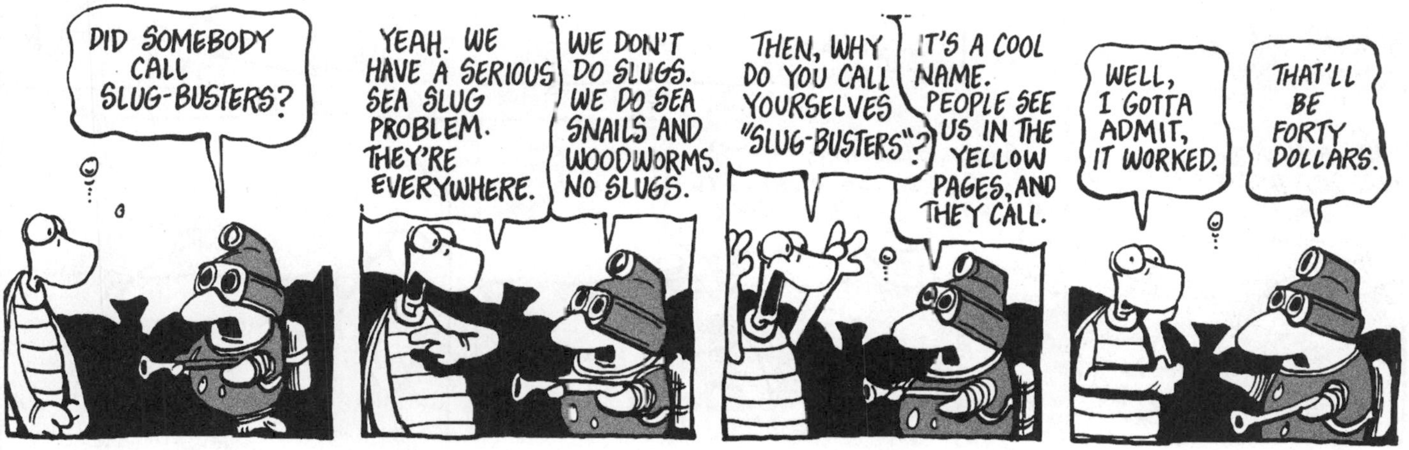
DID SOMEBODY CALL SLUG-BUSTERS?
YEAH. WE HAVE A SERIOUS SEA SLUG PROBLEM. THEY'RE EVERYWHERE.
WE DON'T DO SLUGS. WE DO SEA SNAILS AND WOODWORMS. NO SLUGS.
THEN, WHY DO YOU CALL YOURSELVES "SLUG-BUSTERS"?
IT'S A COOL NAME. PEOPLE SEE US IN THE YELLOW PAGES, AND THEY CALL.
WELL, I GOTTA ADMIT, IT WORKED.
THAT'LL BE FORTY DOLLARS.

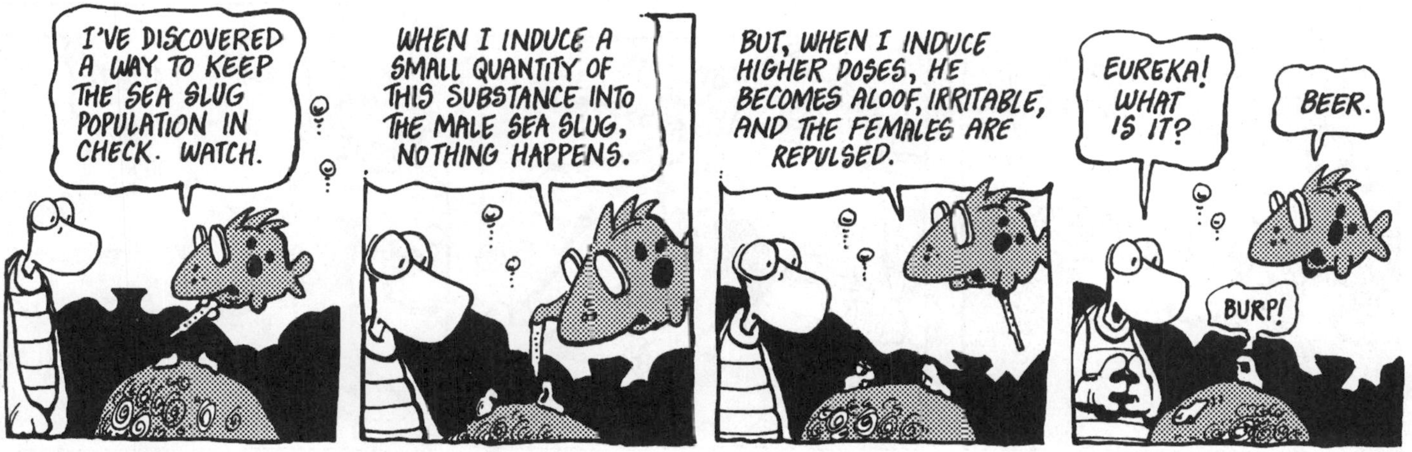
I'VE DISCOVERED A WAY TO KEEP THE SEA SLUG POPULATION IN CHECK. WATCH.
WHEN I INDUCE A SMALL QUANTITY OF THIS SUBSTANCE INTO THE MALE SEA SLUG, NOTHING HAPPENS.
BUT, WHEN I INDUCE HIGHER DOSES, HE BECOMES ALOOF, IRRITABLE, AND THE FEMALES ARE REPULSED.
EUREKA! WHAT IS IT?
BEER.
BURP!

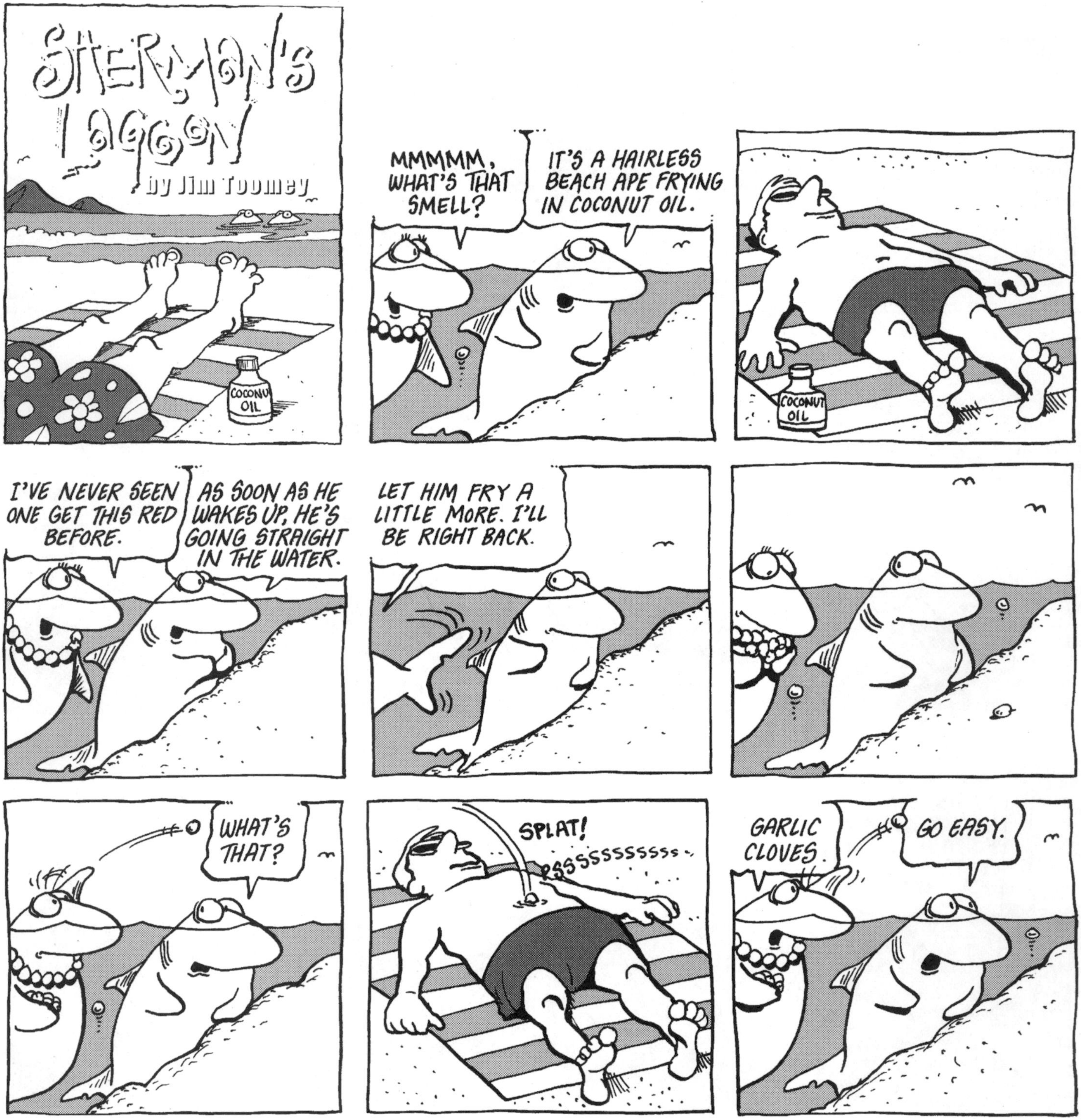
SHERMAN'S LAGOON
by Jim Toomey
COCONUT OIL
MMMMM, WHAT'S THAT SMELL?
IT'S A HAIRLESS BEACH APE FRYING IN COCONUT OIL.
COCONUT OIL
I'VE NEVER SEEN ONE GET THIS RED BEFORE.
AS SOON AS HE WAKES UP, HE'S GOING STRAIGHT IN THE WATER.
LET HIM FRY A LITTLE MORE. I'LL BE RIGHT BACK.
WHAT'S THAT?
SPLAT!
PSSSSSSSSSSSS
GARLIC CLOVES.
GO EASY.

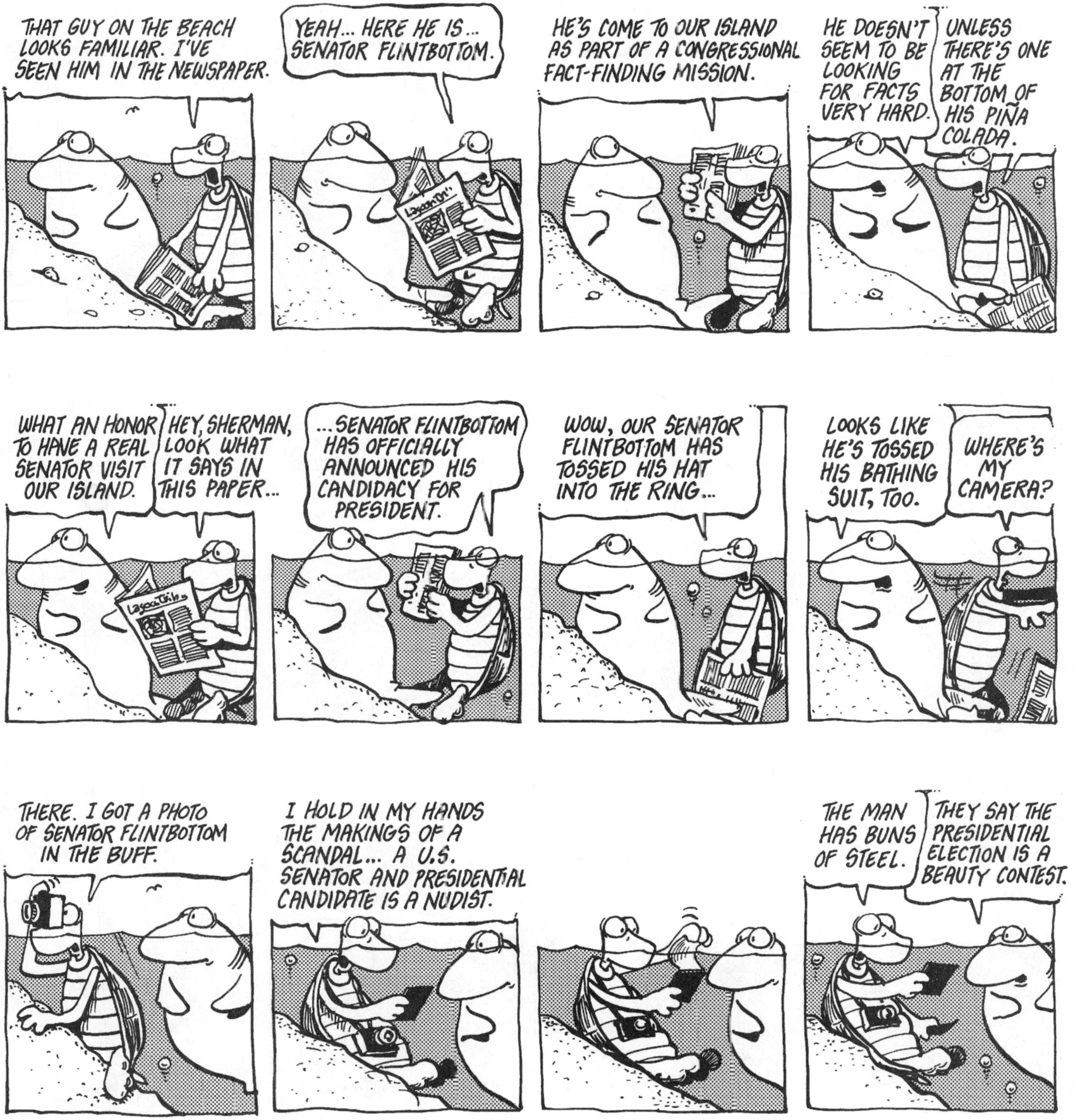
THAT GUY ON THE BEACH LOOKS FAMILIAR. I'VE SEEN HIM IN THE NEWSPAPER.
YEAH... HERE HE IS... SENATOR FLINTBOTTOM.
HE'S COME TO OUR ISLAND AS PART OF A CONGRESSIONAL FACT-FINDING MISSION.
HE DOESN'T SEEM TO BE LOOKING FOR FACTS VERY HARD.
UNLESS THERE'S ONE AT THE BOTTOM OF HIS PIÑA COLADA.
WHAT AN HONOR TO HAVE A REAL SENATOR VISIT OUR ISLAND.
HEY, SHERMAN, LOOK WHAT IT SAYS IN THIS PAPER...
...SENATOR FLINTBOTTOM HAS OFFICIALLY ANNOUNCED HIS CANDIDACY FOR PRESIDENT.
WOW, OUR SENATOR FLINTBOTTOM HAS TOSSED HIS HAT INTO THE RING...
LOOKS LIKE HE'S TOSSED HIS BATHING SUIT, TOO.
WHERE'S MY CAMERA?
THERE. I GOT A PHOTO OF SENATOR FLINTBOTTOM IN THE BUFF.
I HOLD IN MY HANDS THE MAKINGS OF A SCANDAL... A U.S. SENATOR AND PRESIDENTIAL CANDIDATE IS A NUDIST.
THE MAN HAS BUNS OF STEEL.
THEY SAY THE PRESIDENTIAL ELECTION IS A BEAUTY CONTEST.

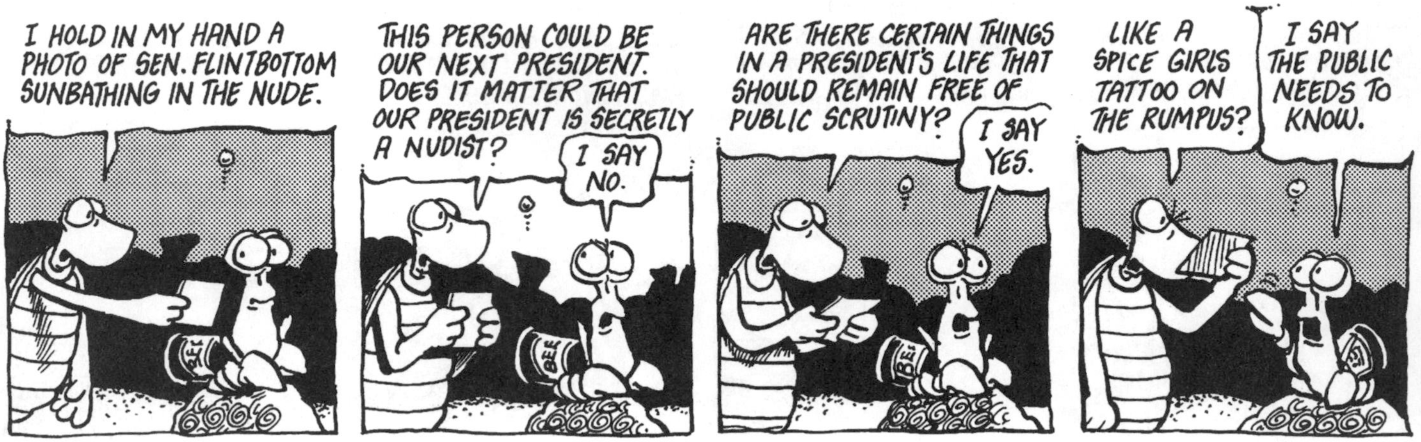
I HOLD IN MY HAND A PHOTO OF SEN. FLINTBOTTOM SUNBATHING IN THE NUDE.
THIS PERSON COULD BE OUR NEXT PRESIDENT. DOES IT MATTER THAT OUR PRESIDENT IS SECRETLY A NUDIST?
I SAY NO.
ARE THERE CERTAIN THINGS IN A PRESIDENT'S LIFE THAT SHOULD REMAIN FREE OF PUBLIC SCRUTINY?
I SAY YES.
LIKE A SPICE GIRLS TATTOO ON THE RUMPUS?
I SAY THE PUBLIC NEEDS TO KNOW.

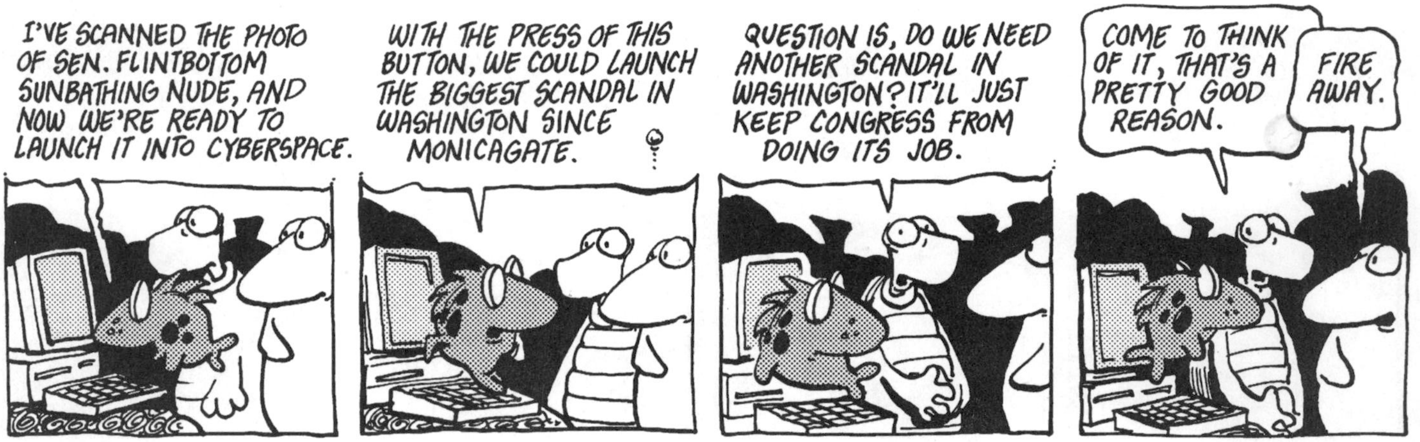
I'VE SCANNED THE PHOTO OF SEN. FLINTBOTTOM SUNBATHING NUDE, AND NOW WE'RE READY TO LAUNCH IT INTO CYBERSPACE.
WITH THE PRESS OF THIS BUTTON, WE COULD LAUNCH THE BIGGEST SCANDAL IN WASHINGTON SINCE MONICAGATE.
QUESTION IS, DO WE NEED ANOTHER SCANDAL IN WASHINGTON? IT'LL JUST KEEP CONGRESS FROM DOING ITS JOB.
COME TO THINK OF IT, THAT'S A PRETTY GOOD REASON.
FIRE AWAY.

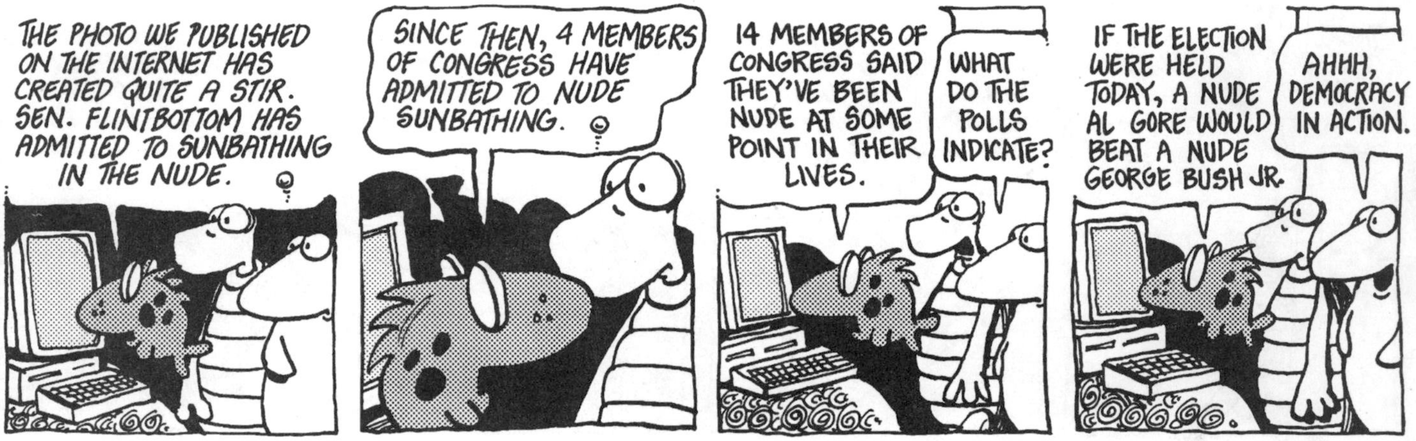
THE PHOTO WE PUBLISHED ON THE INTERNET HAS CREATED QUITE A STIR. SEN. FLINTBOTTOM HAS ADMITTED TO SUNBATHING IN THE NUDE.
SINCE THEN, 4 MEMBERS OF CONGRESS HAVE ADMITTED TO NUDE SUNBATHING.
14 MEMBERS OF CONGRESS SAID THEY'VE BEEN NUDE AT SOME POINT IN THEIR LIVES.
WHAT DO THE POLLS INDICATE?
IF THE ELECTION WERE HELD TODAY, A NUDE AL GORE WOULD BEAT A NUDE GEORGE BUSH JR.
AHHH, DEMOCRACY IN ACTION.

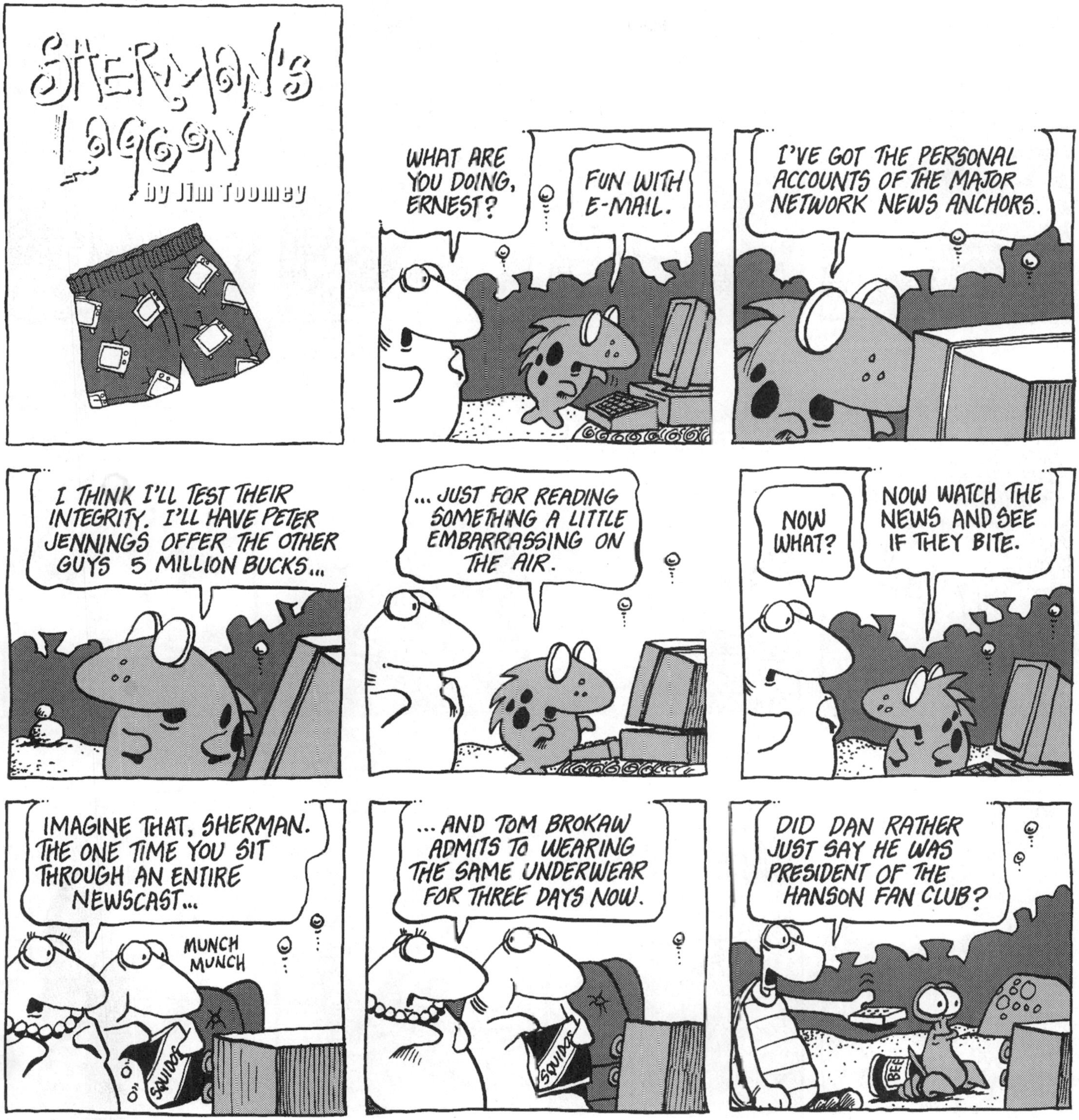
SHERMAN'S LAGOON
by Jim Toomey
WHAT ARE YOU DOING, ERNEST?
FUN WITH E-MAIL.
I'VE GOT THE PERSONAL ACCOUNTS OF THE MAJOR NETWORK NEWS ANCHORS.
I THINK I'LL TEST THEIR INTEGRITY. I'LL HAVE PETER JENNINGS OFFER THE OTHER GUYS 5 MILLION BUCKS...
...JUST FOR READING SOMETHING A LITTLE EMBARRASSING ON THE AIR.
NOW WHAT?
NOW WATCH THE NEWS AND SEE IF THEY BITE.
IMAGINE THAT, SHERMAN. THE ONE TIME YOU SIT THROUGH AN ENTIRE NEWSCAST...
MUNCH MUNCH
SQUIDOS
...AND TOM BROKAW ADMITS TO WEARING THE SAME UNDERWEAR FOR THREE DAYS NOW.
SQUIDOS
DID DAN RATHER JUST SAY HE WAS PRESIDENT OF THE HANSON FAN CLUB?

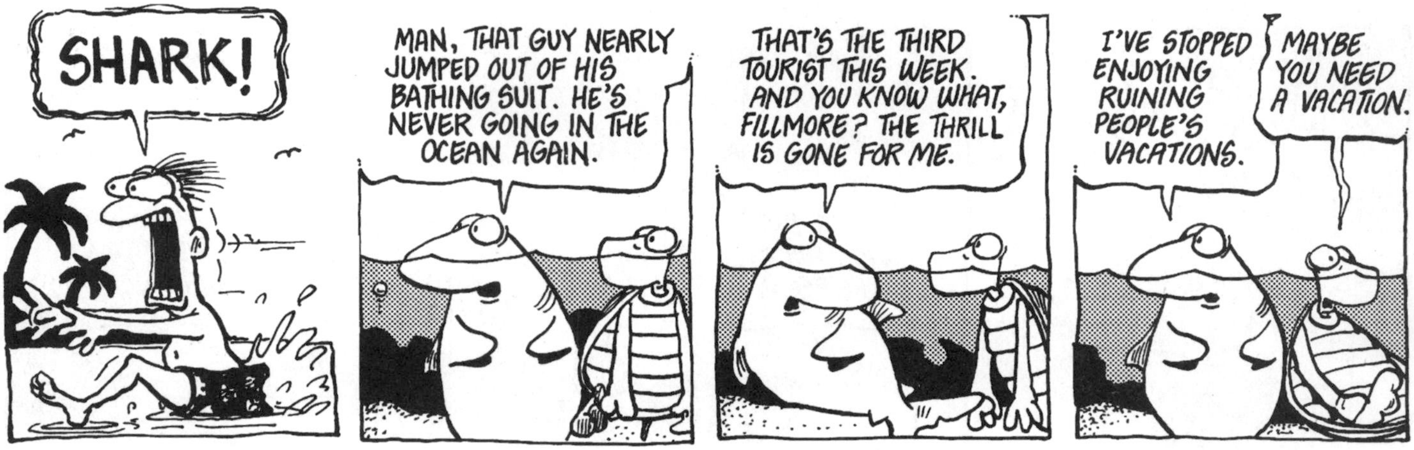
SHARK!
MAN, THAT GUY NEARLY JUMPED OUT OF HIS BATHING SUIT. HE'S NEVER GOING IN THE OCEAN AGAIN.
THAT'S THE THIRD TOURIST THIS WEEK. AND YOU KNOW WHAT, FILLMORE? THE THRILL IS GONE FOR ME.
I'VE STOPPED ENJOYING RUINING PEOPLE'S VACATIONS.
MAYBE YOU NEED A VACATION.

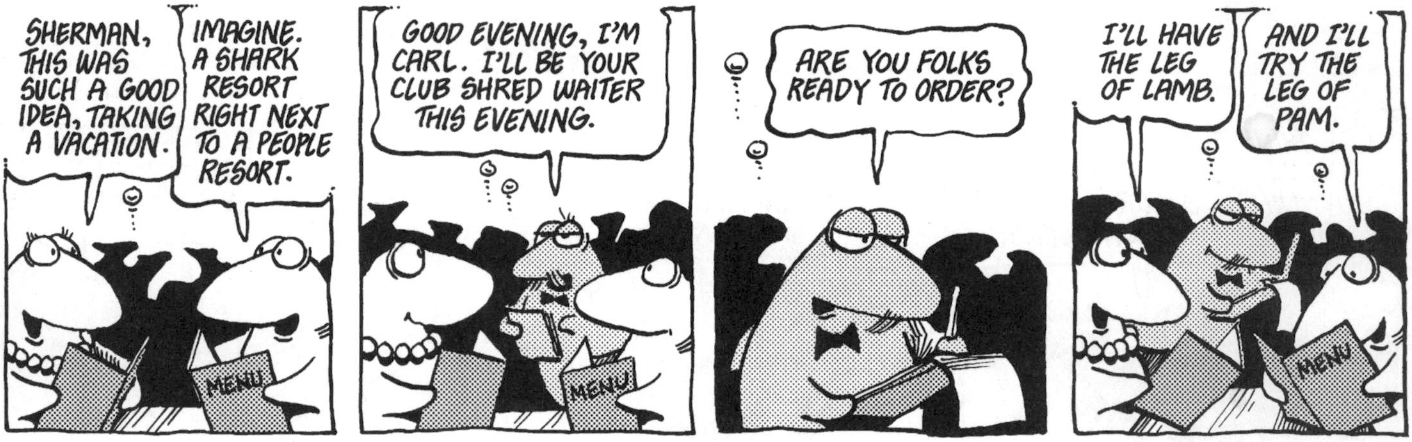
SHERMAN, THIS WAS SUCH A GOOD IDEA, TAKING A VACATION.
IMAGINE. A SHARK RESORT RIGHT NEXT TO A PEOPLE RESORT.
MENU
GOOD EVENING, I'M CARL. I'LL BE YOUR CLUB SHRED WAITER THIS EVENING.
MENU
ARE YOU FOLKS READY TO ORDER?
I'LL HAVE THE LEG OF LAMB.
AND I'LL TRY THE LEG OF PAM.
MENU

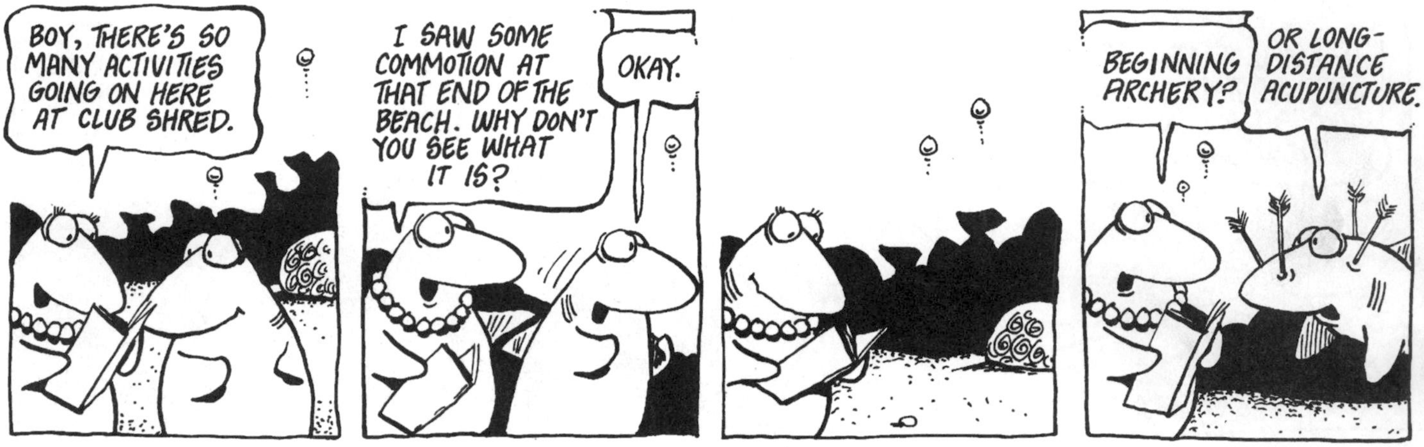
BOY, THERE'S SO MANY ACTIVITIES GOING ON HERE AT CLUB SHRED.
I SAW SOME COMMOTION AT THAT END OF THE BEACH. WHY DON'T YOU SEE WHAT IT IS?
OKAY.
BEGINNING ARCHERY?
OR LONG-DISTANCE ACUPUNCTURE.

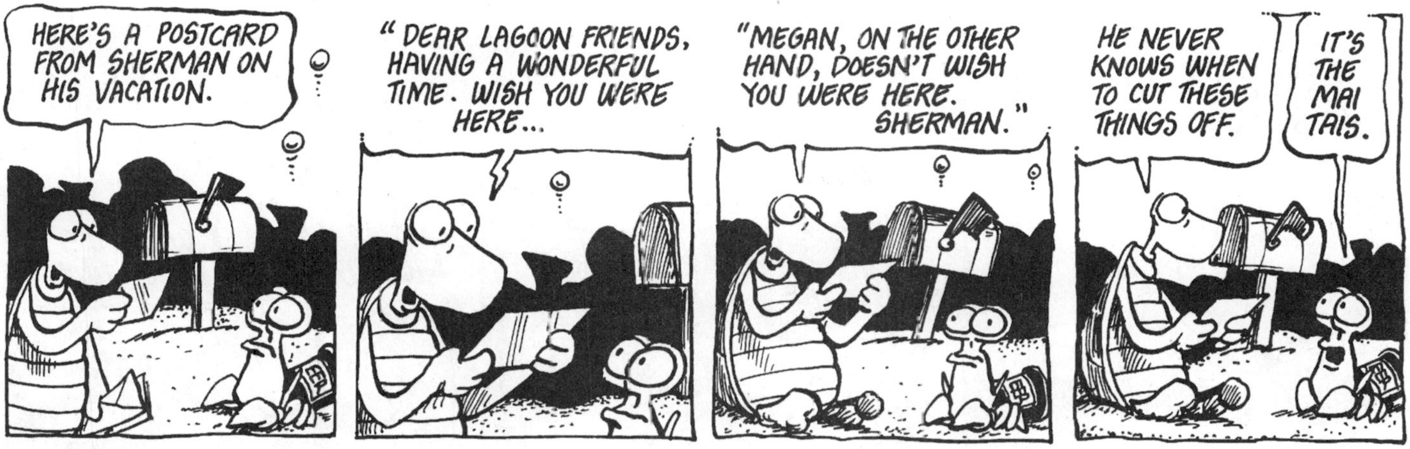
HERE'S A POSTCARD FROM SHERMAN ON HIS VACATION.
"DEAR LAGOON FRIENDS, HAVING A WONDERFUL TIME. WISH YOU WERE HERE...
"MEGAN, ON THE OTHER HAND, DOESN'T WISH YOU WERE HERE. SHERMAN."
HE NEVER KNOWS WHEN TO CUT THESE THINGS OFF.
IT'S THE MAI TAIS.

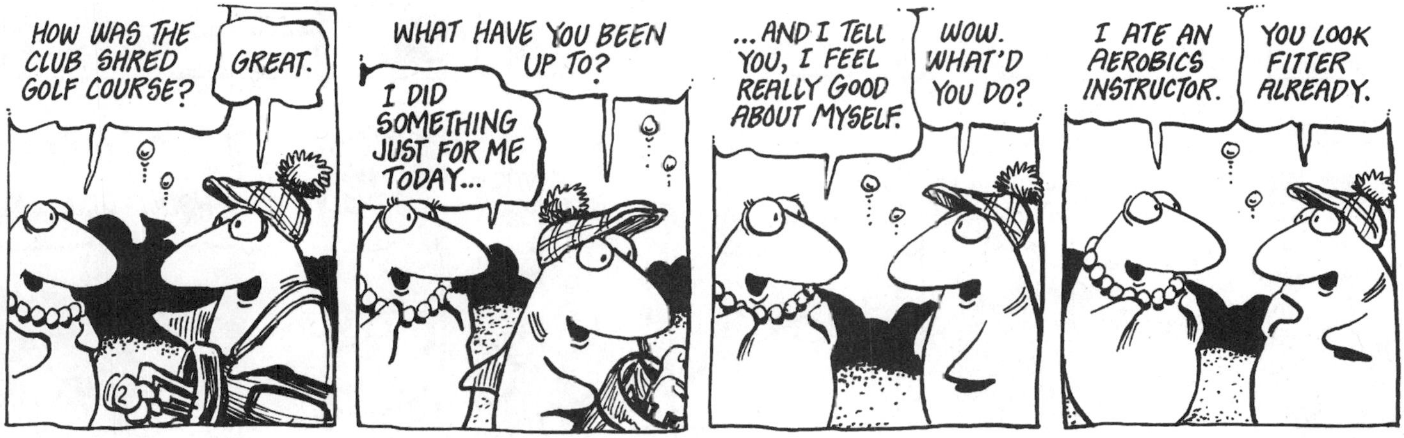
HOW WAS THE CLUB SHRED GOLF COURSE?
GREAT.
WHAT HAVE YOU BEEN UP TO?
I DID SOMETHING JUST FOR ME TODAY...
...AND I TELL YOU, I FEEL REALLY GOOD ABOUT MYSELF.
WOW. WHAT'D YOU DO?
I ATE AN AEROBICS INSTRUCTOR.
YOU LOOK FITTER ALREADY.

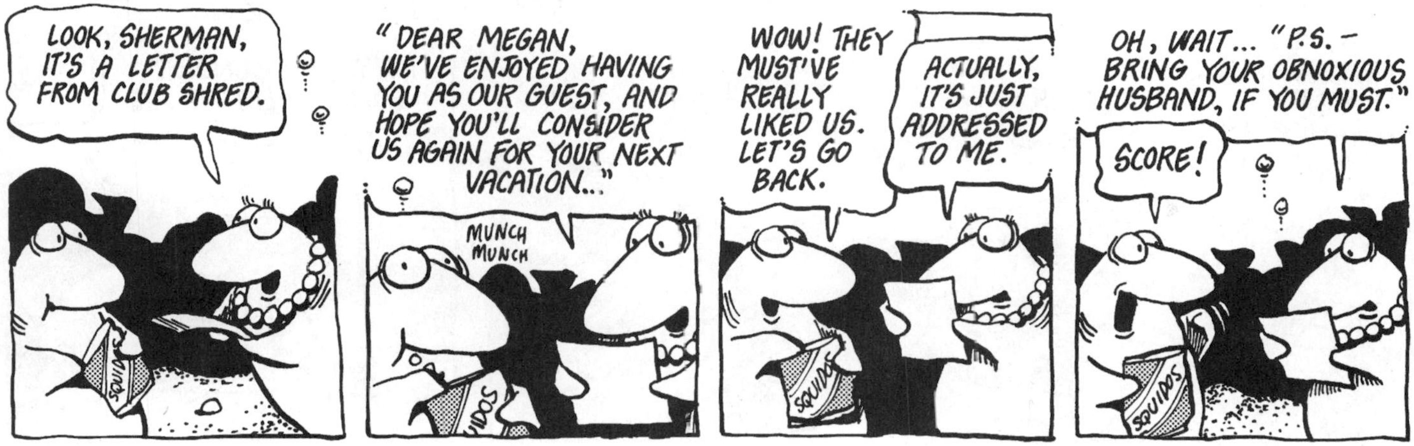
LOOK, SHERMAN, IT'S A LETTER FROM CLUB SHRED.
SQUIDOS
"DEAR MEGAN, WE'VE ENJOYED HAVING YOU AS OUR GUEST, AND HOPE YOU'LL CONSIDER US AGAIN FOR YOUR NEXT VACATION..."
MUNCH MUNCH
WOW! THEY MUST'VE REALLY LIKED US. LET'S GO BACK.
ACTUALLY, IT'S JUST ADDRESSED TO ME.
SQUIDOS
OH, WAIT... "P.S. - BRING YOUR OBNOXIOUS HUSBAND, IF YOU MUST."
SCORE!
SQUIDOS

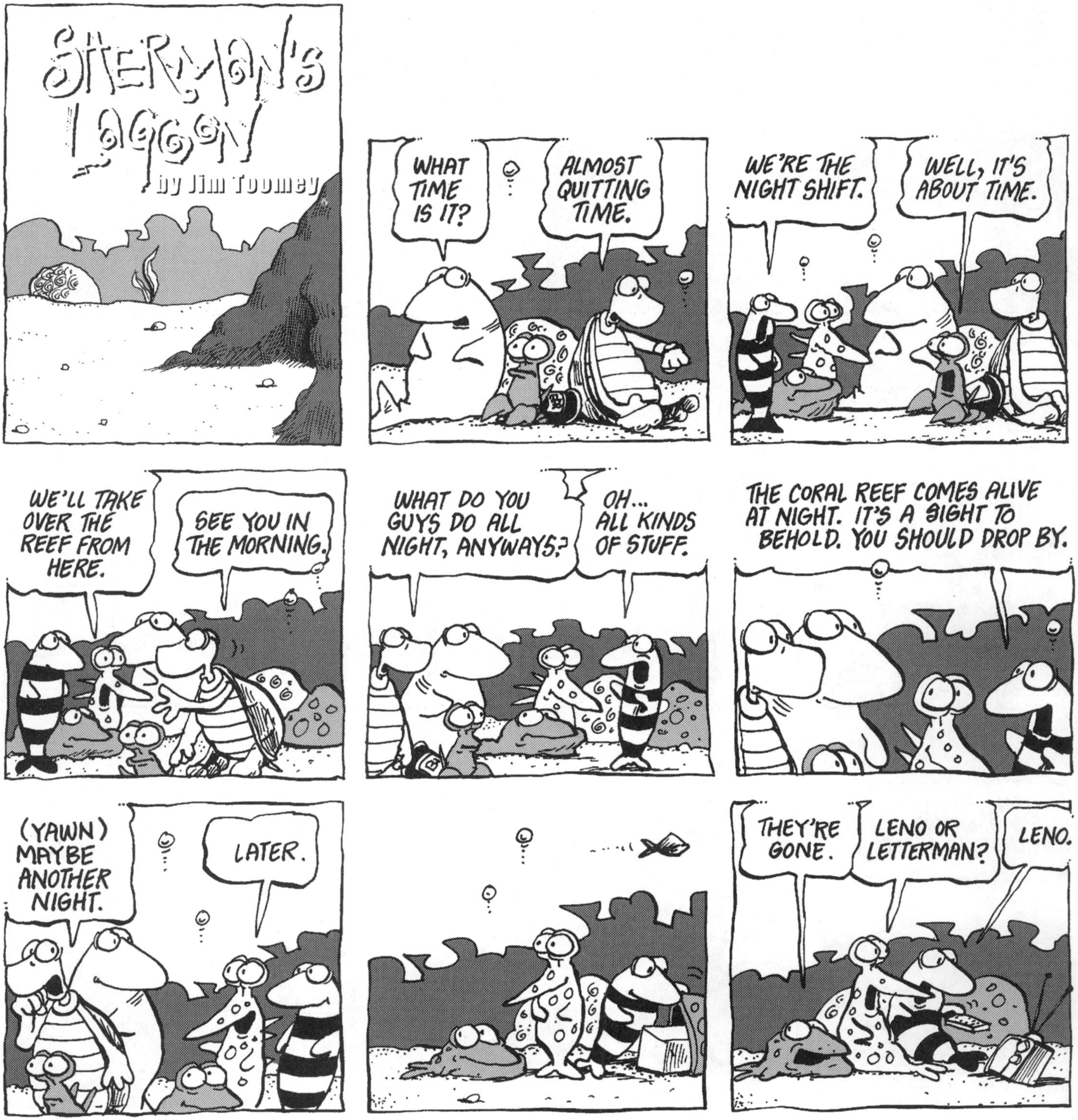
SHERMAN'S LAGOON
by Jim Toomey
WHAT TIME IS IT?
ALMOST QUITTING TIME.
WE'RE THE NIGHT SHIFT.
WELL, IT'S ABOUT TIME.
WE'LL TAKE OVER THE REEF FROM HERE.
SEE YOU IN THE MORNING.
WHAT DO YOU GUYS DO ALL NIGHT, ANYWAYS?
OH... ALL KINDS OF STUFF.
THE CORAL REEF COMES ALIVE AT NIGHT. IT'S A SIGHT TO BEHOLD. YOU SHOULD DROP BY.
(YAWN) MAYBE ANOTHER NIGHT.
LATER.
THEY'RE GONE.
LENO OR LETTERMAN?
LENO.

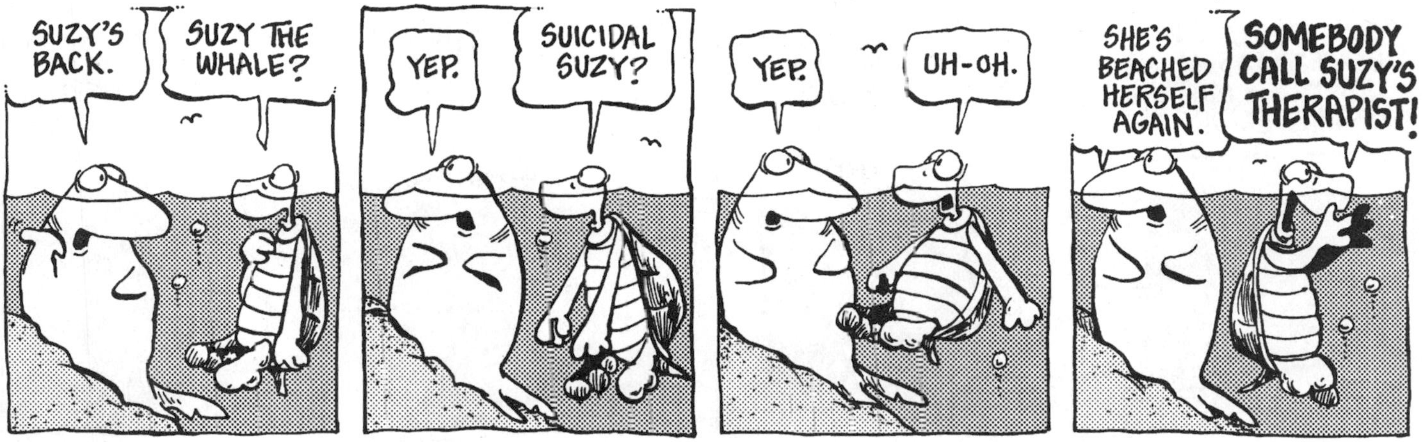
SUZY'S BACK.
SUZY THE WHALE?
YEP.
SUICIDAL SUZY?
YEP.
UH-OH.
SHE'S BEACHED HERSELF AGAIN.
SOMEBODY CALL SUZY'S THERAPIST!

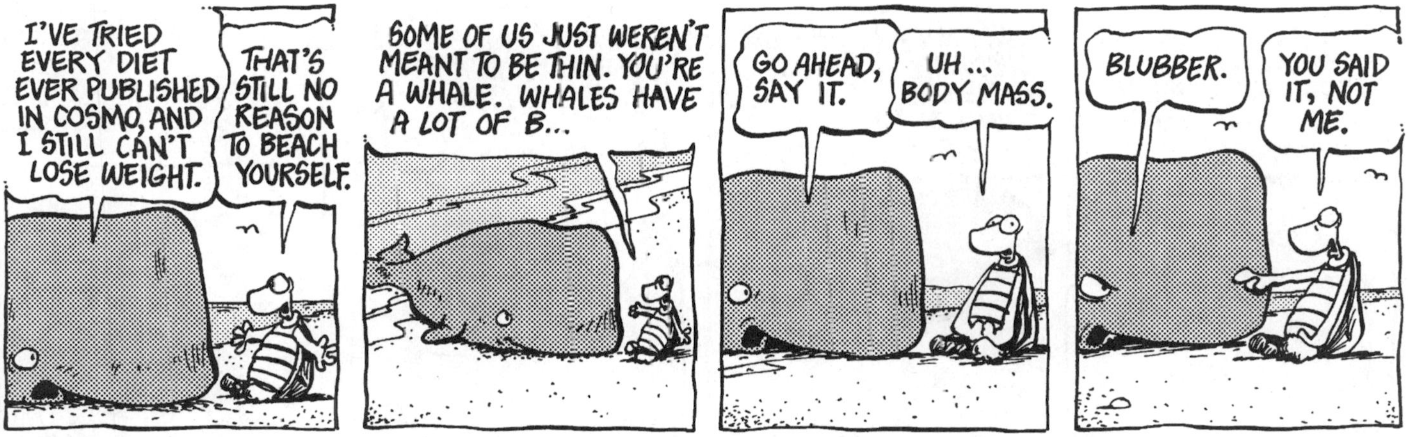
I'VE TRIED EVERY DIET EVER PUBLISHED IN COSMO, AND I STILL CAN'T LOSE WEIGHT.
THAT'S STILL NO REASON TO BEACH YOURSELF.
SOME OF US JUST WEREN'T MEANT TO BE THIN. YOU'RE A WHALE. WHALES HAVE A LOT OF B...
GO AHEAD, SAY IT.
UH... BODY MASS.
BLUBBER.
YOU SAID IT, NOT ME.

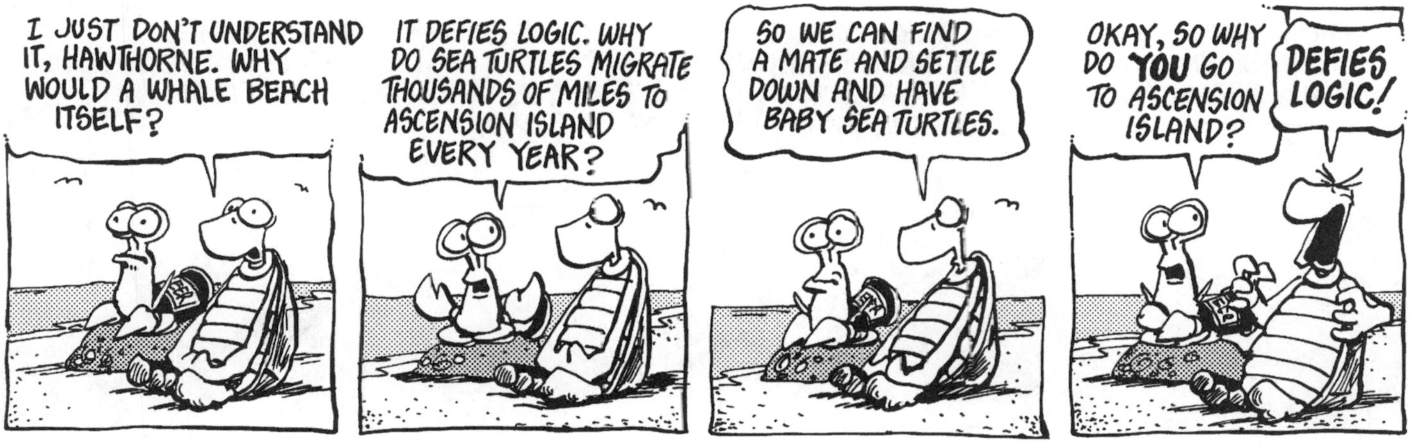
I JUST DON'T UNDERSTAND IT, HAWTHORNE. WHY WOULD A WHALE BEACH ITSELF?
IT DEFIES LOGIC. WHY DO SEA TURTLES MIGRATE THOUSANDS OF MILES TO ASCENSION ISLAND EVERY YEAR?
SO WE CAN FIND A MATE AND SETTLE DOWN AND HAVE BABY SEA TURTLES.
OKAY, SO WHY DO YOU GO TO ASCENSION ISLAND?
DEFIES LOGIC!

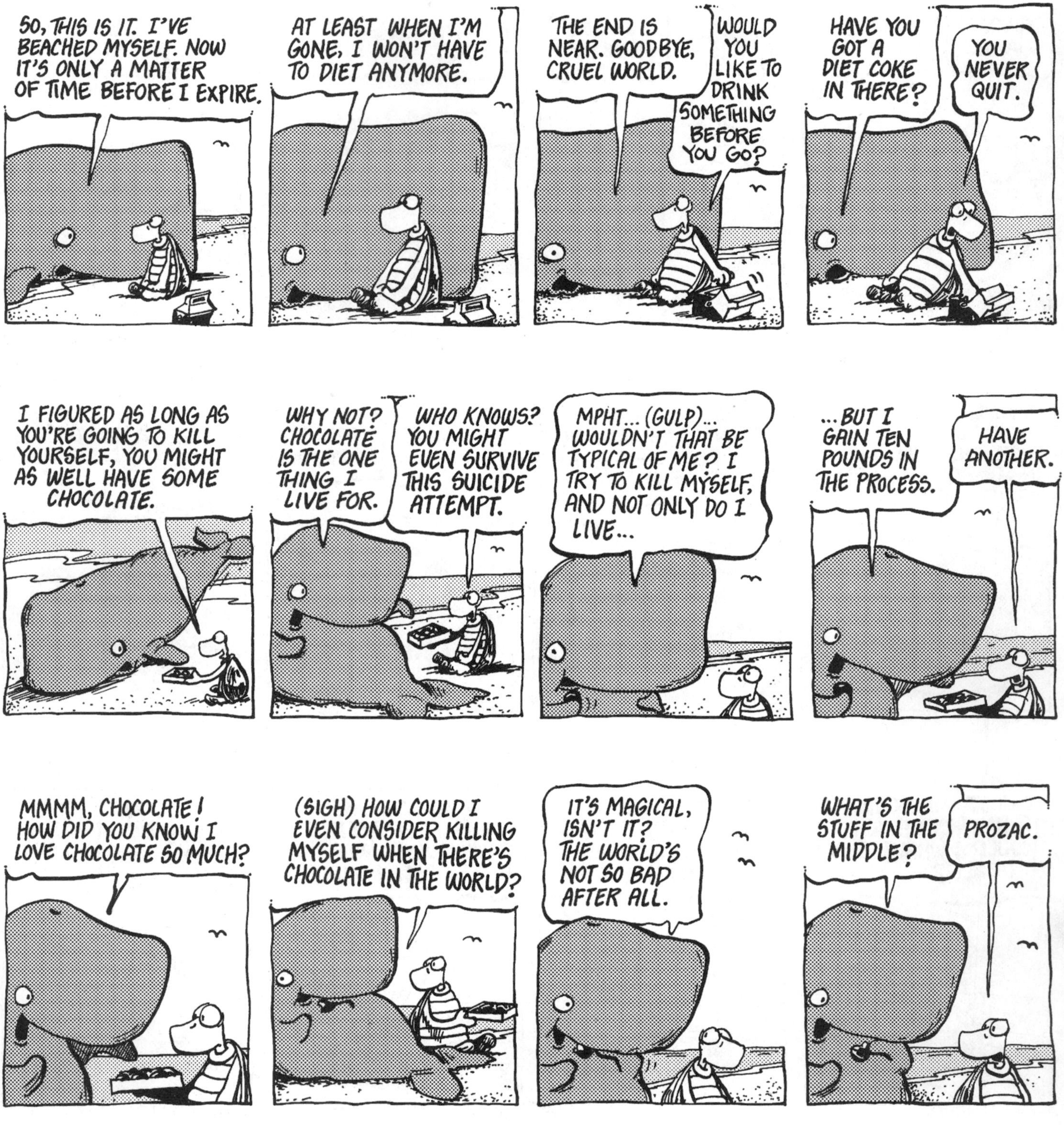
SO, THIS IS IT. I'VE BEACHED MYSELF. NOW IT'S ONLY A MATTER OF TIME BEFORE I EXPIRE.
AT LEAST WHEN I'M GONE, I WON'T HAVE TO DIET ANYMORE.
THE END IS NEAR. GOODBYE, CRUEL WORLD.
WOULD YOU LIKE TO DRINK SOMETHING BEFORE YOU GO?
HAVE YOU GOT A DIET COKE IN THERE?
YOU NEVER QUIT.
I FIGURED AS LONG AS YOU'RE GOING TO KILL YOURSELF, YOU MIGHT AS WELL HAVE SOME CHOCOLATE.
WHY NOT? CHOCOLATE IS THE ONE THING I LIVE FOR.
WHO KNOWS? YOU MIGHT EVEN SURVIVE THIS SUICIDE ATTEMPT.
MPHT... (GULP)... WOULDN'T THAT BE TYPICAL OF ME? I TRY TO KILL MYSELF, AND NOT ONLY DO I LIVE...
...BUT I GAIN TEN POUNDS IN THE PROCESS.
HAVE ANOTHER.
MMMM, CHOCOLATE! HOW DID YOU KNOW I LOVE CHOCOLATE SO MUCH?
(SIGH) HOW COULD I EVEN CONSIDER KILLING MYSELF WHEN THERE'S CHOCOLATE IN THE WORLD?
IT'S MAGICAL, ISN'T IT? THE WORLD'S NOT SO BAD AFTER ALL.
WHAT'S THE STUFF IN THE MIDDLE?
PROZAC.

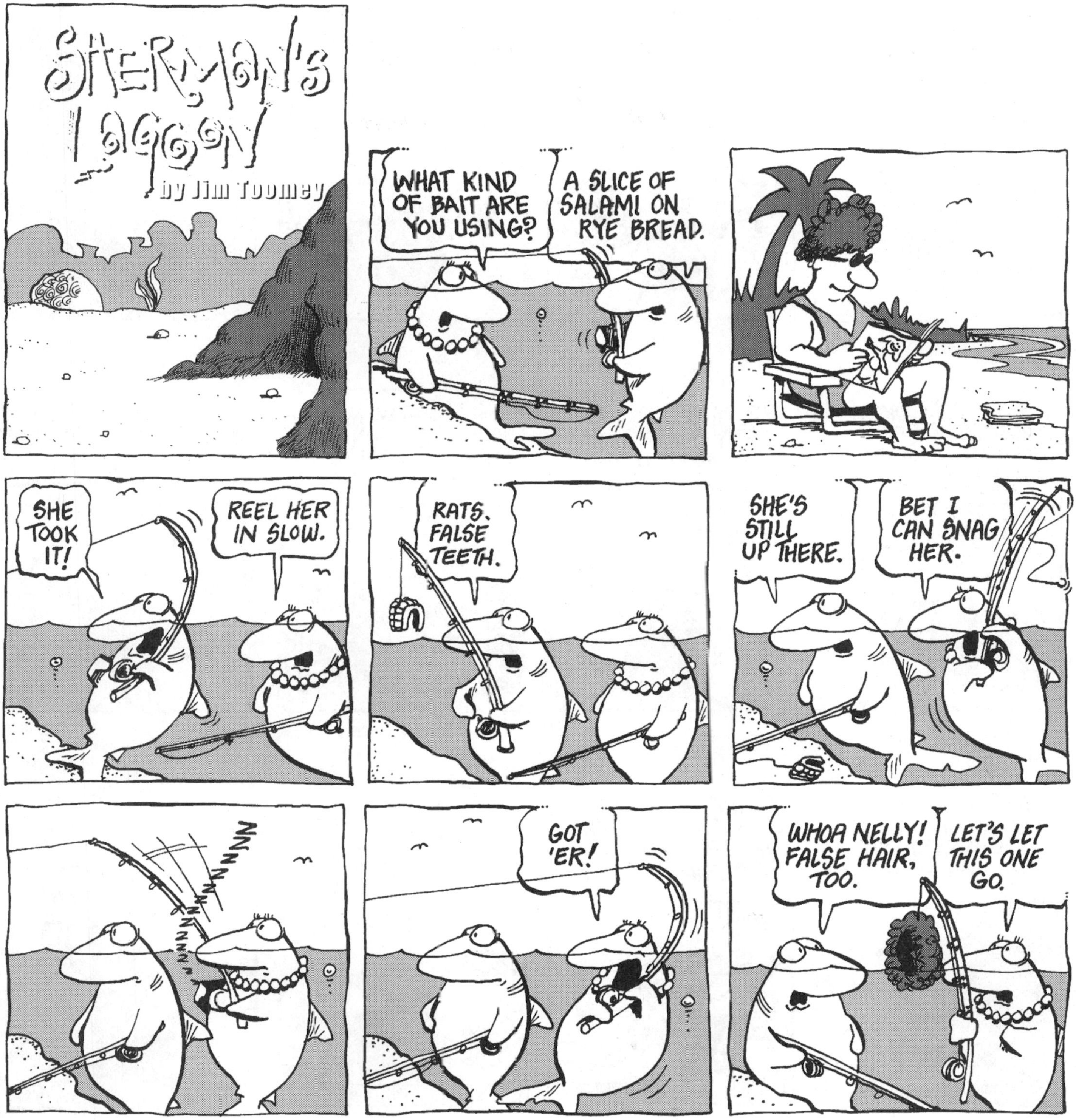
SHERMAN'S LAGOON
by Jim Toomey
WHAT KIND OF BAIT ARE YOU USING?
A SLICE OF SALAMI ON RYE BREAD.
SHE TOOK IT!
REEL HER IN SLOW.
RATS. FALSE TEETH.
SHE'S STILL UP THERE.
BET I CAN SNAG HER.
GOT 'ER!
WHOA NELLY! FALSE HAIR, TOO.
LET'S LET THIS ONE GO.

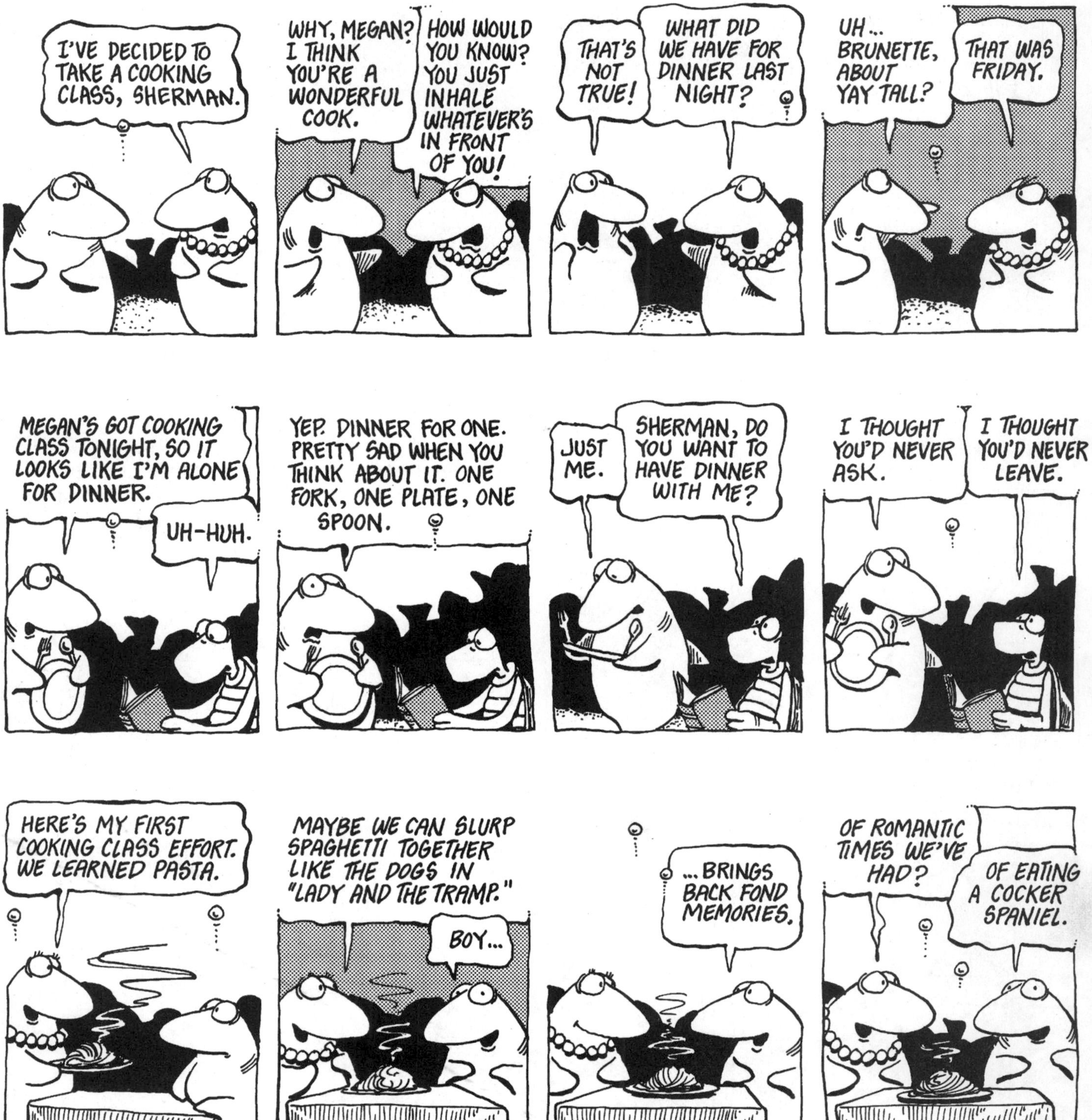
I'VE DECIDED TO TAKE A COOKING CLASS, SHERMAN.
WHY, MEGAN? I THINK YOU'RE A WONDERFUL COOK.
HOW WOULD YOU KNOW? YOU JUST INHALE WHATEVER'S IN FRONT OF YOU!
THAT'S NOT TRUE!
WHAT DID WE HAVE FOR DINNER LAST NIGHT?
UH... BRUNETTE, ABOUT YAY TALL?
THAT WAS FRIDAY.
MEGAN'S GOT COOKING CLASS TONIGHT, SO IT LOOKS LIKE I'M ALONE FOR DINNER.
UH-HUH.
YEP. DINNER FOR ONE. PRETTY SAD WHEN YOU THINK ABOUT IT. ONE FORK, ONE PLATE, ONE SPOON.
JUST ME.
SHERMAN, DO YOU WANT TO HAVE DINNER WITH ME?
I THOUGHT YOU'D NEVER ASK.
I THOUGHT YOU'D NEVER LEAVE.
HERE'S MY FIRST COOKING CLASS EFFORT. WE LEARNED PASTA.
MAYBE WE CAN SLURP SPAGHETTI TOGETHER LIKE THE DOGS IN "LADY AND THE TRAMP."
BOY...
...BRINGS BACK FOND MEMORIES.
OF ROMANTIC TIMES WE'VE HAD?
OF EATING A COCKER SPANIEL.

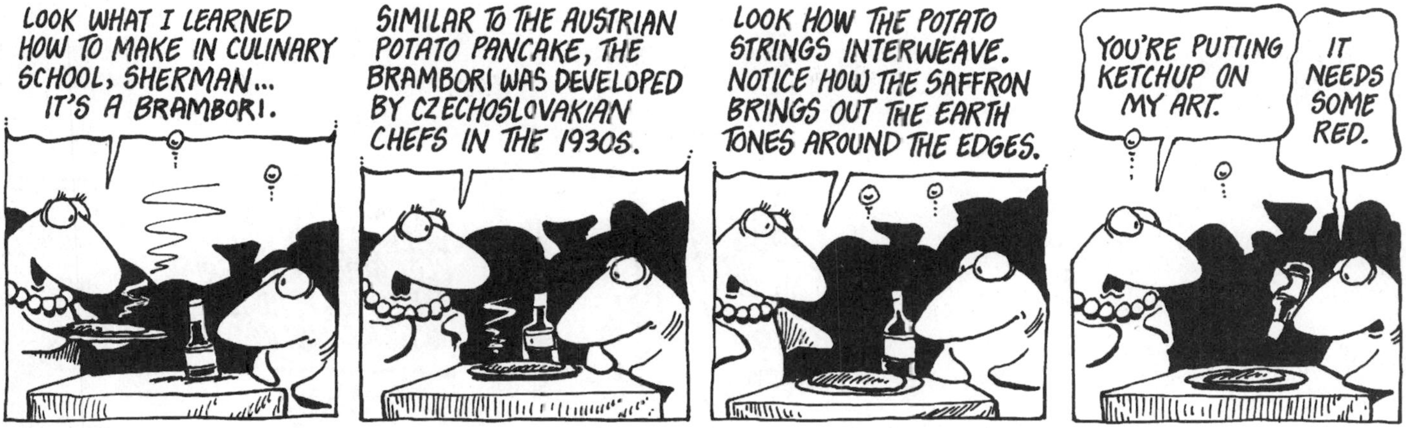
LOOK WHAT I LEARNED HOW TO MAKE IN CULINARY SCHOOL, SHERMAN... IT'S A BRAMBORI.
SIMILAR TO THE AUSTRIAN POTATO PANCAKE, THE BRAMBORI WAS DEVELOPED BY CZECHOSLOVAKIAN CHEFS IN THE 1930S.
LOOK HOW THE POTATO STRINGS INTERWEAVE. NOTICE HOW THE SAFFRON BRINGS OUT THE EARTH TONES AROUND THE EDGES.
YOU'RE PUTTING KETCHUP ON MY ART.
IT NEEDS SOME RED.

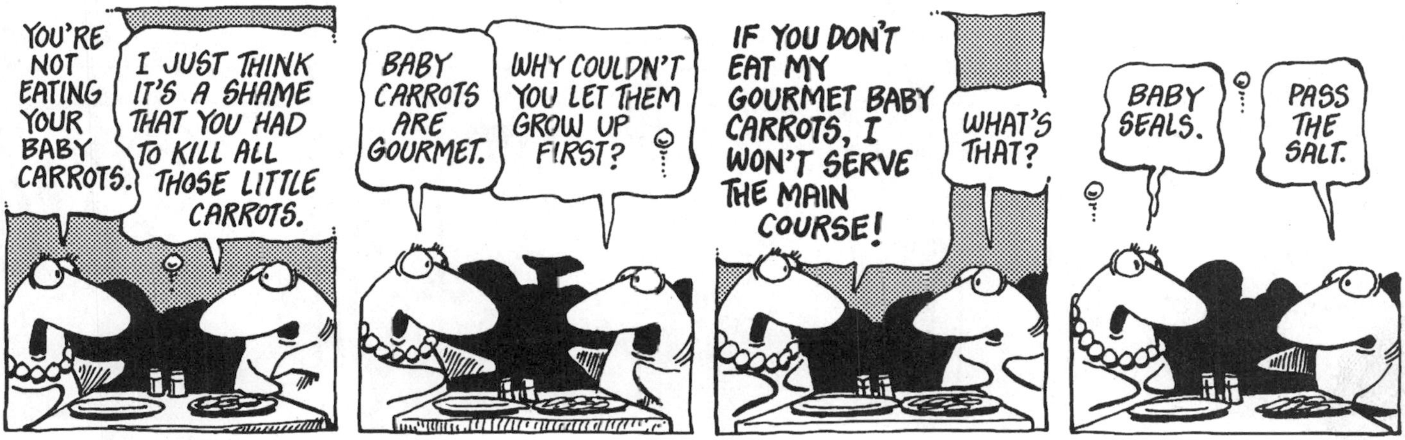
YOU'RE NOT EATING YOUR BABY CARROTS.
I JUST THINK IT'S A SHAME THAT YOU HAD TO KILL ALL THOSE LITTLE CARROTS.
BABY CARROTS ARE GOURMET.
WHY COULDN'T YOU LET THEM GROW UP FIRST?
IF YOU DON'T EAT MY GOURMET BABY CARROTS, I WON'T SERVE THE MAIN COURSE!
WHAT'S THAT?
BABY SEALS.
PASS THE SALT.

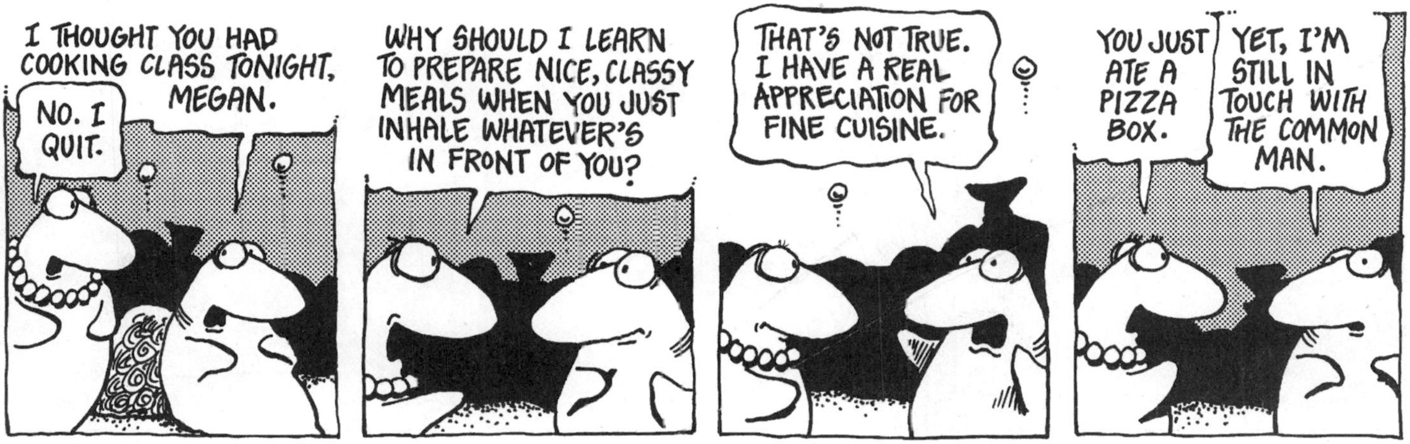
I THOUGHT YOU HAD COOKING CLASS TONIGHT, MEGAN.
NO. I QUIT.
WHY SHOULD I LEARN TO PREPARE NICE, CLASSY MEALS WHEN YOU JUST INHALE WHATEVER'S IN FRONT OF YOU?
THAT'S NOT TRUE. I HAVE A REAL APPRECIATION FOR FINE CUISINE.
YOU JUST ATE A PIZZA BOX.
YET, I'M STILL IN TOUCH WITH THE COMMON MAN.

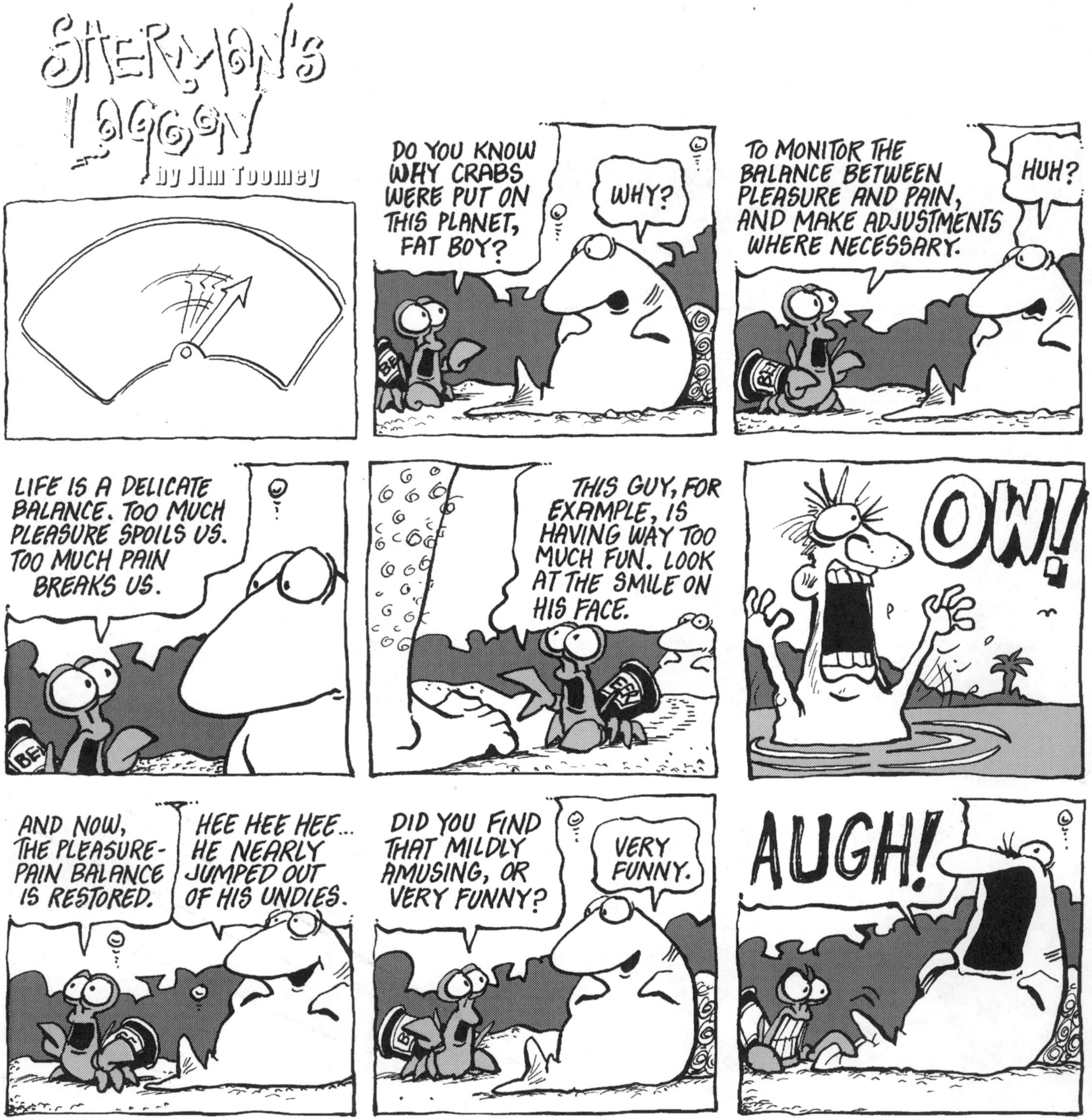

Sherman's Lagoon
by Jim Toomey
DO YOU KNOW WHY CRABS WERE PUT ON THIS PLANET, FAT BOY?
WHY?
TO MONITOR THE BALANCE BETWEEN PLEASURE AND PAIN, AND MAKE ADJUSTMENTS WHERE NECESSARY.
HUH?
LIFE IS A DELICATE BALANCE. TOO MUCH PLEASURE SPOILS US. TOO MUCH PAIN BREAKS US.
THIS GUY, FOR EXAMPLE, IS HAVING WAY TOO MUCH FUN. LOOK AT THE SMILE ON HIS FACE.
OW!
AND NOW, THE PLEASURE-PAIN BALANCE IS RESTORED.
HEE HEE HEE... HE NEARLY JUMPED OUT OF HIS UNDIES.
DID YOU FIND THAT MILDLY AMUSING, OR VERY FUNNY?
VERY FUNNY.
AUGH!

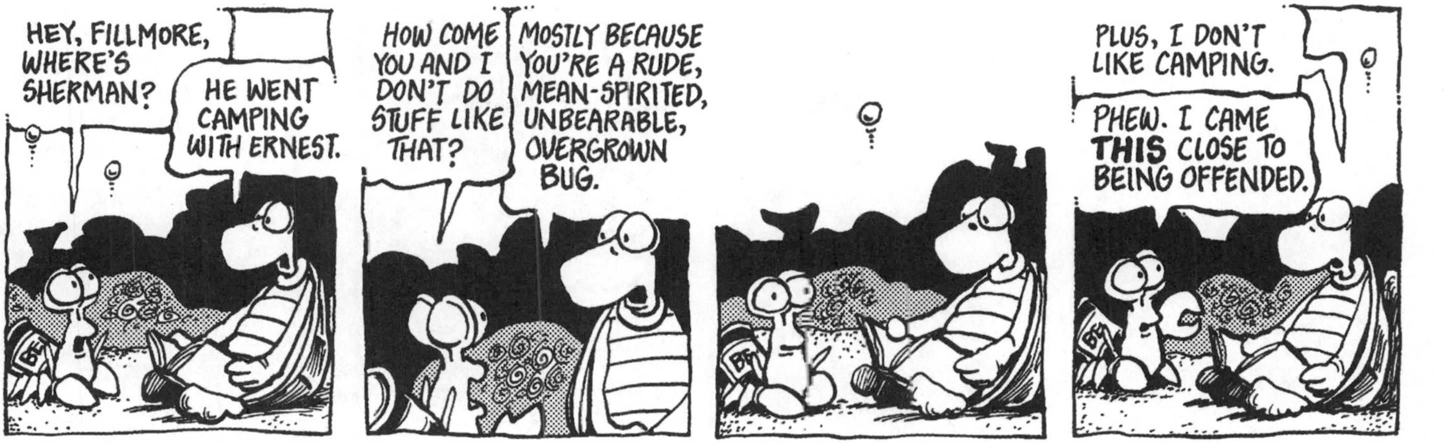
HEY, FILLMORE, WHERE'S SHERMAN?
HE WENT CAMPING WITH ERNEST.
HOW COME YOU AND I DON'T DO STUFF LIKE THAT?
MOSTLY BECAUSE YOU'RE A RUDE, MEAN-SPIRITED, UNBEARABLE, OVERGROWN BUG.
PLUS, I DON'T LIKE CAMPING.
PHEW. I CAME THIS CLOSE TO BEING OFFENDED.

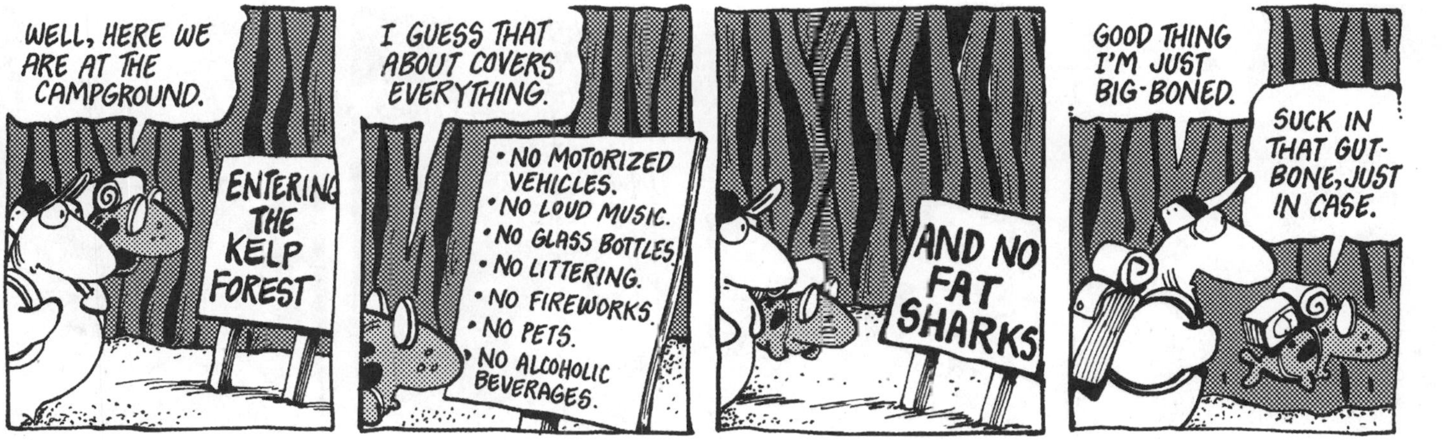
WELL, HERE WE ARE AT THE CAMPGROUND.
ENTERING THE KELP FOREST
I GUESS THAT ABOUT COVERS EVERYTHING.
• NO MOTORIZED VEHICLES.
• NO LOUD MUSIC.
• NO GLASS BOTTLES.
• NO LITTERING.
• NO FIREWORKS.
• NO PETS.
• NO ALCOHOLIC BEVERAGES.
AND NO FAT SHARKS
GOOD THING I'M JUST BIG-BONED.
SUCK IN THAT GUT-BONE, JUST IN CASE.

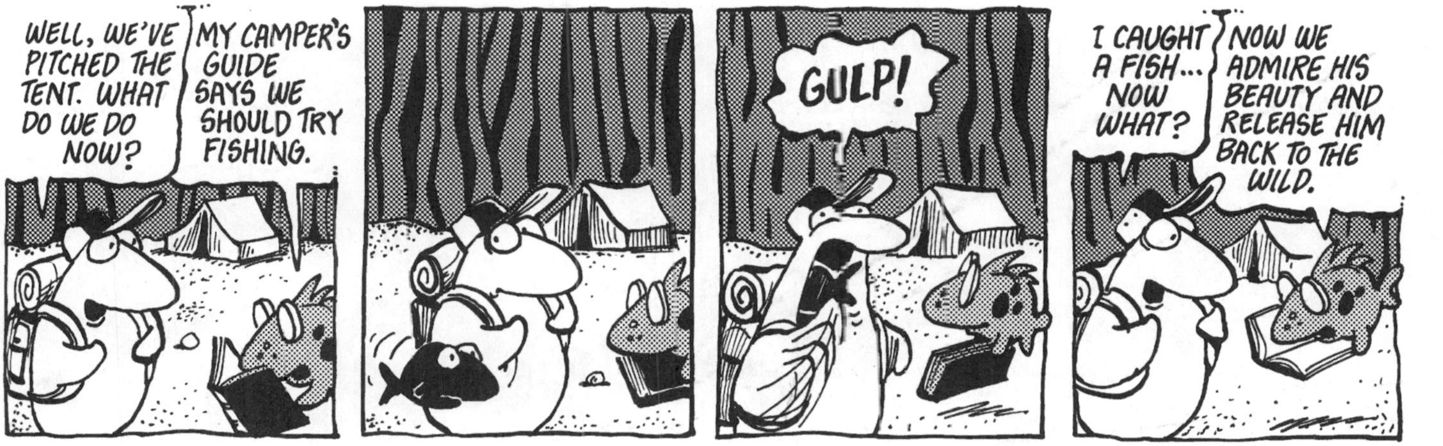
WELL, WE'VE PITCHED THE TENT. WHAT DO WE DO NOW?
MY CAMPER'S GUIDE SAYS WE SHOULD TRY FISHING.
GULP!
I CAUGHT A FISH... NOW WHAT?
NOW WE ADMIRE HIS BEAUTY AND RELEASE HIM BACK TO THE WILD.

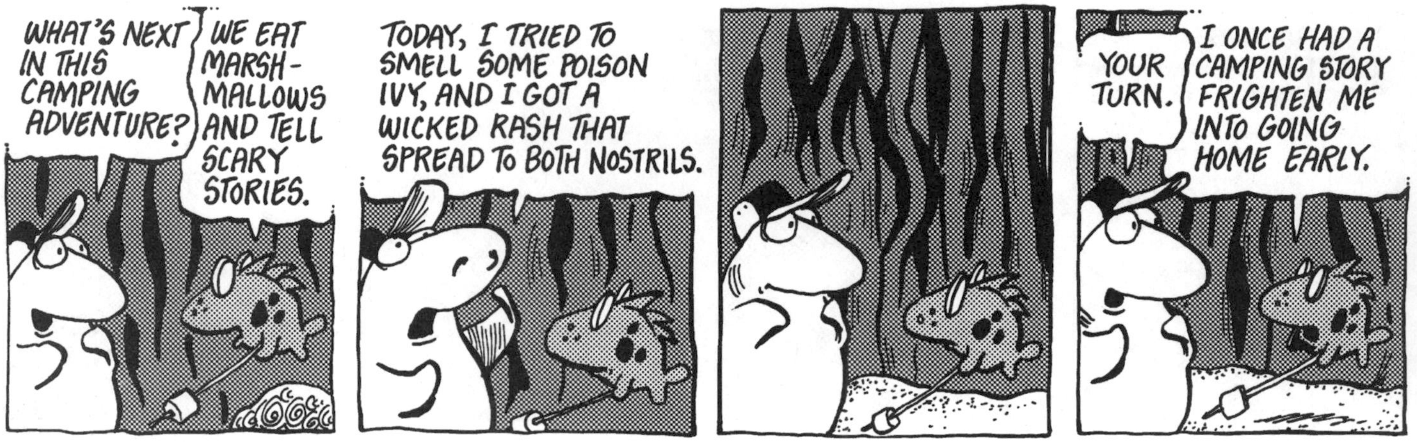
WHAT'S NEXT IN THIS CAMPING ADVENTURE?
WE EAT MARSH-MALLOWS AND TELL SCARY STORIES.
TODAY, I TRIED TO SMELL SOME POISON IVY, AND I GOT A WICKED RASH THAT SPREAD TO BOTH NOSTRILS.
YOUR TURN.
I ONCE HAD A CAMPING STORY FRIGHTEN ME INTO GOING HOME EARLY.

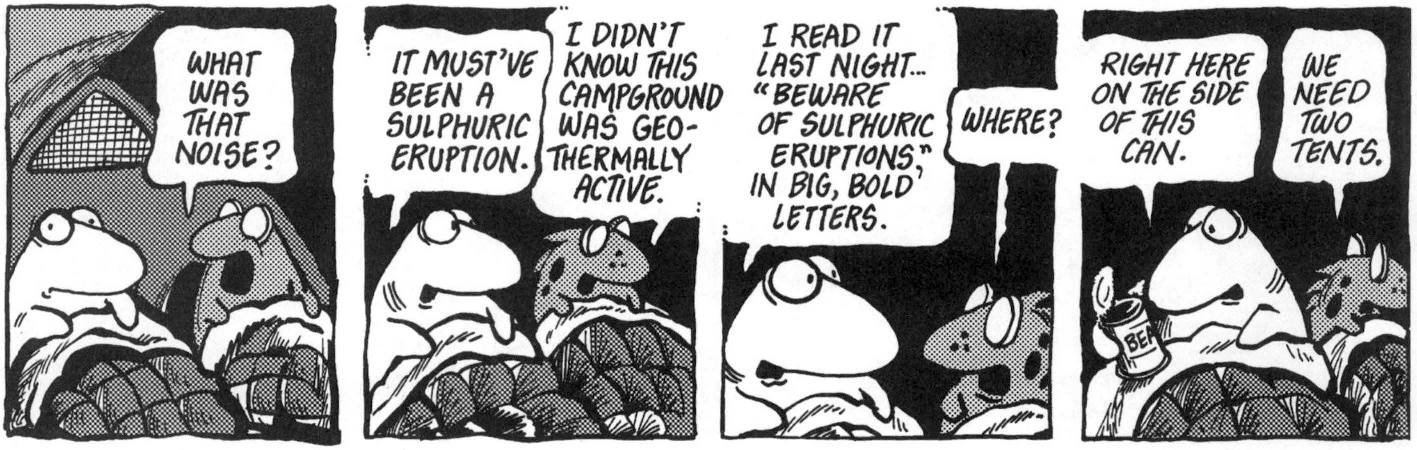
WHAT WAS THAT NOISE?
IT MUST'VE BEEN A SULPHURIC ERUPTION.
I DIDN'T KNOW THIS CAMPGROUND WAS GEO-THERMALLY ACTIVE.
I READ IT LAST NIGHT... "BEWARE OF SULPHURIC ERUPTIONS," IN BIG, BOLD LETTERS.
WHERE?
RIGHT HERE ON THE SIDE OF THIS CAN.
WE NEED TWO TENTS.

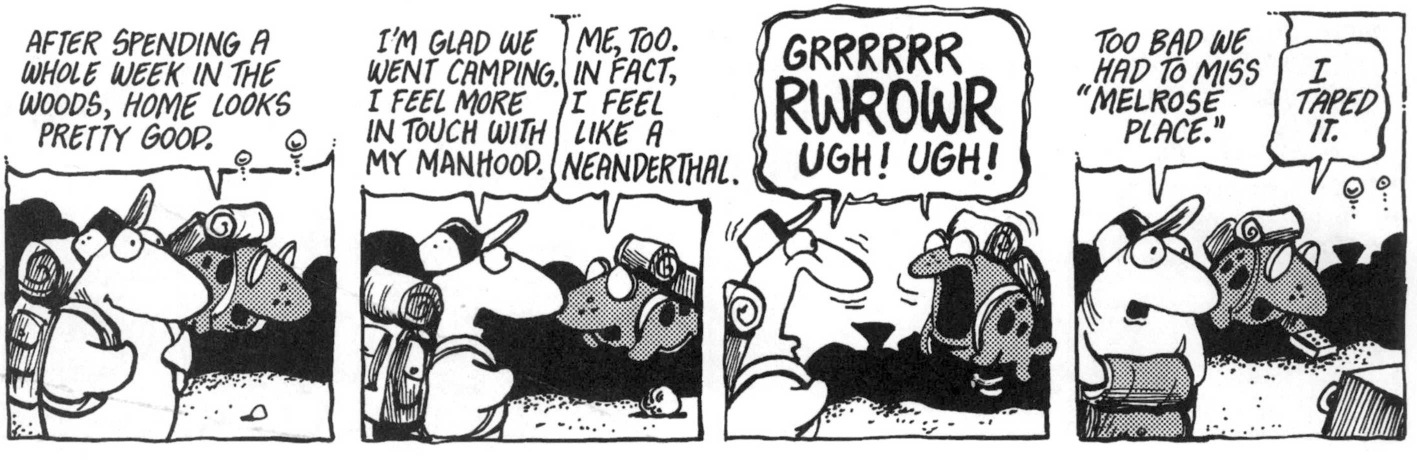
AFTER SPENDING A WHOLE WEEK IN THE WOODS, HOME LOOKS PRETTY GOOD.
I'M GLAD WE WENT CAMPING. I FEEL MORE IN TOUCH WITH MY MANHOOD.
ME, TOO. IN FACT, I FEEL LIKE A NEANDERTHAL.
GRRRRRR RWROWR UGH! UGH!
TOO BAD WE HAD TO MISS "MELROSE PLACE."
I TAPED IT.

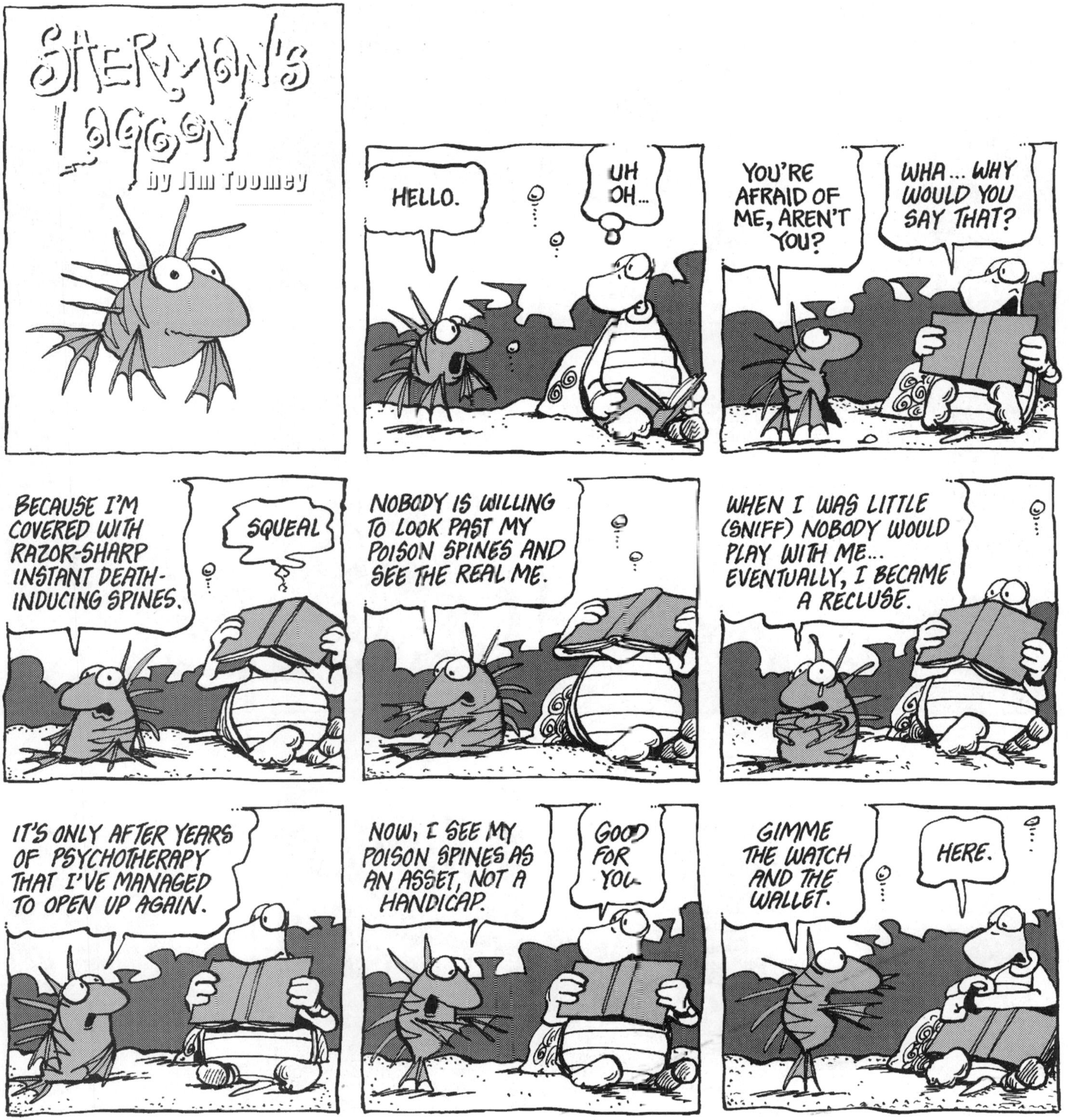
SHERMAN'S LAGOON
by Jim Toomey
HELLO.
UH OH...
YOU'RE AFRAID OF ME, AREN'T YOU?
WHA... WHY WOULD YOU SAY THAT?
BECAUSE I'M COVERED WITH RAZOR-SHARP INSTANT DEATH-INDUCING SPINES.
SQUEAL
NOBODY IS WILLING TO LOOK PAST MY POISON SPINES AND SEE THE REAL ME.
WHEN I WAS LITTLE (SNIFF) NOBODY WOULD PLAY WITH ME... EVENTUALLY, I BECAME A RECLUSE.
IT'S ONLY AFTER YEARS OF PSYCHOTHERAPY THAT I'VE MANAGED TO OPEN UP AGAIN.
NOW, I SEE MY POISON SPINES AS AN ASSET, NOT A HANDICAP.
GOOD FOR YOU.
GIMME THE WATCH AND THE WALLET.
HERE.

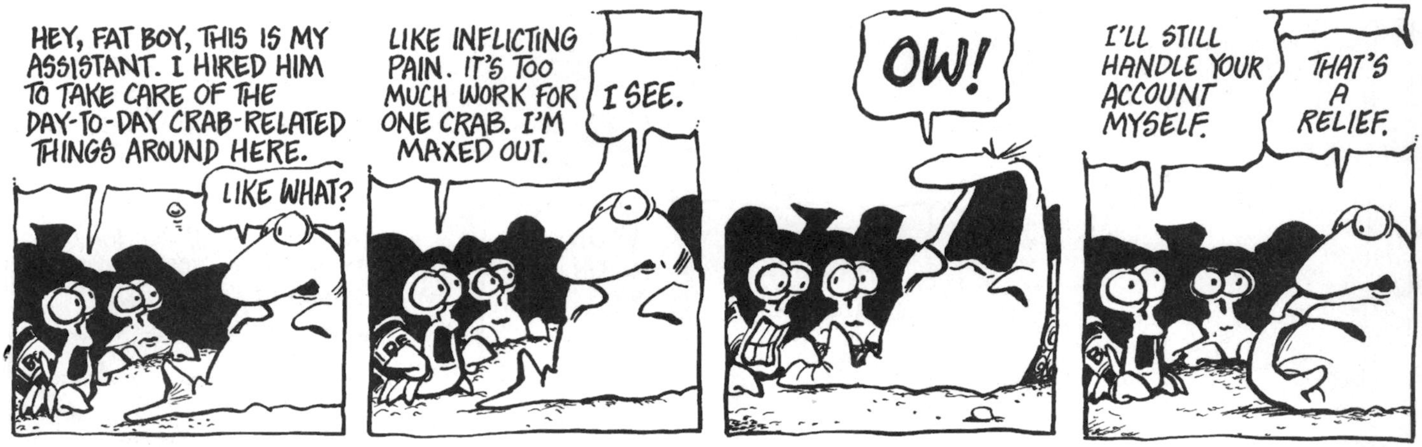
HEY, FAT BOY, THIS IS MY ASSISTANT. I HIRED HIM TO TAKE CARE OF THE DAY-TO-DAY CRAB-RELATED THINGS AROUND HERE.
LIKE WHAT?
LIKE INFLICTING PAIN. IT'S TOO MUCH WORK FOR ONE CRAB. I'M MAXED OUT.
I SEE.
OW!
I'LL STILL HANDLE YOUR ACCOUNT MYSELF.
THAT'S A RELIEF.

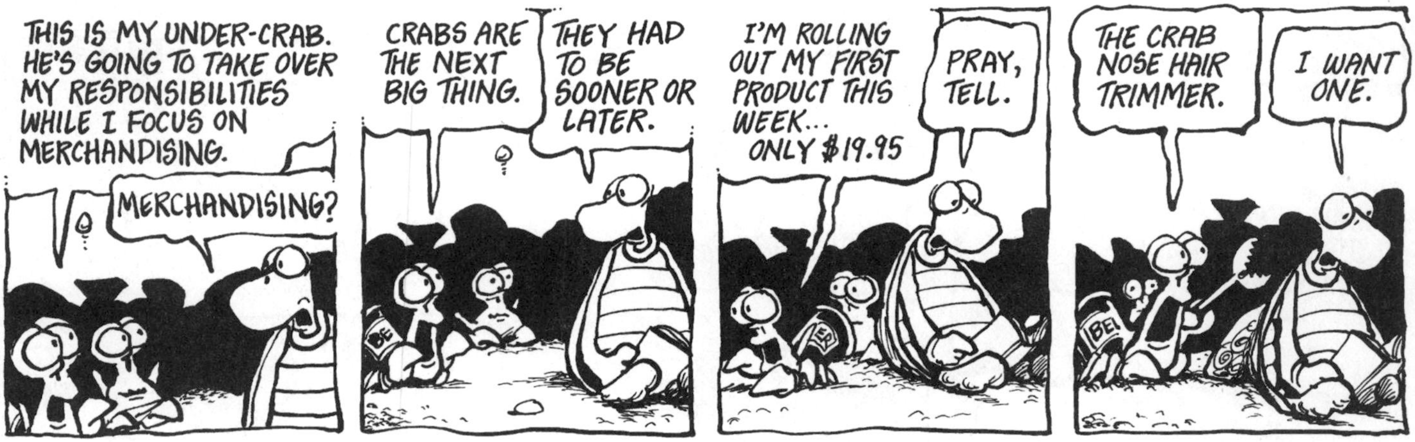
THIS IS MY UNDER-CRAB. HE'S GOING TO TAKE OVER MY RESPONSIBILITIES WHILE I FOCUS ON MERCHANDISING.
MERCHANDISING?
CRABS ARE THE NEXT BIG THING.
THEY HAD TO BE SOONER OR LATER.
I'M ROLLING OUT MY FIRST PRODUCT THIS WEEK... ONLY $19.95
PRAY, TELL.
THE CRAB NOSE HAIR TRIMMER.
I WANT ONE.

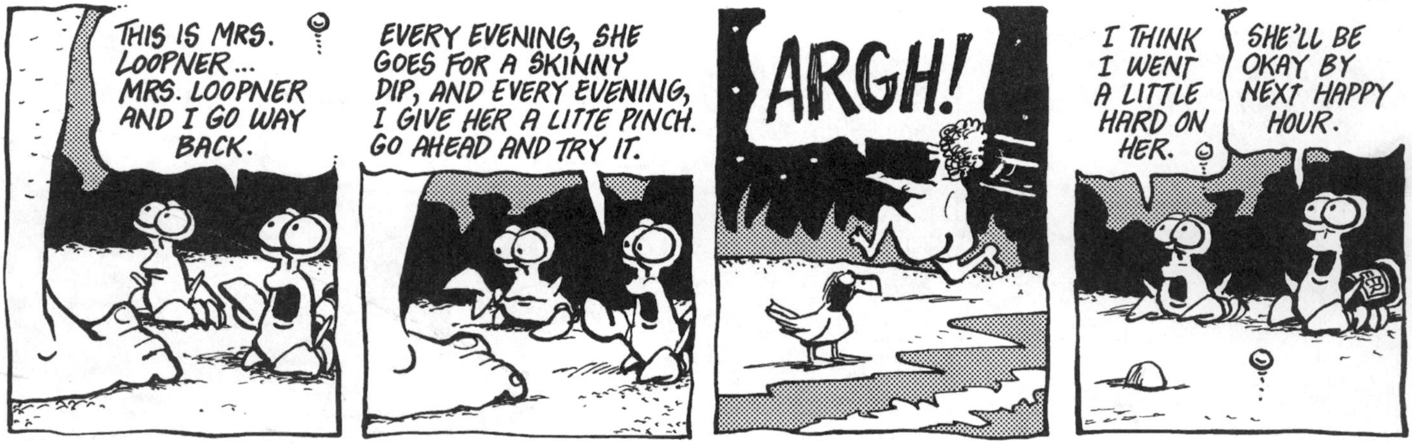
THIS IS MRS. LOOPNER... MRS. LOOPNER AND I GO WAY BACK.
EVERY EVENING, SHE GOES FOR A SKINNY DIP, AND EVERY EVENING, I GIVE HER A LITTE PINCH. GO AHEAD AND TRY IT.
ARGH!
I THINK I WENT A LITTLE HARD ON HER.
SHE'LL BE OKAY BY NEXT HAPPY HOUR.

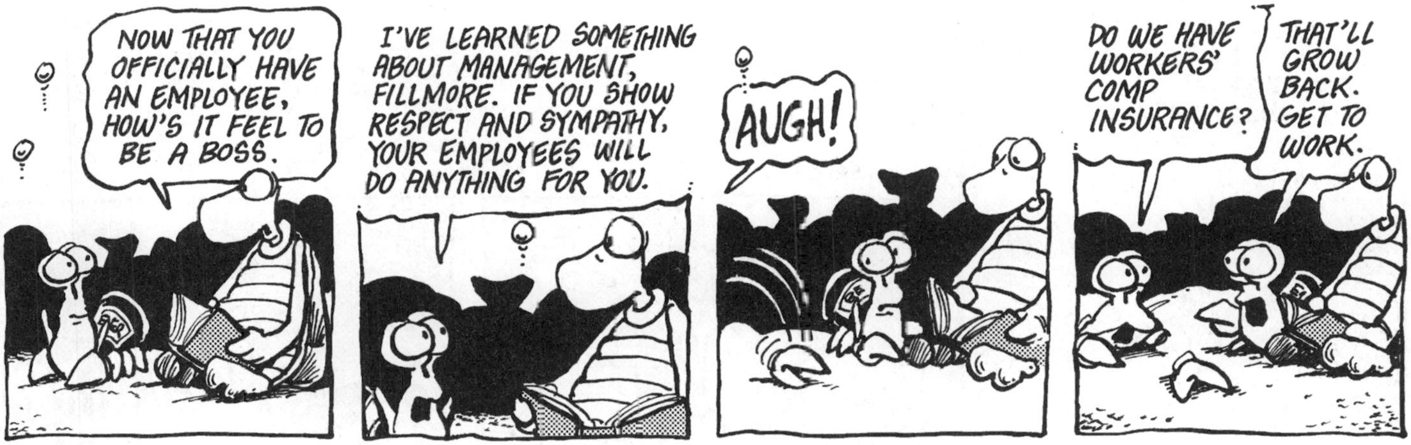
NOW THAT YOU OFFICIALLY HAVE AN EMPLOYEE, HOW'S IT FEEL TO BE A BOSS.
I'VE LEARNED SOMETHING ABOUT MANAGEMENT, FILLMORE. IF YOU SHOW RESPECT AND SYMPATHY, YOUR EMPLOYEES WILL DO ANYTHING FOR YOU.
AUGH!
DO WE HAVE WORKERS' COMP INSURANCE?
THAT'LL GROW BACK. GET TO WORK.

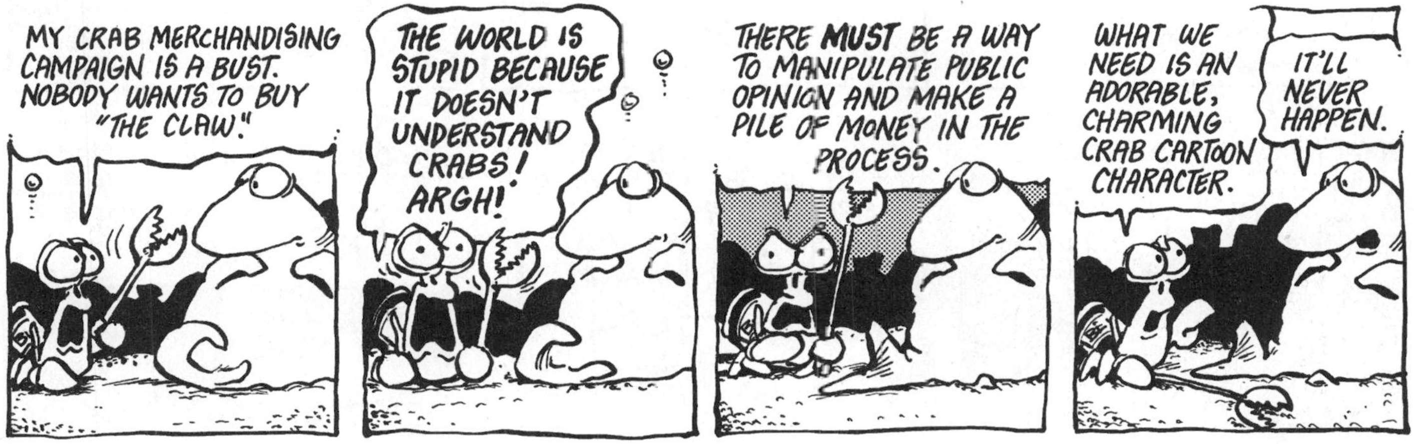
MY CRAB MERCHANDISING CAMPAIGN IS A BUST. NOBODY WANTS TO BUY "THE CLAW."
THE WORLD IS STUPID BECAUSE IT DOESN'T UNDERSTAND CRABS! ARGH!
THERE MUST BE A WAY TO MANIPULATE PUBLIC OPINION AND MAKE A PILE OF MONEY IN THE PROCESS.
WHAT WE NEED IS AN ADORABLE, CHARMING CRAB CARTOON CHARACTER.
IT'LL NEVER HAPPEN.

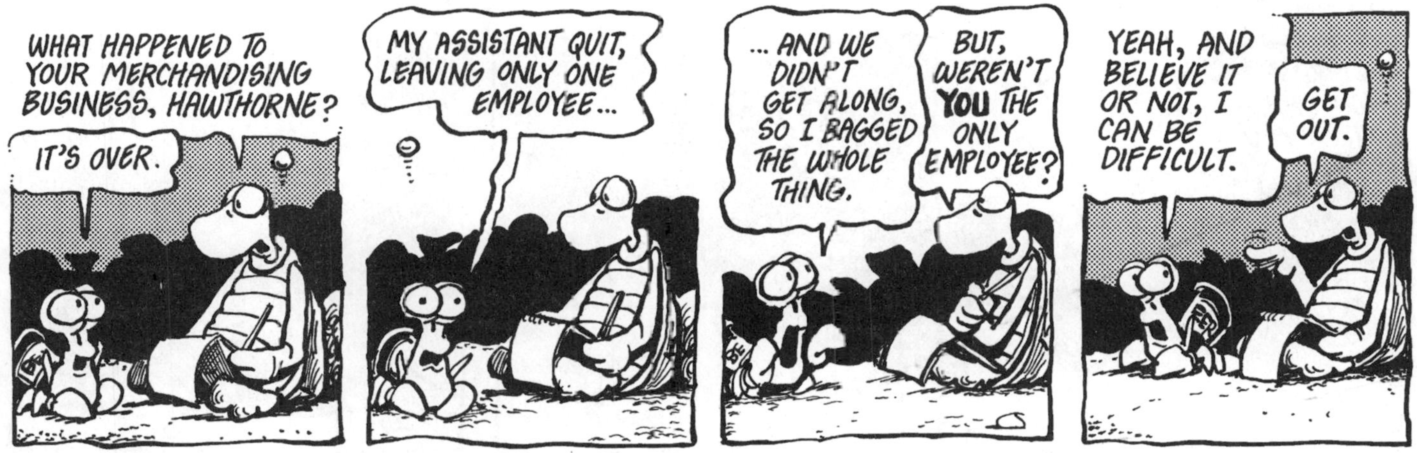
WHAT HAPPENED TO YOUR MERCHANDISING BUSINESS, HAWTHORNE?
IT'S OVER.
MY ASSISTANT QUIT, LEAVING ONLY ONE EMPLOYEE...
... AND WE DIDN'T GET ALONG, SO I BAGGED THE WHOLE THING.
BUT, WEREN'T YOU THE ONLY EMPLOYEE?
YEAH, AND BELIEVE IT OR NOT, I CAN BE DIFFICULT.
GET OUT.

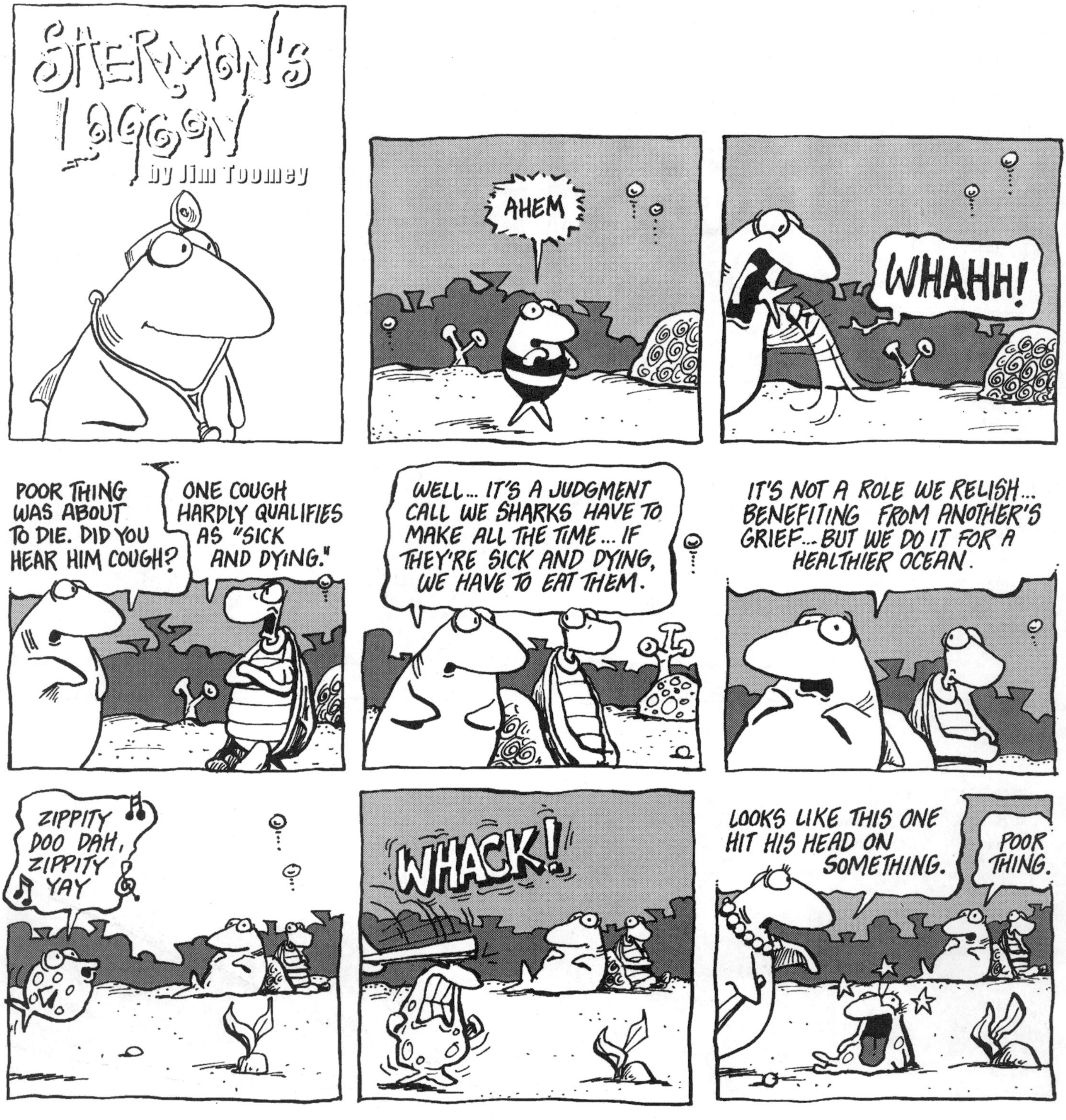
SHERMAN'S LAGOON
by Jim Toomey
AHEM
WHAHH!
POOR THING WAS ABOUT TO DIE. DID YOU HEAR HIM COUGH?
ONE COUGH HARDLY QUALIFIES AS "SICK AND DYING."
WELL... IT'S A JUDGMENT CALL WE SHARKS HAVE TO MAKE ALL THE TIME... IF THEY'RE SICK AND DYING, WE HAVE TO EAT THEM.
IT'S NOT A ROLE WE RELISH... BENEFITING FROM ANOTHER'S GRIEF... BUT WE DO IT FOR A HEALTHIER OCEAN.
ZIPPITY DOO DAH, ZIPPITY YAY
WHACK!
LOOKS LIKE THIS ONE HIT HIS HEAD ON SOMETHING.
POOR THING.

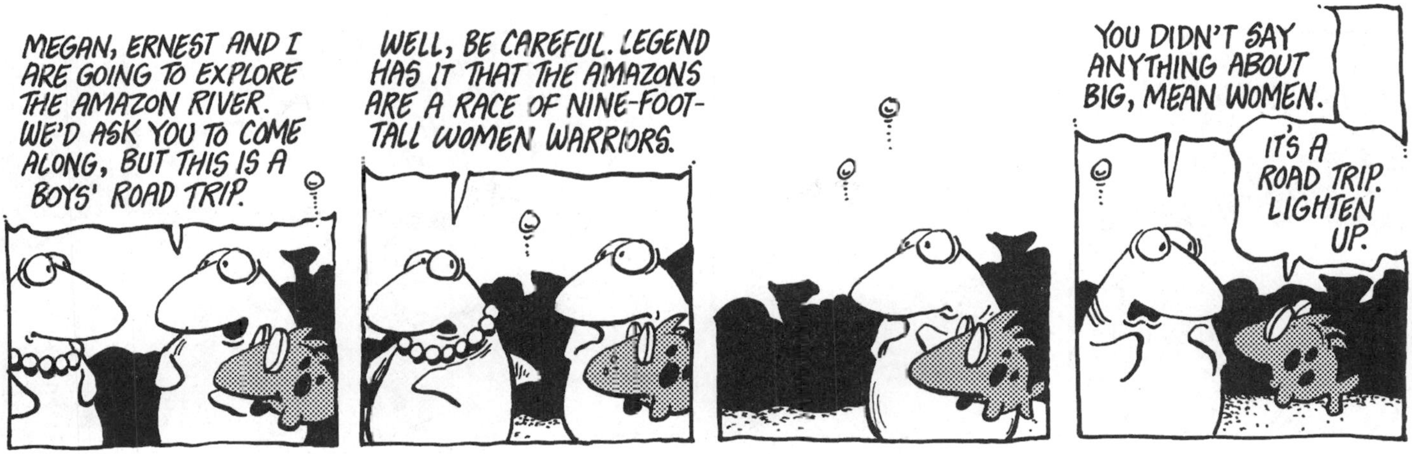
MEGAN, ERNEST AND I ARE GOING TO EXPLORE THE AMAZON RIVER. WE'D ASK YOU TO COME ALONG, BUT THIS IS A BOYS' ROAD TRIP.
WELL, BE CAREFUL. LEGEND HAS IT THAT THE AMAZONS ARE A RACE OF NINE-FOOT-TALL WOMEN WARRIORS.
YOU DIDN'T SAY ANYTHING ABOUT BIG, MEAN WOMEN.
IT'S A ROAD TRIP. LIGHTEN UP.

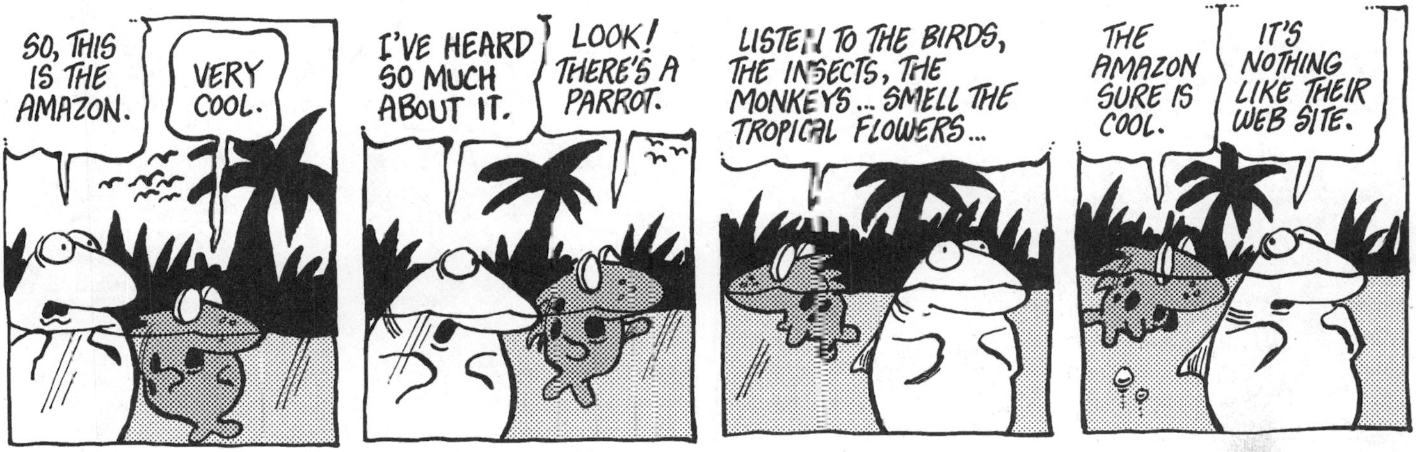
SO, THIS IS THE AMAZON.
VERY COOL.
I'VE HEARD SO MUCH ABOUT IT.
LOOK! THERE'S A PARROT.
LISTEN TO THE BIRDS, THE INSECTS, THE MONKEYS... SMELL THE TROPICAL FLOWERS...
THE AMAZON SURE IS COOL.
IT'S NOTHING LIKE THEIR WEB SITE.

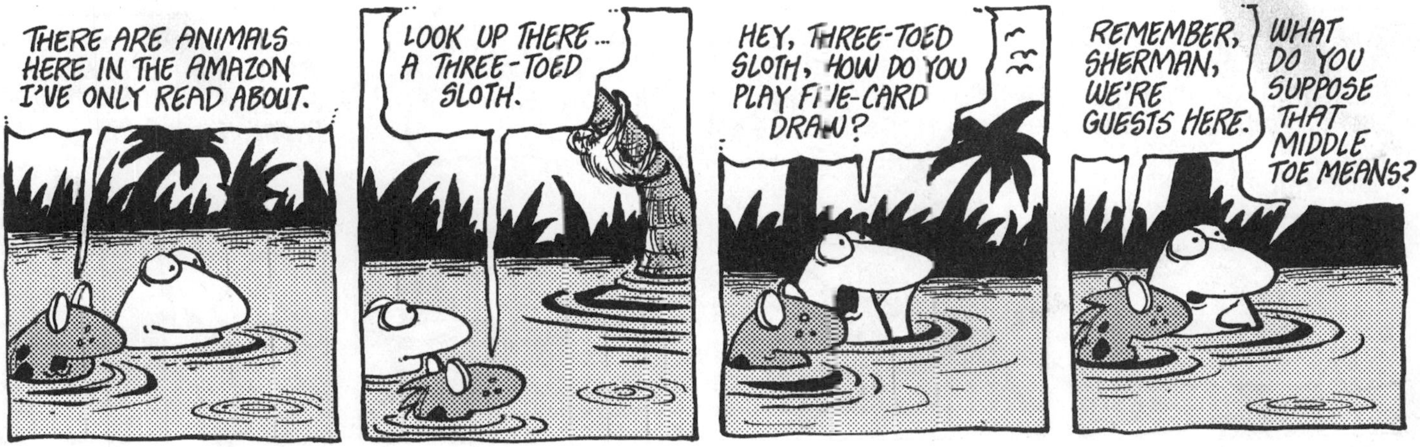
THERE ARE ANIMALS HERE IN THE AMAZON I'VE ONLY READ ABOUT.
LOOK UP THERE... A THREE-TOED SLOTH.
HEY, THREE-TOED SLOTH, HOW DO YOU PLAY FIVE-CARD DRAW?
REMEMBER, SHERMAN, WE'RE GUESTS HERE.
WHAT DO YOU SUPPOSE THAT MIDDLE TOE MEANS?

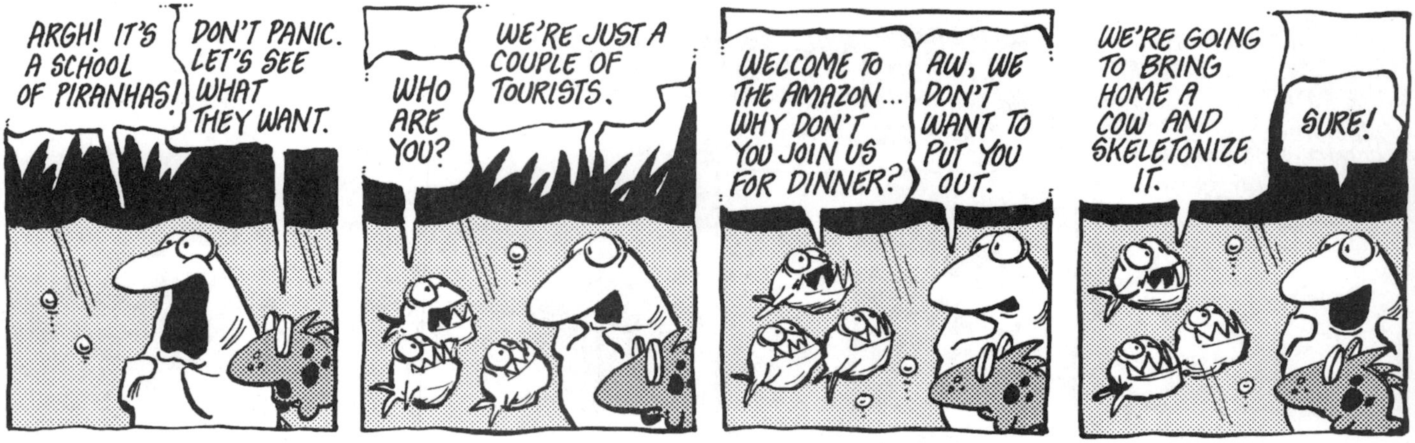
ARGH! IT'S A SCHOOL OF PIRANHAS!
DON'T PANIC. LET'S SEE WHAT THEY WANT.
WHO ARE YOU?
WE'RE JUST A COUPLE OF TOURISTS.
WELCOME TO THE AMAZON... WHY DON'T YOU JOIN US FOR DINNER?
AW, WE DON'T WANT TO PUT YOU OUT.
WE'RE GOING TO BRING HOME A COW AND SKELETONIZE IT.
SURE!

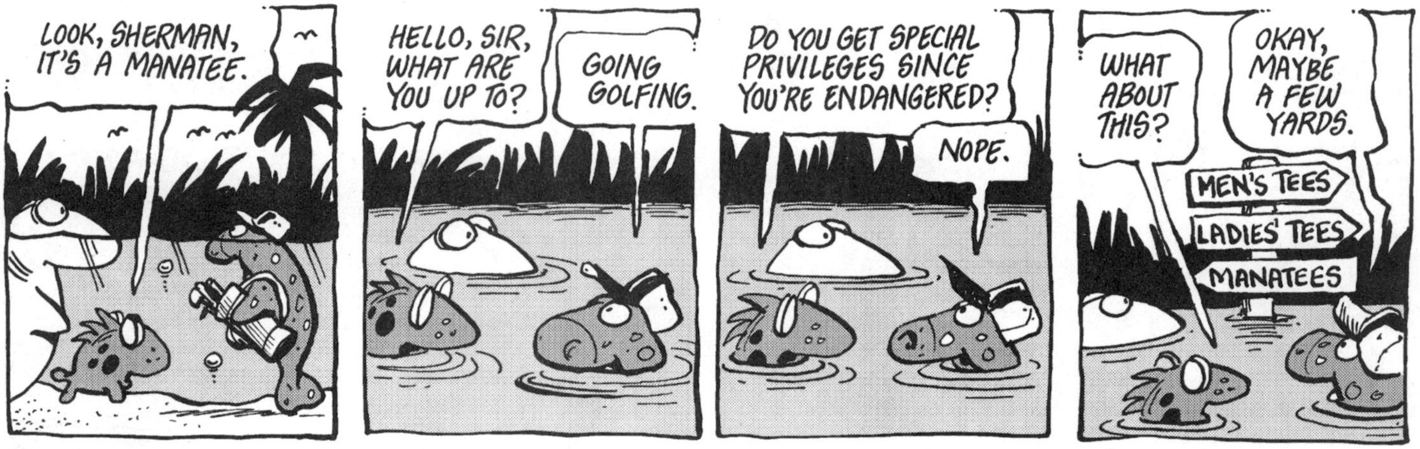
LOOK, SHERMAN, IT'S A MANATEE.
HELLO, SIR, WHAT ARE YOU UP TO?
GOING GOLFING.
DO YOU GET SPECIAL PRIVILEGES SINCE YOU'RE ENDANGERED?
NOPE.
WHAT ABOUT THIS?
OKAY, MAYBE A FEW YARDS.
MEN'S TEES
LADIES' TEES
MANATEES

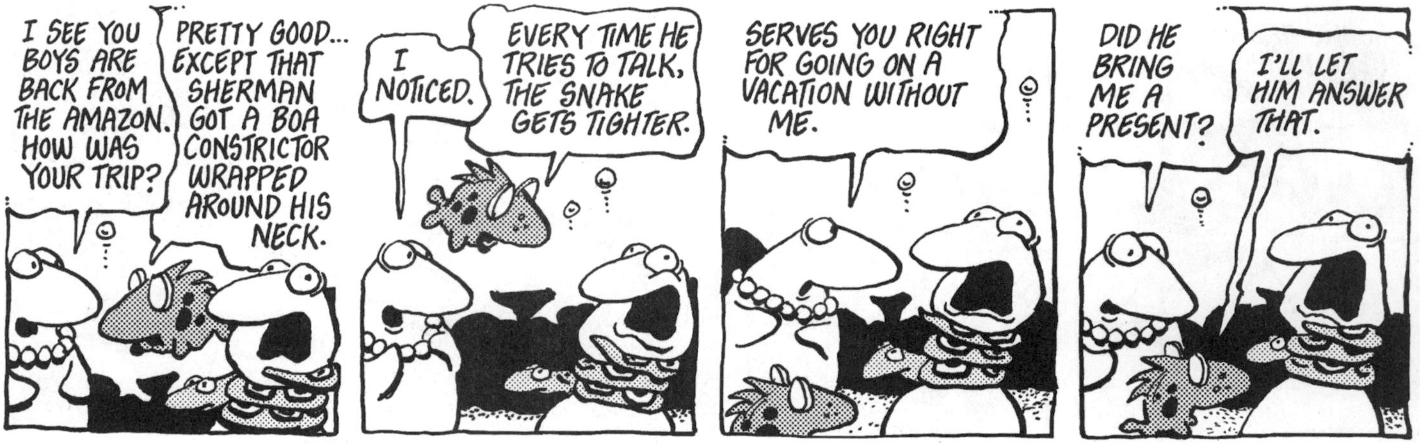
I SEE YOU BOYS ARE BACK FROM THE AMAZON. HOW WAS YOUR TRIP?
PRETTY GOOD... EXCEPT THAT SHERMAN GOT A BOA CONSTRICTOR WRAPPED AROUND HIS NECK.
I NOTICED.
EVERY TIME HE TRIES TO TALK, THE SNAKE GETS TIGHTER.
SERVES YOU RIGHT FOR GOING ON A VACATION WITHOUT ME.
DID HE BRING ME A PRESENT?
I'LL LET HIM ANSWER THAT.

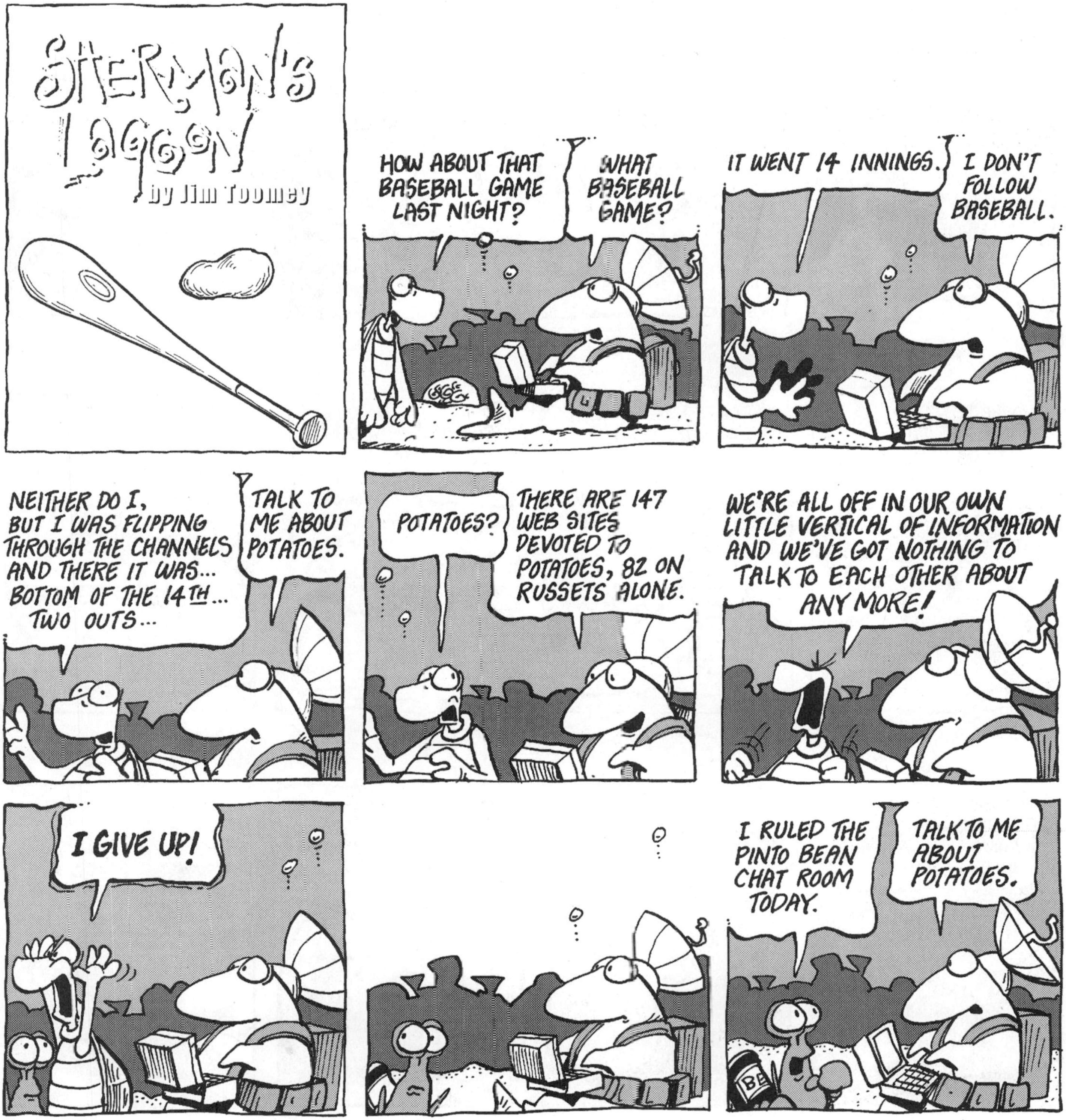
SHERMAN'S LAGOON
by Jim Toomey
HOW ABOUT THAT BASEBALL GAME LAST NIGHT?
WHAT BASEBALL GAME?
IT WENT 14 INNINGS.
I DON'T FOLLOW BASEBALL.
NEITHER DO I, BUT I WAS FLIPPING THROUGH THE CHANNELS AND THERE IT WAS... BOTTOM OF THE 14TH... TWO OUTS...
TALK TO ME ABOUT POTATOES.
POTATOES?
THERE ARE 147 WEB SITES DEVOTED TO POTATOES, 82 ON RUSSETS ALONE.
WE'RE ALL OFF IN OUR OWN LITTLE VERTICAL OF INFORMATION AND WE'VE GOT NOTHING TO TALK TO EACH OTHER ABOUT ANY MORE!
I GIVE UP!
I RULED THE PINTO BEAN CHAT ROOM TODAY.
TALK TO ME ABOUT POTATOES.

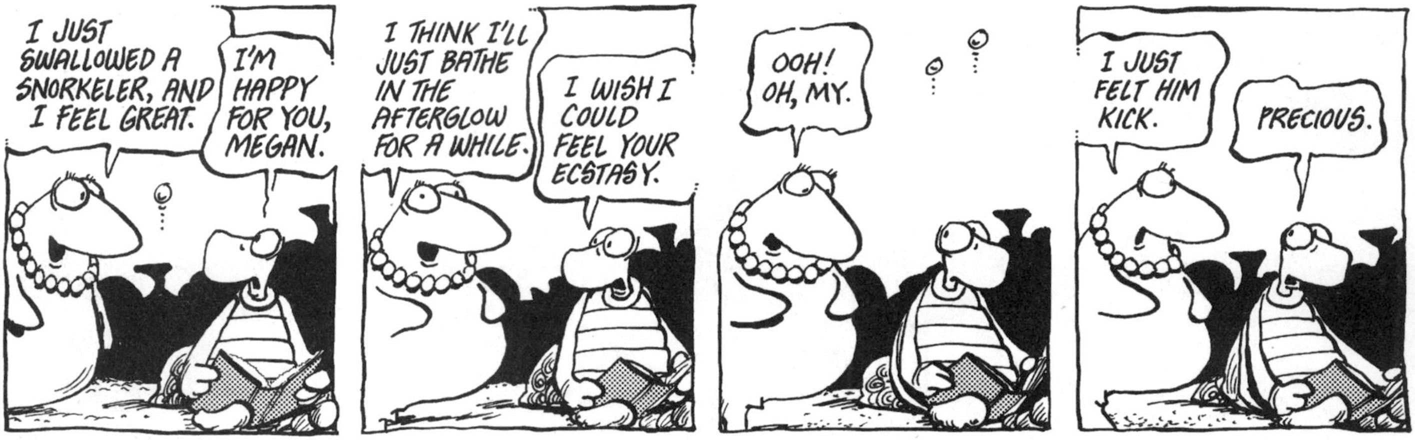
I JUST SWALLOWED A SNORKELER, AND I FEEL GREAT.
I'M HAPPY FOR YOU, MEGAN.
I THINK I'LL JUST BATHE IN THE AFTERGLOW FOR A WHILE.
I WISH I COULD FEEL YOUR ECSTASY.
OOH! OH, MY.
I JUST FELT HIM KICK.
PRECIOUS.

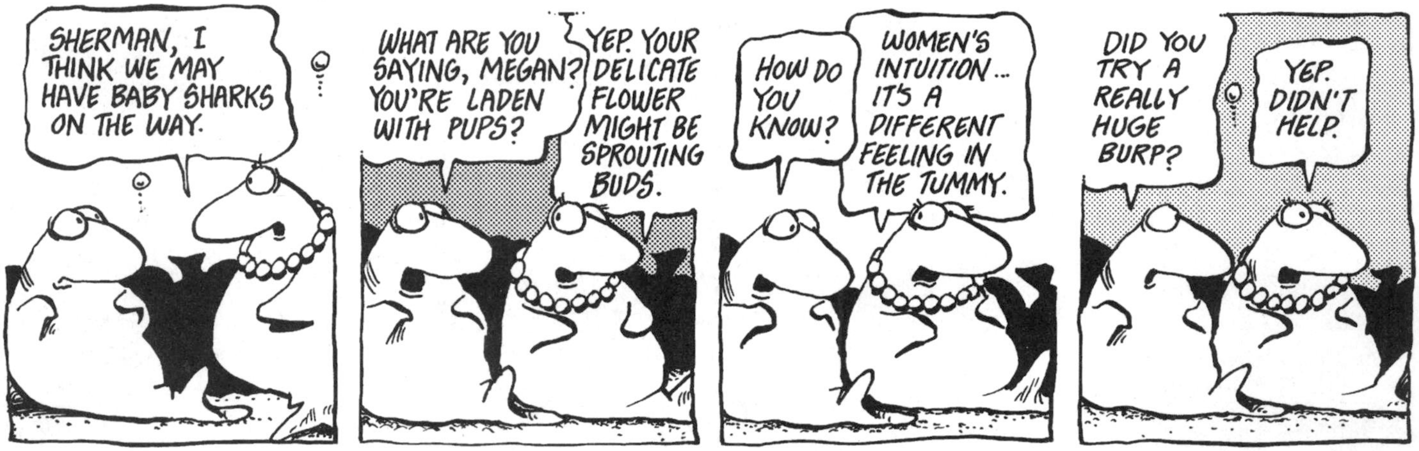
SHERMAN, I THINK WE MAY HAVE BABY SHARKS ON THE WAY.
WHAT ARE YOU SAYING, MEGAN? YOU'RE LADEN WITH PUPS?
YEP. YOUR DELICATE FLOWER MIGHT BE SPROUTING BUDS.
HOW DO YOU KNOW?
WOMEN'S INTUITION... IT'S A DIFFERENT FEELING IN THE TUMMY.
DID YOU TRY A REALLY HUGE BURP?
YEP. DIDN'T HELP.

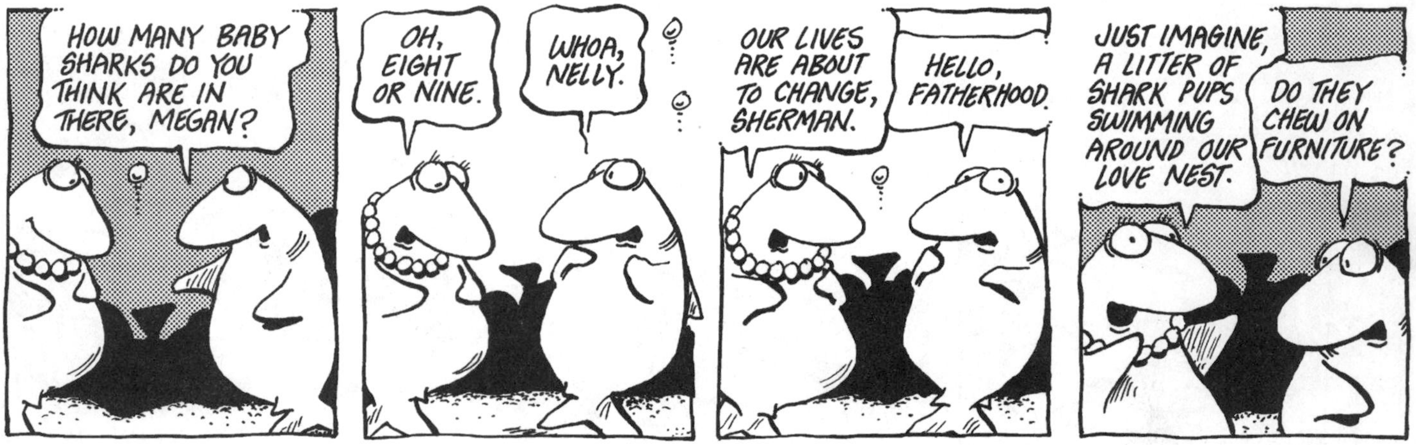
HOW MANY BABY SHARKS DO YOU THINK ARE IN THERE, MEGAN?
OH, EIGHT OR NINE.
WHOA, NELLY.
OUR LIVES ARE ABOUT TO CHANGE, SHERMAN.
HELLO, FATHERHOOD.
JUST IMAGINE, A LITTER OF SHARK PUPS SWIMMING AROUND OUR LOVE NEST.
DO THEY CHEW ON FURNITURE?

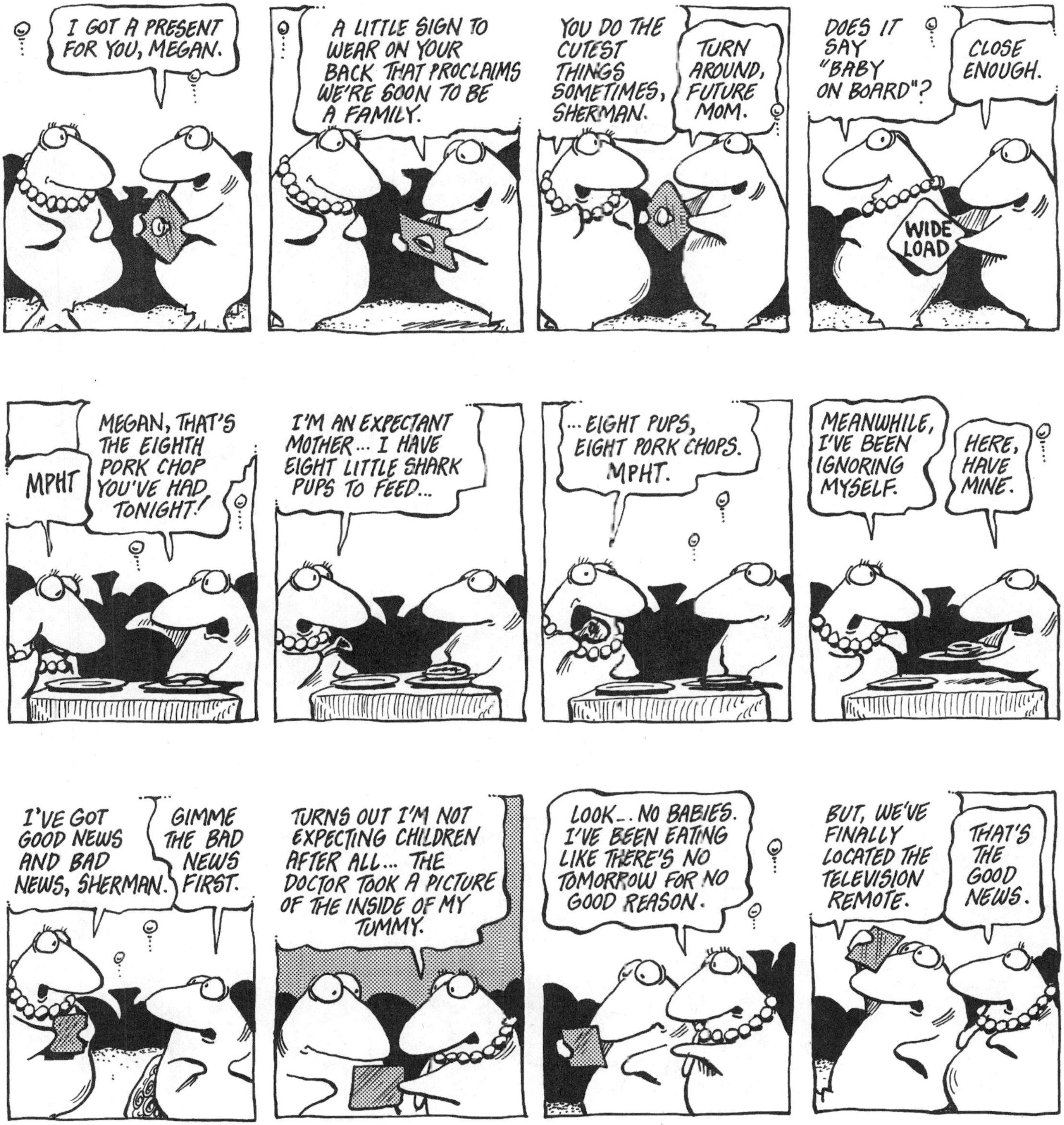
I GOT A PRESENT FOR YOU, MEGAN.
A LITTLE SIGN TO WEAR ON YOUR BACK THAT PROCLAIMS WE'RE SOON TO BE A FAMILY.
YOU DO THE CUTEST THINGS SOMETIMES, SHERMAN.
TURN AROUND, FUTURE MOM.
DOES IT SAY "BABY ON BOARD"?
CLOSE ENOUGH.
WIDE LOAD
MPHT
MEGAN, THAT'S THE EIGHTH PORK CHOP YOU'VE HAD TONIGHT!
I'M AN EXPECTANT MOTHER... I HAVE EIGHT LITTLE SHARK PUPS TO FEED...
...EIGHT PUPS, EIGHT PORK CHOPS. MPHT.
MEANWHILE, I'VE BEEN IGNORING MYSELF.
HERE, HAVE MINE.
I'VE GOT GOOD NEWS AND BAD NEWS, SHERMAN.
GIMME THE BAD NEWS FIRST.
TURNS OUT I'M NOT EXPECTING CHILDREN AFTER ALL... THE DOCTOR TOOK A PICTURE OF THE INSIDE OF MY TUMMY.
LOOK... NO BABIES. I'VE BEEN EATING LIKE THERE'S NO TOMORROW FOR NO GOOD REASON.
BUT, WE'VE FINALLY LOCATED THE TELEVISION REMOTE.
THAT'S THE GOOD NEWS.

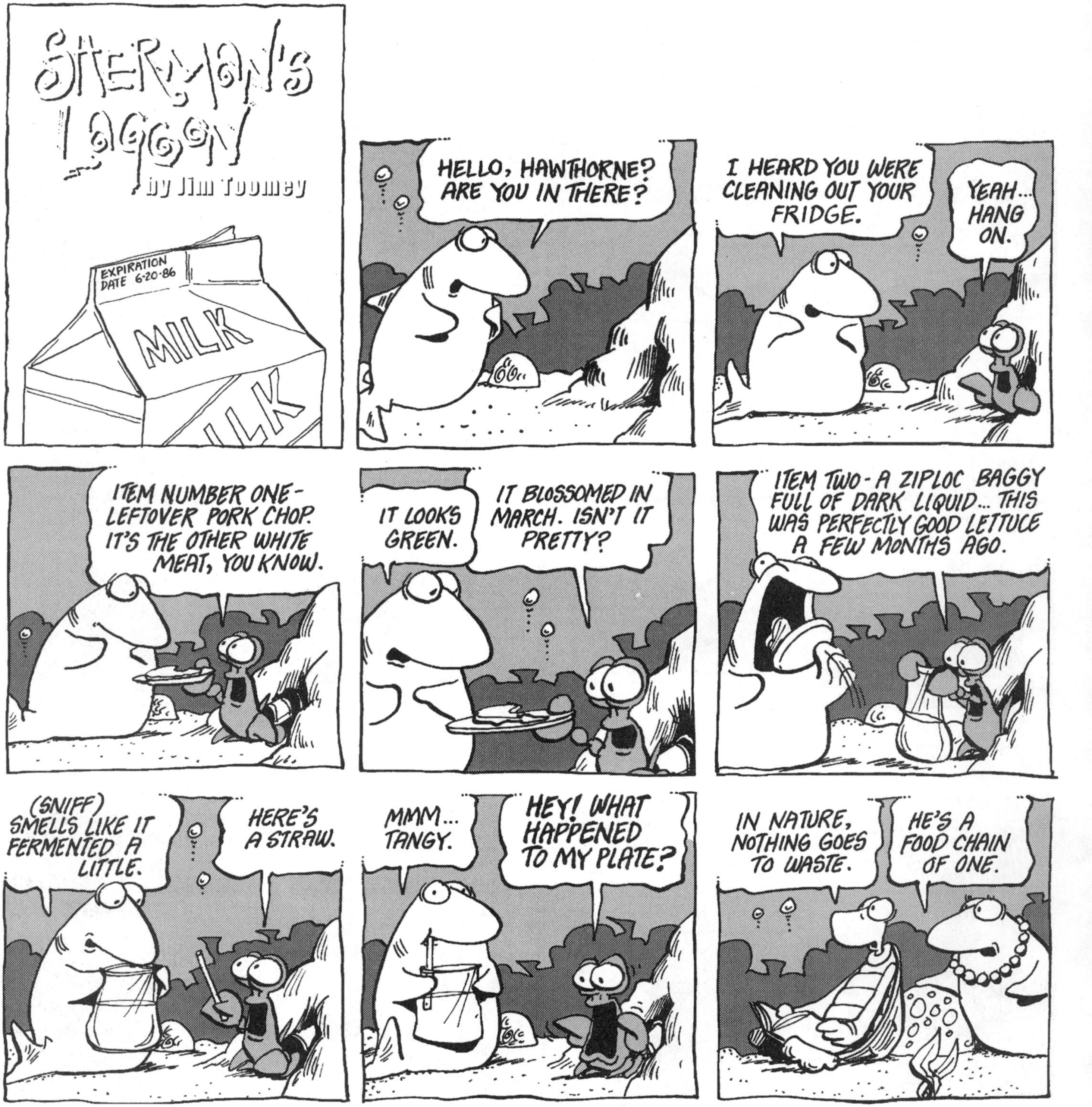
SHERMAN'S LAGOON
by Jim Toomey
EXPIRATION DATE 6-20-86
MILK
HELLO, HAWTHORNE? ARE YOU IN THERE?
I HEARD YOU WERE CLEANING OUT YOUR FRIDGE.
YEAH... HANG ON.
ITEM NUMBER ONE- LEFTOVER PORK CHOP. IT'S THE OTHER WHITE MEAT, YOU KNOW.
IT LOOKS GREEN.
IT BLOSSOMED IN MARCH. ISN'T IT PRETTY?
ITEM TWO - A ZIPLOC BAGGY FULL OF DARK LIQUID... THIS WAS PERFECTLY GOOD LETTUCE A FEW MONTHS AGO.
(SNIFF) SMELLS LIKE IT FERMENTED A LITTLE.
HERE'S A STRAW.
MMM... TANGY.
HEY! WHAT HAPPENED TO MY PLATE?
IN NATURE, NOTHING GOES TO WASTE.
HE'S A FOOD CHAIN OF ONE.

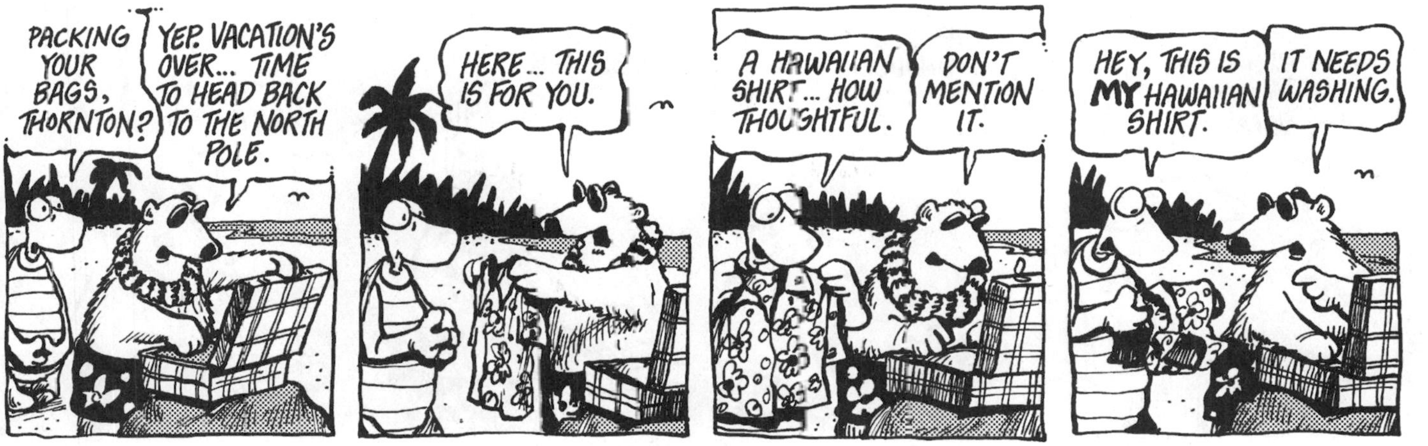
PACKING YOUR BAGS, THORNTON?
YEP. VACATION'S OVER... TIME TO HEAD BACK TO THE NORTH POLE.
HERE... THIS IS FOR YOU.
A HAWAIIAN SHIRT... HOW THOUGHTFUL.
DON'T MENTION IT.
HEY, THIS IS MY HAWAIIAN SHIRT.
IT NEEDS WASHING.

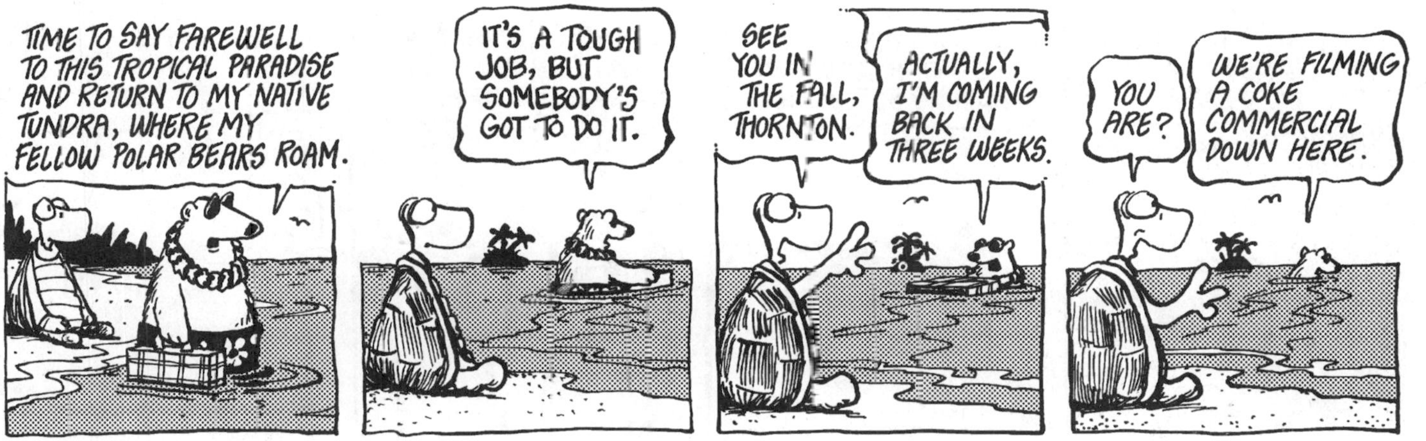
TIME TO SAY FAREWELL TO THIS TROPICAL PARADISE AND RETURN TO MY NATIVE TUNDRA, WHERE MY FELLOW POLAR BEARS ROAM.
IT'S A TOUGH JOB, BUT SOMEBODY'S GOT TO DO IT.
SEE YOU IN THE FALL, THORNTON.
ACTUALLY, I'M COMING BACK IN THREE WEEKS.
YOU ARE?
WE'RE FILMING A COKE COMMERCIAL DOWN HERE.

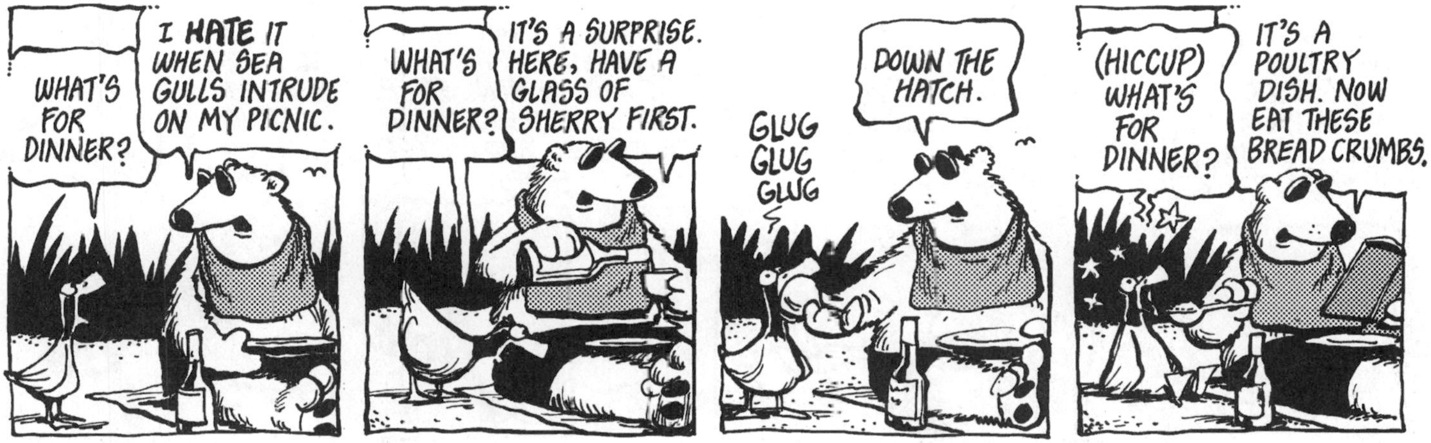
WHAT'S FOR DINNER?
I HATE IT WHEN SEA GULLS INTRUDE ON MY PICNIC.
WHAT'S FOR DINNER?
IT'S A SURPRISE. HERE, HAVE A GLASS OF SHERRY FIRST.
GLUG GLUG GLUG
DOWN THE HATCH.
(HICCUP) WHAT'S FOR DINNER?
IT'S A POULTRY DISH. NOW EAT THESE BREAD CRUMBS.

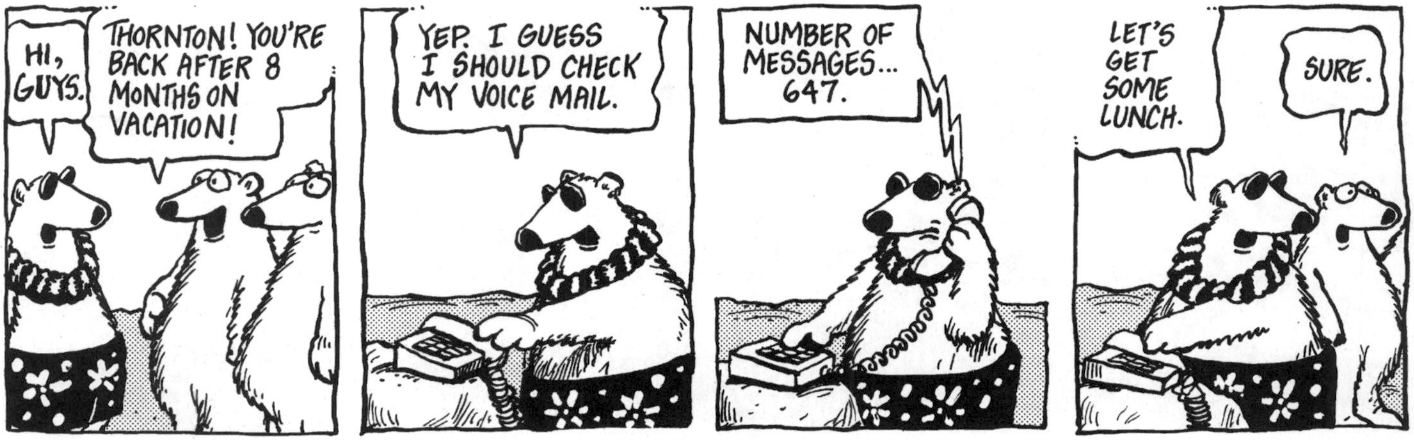
HI, GUYS.
THORNTON! YOU'RE BACK AFTER 8 MONTHS ON VACATION!
YEP. I GUESS I SHOULD CHECK MY VOICE MAIL.
NUMBER OF MESSAGES... 647.
LET'S GET SOME LUNCH.
SURE.

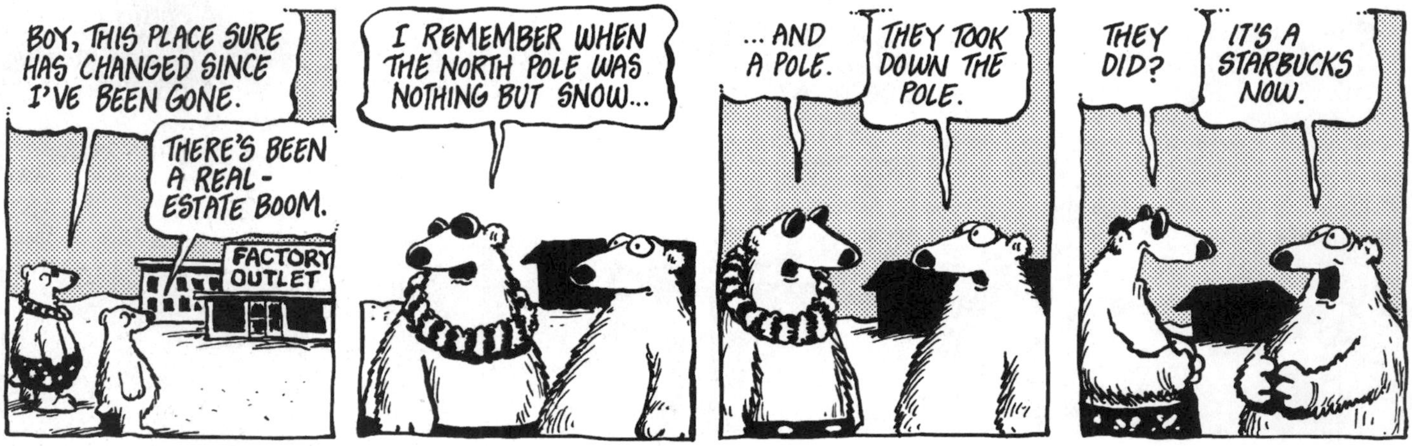
BOY, THIS PLACE SURE HAS CHANGED SINCE I'VE BEEN GONE.
THERE'S BEEN A REAL-ESTATE BOOM.
FACTORY OUTLET
I REMEMBER WHEN THE NORTH POLE WAS NOTHING BUT SNOW...
... AND A POLE.
THEY TOOK DOWN THE POLE.
THEY DID?
IT'S A STARBUCKS NOW.

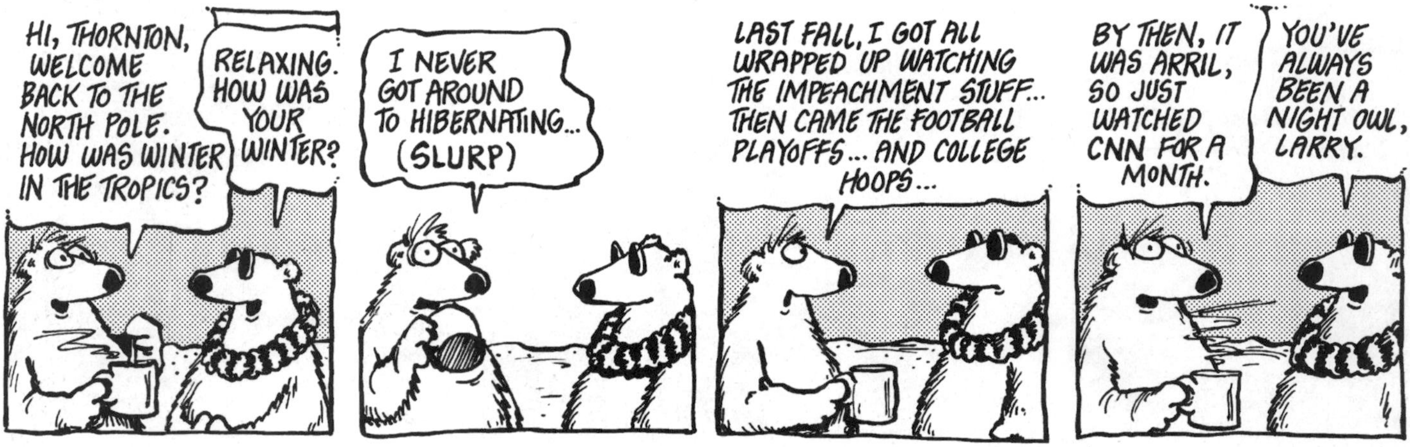
HI, THORNTON, WELCOME BACK TO THE NORTH POLE. HOW WAS WINTER IN THE TROPICS?
RELAXING. HOW WAS YOUR WINTER?
I NEVER GOT AROUND TO HIBERNATING... (SLURP)
LAST FALL, I GOT ALL WRAPPED UP WATCHING THE IMPEACHMENT STUFF... THEN CAME THE FOOTBALL PLAYOFFS ... AND COLLEGE HOOPS...
BY THEN, IT WAS APRIL, SO JUST WATCHED CNN FOR A MONTH.
YOU'VE ALWAYS BEEN A NIGHT OWL, LARRY.

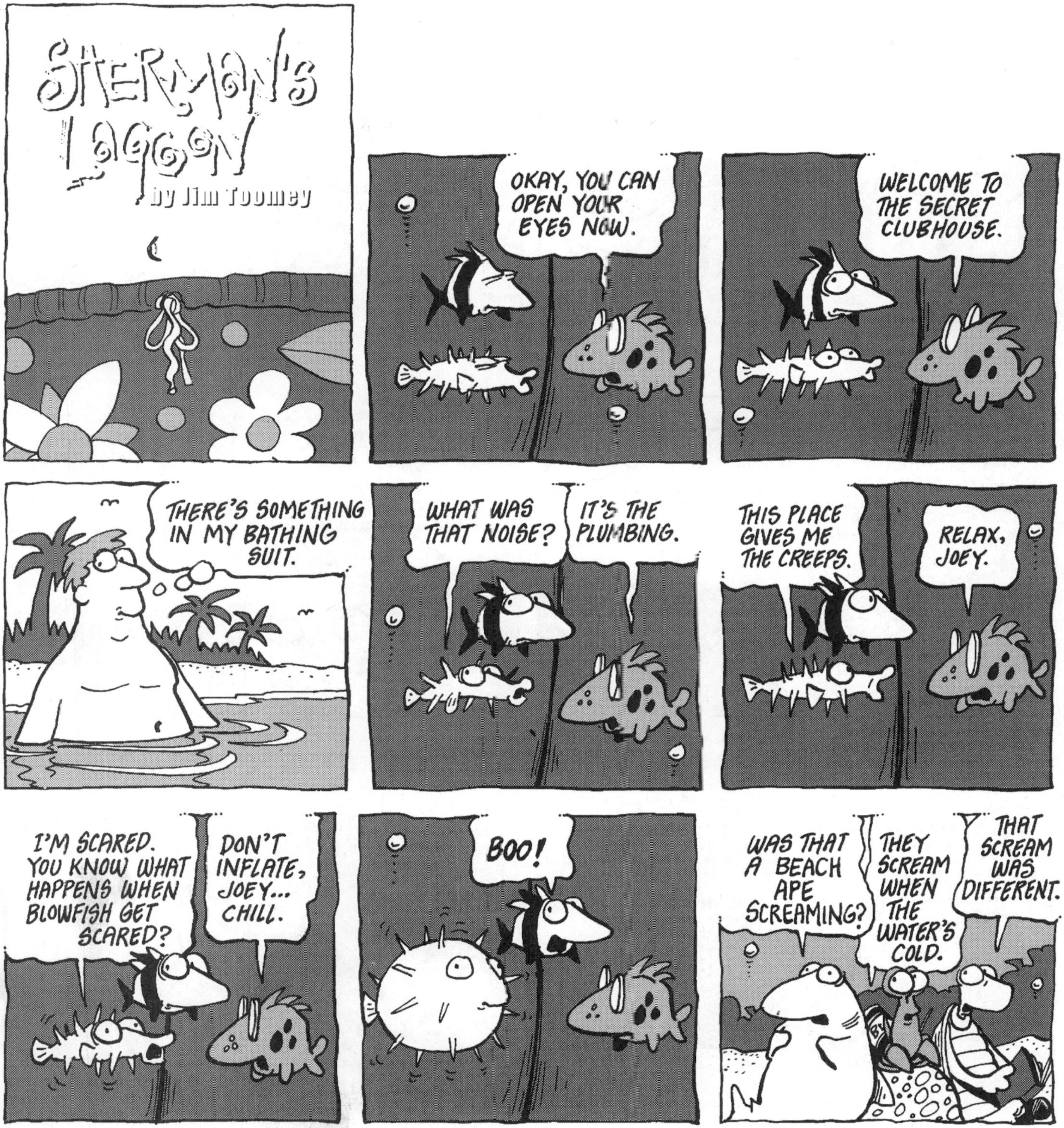
SHERMAN'S LAGOON
by Jim Toomey
OKAY, YOU CAN OPEN YOUR EYES NOW.
WELCOME TO THE SECRET CLUBHOUSE.
THERE'S SOMETHING IN MY BATHING SUIT.
WHAT WAS THAT NOISE?
IT'S THE PLUMBING.
THIS PLACE GIVES ME THE CREEPS.
RELAX, JOEY.
I'M SCARED. YOU KNOW WHAT HAPPENS WHEN BLOWFISH GET SCARED?
DON'T INFLATE, JOEY... CHILL.
BOO!
WAS THAT A BEACH APE SCREAMING?
THEY SCREAM WHEN THE WATER'S COLD.
THAT SCREAM WAS DIFFERENT.

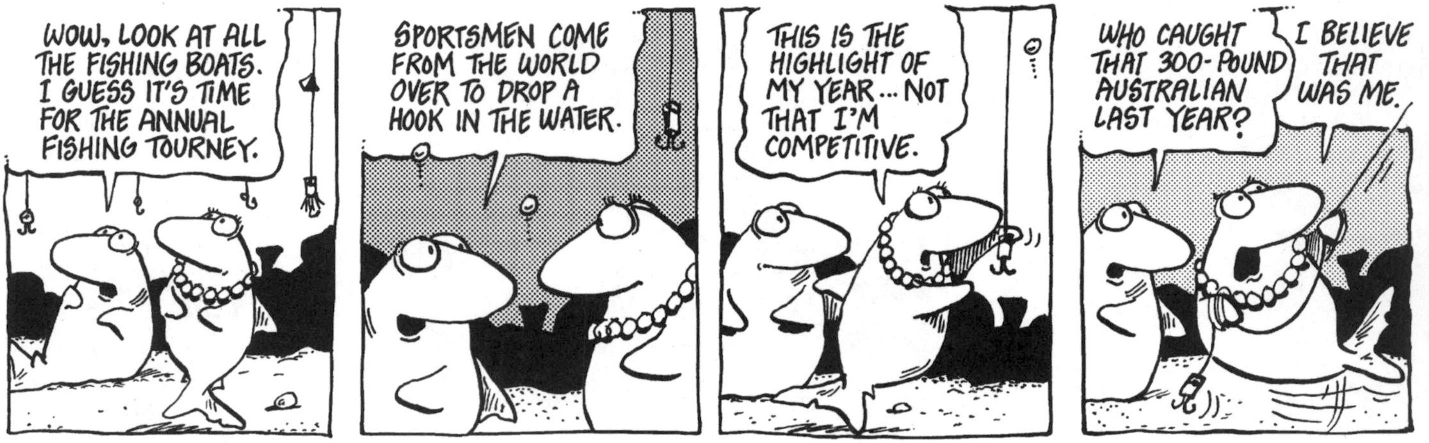
WOW, LOOK AT ALL THE FISHING BOATS. I GUESS IT'S TIME FOR THE ANNUAL FISHING TOURNEY.
SPORTSMEN COME FROM THE WORLD OVER TO DROP A HOOK IN THE WATER.
THIS IS THE HIGHLIGHT OF MY YEAR... NOT THAT I'M COMPETITIVE.
WHO CAUGHT THAT 300-POUND AUSTRALIAN LAST YEAR?
I BELIEVE THAT WAS ME.

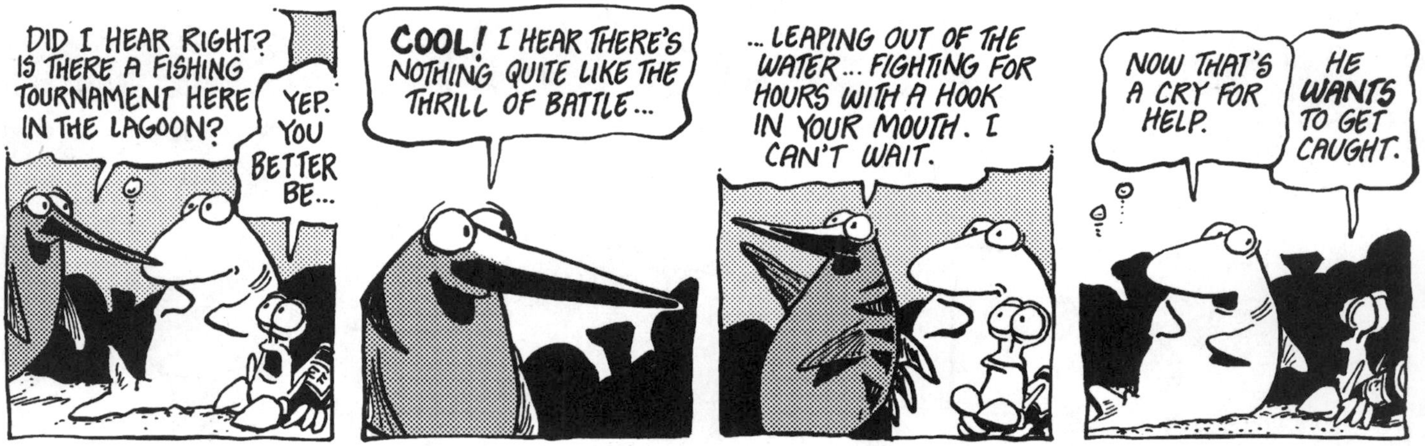
DID I HEAR RIGHT? IS THERE A FISHING TOURNAMENT HERE IN THE LAGOON?
YEP. YOU BETTER BE...
COOL! I HEAR THERE'S NOTHING QUITE LIKE THE THRILL OF BATTLE...
... LEAPING OUT OF THE WATER... FIGHTING FOR HOURS WITH A HOOK IN YOUR MOUTH. I CAN'T WAIT.
NOW THAT'S A CRY FOR HELP.
HE WANTS TO GET CAUGHT.

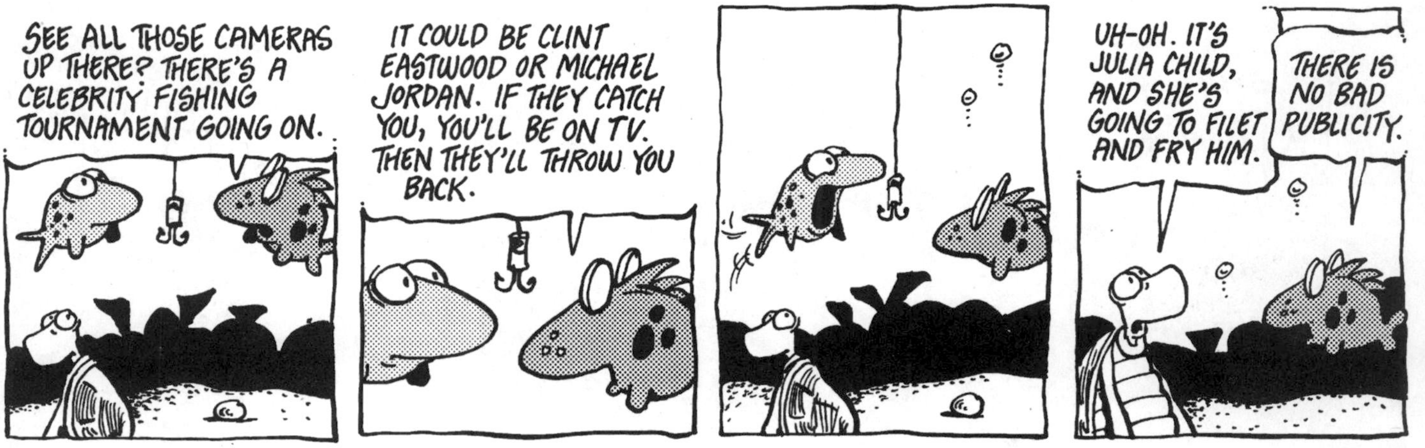
SEE ALL THOSE CAMERAS UP THERE? THERE'S A CELEBRITY FISHING TOURNAMENT GOING ON.
IT COULD BE CLINT EASTWOOD OR MICHAEL JORDAN. IF THEY CATCH YOU, YOU'LL BE ON TV. THEN THEY'LL THROW YOU BACK.
UH-OH. IT'S JULIA CHILD, AND SHE'S GOING TO FILET AND FRY HIM.
THERE IS NO BAD PUBLICITY.

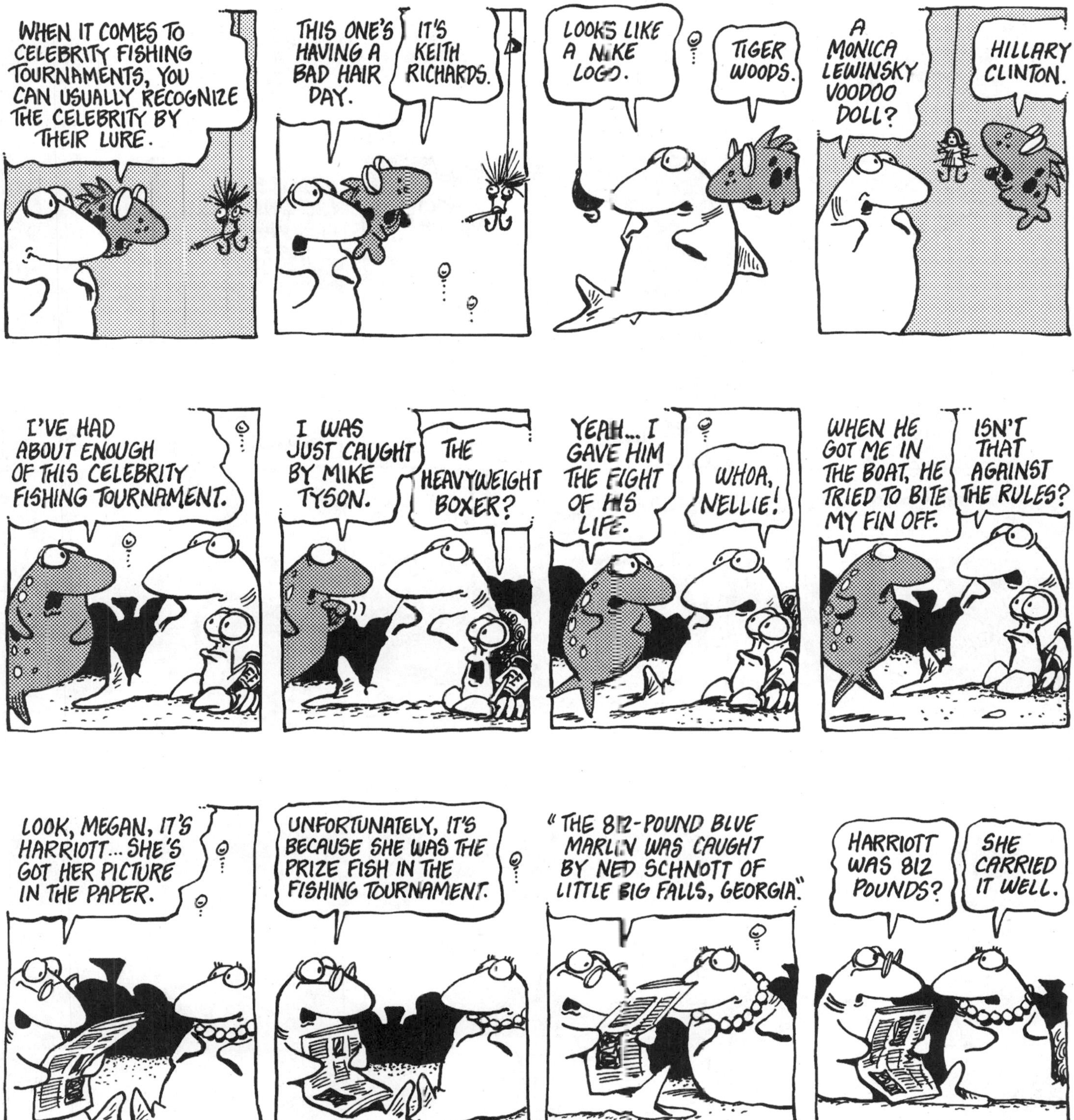

WHEN IT COMES TO CELEBRITY FISHING TOURNAMENTS, YOU CAN USUALLY RECOGNIZE THE CELEBRITY BY THEIR LURE.
THIS ONE'S HAVING A BAD HAIR DAY.
IT'S KEITH RICHARDS.
LOOKS LIKE A NIKE LOGO.
TIGER WOODS.
A MONICA LEWINSKY VOODOO DOLL?
HILLARY CLINTON.
I'VE HAD ABOUT ENOUGH OF THIS CELEBRITY FISHING TOURNAMENT.
I WAS JUST CAUGHT BY MIKE TYSON.
THE HEAVYWEIGHT BOXER?
YEAH... I GAVE HIM THE FIGHT OF HIS LIFE.
WHOA, NELLIE!
WHEN HE GOT ME IN THE BOAT, HE TRIED TO BITE MY FIN OFF.
ISN'T THAT AGAINST THE RULES?
LOOK, MEGAN, IT'S HARRIOTT... SHE'S GOT HER PICTURE IN THE PAPER.
UNFORTUNATELY, IT'S BECAUSE SHE WAS THE PRIZE FISH IN THE FISHING TOURNAMENT.
"THE 812-POUND BLUE MARLIN WAS CAUGHT BY NED SCHNOTT OF LITTLE BIG FALLS, GEORGIA."
HARRIOTT WAS 812 POUNDS?
SHE CARRIED IT WELL.

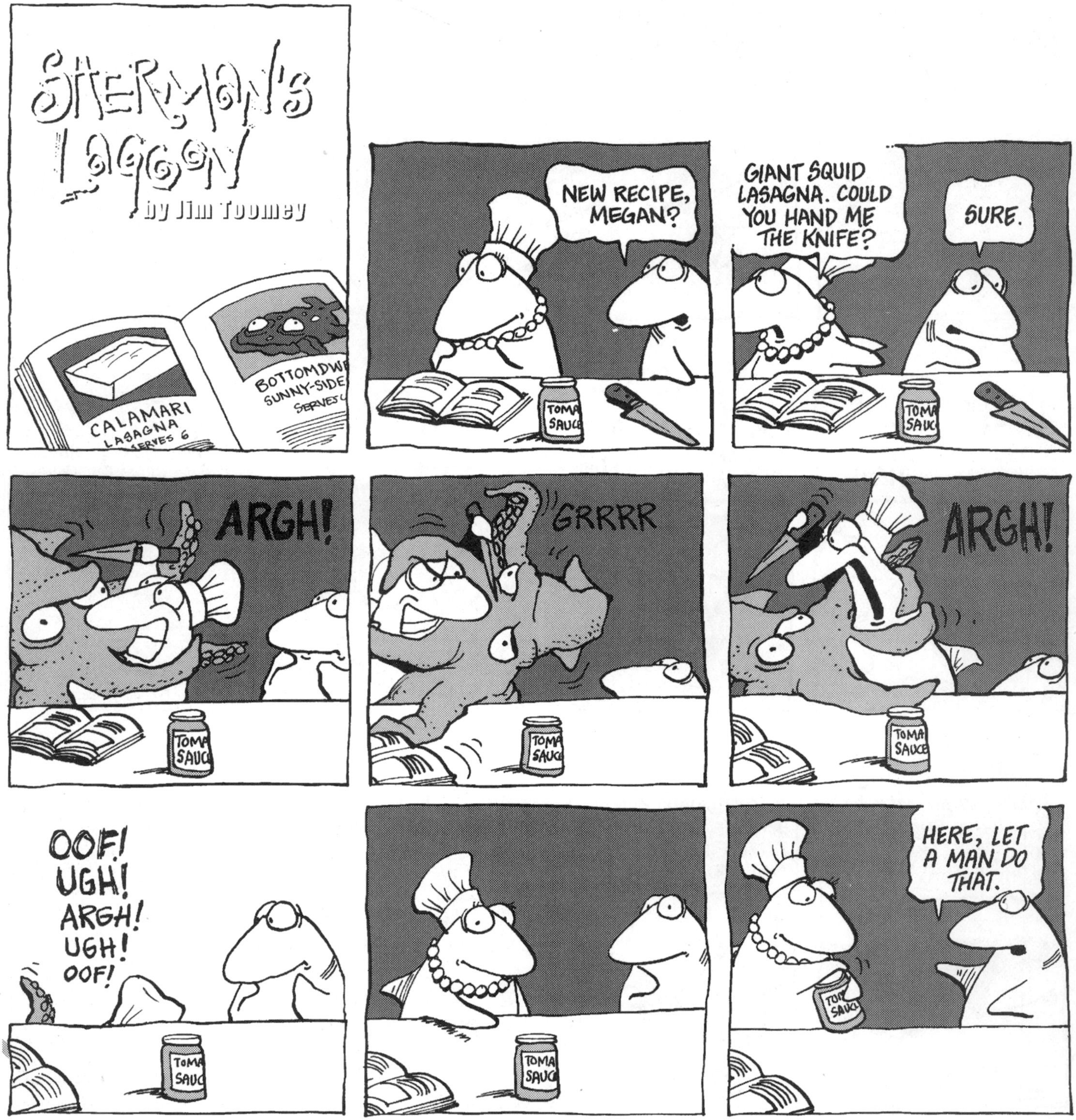
SHERMAN'S LAGOON
by Jim Toomey
CALAMARI LASAGNA
SERVES 6
BOTTOMDWE
SUNNY-SIDE
NEW RECIPE, MEGAN?
TOMA SAUCE
GIANT SQUID LASAGNA. COULD YOU HAND ME THE KNIFE?
SURE.
ARGH!
GRRRR
ARGH!
OOF!
UGH!
ARGH!
UGH!
OOF!
HERE, LET A MAN DO THAT.

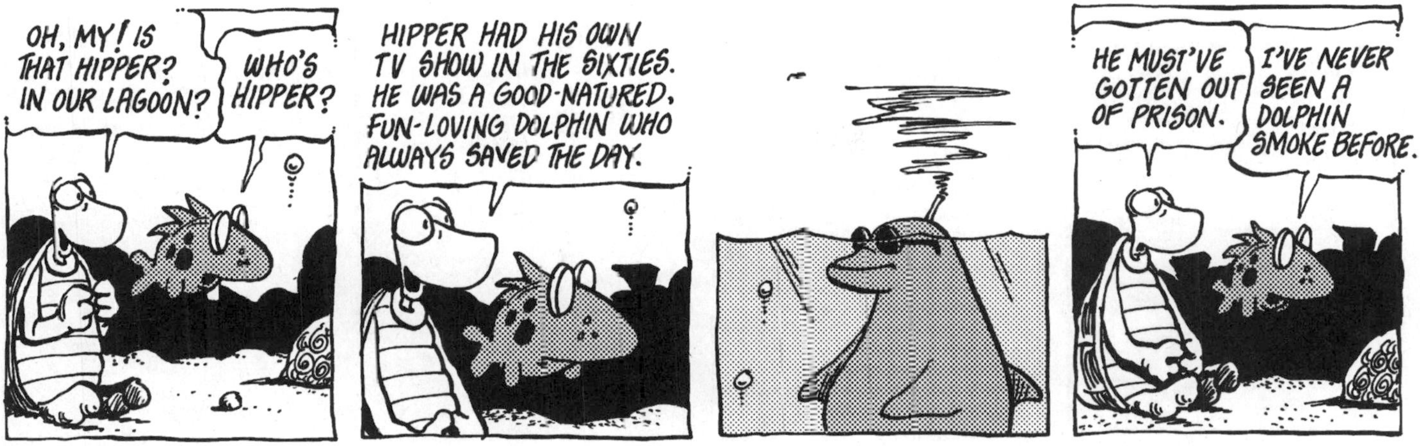
OH, MY! IS THAT HIPPER? IN OUR LAGOON?
WHO'S HIPPER?
HIPPER HAD HIS OWN TV SHOW IN THE SIXTIES. HE WAS A GOOD-NATURED, FUN-LOVING DOLPHIN WHO ALWAYS SAVED THE DAY.
HE MUST'VE GOTTEN OUT OF PRISON.
I'VE NEVER SEEN A DOLPHIN SMOKE BEFORE.

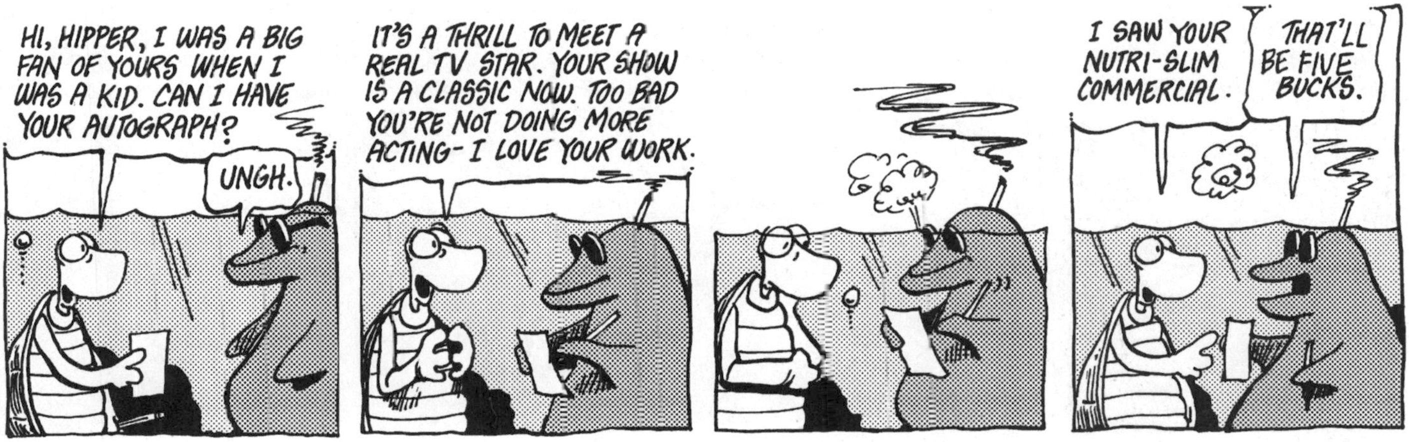
HI, HIPPER, I WAS A BIG FAN OF YOURS WHEN I WAS A KID. CAN I HAVE YOUR AUTOGRAPH?
UNGH.
IT'S A THRILL TO MEET A REAL TV STAR. YOUR SHOW IS A CLASSIC NOW. TOO BAD YOU'RE NOT DOING MORE ACTING- I LOVE YOUR WORK.
I SAW YOUR NUTRI-SLIM COMMERCIAL.
THAT'LL BE FIVE BUCKS.

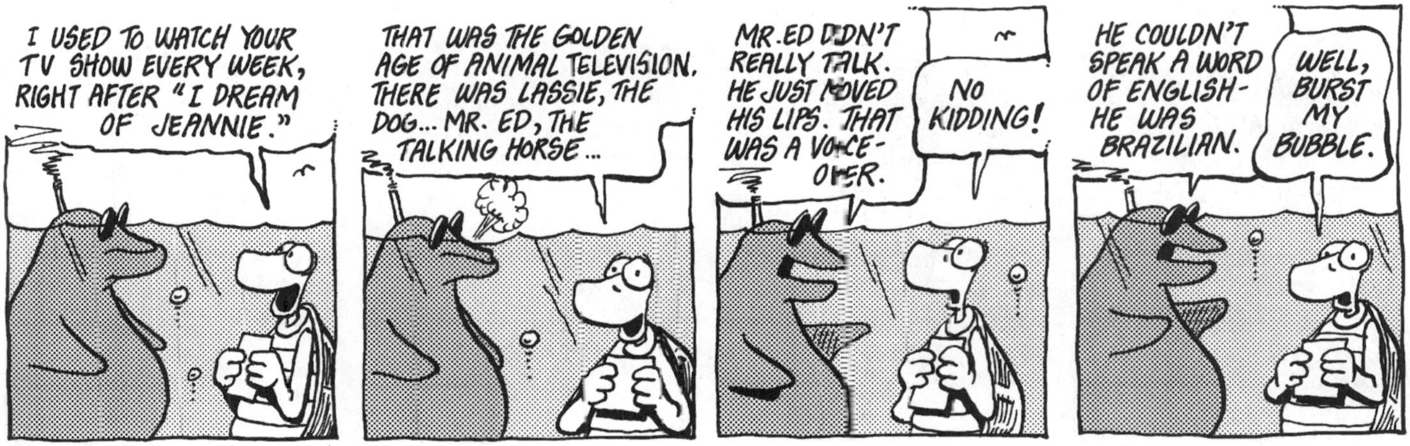
I USED TO WATCH YOUR TV SHOW EVERY WEEK, RIGHT AFTER "I DREAM OF JEANNIE."
THAT WAS THE GOLDEN AGE OF ANIMAL TELEVISION. THERE WAS LASSIE, THE DOG... MR. ED, THE TALKING HORSE...
MR. ED DIDN'T REALLY TALK. HE JUST MOVED HIS LIPS. THAT WAS A VOICE-OVER.
NO KIDDING!
HE COULDN'T SPEAK A WORD OF ENGLISH- HE WAS BRAZILIAN.
WELL, BURST MY BUBBLE.

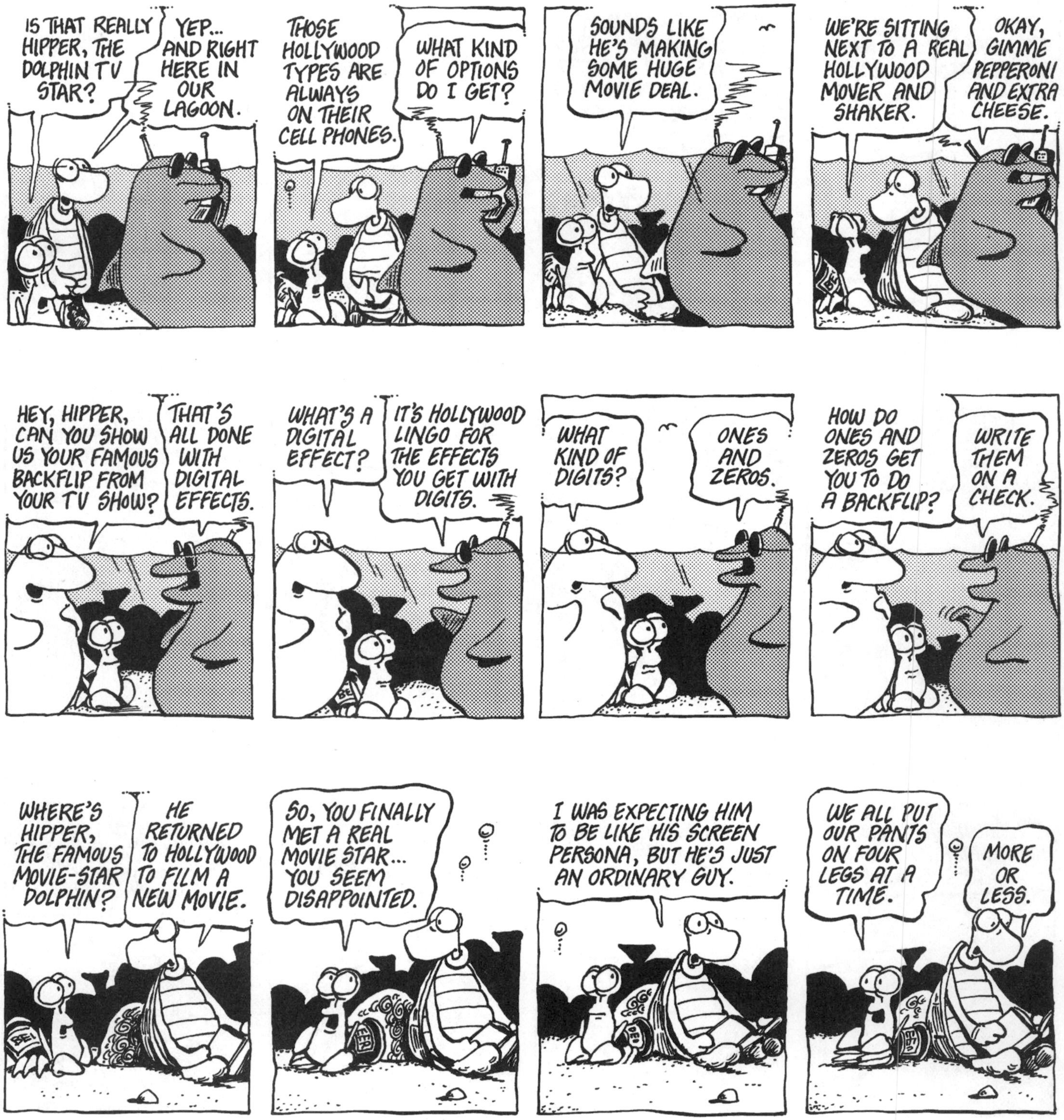
IS THAT REALLY HIPPER, THE DOLPHIN TV STAR?
YEP... AND RIGHT HERE IN OUR LAGOON.
THOSE HOLLYWOOD TYPES ARE ALWAYS ON THEIR CELL PHONES.
WHAT KIND OF OPTIONS DO I GET?
SOUNDS LIKE HE'S MAKING SOME HUGE MOVIE DEAL.
WE'RE SITTING NEXT TO A REAL HOLLYWOOD MOVER AND SHAKER.
OKAY, GIMME PEPPERONI AND EXTRA CHEESE.
HEY, HIPPER, CAN YOU SHOW US YOUR FAMOUS BACKFLIP FROM YOUR TV SHOW?
THAT'S ALL DONE WITH DIGITAL EFFECTS.
WHAT'S A DIGITAL EFFECT?
IT'S HOLLYWOOD LINGO FOR THE EFFECTS YOU GET WITH DIGITS.
WHAT KIND OF DIGITS?
ONES AND ZEROS.
HOW DO ONES AND ZEROS GET YOU TO DO A BACKFLIP?
WRITE THEM ON A CHECK.
WHERE'S HIPPER, THE FAMOUS MOVIE-STAR DOLPHIN?
HE RETURNED TO HOLLYWOOD TO FILM A NEW MOVIE.
SO, YOU FINALLY MET A REAL MOVIE STAR... YOU SEEM DISAPPOINTED.
I WAS EXPECTING HIM TO BE LIKE HIS SCREEN PERSONA, BUT HE'S JUST AN ORDINARY GUY.
WE ALL PUT OUR PANTS ON FOUR LEGS AT A TIME.
MORE OR LESS.

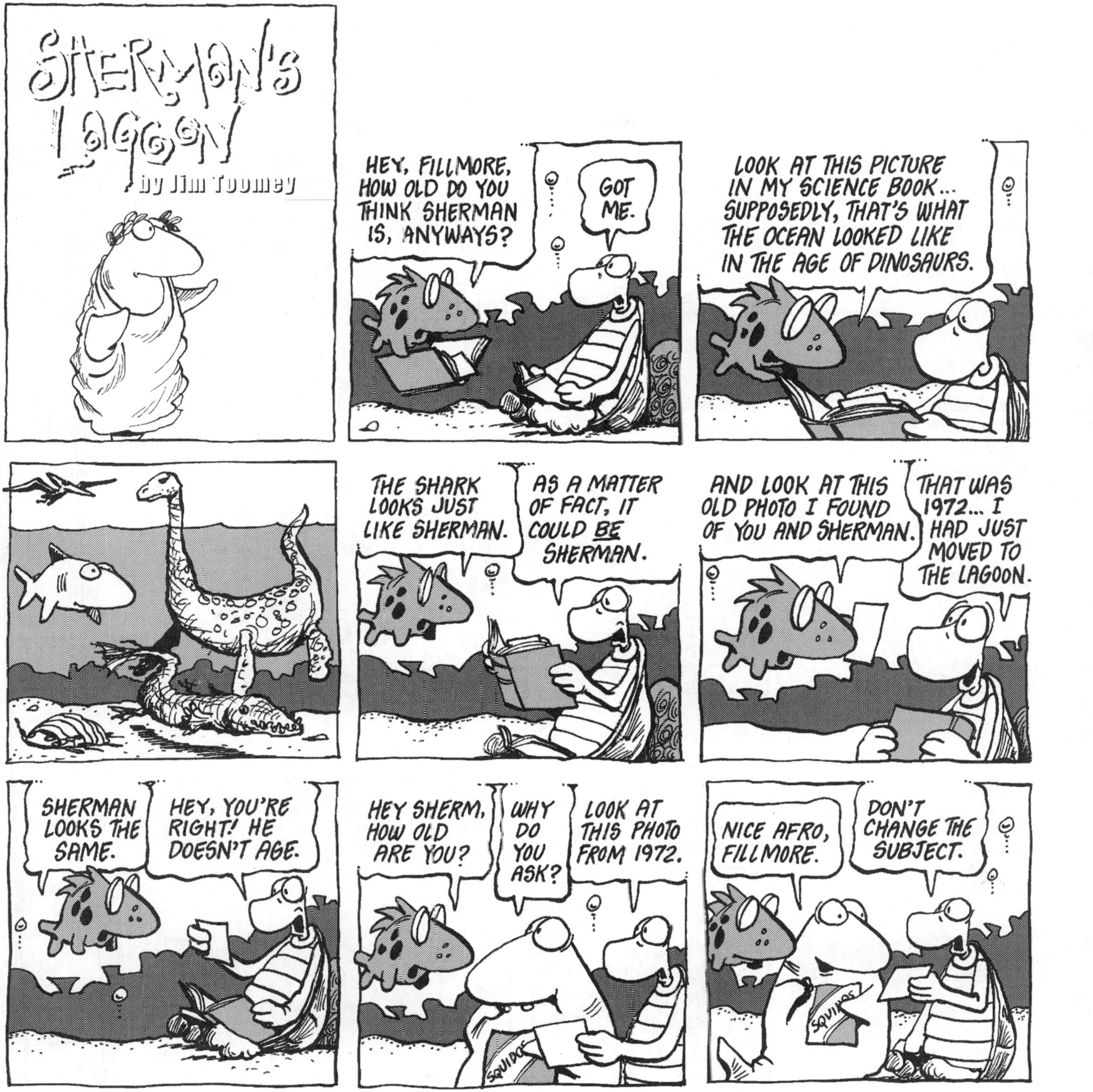
SHERMAN'S LAGOON
by Jim Toomey
HEY, FILLMORE, HOW OLD DO YOU THINK SHERMAN IS, ANYWAYS?
GOT ME.
LOOK AT THIS PICTURE IN MY SCIENCE BOOK... SUPPOSEDLY, THAT'S WHAT THE OCEAN LOOKED LIKE IN THE AGE OF DINOSAURS.
THE SHARK LOOKS JUST LIKE SHERMAN.
AS A MATTER OF FACT, IT COULD BE SHERMAN.
AND LOOK AT THIS OLD PHOTO I FOUND OF YOU AND SHERMAN.
THAT WAS 1972... I HAD JUST MOVED TO THE LAGOON.
SHERMAN LOOKS THE SAME.
HEY, YOU'RE RIGHT! HE DOESN'T AGE.
HEY SHERM, HOW OLD ARE YOU?
WHY DO YOU ASK?
LOOK AT THIS PHOTO FROM 1972.
SQUIDOS
NICE AFRO, FILLMORE.
DON'T CHANGE THE SUBJECT.
SQUIDOS

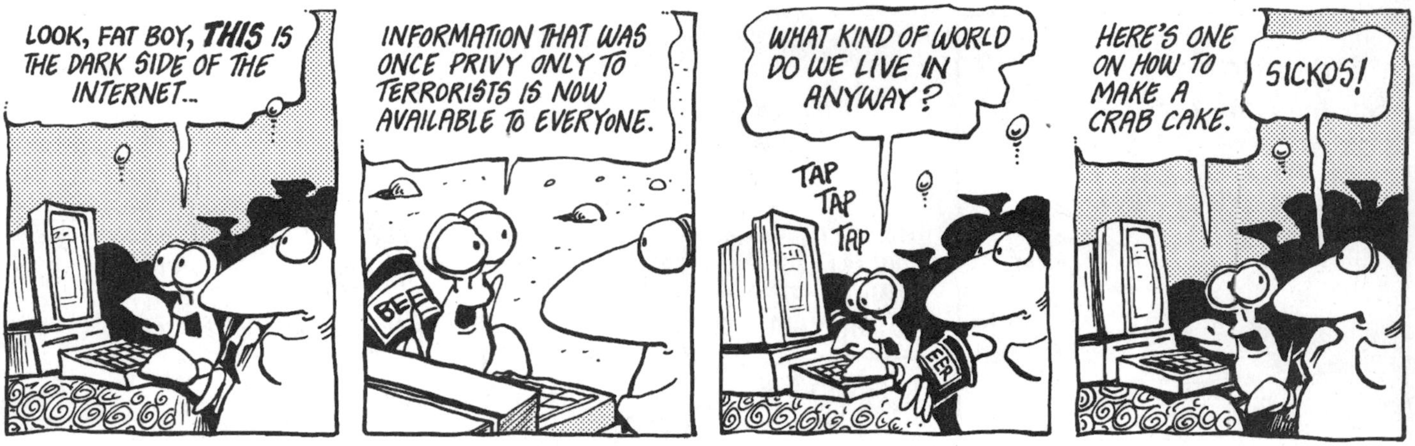
LOOK, FAT BOY, **THIS** IS THE DARK SIDE OF THE INTERNET...
INFORMATION THAT WAS ONCE PRIVY ONLY TO TERRORISTS IS NOW AVAILABLE TO EVERYONE.
TAP TAP TAP
WHAT KIND OF WORLD DO WE LIVE IN ANYWAY?
HERE'S ONE ON HOW TO MAKE A CRAB CAKE.
SICKOS!

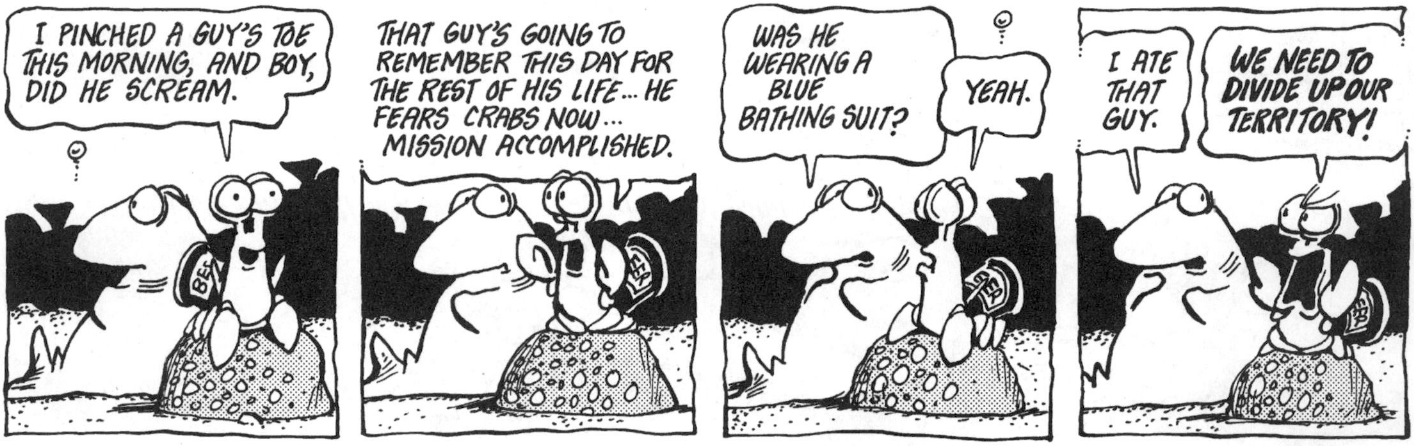
I PINCHED A GUY'S TOE THIS MORNING, AND BOY, DID HE SCREAM.
THAT GUY'S GOING TO REMEMBER THIS DAY FOR THE REST OF HIS LIFE... HE FEARS CRABS NOW... MISSION ACCOMPLISHED.
WAS HE WEARING A BLUE BATHING SUIT?
YEAH.
I ATE THAT GUY.
**WE NEED TO DIVIDE UP OUR TERRITORY!**

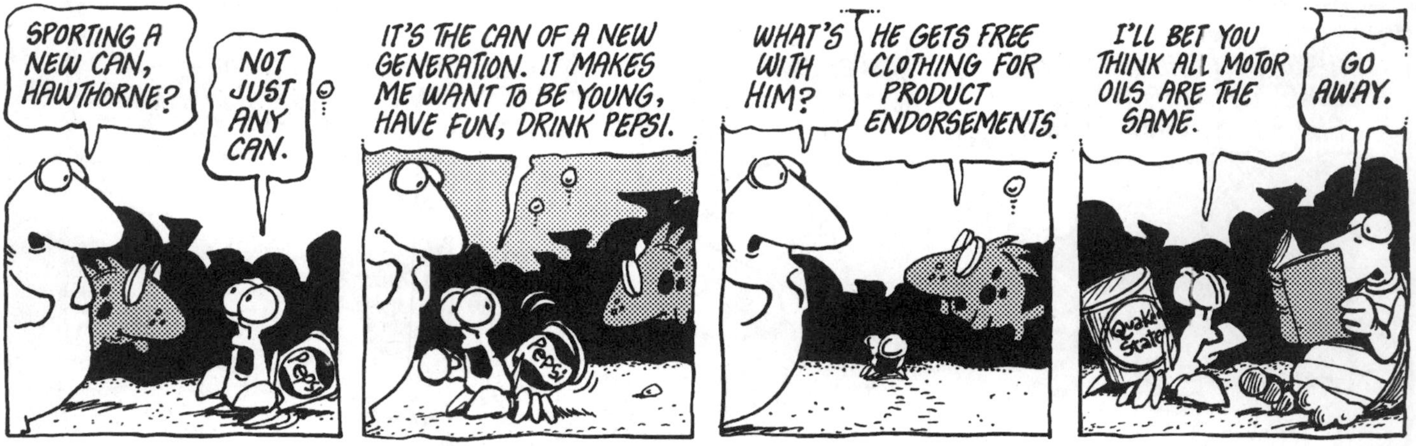
SPORTING A NEW CAN, HAWTHORNE?
NOT JUST ANY CAN.
IT'S THE CAN OF A NEW GENERATION. IT MAKES ME WANT TO BE YOUNG, HAVE FUN, DRINK PEPSI.
Pepsi
WHAT'S WITH HIM?
HE GETS FREE CLOTHING FOR PRODUCT ENDORSEMENTS.
I'LL BET YOU THINK ALL MOTOR OILS ARE THE SAME.
GO AWAY.

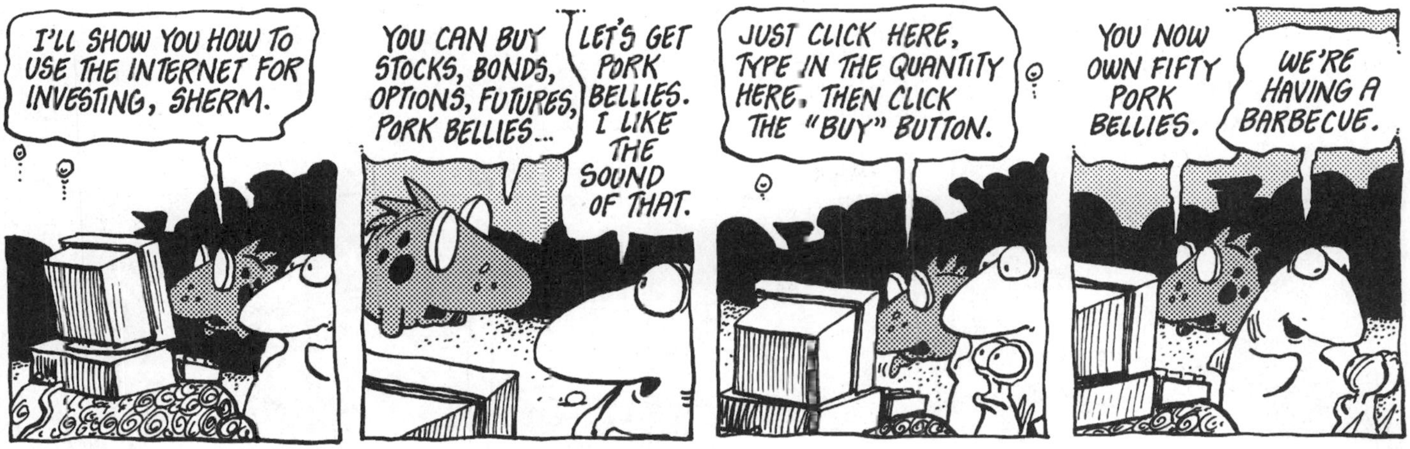
I'LL SHOW YOU HOW TO USE THE INTERNET FOR INVESTING, SHERM.
YOU CAN BUY STOCKS, BONDS, OPTIONS, FUTURES, PORK BELLIES...
LET'S GET PORK BELLIES. I LIKE THE SOUND OF THAT.
JUST CLICK HERE, TYPE IN THE QUANTITY HERE, THEN CLICK THE "BUY" BUTTON.
YOU NOW OWN FIFTY PORK BELLIES.
WE'RE HAVING A BARBECUE.

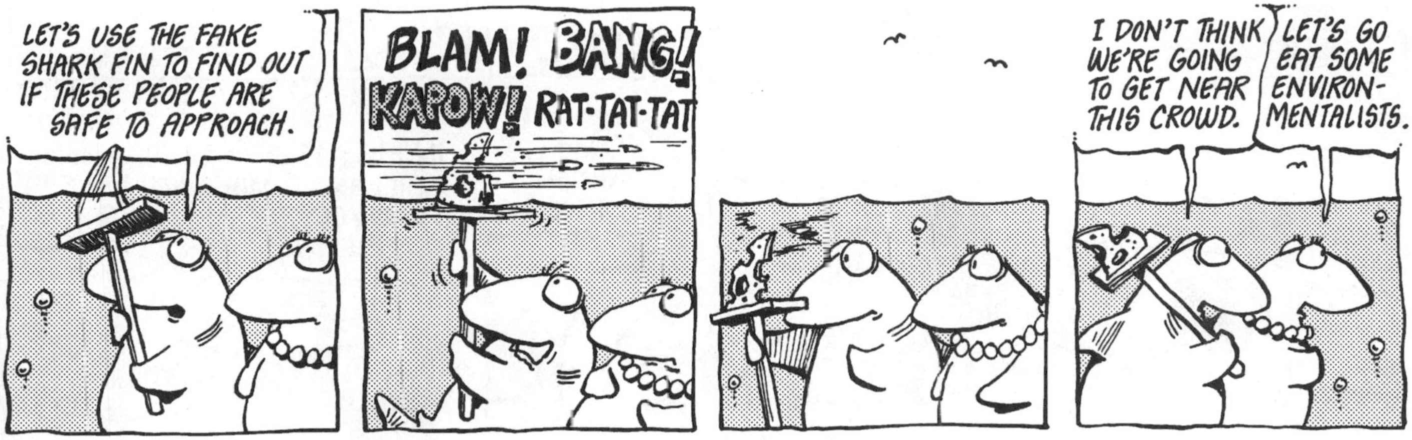
LET'S USE THE FAKE SHARK FIN TO FIND OUT IF THESE PEOPLE ARE SAFE TO APPROACH.
BLAM! BANG! KAPOW! RAT-TAT-TAT
I DON'T THINK WE'RE GOING TO GET NEAR THIS CROWD.
LET'S GO EAT SOME ENVIRON-MENTALISTS.

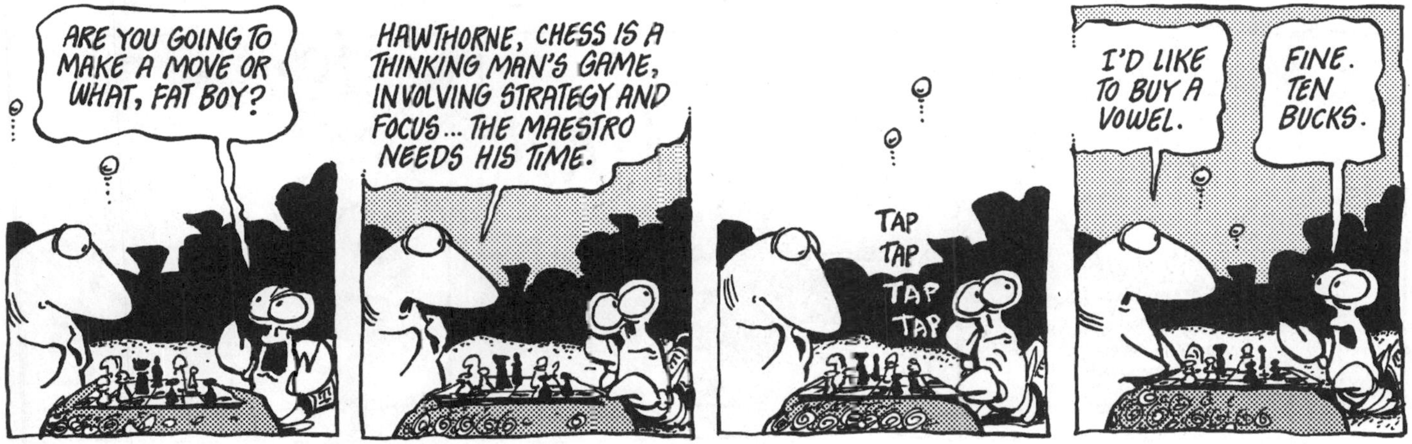
ARE YOU GOING TO MAKE A MOVE OR WHAT, FAT BOY?
HAWTHORNE, CHESS IS A THINKING MAN'S GAME, INVOLVING STRATEGY AND FOCUS... THE MAESTRO NEEDS HIS TIME.
TAP TAP TAP TAP
I'D LIKE TO BUY A VOWEL.
FINE. TEN BUCKS.

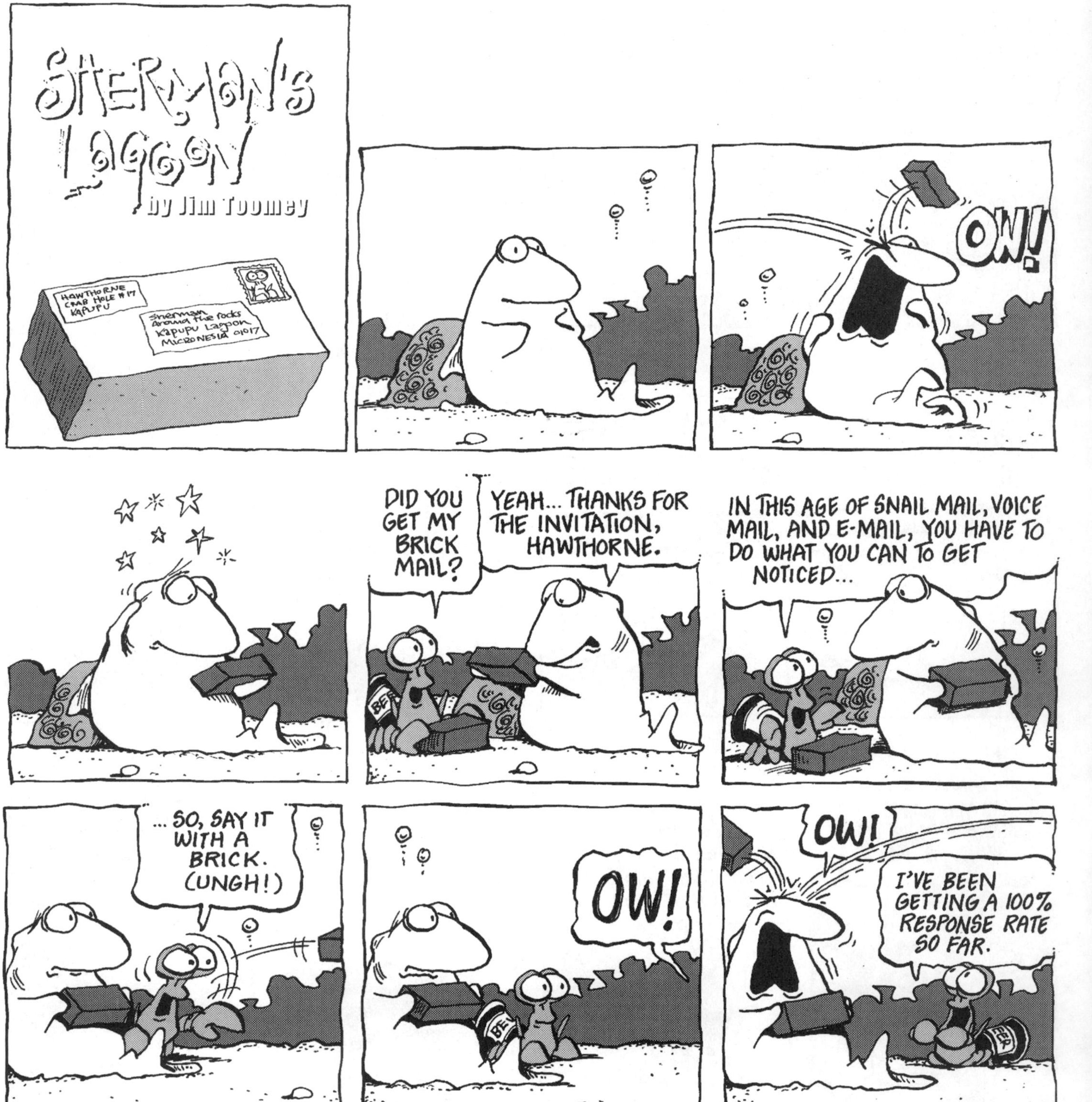

SHERMAN'S LAGOON
by Jim Toomey
HAWTHORNE
CRAB HOLE # 17
KAPUPU
Sherman
Around the rocks
Kapupu Lagoon
MICRONESIA 01017
OW!
DID YOU GET MY BRICK MAIL?
YEAH... THANKS FOR THE INVITATION, HAWTHORNE.
IN THIS AGE OF SNAIL MAIL, VOICE MAIL, AND E-MAIL, YOU HAVE TO DO WHAT YOU CAN TO GET NOTICED...
... SO, SAY IT WITH A BRICK. (UNGH!)
OW!
OW!
I'VE BEEN GETTING A 100% RESPONSE RATE SO FAR.

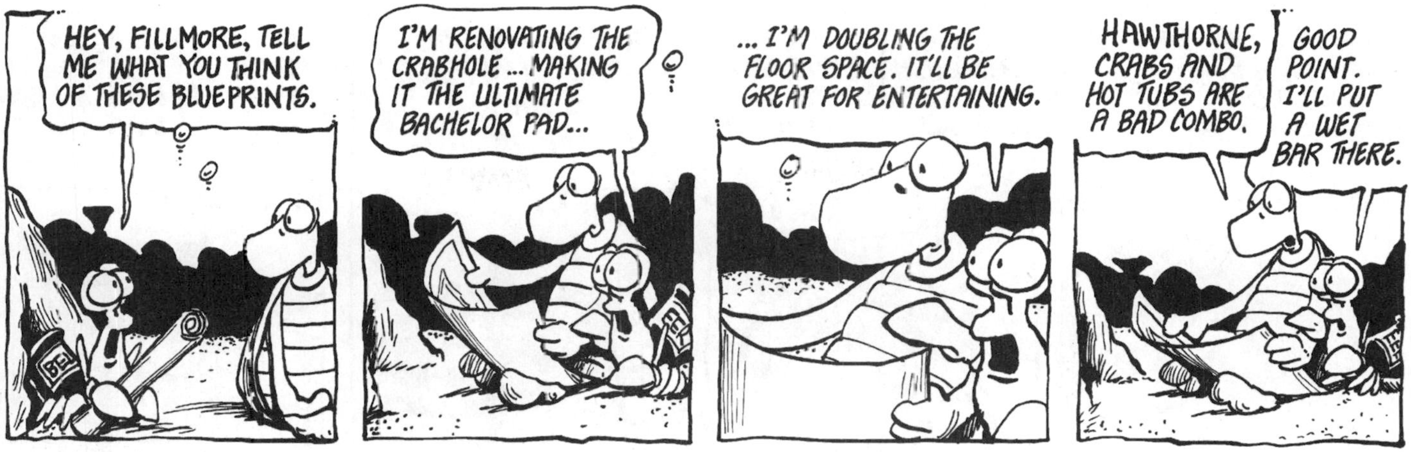
HEY, FILLMORE, TELL ME WHAT YOU THINK OF THESE BLUEPRINTS.
I'M RENOVATING THE CRABHOLE ... MAKING IT THE ULTIMATE BACHELOR PAD...
... I'M DOUBLING THE FLOOR SPACE. IT'LL BE GREAT FOR ENTERTAINING.
HAWTHORNE, CRABS AND HOT TUBS ARE A BAD COMBO.
GOOD POINT. I'LL PUT A WET BAR THERE.

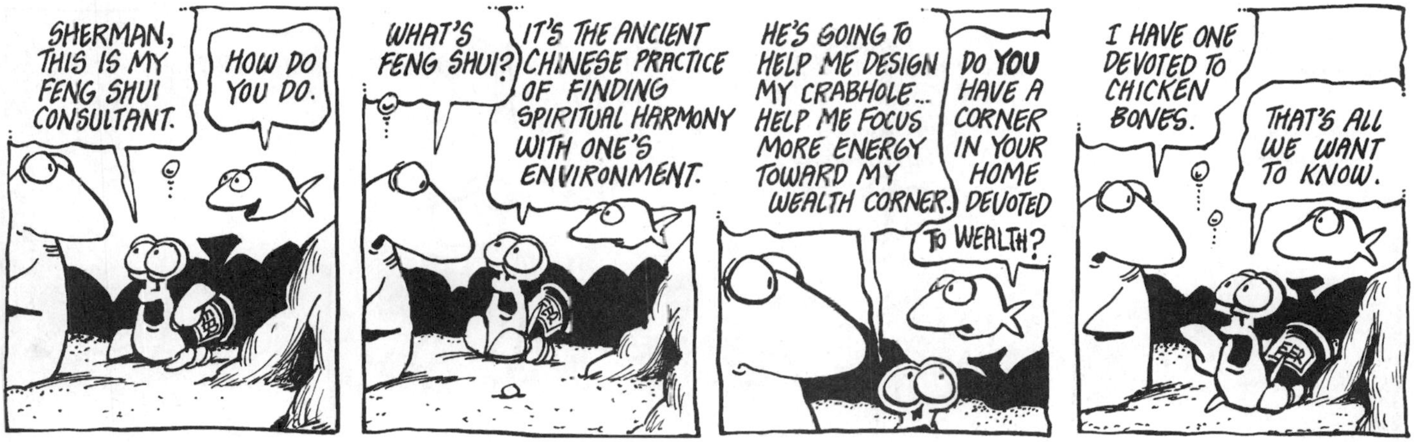
SHERMAN, THIS IS MY FENG SHUI CONSULTANT.
HOW DO YOU DO.
WHAT'S FENG SHUI?
IT'S THE ANCIENT CHINESE PRACTICE OF FINDING SPIRITUAL HARMONY WITH ONE'S ENVIRONMENT.
HE'S GOING TO HELP ME DESIGN MY CRABHOLE... HELP ME FOCUS MORE ENERGY TOWARD MY WEALTH CORNER.
DO YOU HAVE A CORNER IN YOUR HOME DEVOTED TO WEALTH?
I HAVE ONE DEVOTED TO CHICKEN BONES.
THAT'S ALL WE WANT TO KNOW.

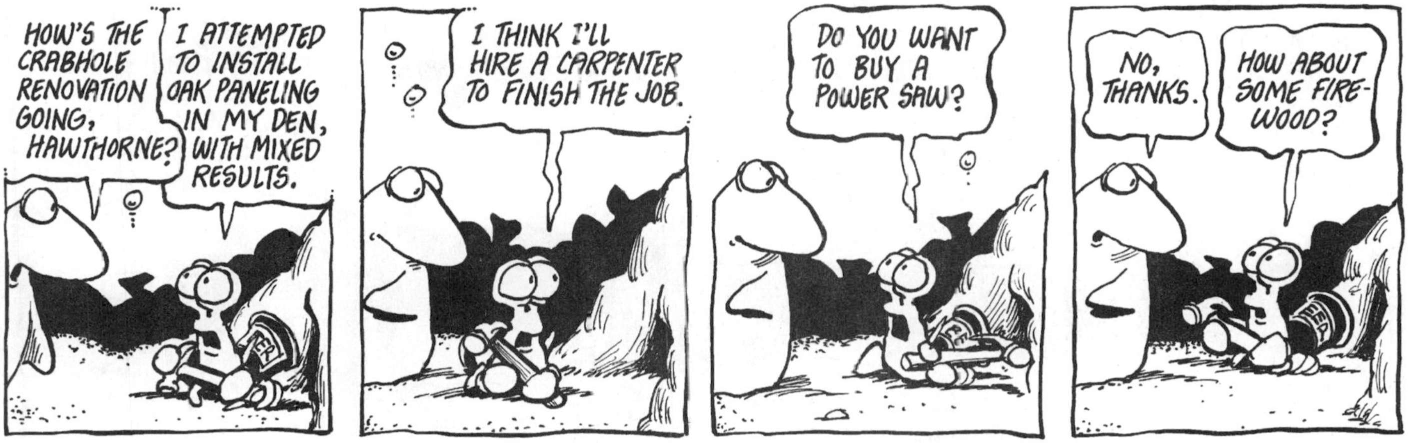
HOW'S THE CRABHOLE RENOVATION GOING, HAWTHORNE?
I ATTEMPTED TO INSTALL OAK PANELING IN MY DEN, WITH MIXED RESULTS.
I THINK I'LL HIRE A CARPENTER TO FINISH THE JOB.
DO YOU WANT TO BUY A POWER SAW?
NO, THANKS.
HOW ABOUT SOME FIRE-WOOD?

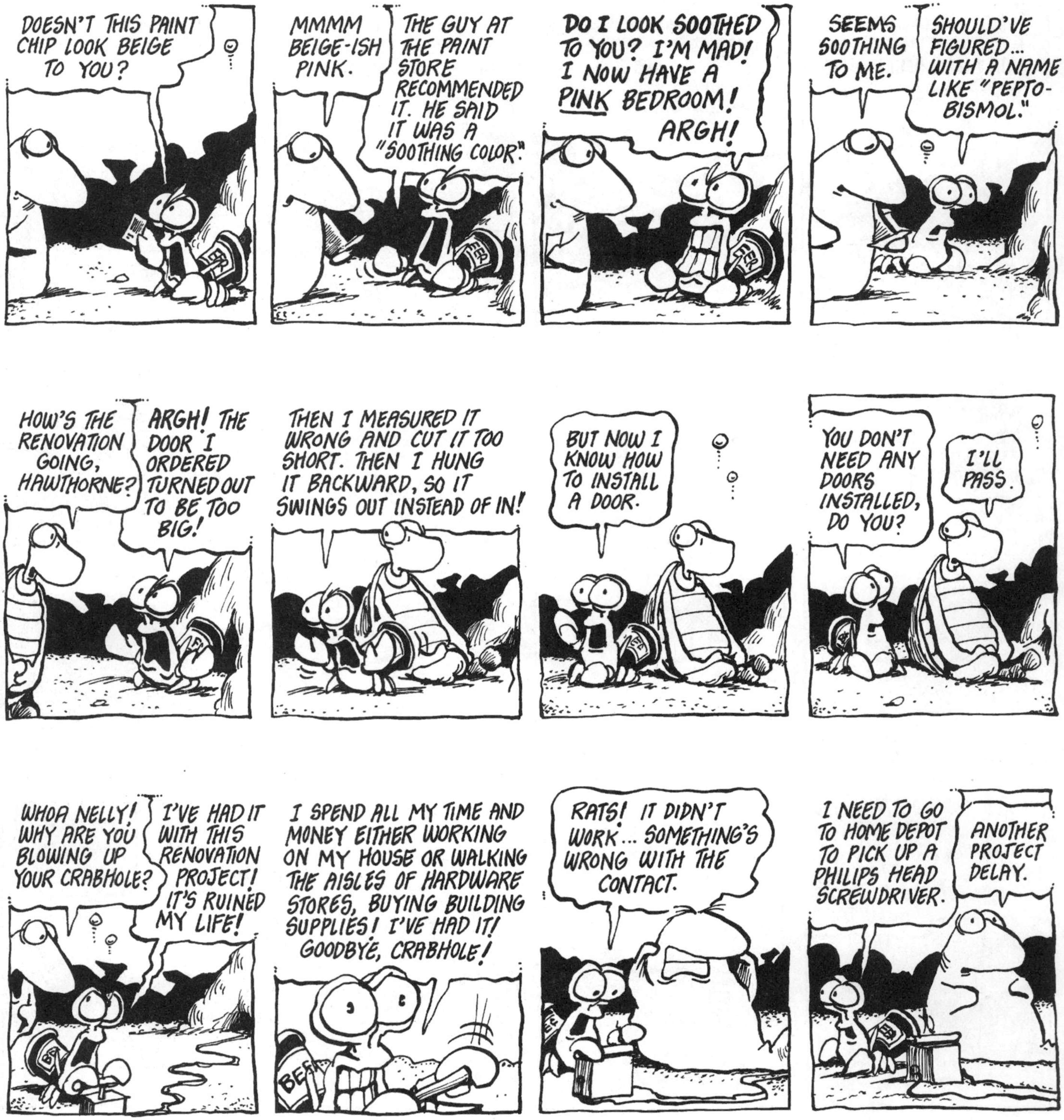
DOESN'T THIS PAINT CHIP LOOK BEIGE TO YOU?
MMMM BEIGE-ISH PINK.
THE GUY AT THE PAINT STORE RECOMMENDED IT. HE SAID IT WAS A "SOOTHING COLOR."
DO I LOOK SOOTHED TO YOU? I'M MAD! I NOW HAVE A PINK BEDROOM! ARGH!
SEEMS SOOTHING TO ME.
SHOULD'VE FIGURED... WITH A NAME LIKE "PEPTO-BISMOL."
HOW'S THE RENOVATION GOING, HAWTHORNE?
ARGH! THE DOOR I ORDERED TURNED OUT TO BE TOO BIG!
THEN I MEASURED IT WRONG AND CUT IT TOO SHORT. THEN I HUNG IT BACKWARD, SO IT SWINGS OUT INSTEAD OF IN!
BUT NOW I KNOW HOW TO INSTALL A DOOR.
YOU DON'T NEED ANY DOORS INSTALLED, DO YOU?
I'LL PASS.
WHOA NELLY! WHY ARE YOU BLOWING UP YOUR CRABHOLE?
I'VE HAD IT WITH THIS RENOVATION PROJECT! IT'S RUINED MY LIFE!
I SPEND ALL MY TIME AND MONEY EITHER WORKING ON MY HOUSE OR WALKING THE AISLES OF HARDWARE STORES, BUYING BUILDING SUPPLIES! I'VE HAD IT! GOODBYE, CRABHOLE!
RATS! IT DIDN'T WORK... SOMETHING'S WRONG WITH THE CONTACT.
I NEED TO GO TO HOME DEPOT TO PICK UP A PHILIPS HEAD SCREWDRIVER.
ANOTHER PROJECT DELAY.

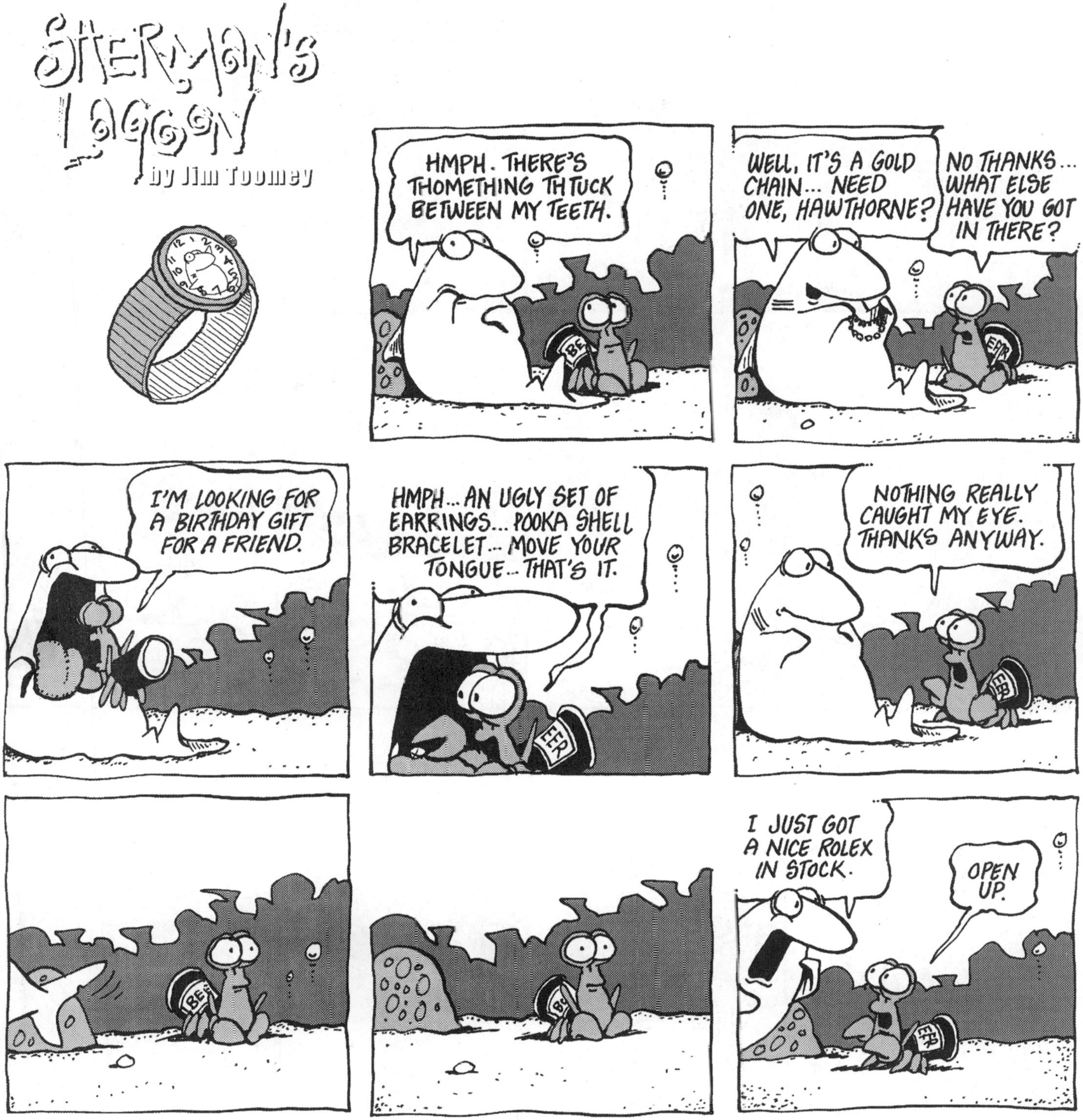
SHERMAN'S LAGOON
by Jim Toomey
HMPH. THERE'S THOMETHING THTUCK BETWEEN MY TEETH.
WELL, IT'S A GOLD CHAIN... NEED ONE, HAWTHORNE?
NO THANKS... WHAT ELSE HAVE YOU GOT IN THERE?
I'M LOOKING FOR A BIRTHDAY GIFT FOR A FRIEND.
HMPH... AN UGLY SET OF EARRINGS... POOKA SHELL BRACELET... MOVE YOUR TONGUE... THAT'S IT.
NOTHING REALLY CAUGHT MY EYE. THANKS ANYWAY.
I JUST GOT A NICE ROLEX IN STOCK.
OPEN UP.

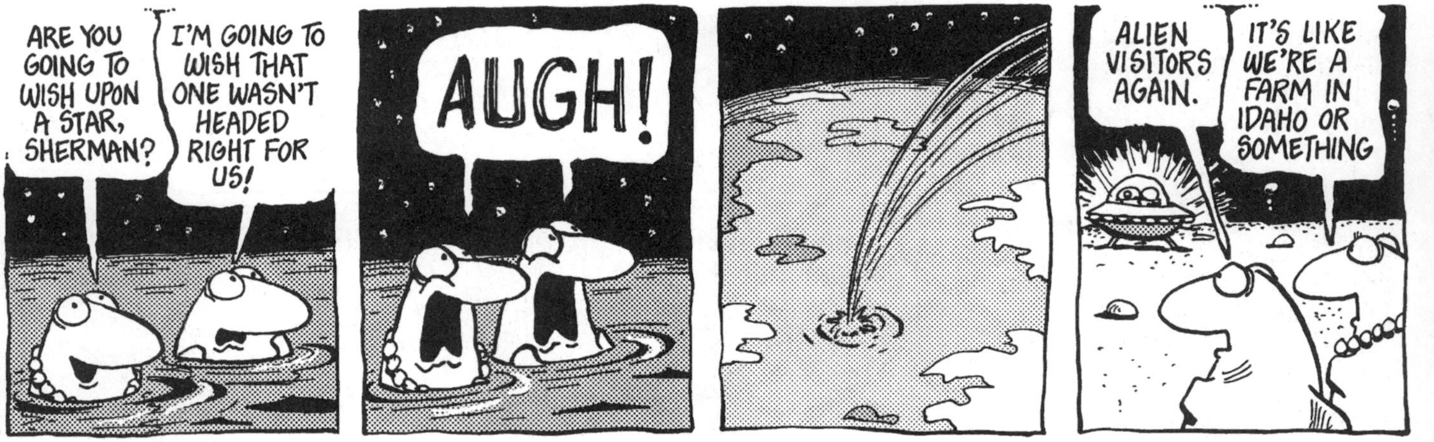
ARE YOU GOING TO WISH UPON A STAR, SHERMAN?
I'M GOING TO WISH THAT ONE WASN'T HEADED RIGHT FOR US!
AUGH!
ALIEN VISITORS AGAIN.
IT'S LIKE WE'RE A FARM IN IDAHO OR SOMETHING

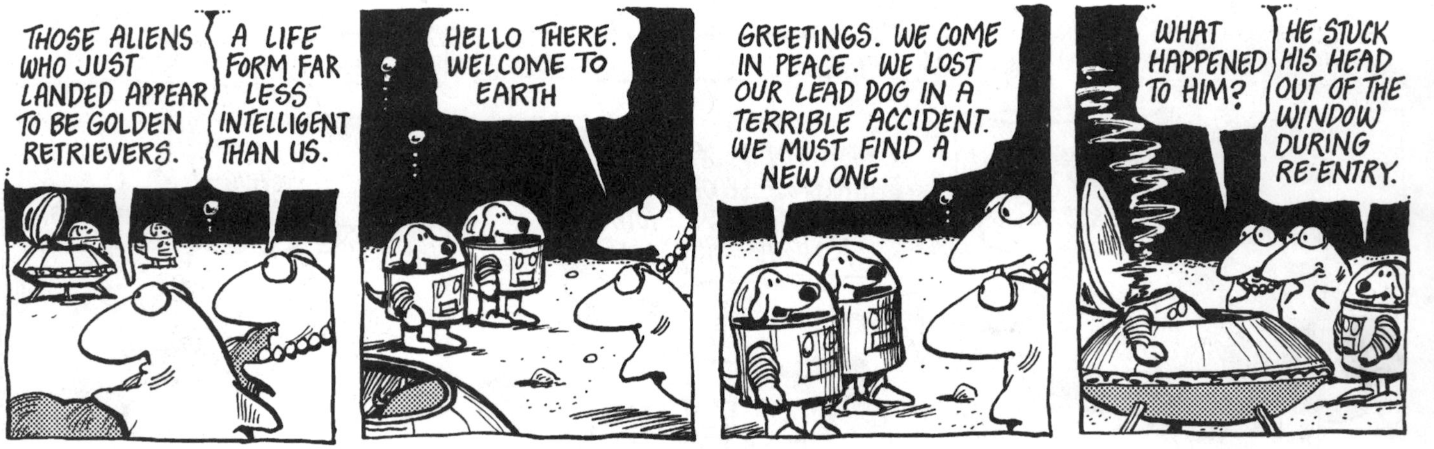
THOSE ALIENS WHO JUST LANDED APPEAR TO BE GOLDEN RETRIEVERS.
A LIFE FORM FAR LESS INTELLIGENT THAN US.
HELLO THERE. WELCOME TO EARTH
GREETINGS. WE COME IN PEACE. WE LOST OUR LEAD DOG IN A TERRIBLE ACCIDENT. WE MUST FIND A NEW ONE.
WHAT HAPPENED TO HIM?
HE STUCK HIS HEAD OUT OF THE WINDOW DURING RE-ENTRY.

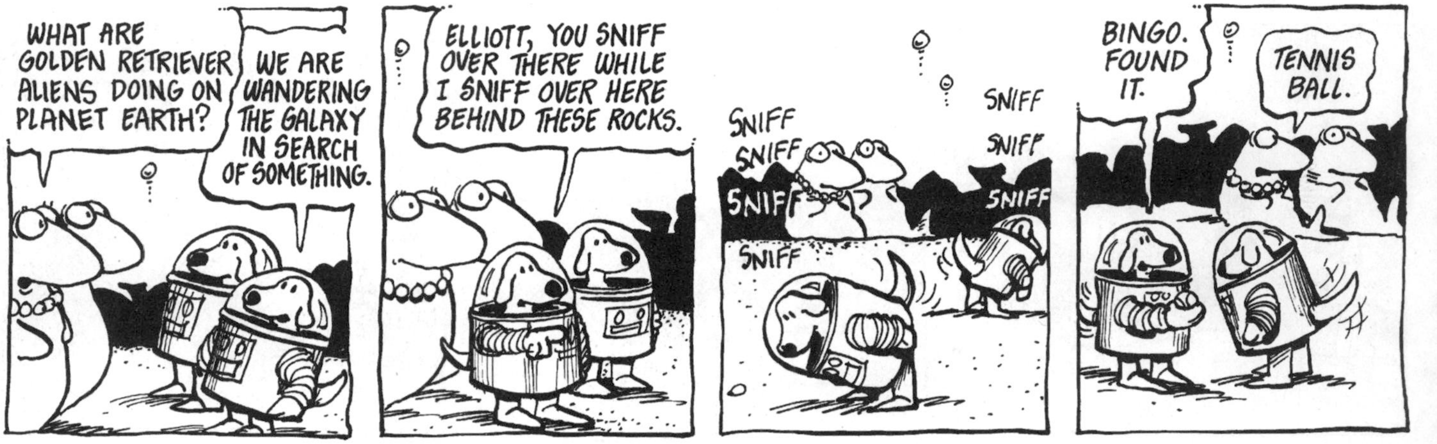
WHAT ARE GOLDEN RETRIEVER ALIENS DOING ON PLANET EARTH?
WE ARE WANDERING THE GALAXY IN SEARCH OF SOMETHING.
ELLIOTT, YOU SNIFF OVER THERE WHILE I SNIFF OVER HERE BEHIND THESE ROCKS.
SNIFF
SNIFF
SNIFF
SNIFF
SNIFF
SNIFF
SNIFF
BINGO. FOUND IT.
TENNIS BALL.

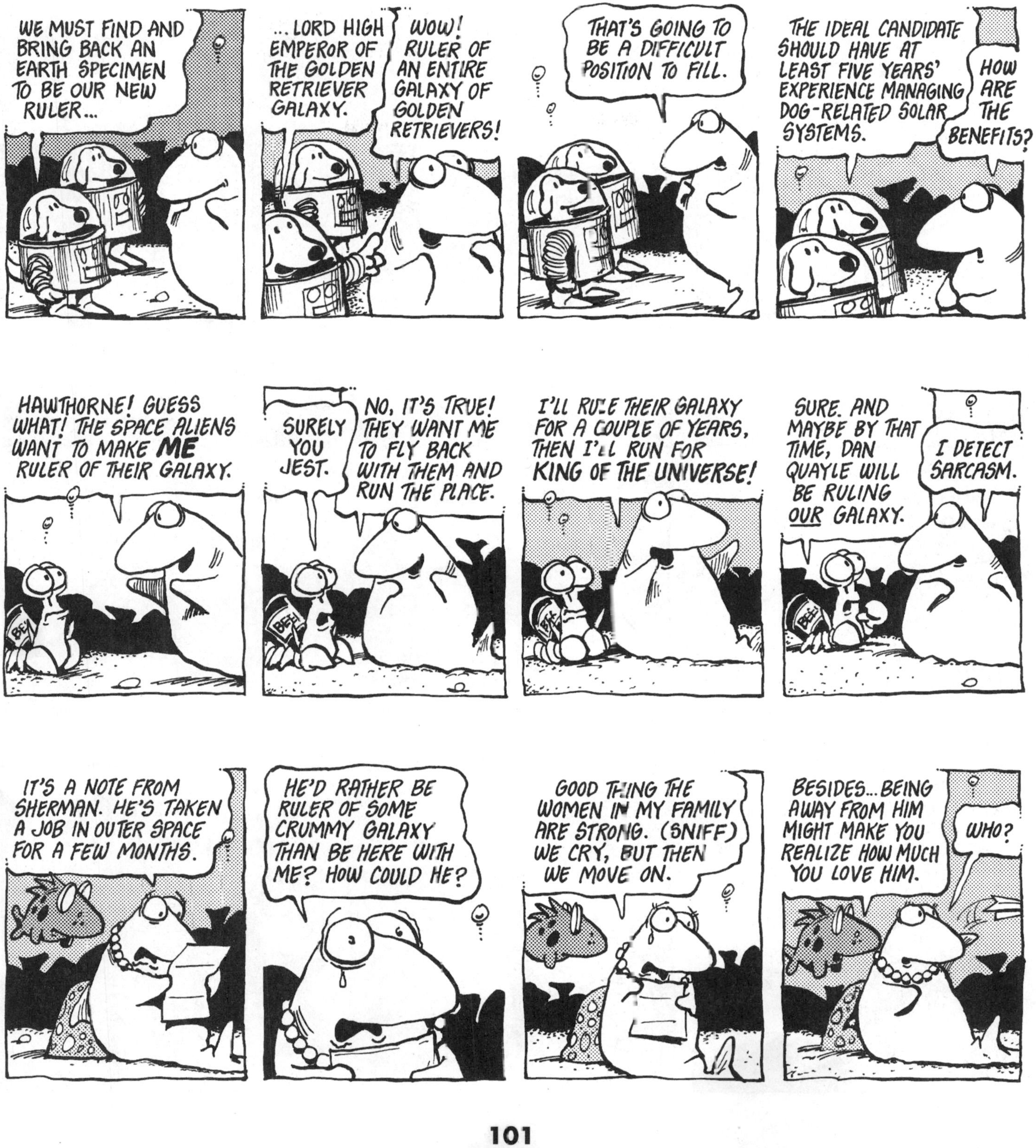

WE MUST FIND AND BRING BACK AN EARTH SPECIMEN TO BE OUR NEW RULER...
...LORD HIGH EMPEROR OF THE GOLDEN RETRIEVER GALAXY.
WOW! RULER OF AN ENTIRE GALAXY OF GOLDEN RETRIEVERS!
THAT'S GOING TO BE A DIFFICULT POSITION TO FILL.
THE IDEAL CANDIDATE SHOULD HAVE AT LEAST FIVE YEARS' EXPERIENCE MANAGING DOG-RELATED SOLAR SYSTEMS.
HOW ARE THE BENEFITS?
HAWTHORNE! GUESS WHAT! THE SPACE ALIENS WANT TO MAKE ME RULER OF THEIR GALAXY.
SURELY YOU JEST.
NO, IT'S TRUE! THEY WANT ME TO FLY BACK WITH THEM AND RUN THE PLACE.
I'LL RULE THEIR GALAXY FOR A COUPLE OF YEARS, THEN I'LL RUN FOR KING OF THE UNIVERSE!
SURE. AND MAYBE BY THAT TIME, DAN QUAYLE WILL BE RULING OUR GALAXY.
I DETECT SARCASM.
IT'S A NOTE FROM SHERMAN. HE'S TAKEN A JOB IN OUTER SPACE FOR A FEW MONTHS.
HE'D RATHER BE RULER OF SOME CRUMMY GALAXY THAN BE HERE WITH ME? HOW COULD HE?
GOOD THING THE WOMEN IN MY FAMILY ARE STRONG. (SNIFF) WE CRY, BUT THEN WE MOVE ON.
BESIDES... BEING AWAY FROM HIM MIGHT MAKE YOU REALIZE HOW MUCH YOU LOVE HIM.
WHO?

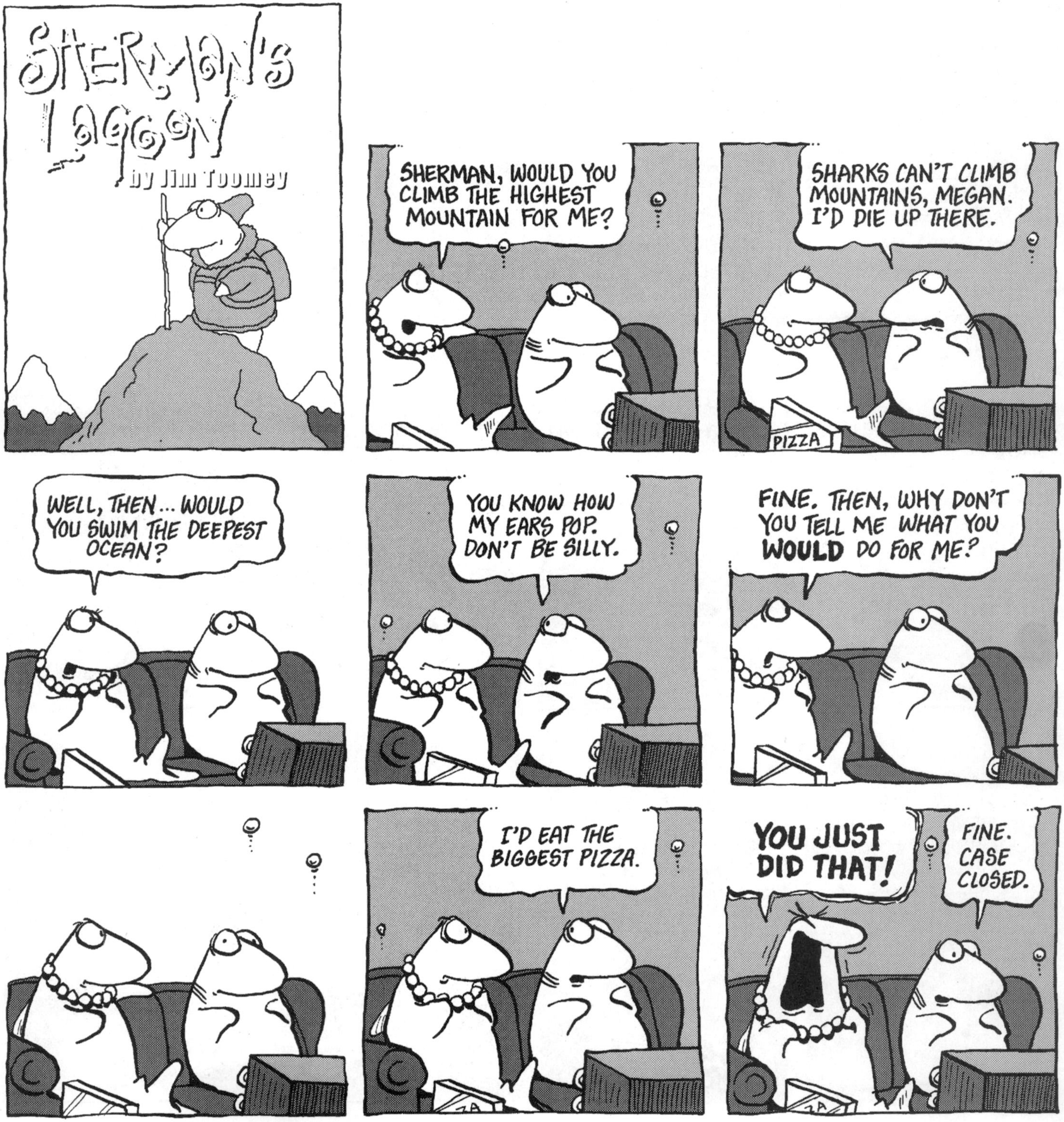
SHERMAN'S LAGOON
by Jim Toomey
SHERMAN, WOULD YOU CLIMB THE HIGHEST MOUNTAIN FOR ME?
SHARKS CAN'T CLIMB MOUNTAINS, MEGAN. I'D DIE UP THERE.
PIZZA
WELL, THEN... WOULD YOU SWIM THE DEEPEST OCEAN?
YOU KNOW HOW MY EARS POP. DON'T BE SILLY.
FINE. THEN, WHY DON'T YOU TELL ME WHAT YOU WOULD DO FOR ME?
I'D EAT THE BIGGEST PIZZA.
YOU JUST DID THAT!
FINE. CASE CLOSED.

A long time ago, in a galaxy far, far away, the Intergalactic Trade Federation put a blockade on planet Nanoo-Nanoo, limiting the number of Star Wars collectible action figures it could import.

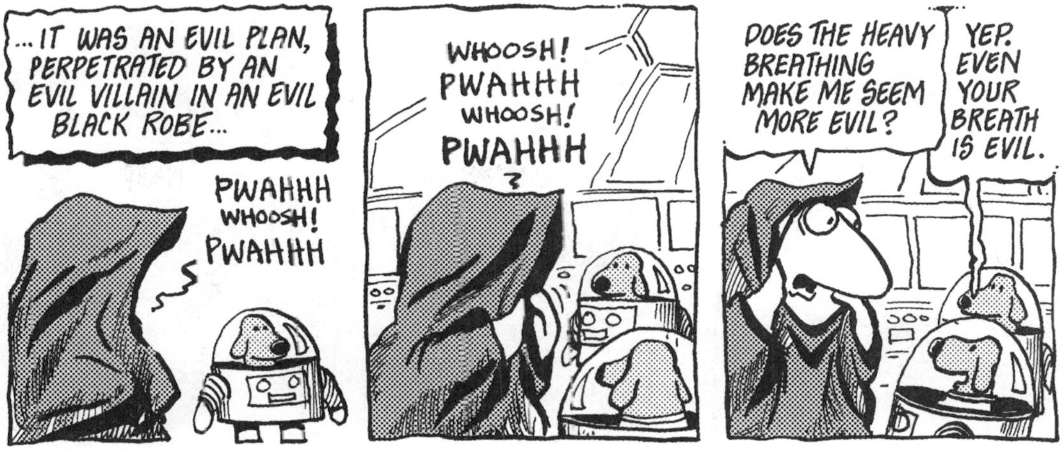
...IT WAS AN EVIL PLAN, PERPETRATED BY AN EVIL VILLAIN IN AN EVIL BLACK ROBE...
PWAHHH
WHOOSH!
PWAHHH
WHOOSH!
PWAHHH
WHOOSH!
PWAHHH
DOES THE HEAVY BREATHING MAKE ME SEEM MORE EVIL?
YEP. EVEN YOUR BREATH IS EVIL.

The Intergalactic Trade Federation's blockade of planet Nanoo-Nanoo continued, bringing much distress to its inhabitants. Meanwhile, Queen Amana Radarrange was plotting a strategy to save her planet.

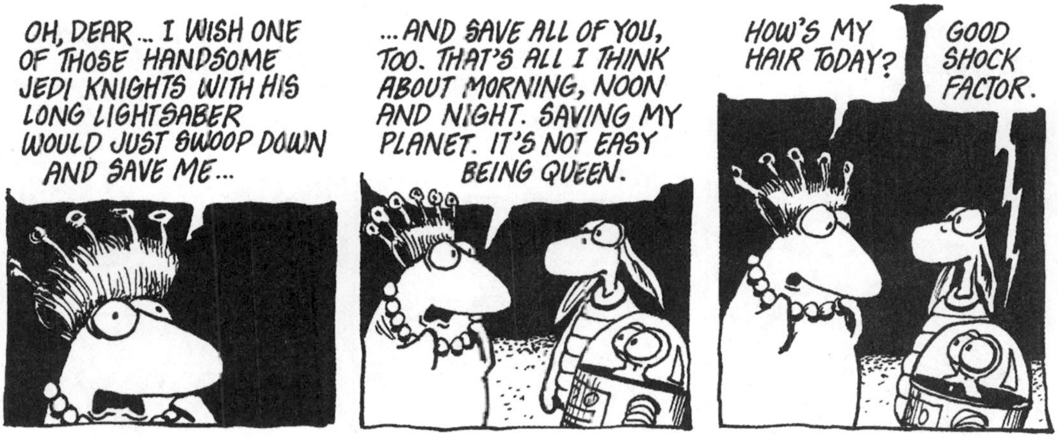
OH, DEAR... I WISH ONE OF THOSE HANDSOME JEDI KNIGHTS WITH HIS LONG LIGHTSABER WOULD JUST SWOOP DOWN AND SAVE ME...
...AND SAVE ALL OF YOU, TOO. THAT'S ALL I THINK ABOUT MORNING, NOON AND NIGHT. SAVING MY PLANET. IT'S NOT EASY BEING QUEEN.
HOW'S MY HAIR TODAY?
GOOD SHOCK FACTOR.

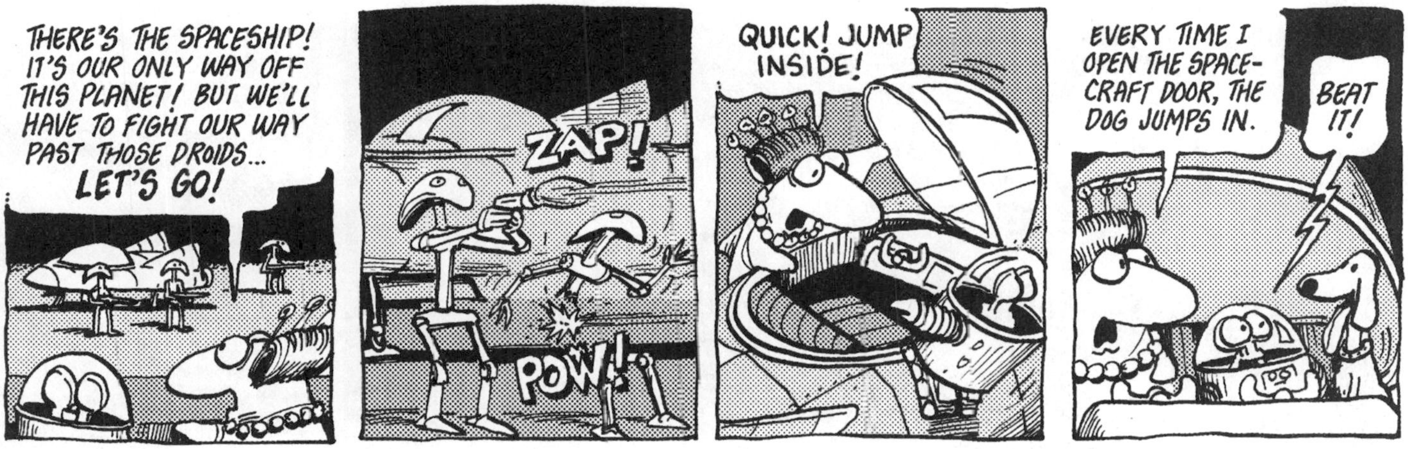
THERE'S THE SPACESHIP! IT'S OUR ONLY WAY OFF THIS PLANET! BUT WE'LL HAVE TO FIGHT OUR WAY PAST THOSE DROIDS... LET'S GO!
ZAP!
POW!
QUICK! JUMP INSIDE!
EVERY TIME I OPEN THE SPACECRAFT DOOR, THE DOG JUMPS IN.
BEAT IT!

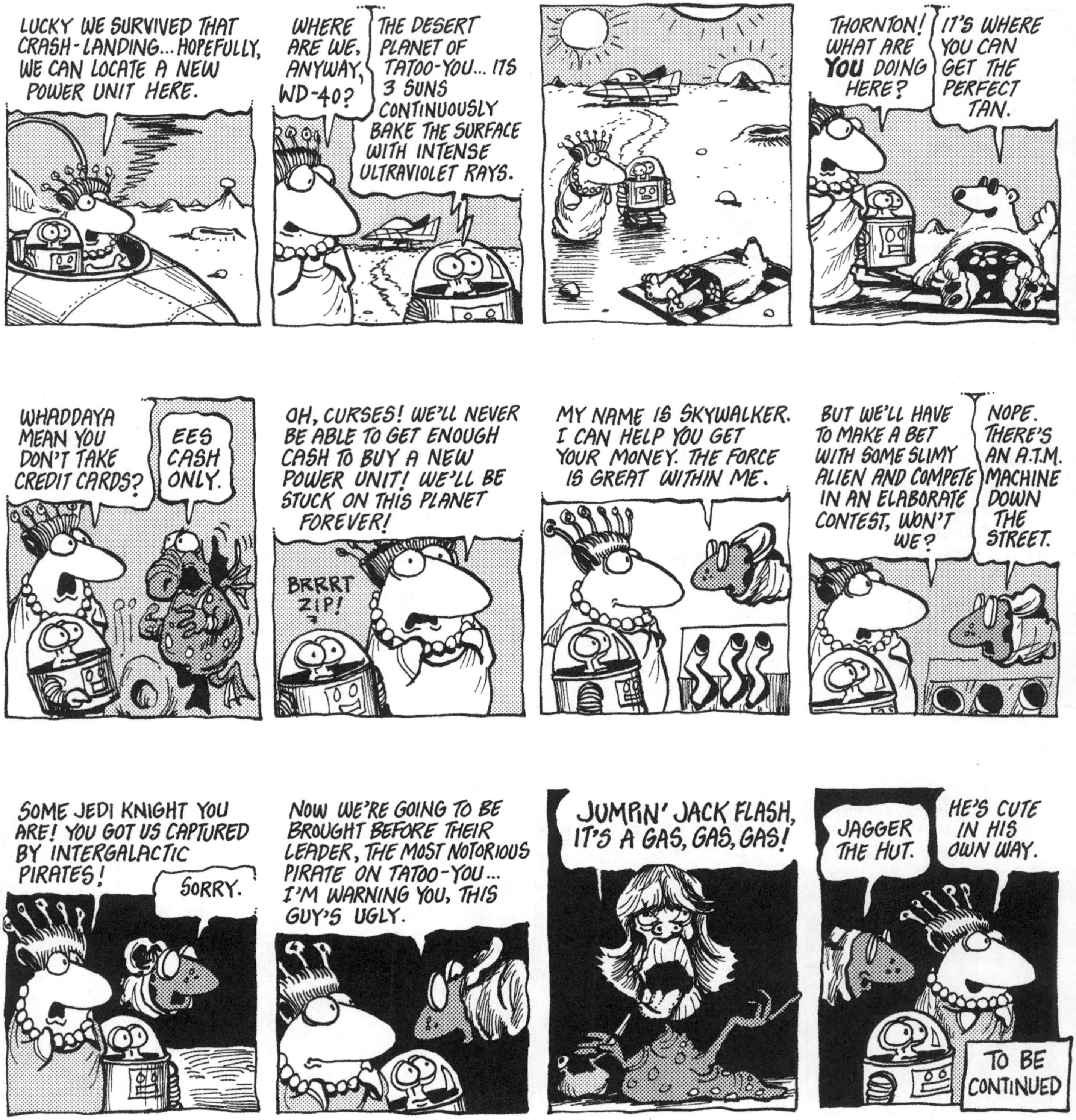
LUCKY WE SURVIVED THAT CRASH-LANDING... HOPEFULLY, WE CAN LOCATE A NEW POWER UNIT HERE.
WHERE ARE WE, ANYWAY, WD-40?
THE DESERT PLANET OF TATOO-YOU... ITS 3 SUNS CONTINUOUSLY BAKE THE SURFACE WITH INTENSE ULTRAVIOLET RAYS.
THORNTON! WHAT ARE **YOU** DOING HERE?
IT'S WHERE YOU CAN GET THE PERFECT TAN.
WHADDAYA MEAN YOU DON'T TAKE CREDIT CARDS?
EES CASH ONLY.
OH, CURSES! WE'LL NEVER BE ABLE TO GET ENOUGH CASH TO BUY A NEW POWER UNIT! WE'LL BE STUCK ON THIS PLANET FOREVER!
BRRRT ZIP!
MY NAME IS SKYWALKER. I CAN HELP YOU GET YOUR MONEY. THE FORCE IS GREAT WITHIN ME.
BUT WE'LL HAVE TO MAKE A BET WITH SOME SLIMY ALIEN AND COMPETE IN AN ELABORATE CONTEST, WON'T WE?
NOPE. THERE'S AN A.T.M. MACHINE DOWN THE STREET.
SOME JEDI KNIGHT YOU ARE! YOU GOT US CAPTURED BY INTERGALACTIC PIRATES!
SORRY.
NOW WE'RE GOING TO BE BROUGHT BEFORE THEIR LEADER, THE MOST NOTORIOUS PIRATE ON TATOO-YOU... I'M WARNING YOU, THIS GUY'S UGLY.
JUMPIN' JACK FLASH, IT'S A GAS, GAS, GAS!
JAGGER THE HUT.
HE'S CUTE IN HIS OWN WAY.
TO BE CONTINUED

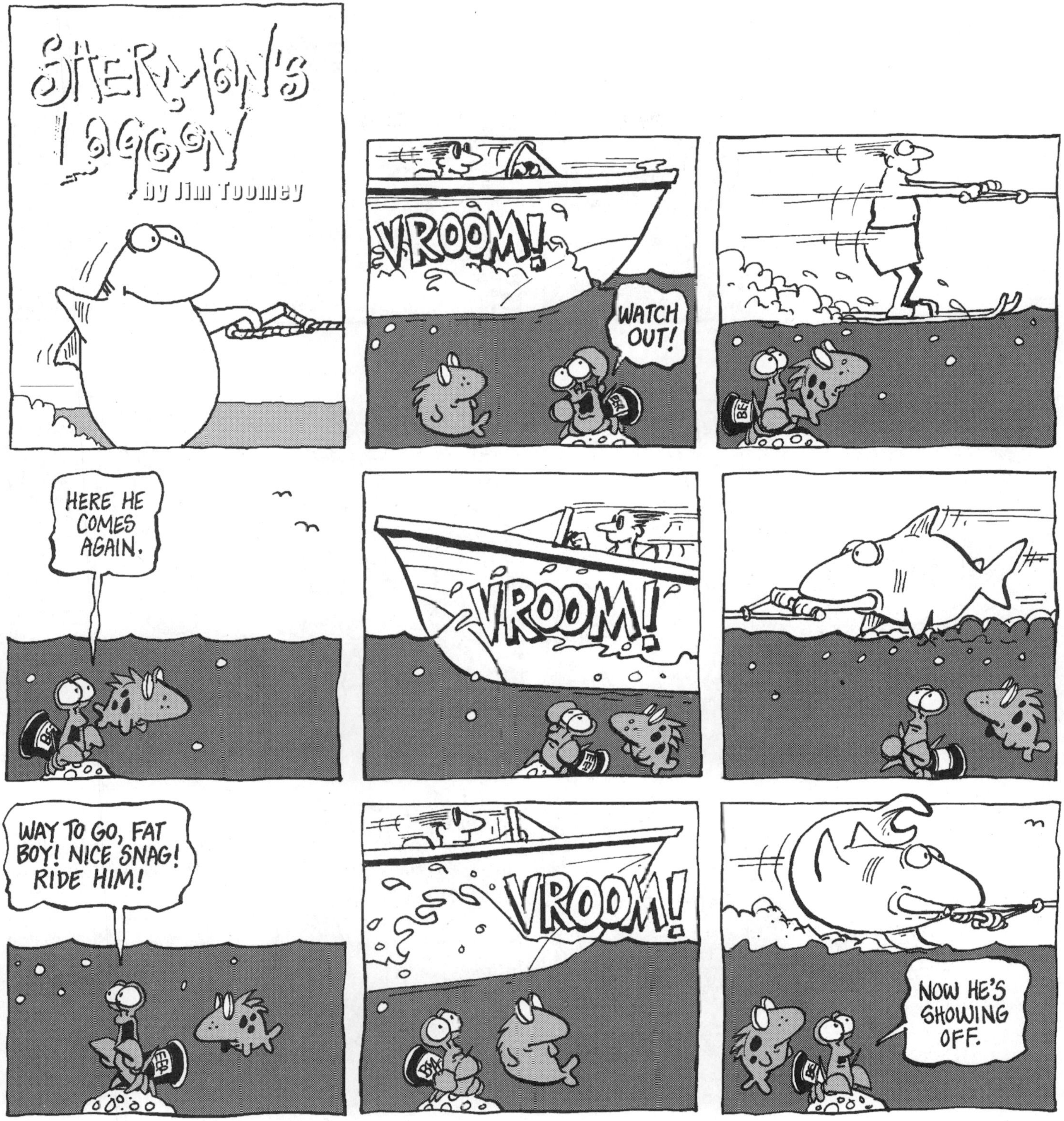
SHERMAN'S LAGOON
by Jim Toomey
VROOM!
WATCH OUT!
HERE HE COMES AGAIN.
VROOM!
WAY TO GO, FAT BOY! NICE SNAG! RIDE HIM!
VROOM!
NOW HE'S SHOWING OFF.

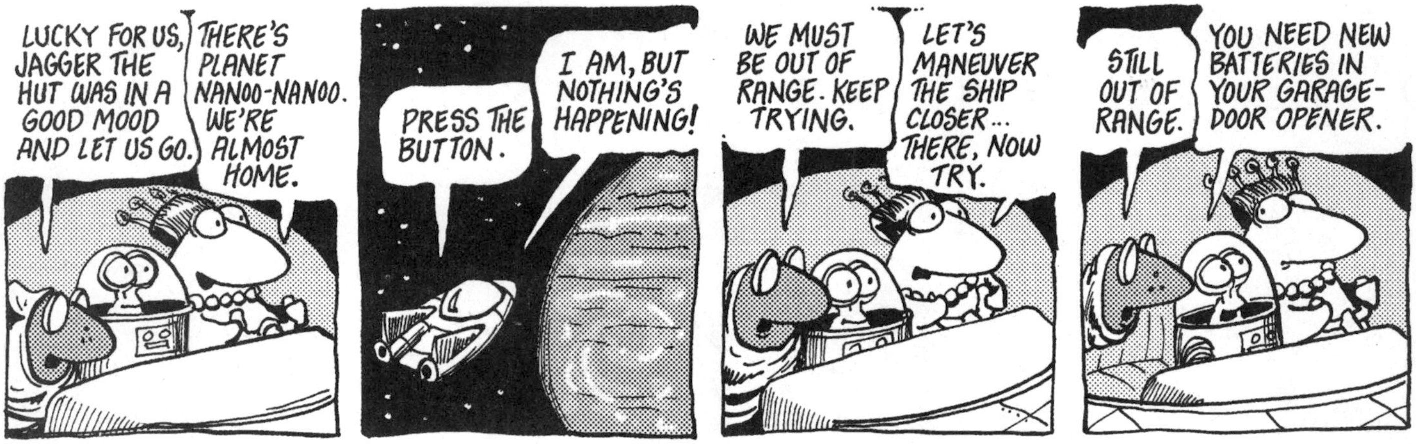
LUCKY FOR US, JAGGER THE HUT WAS IN A GOOD MOOD AND LET US GO.
THERE'S PLANET NANOO-NANOO. WE'RE ALMOST HOME.
PRESS THE BUTTON.
I AM, BUT NOTHING'S HAPPENING!
WE MUST BE OUT OF RANGE. KEEP TRYING.
LET'S MANEUVER THE SHIP CLOSER... THERE, NOW TRY.
STILL OUT OF RANGE.
YOU NEED NEW BATTERIES IN YOUR GARAGE-DOOR OPENER.

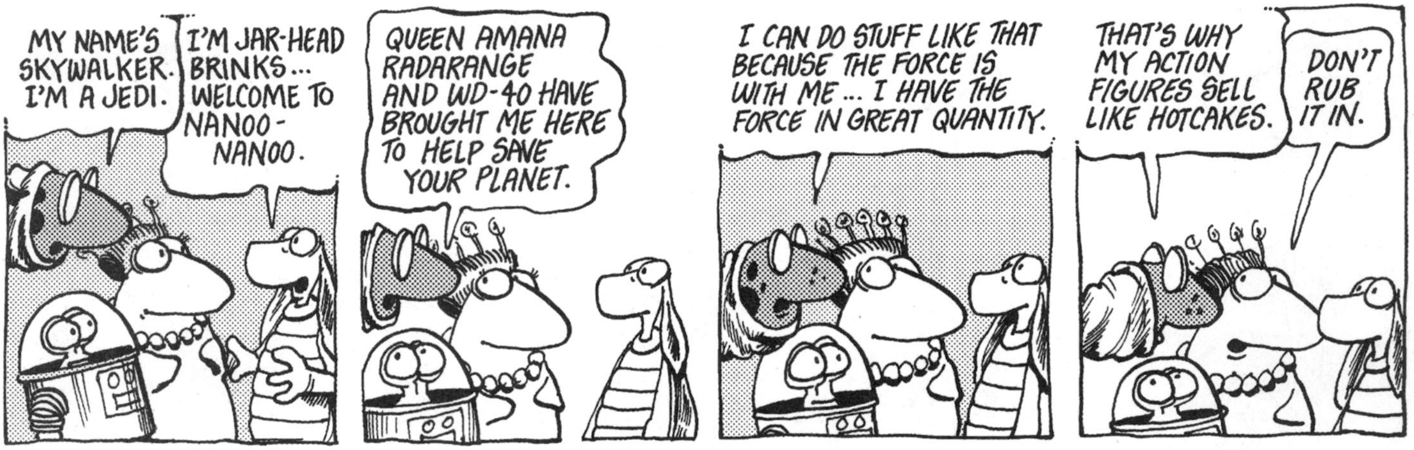
MY NAME'S SKYWALKER. I'M A JEDI.
I'M JAR-HEAD BRINKS... WELCOME TO NANOO-NANOO.
QUEEN AMANA RADARANGE AND WD-40 HAVE BROUGHT ME HERE TO HELP SAVE YOUR PLANET.
I CAN DO STUFF LIKE THAT BECAUSE THE FORCE IS WITH ME... I HAVE THE FORCE IN GREAT QUANTITY.
THAT'S WHY MY ACTION FIGURES SELL LIKE HOTCAKES.
DON'T RUB IT IN.

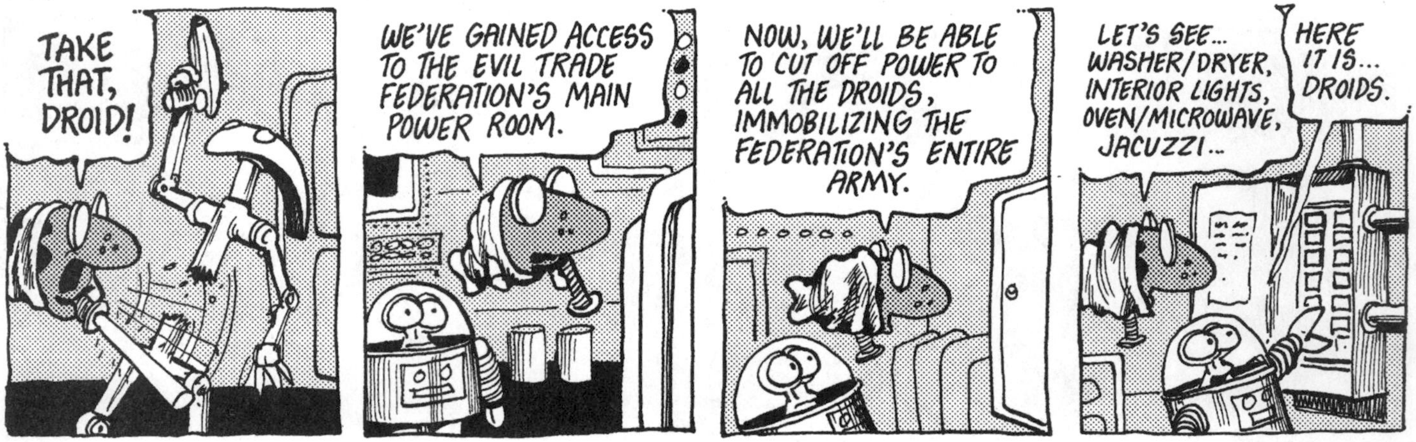
TAKE THAT, DROID!
WE'VE GAINED ACCESS TO THE EVIL TRADE FEDERATION'S MAIN POWER ROOM.
NOW, WE'LL BE ABLE TO CUT OFF POWER TO ALL THE DROIDS, IMMOBILIZING THE FEDERATION'S ENTIRE ARMY.
LET'S SEE... WASHER/DRYER, INTERIOR LIGHTS, OVEN/MICROWAVE, JACUZZI...
HERE IT IS... DROIDS.

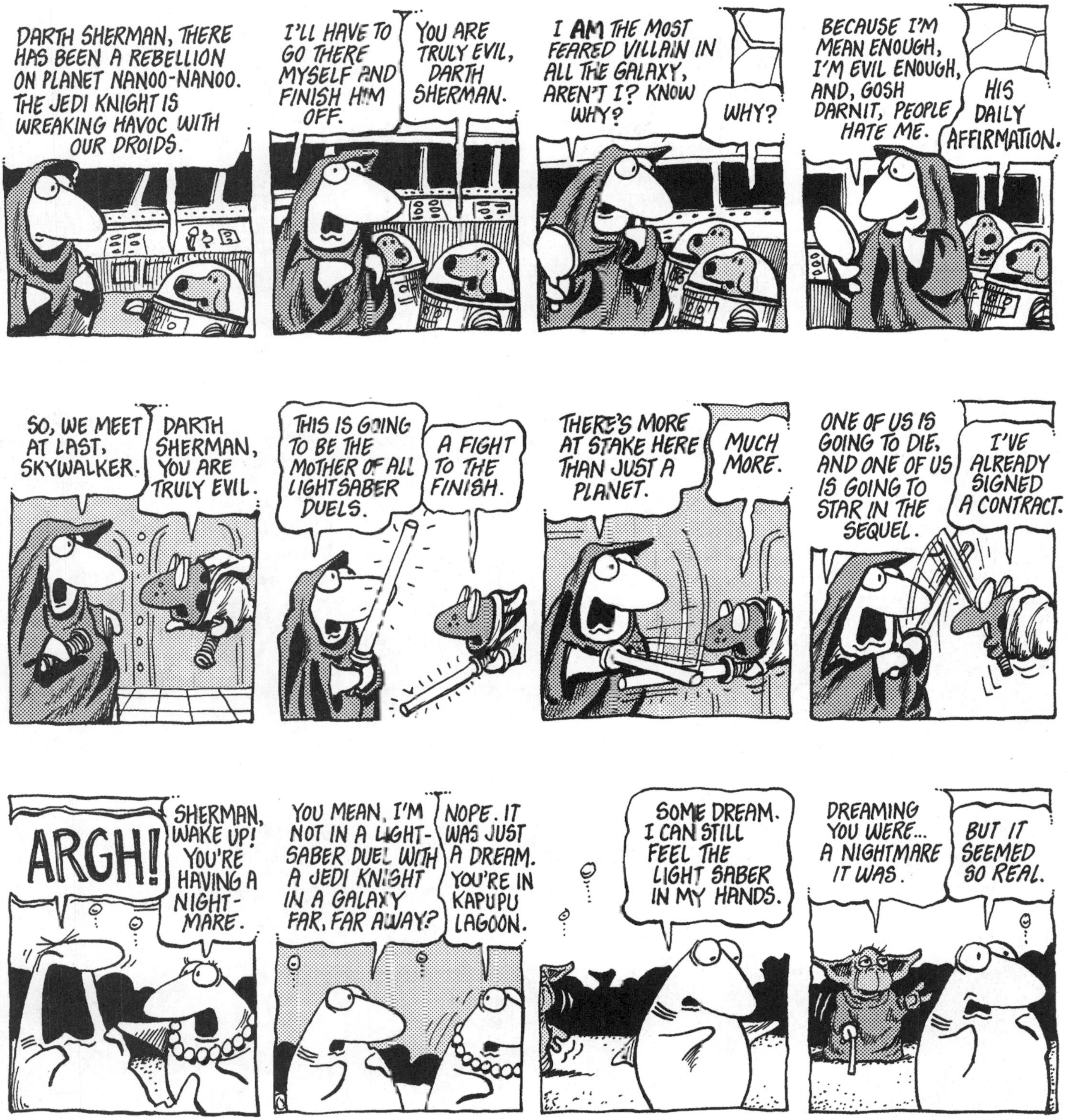
DARTH SHERMAN, THERE HAS BEEN A REBELLION ON PLANET NANOO-NANOO. THE JEDI KNIGHT IS WREAKING HAVOC WITH OUR DROIDS.
I'LL HAVE TO GO THERE MYSELF AND FINISH HIM OFF.
YOU ARE TRULY EVIL, DARTH SHERMAN.
I AM THE MOST FEARED VILLAIN IN ALL THE GALAXY, AREN'T I? KNOW WHY?
WHY?
BECAUSE I'M MEAN ENOUGH, I'M EVIL ENOUGH, AND, GOSH DARNIT, PEOPLE HATE ME.
HIS DAILY AFFIRMATION.
SO, WE MEET AT LAST, SKYWALKER.
DARTH SHERMAN, YOU ARE TRULY EVIL.
THIS IS GOING TO BE THE MOTHER OF ALL LIGHTSABER DUELS.
A FIGHT TO THE FINISH.
THERE'S MORE AT STAKE HERE THAN JUST A PLANET.
MUCH MORE.
ONE OF US IS GOING TO DIE, AND ONE OF US IS GOING TO STAR IN THE SEQUEL.
I'VE ALREADY SIGNED A CONTRACT.
ARGH!
SHERMAN, WAKE UP! YOU'RE HAVING A NIGHT-MARE.
YOU MEAN, I'M NOT IN A LIGHT-SABER DUEL WITH A JEDI KNIGHT IN A GALAXY FAR, FAR AWAY?
NOPE. IT WAS JUST A DREAM. YOU'RE IN KAPUPU LAGOON.
SOME DREAM. I CAN STILL FEEL THE LIGHT SABER IN MY HANDS.
DREAMING YOU WERE... A NIGHTMARE IT WAS.
BUT IT SEEMED SO REAL.

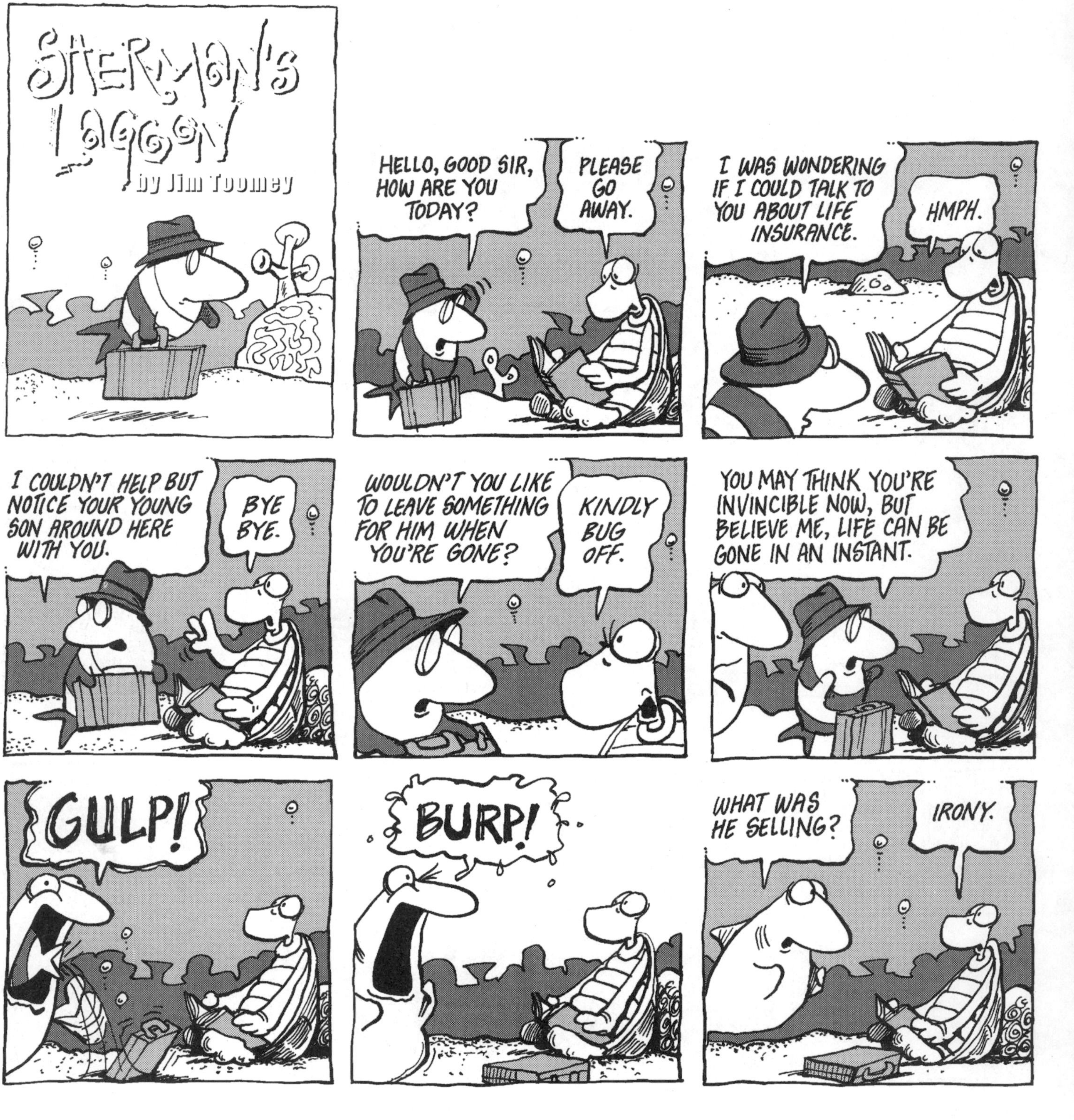
SHERMAN'S LAGOON
by Jim Toomey
HELLO, GOOD SIR, HOW ARE YOU TODAY?
PLEASE GO AWAY.
I WAS WONDERING IF I COULD TALK TO YOU ABOUT LIFE INSURANCE.
HMPH.
I COULDN'T HELP BUT NOTICE YOUR YOUNG SON AROUND HERE WITH YOU.
BYE BYE.
WOULDN'T YOU LIKE TO LEAVE SOMETHING FOR HIM WHEN YOU'RE GONE?
KINDLY BUG OFF.
YOU MAY THINK YOU'RE INVINCIBLE NOW, BUT BELIEVE ME, LIFE CAN BE GONE IN AN INSTANT.
GULP!
BURP!
WHAT WAS HE SELLING?
IRONY.

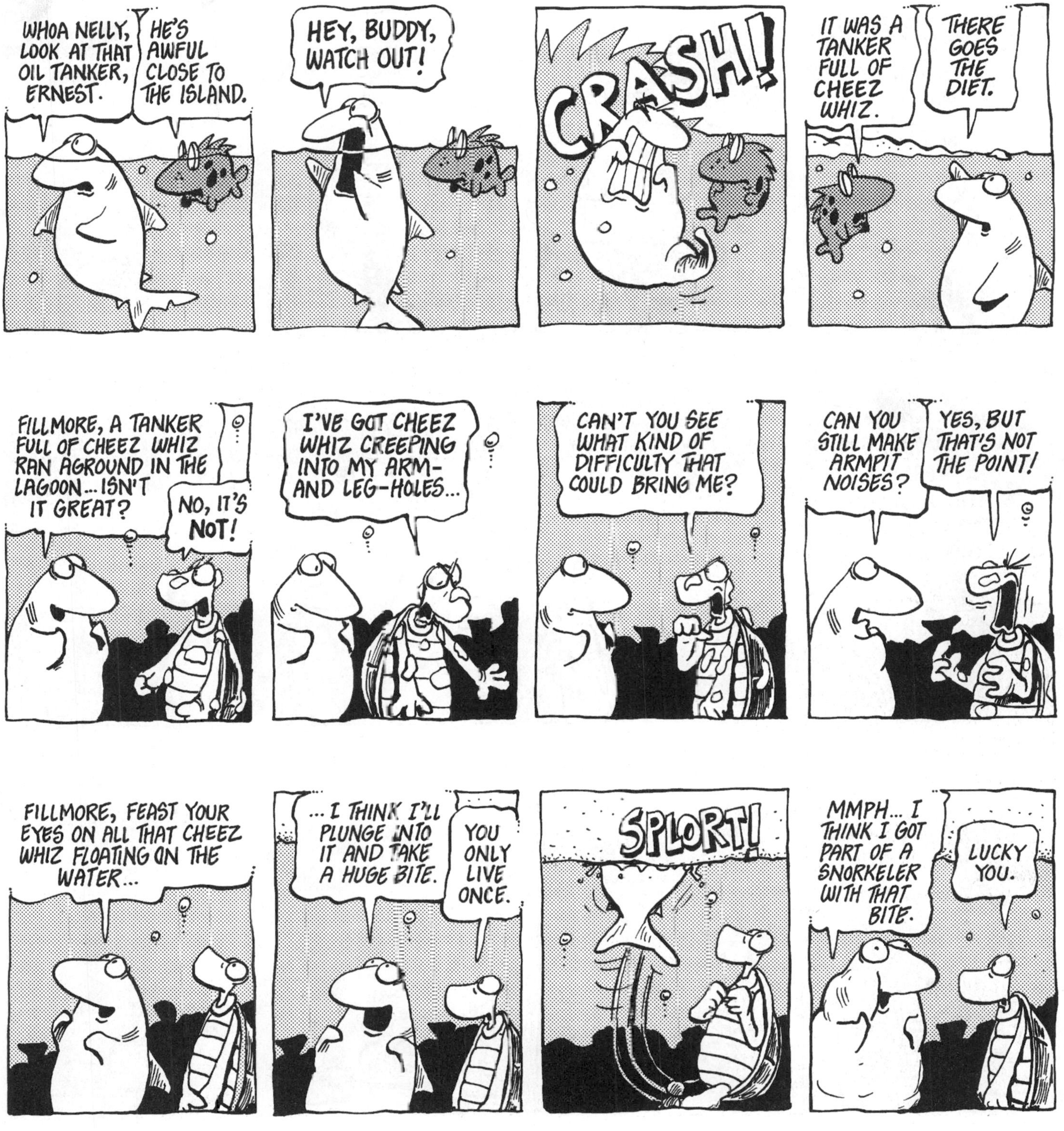
WHOA NELLY, LOOK AT THAT OIL TANKER, ERNEST.
HE'S AWFUL CLOSE TO THE ISLAND.
HEY, BUDDY, WATCH OUT!
CRASH!
IT WAS A TANKER FULL OF CHEEZ WHIZ.
THERE GOES THE DIET.
FILLMORE, A TANKER FULL OF CHEEZ WHIZ RAN AGROUND IN THE LAGOON... ISN'T IT GREAT?
NO, IT'S NOT!
I'VE GOT CHEEZ WHIZ CREEPING INTO MY ARM- AND LEG-HOLES...
CAN'T YOU SEE WHAT KIND OF DIFFICULTY THAT COULD BRING ME?
CAN YOU STILL MAKE ARMPIT NOISES?
YES, BUT THAT'S NOT THE POINT!
FILLMORE, FEAST YOUR EYES ON ALL THAT CHEEZ WHIZ FLOATING ON THE WATER...
...I THINK I'LL PLUNGE INTO IT AND TAKE A HUGE BITE.
YOU ONLY LIVE ONCE.
SPLORT!
MMPH... I THINK I GOT PART OF A SNORKELER WITH THAT BITE.
LUCKY YOU.

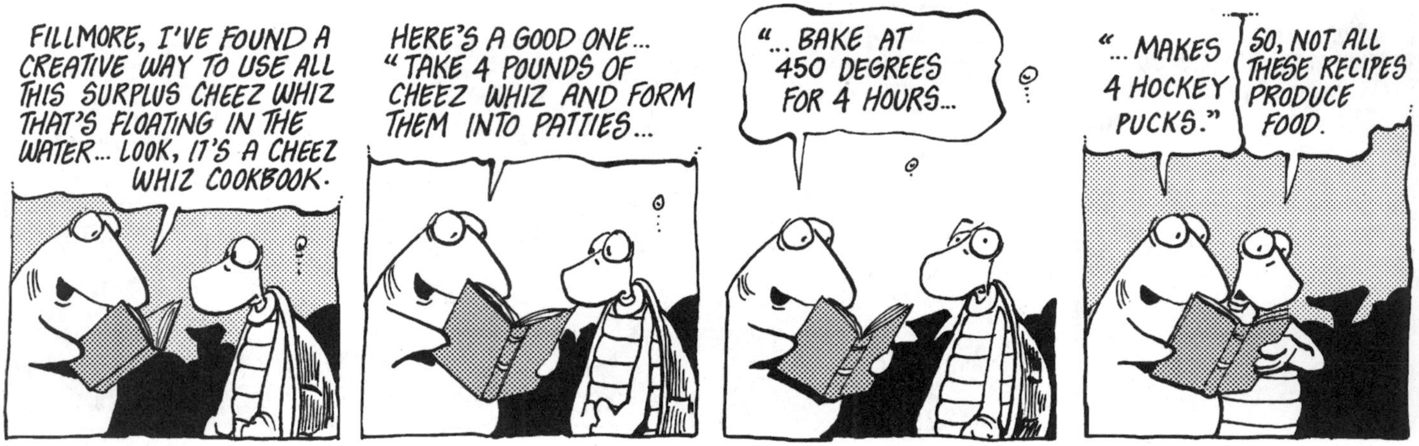
FILLMORE, I'VE FOUND A CREATIVE WAY TO USE ALL THIS SURPLUS CHEEZ WHIZ THAT'S FLOATING IN THE WATER... LOOK, IT'S A CHEEZ WHIZ COOKBOOK.
HERE'S A GOOD ONE... "TAKE 4 POUNDS OF CHEEZ WHIZ AND FORM THEM INTO PATTIES...
"... BAKE AT 450 DEGREES FOR 4 HOURS...
"... MAKES 4 HOCKEY PUCKS."
SO, NOT ALL THESE RECIPES PRODUCE FOOD.

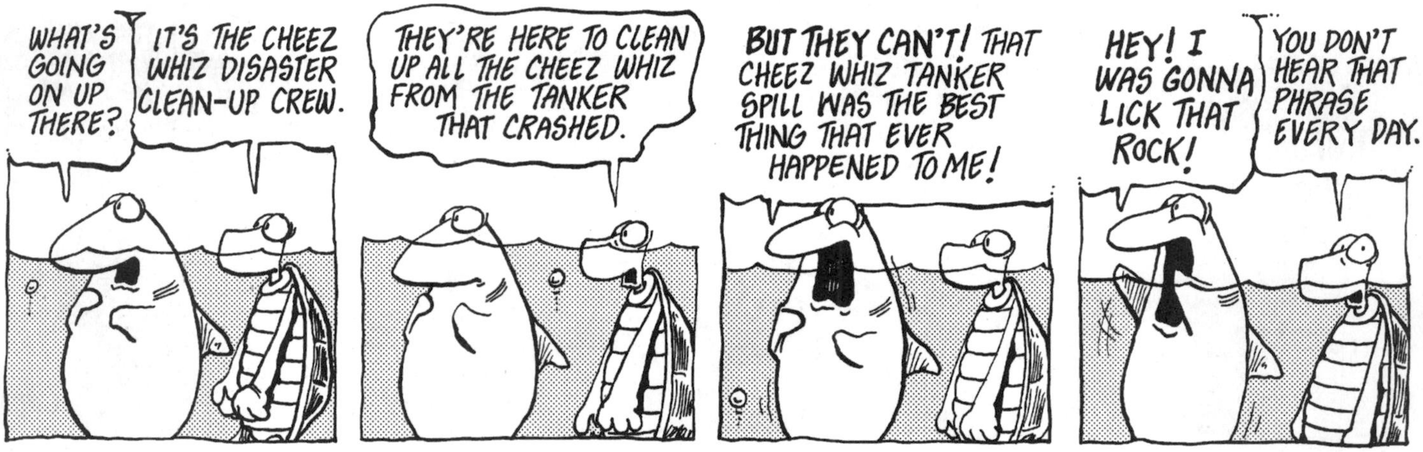
WHAT'S GOING ON UP THERE?
IT'S THE CHEEZ WHIZ DISASTER CLEAN-UP CREW.
THEY'RE HERE TO CLEAN UP ALL THE CHEEZ WHIZ FROM THE TANKER THAT CRASHED.
BUT THEY CAN'T! THAT CHEEZ WHIZ TANKER SPILL WAS THE BEST THING THAT EVER HAPPENED TO ME!
HEY! I WAS GONNA LICK THAT ROCK!
YOU DON'T HEAR THAT PHRASE EVERY DAY.

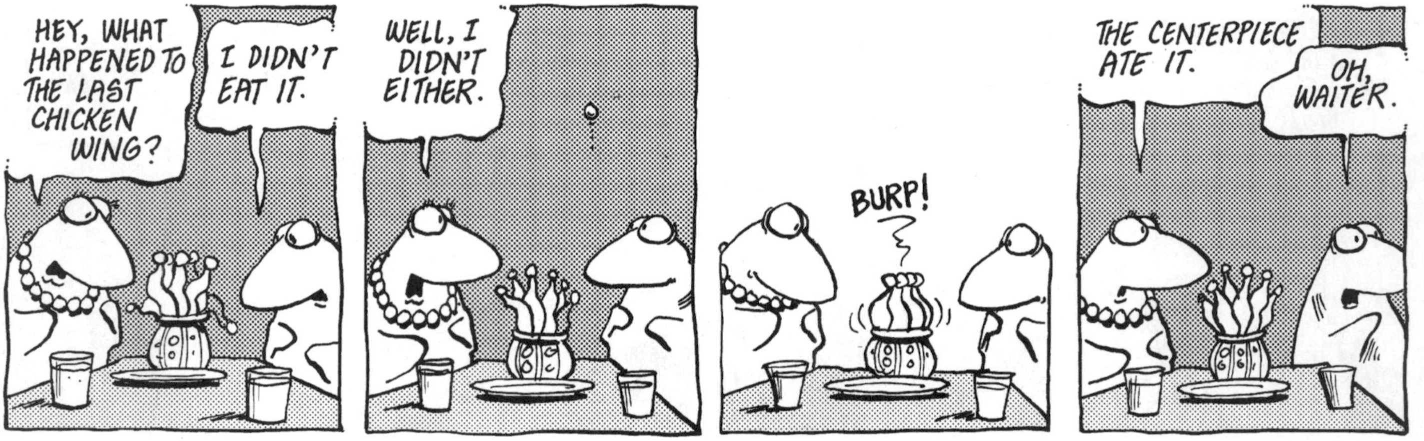
HEY, WHAT HAPPENED TO THE LAST CHICKEN WING?
I DIDN'T EAT IT.
WELL, I DIDN'T EITHER.
BURP!
THE CENTERPIECE ATE IT.
OH, WAITER.

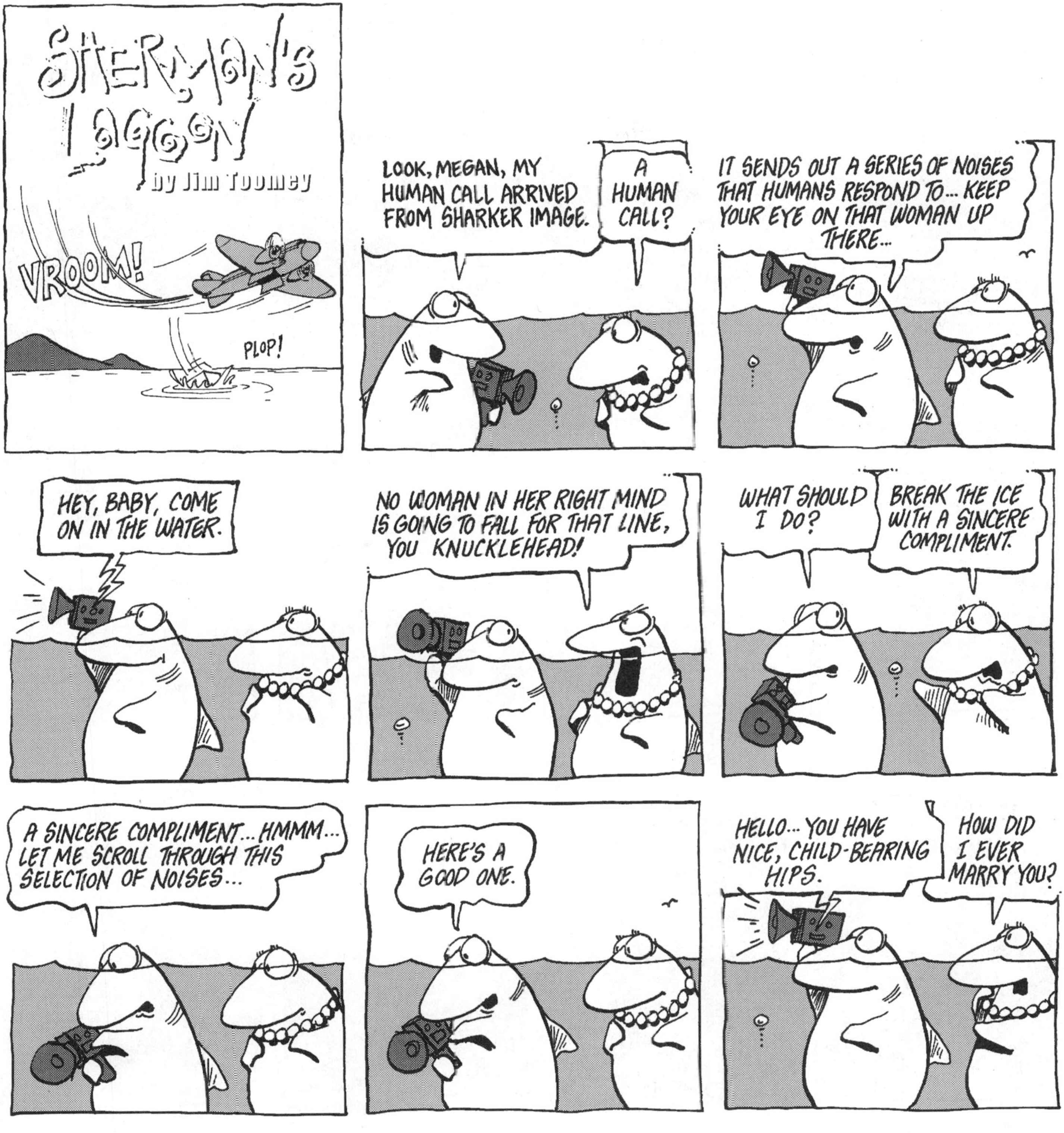
SHERMAN'S LAGOON
by Jim Toomey
VROOM!
PLOP!
LOOK, MEGAN, MY HUMAN CALL ARRIVED FROM SHARKER IMAGE.
A HUMAN CALL?
IT SENDS OUT A SERIES OF NOISES THAT HUMANS RESPOND TO... KEEP YOUR EYE ON THAT WOMAN UP THERE...
HEY, BABY, COME ON IN THE WATER.
NO WOMAN IN HER RIGHT MIND IS GOING TO FALL FOR THAT LINE, YOU KNUCKLEHEAD!
WHAT SHOULD I DO?
BREAK THE ICE WITH A SINCERE COMPLIMENT.
A SINCERE COMPLIMENT... HMMM... LET ME SCROLL THROUGH THIS SELECTION OF NOISES...
HERE'S A GOOD ONE.
HELLO... YOU HAVE NICE, CHILD-BEARING HIPS.
HOW DID I EVER MARRY YOU?

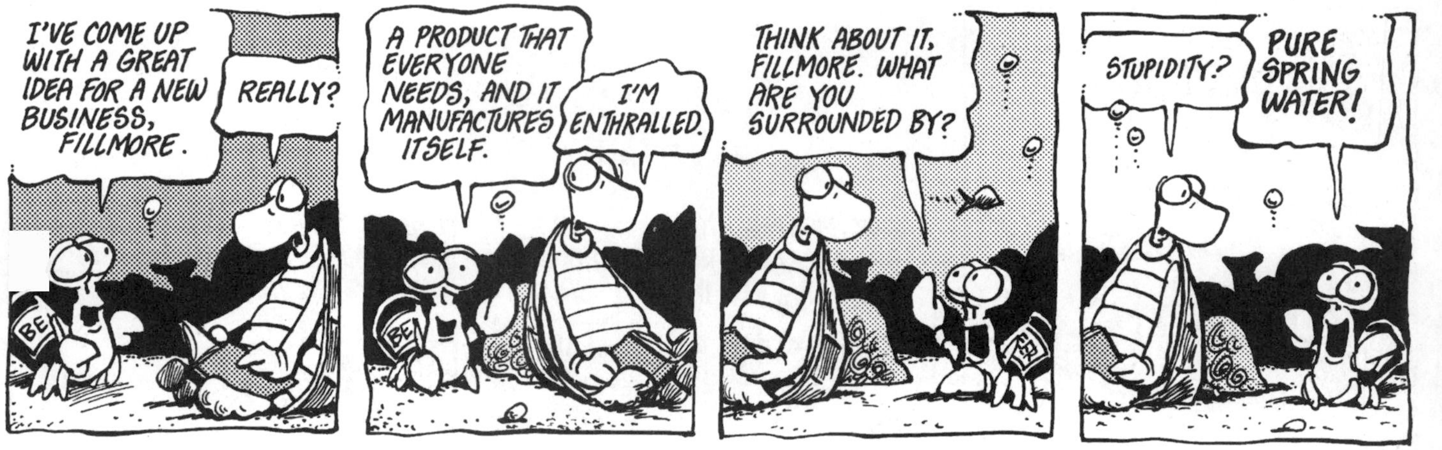
I'VE COME UP WITH A GREAT IDEA FOR A NEW BUSINESS, FILLMORE.
REALLY?
A PRODUCT THAT EVERYONE NEEDS, AND IT MANUFACTURES ITSELF.
I'M ENTHRALLED.
THINK ABOUT IT, FILLMORE. WHAT ARE YOU SURROUNDED BY?
STUPIDITY?
PURE SPRING WATER!

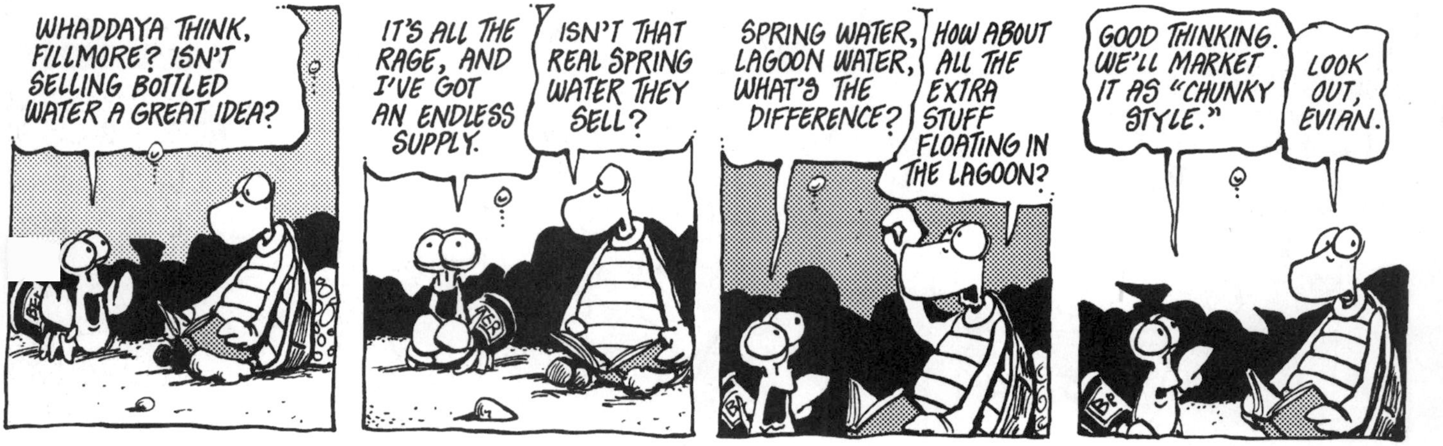
WHADDAYA THINK, FILLMORE? ISN'T SELLING BOTTLED WATER A GREAT IDEA?
IT'S ALL THE RAGE, AND I'VE GOT AN ENDLESS SUPPLY.
ISN'T THAT REAL SPRING WATER THEY SELL?
SPRING WATER, LAGOON WATER, WHAT'S THE DIFFERENCE?
HOW ABOUT ALL THE EXTRA STUFF FLOATING IN THE LAGOON?
GOOD THINKING. WE'LL MARKET IT AS "CHUNKY STYLE."
LOOK OUT, EVIAN.

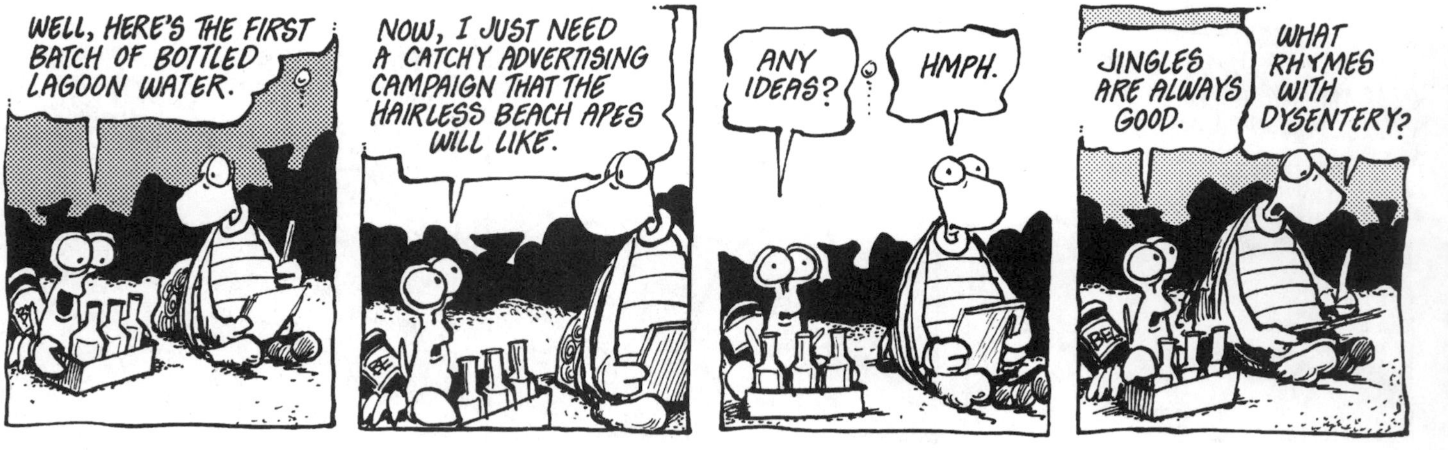
WELL, HERE'S THE FIRST BATCH OF BOTTLED LAGOON WATER.
NOW, I JUST NEED A CATCHY ADVERTISING CAMPAIGN THAT THE HAIRLESS BEACH APES WILL LIKE.
ANY IDEAS?
HMPH.
JINGLES ARE ALWAYS GOOD.
WHAT RHYMES WITH DYSENTERY?

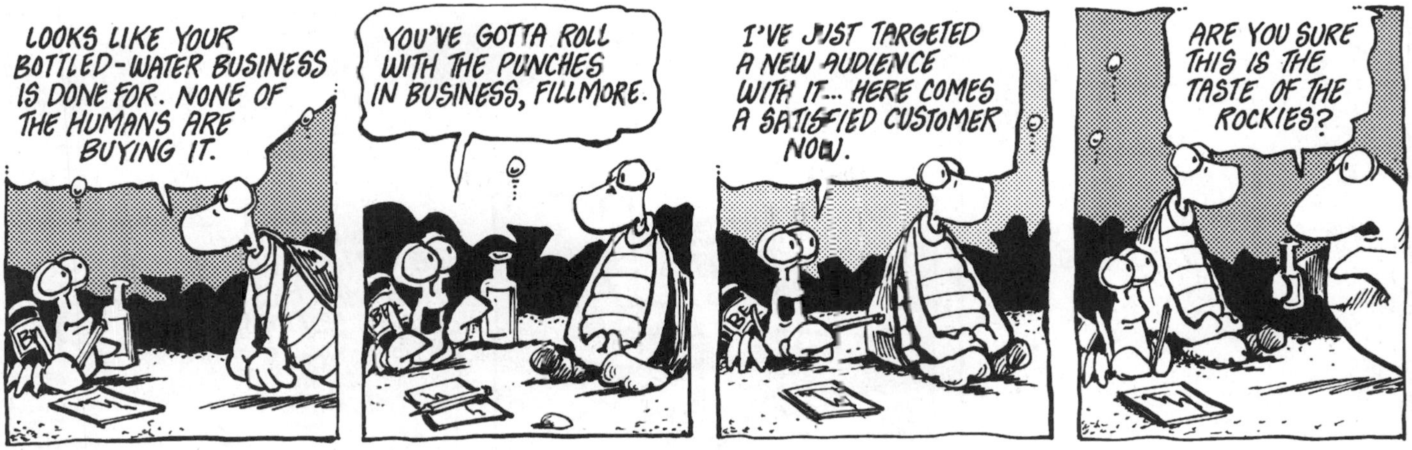
LOOKS LIKE YOUR BOTTLED-WATER BUSINESS IS DONE FOR. NONE OF THE HUMANS ARE BUYING IT.
YOU'VE GOTTA ROLL WITH THE PUNCHES IN BUSINESS, FILLMORE.
I'VE JUST TARGETED A NEW AUDIENCE WITH IT... HERE COMES A SATISFIED CUSTOMER NOW.
ARE YOU SURE THIS IS THE TASTE OF THE ROCKIES?

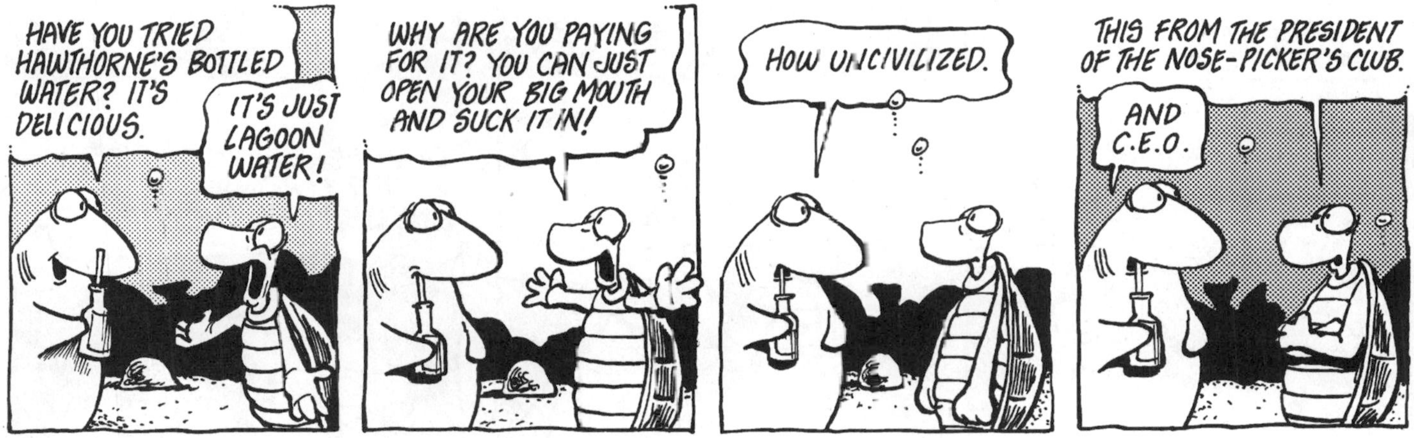
HAVE YOU TRIED HAWTHORNE'S BOTTLED WATER? IT'S DELICIOUS.
IT'S JUST LAGOON WATER!
WHY ARE YOU PAYING FOR IT? YOU CAN JUST OPEN YOUR BIG MOUTH AND SUCK IT IN!
HOW UNCIVILIZED.
THIS FROM THE PRESIDENT OF THE NOSE-PICKER'S CLUB.
AND C.E.O.

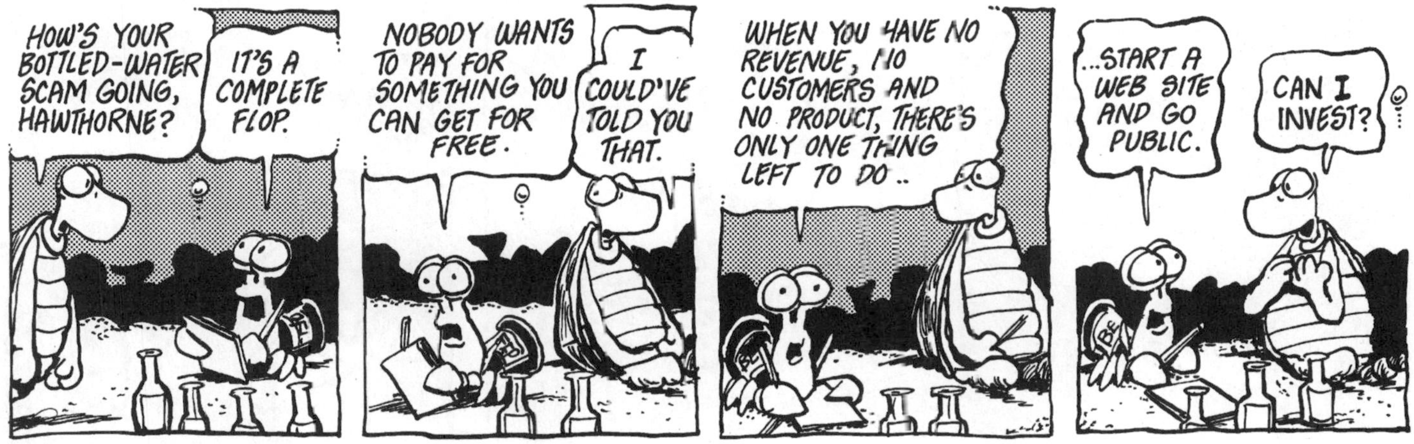
HOW'S YOUR BOTTLED-WATER SCAM GOING, HAWTHORNE?
IT'S A COMPLETE FLOP.
NOBODY WANTS TO PAY FOR SOMETHING YOU CAN GET FOR FREE.
I COULD'VE TOLD YOU THAT.
WHEN YOU HAVE NO REVENUE, NO CUSTOMERS AND NO PRODUCT, THERE'S ONLY ONE THING LEFT TO DO..
...START A WEB SITE AND GO PUBLIC.
CAN I INVEST?

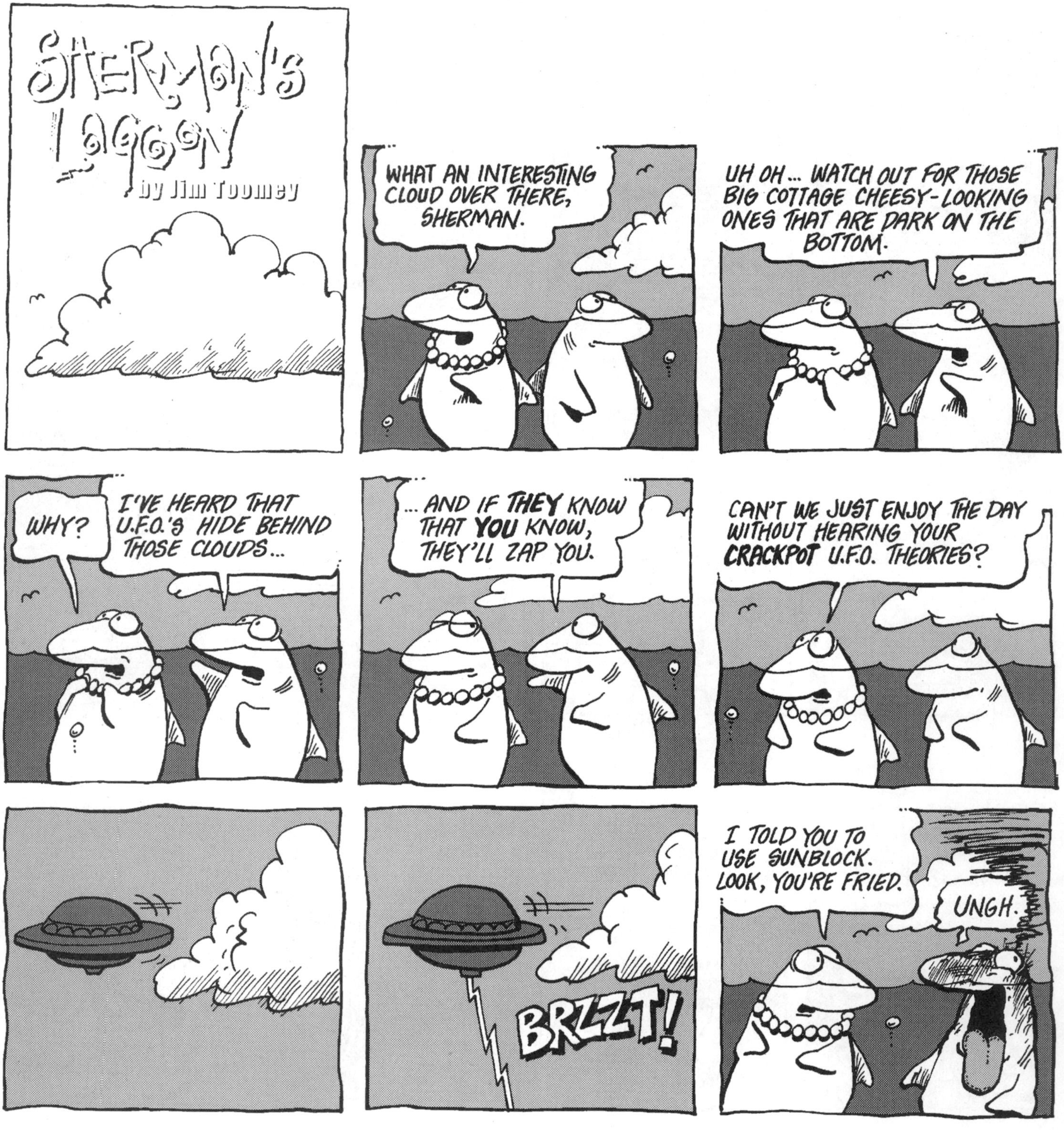
SHERMAN'S LAGOON
by Jim Toomey
WHAT AN INTERESTING CLOUD OVER THERE, SHERMAN.
UH OH... WATCH OUT FOR THOSE BIG COTTAGE CHEESY-LOOKING ONES THAT ARE DARK ON THE BOTTOM.
WHY?
I'VE HEARD THAT U.F.O.'S HIDE BEHIND THOSE CLOUDS...
...AND IF THEY KNOW THAT YOU KNOW, THEY'LL ZAP YOU.
CAN'T WE JUST ENJOY THE DAY WITHOUT HEARING YOUR CRACKPOT U.F.O. THEORIES?
BRZZT!
I TOLD YOU TO USE SUNBLOCK. LOOK, YOU'RE FRIED.
UNGH.

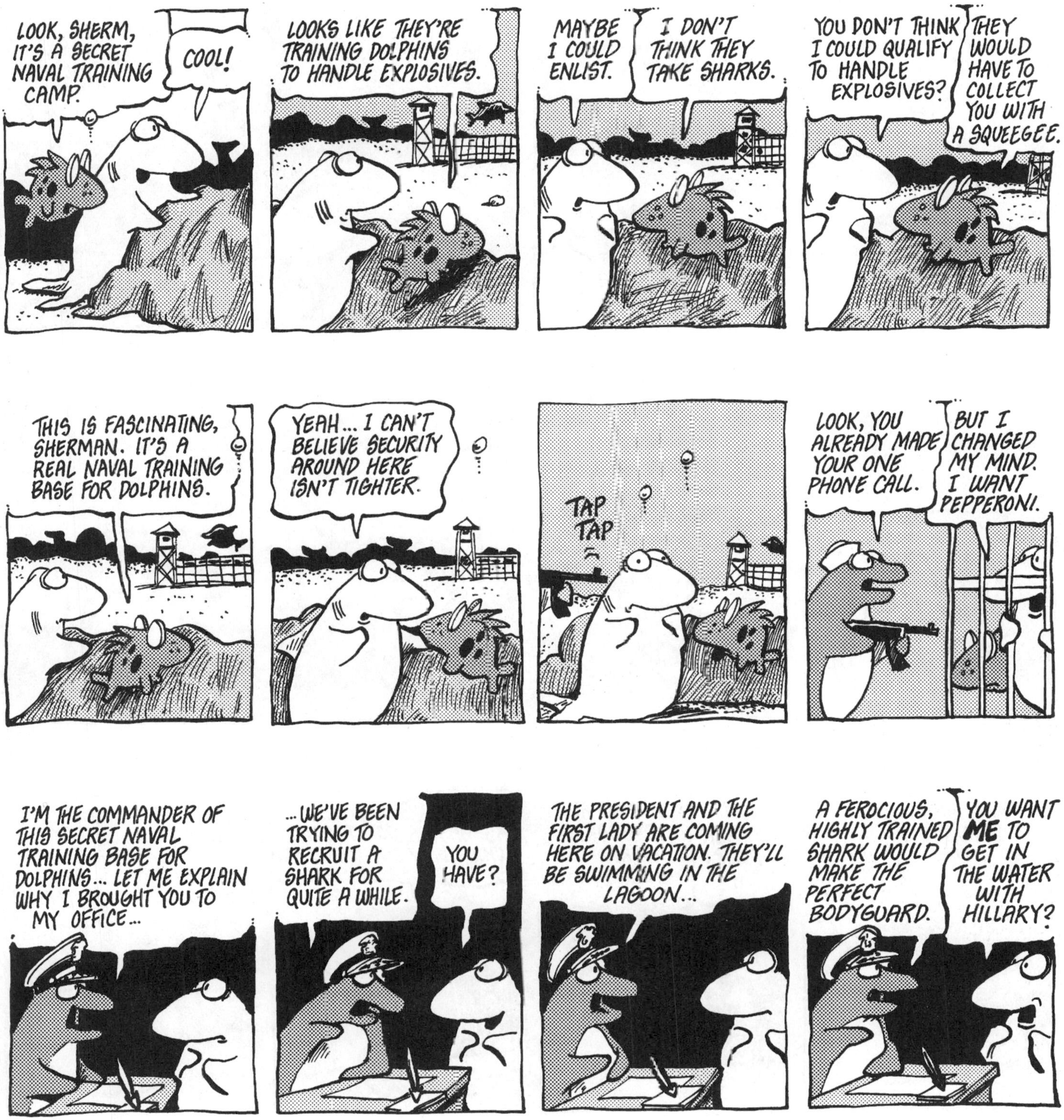
LOOK, SHERM, IT'S A SECRET NAVAL TRAINING CAMP.
COOL!
LOOKS LIKE THEY'RE TRAINING DOLPHINS TO HANDLE EXPLOSIVES.
MAYBE I COULD ENLIST.
I DON'T THINK THEY TAKE SHARKS.
YOU DON'T THINK I COULD QUALIFY TO HANDLE EXPLOSIVES?
THEY WOULD HAVE TO COLLECT YOU WITH A SQUEEGEE.
THIS IS FASCINATING, SHERMAN. IT'S A REAL NAVAL TRAINING BASE FOR DOLPHINS.
YEAH... I CAN'T BELIEVE SECURITY AROUND HERE ISN'T TIGHTER.
TAP TAP
LOOK, YOU ALREADY MADE YOUR ONE PHONE CALL.
BUT I CHANGED MY MIND. I WANT PEPPERONI.
I'M THE COMMANDER OF THIS SECRET NAVAL TRAINING BASE FOR DOLPHINS... LET ME EXPLAIN WHY I BROUGHT YOU TO MY OFFICE...
...WE'VE BEEN TRYING TO RECRUIT A SHARK FOR QUITE A WHILE.
YOU HAVE?
THE PRESIDENT AND THE FIRST LADY ARE COMING HERE ON VACATION. THEY'LL BE SWIMMING IN THE LAGOON...
A FEROCIOUS, HIGHLY TRAINED SHARK WOULD MAKE THE PERFECT BODYGUARD.
YOU WANT ME TO GET IN THE WATER WITH HILLARY?

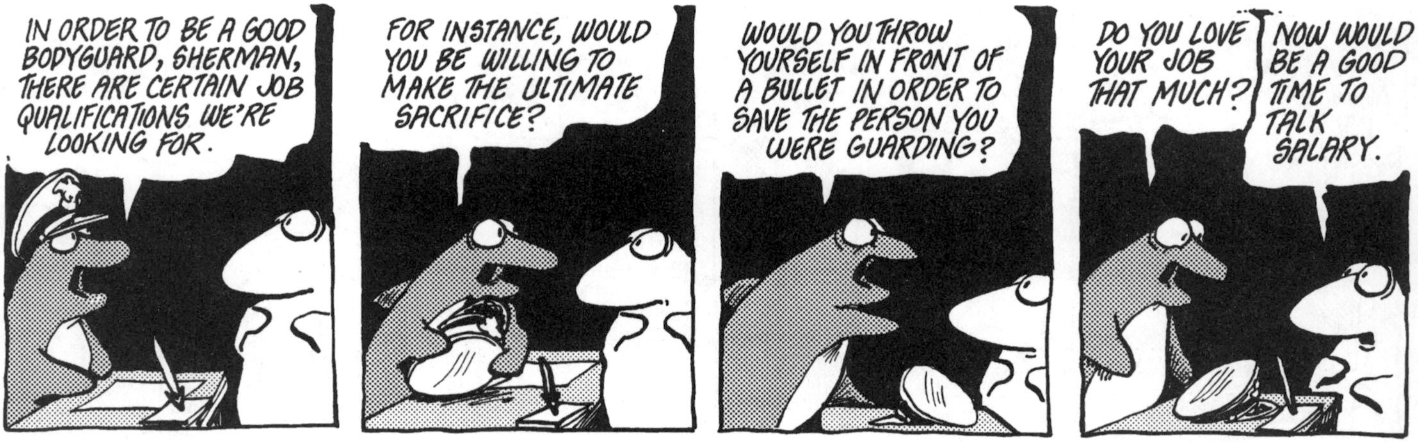
IN ORDER TO BE A GOOD BODYGUARD, SHERMAN, THERE ARE CERTAIN JOB QUALIFICATIONS WE'RE LOOKING FOR.
FOR INSTANCE, WOULD YOU BE WILLING TO MAKE THE ULTIMATE SACRIFICE?
WOULD YOU THROW YOURSELF IN FRONT OF A BULLET IN ORDER TO SAVE THE PERSON YOU WERE GUARDING?
DO YOU LOVE YOUR JOB THAT MUCH?
NOW WOULD BE A GOOD TIME TO TALK SALARY.

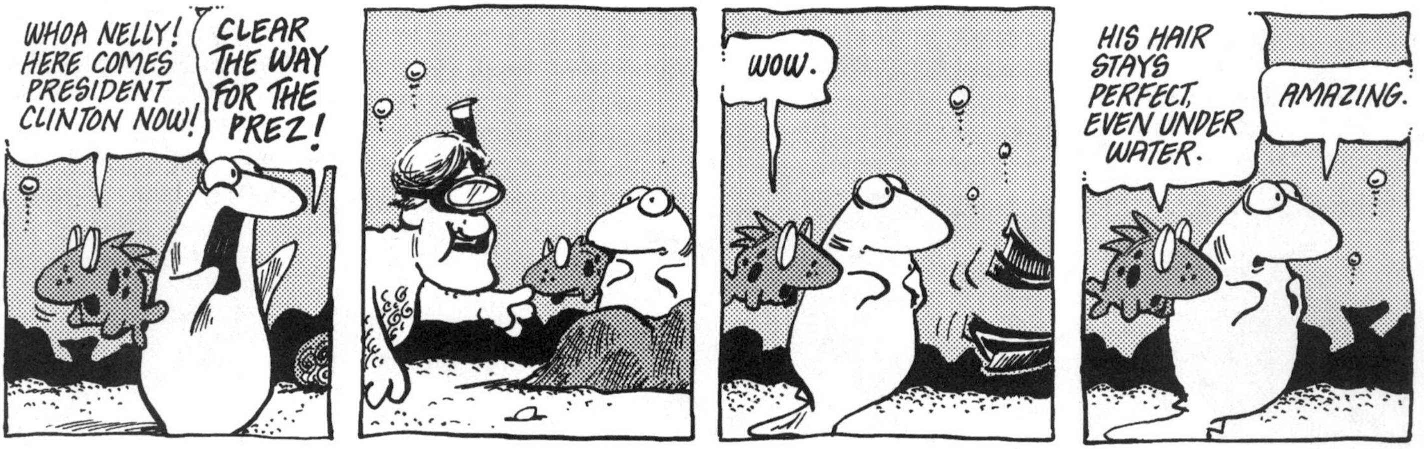
WHOA NELLY! HERE COMES PRESIDENT CLINTON NOW!
CLEAR THE WAY FOR THE PREZ!
WOW.
HIS HAIR STAYS PERFECT, EVEN UNDER WATER.
AMAZING.

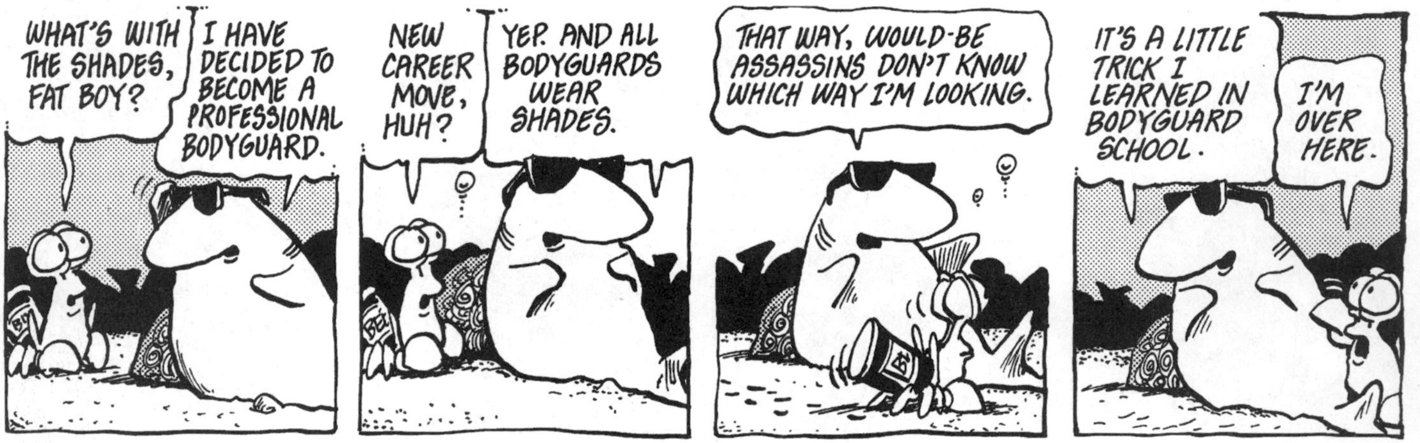
WHAT'S WITH THE SHADES, FAT BOY?
I HAVE DECIDED TO BECOME A PROFESSIONAL BODYGUARD.
NEW CAREER MOVE, HUH?
YEP. AND ALL BODYGUARDS WEAR SHADES.
THAT WAY, WOULD-BE ASSASSINS DON'T KNOW WHICH WAY I'M LOOKING.
IT'S A LITTLE TRICK I LEARNED IN BODYGUARD SCHOOL.
I'M OVER HERE.

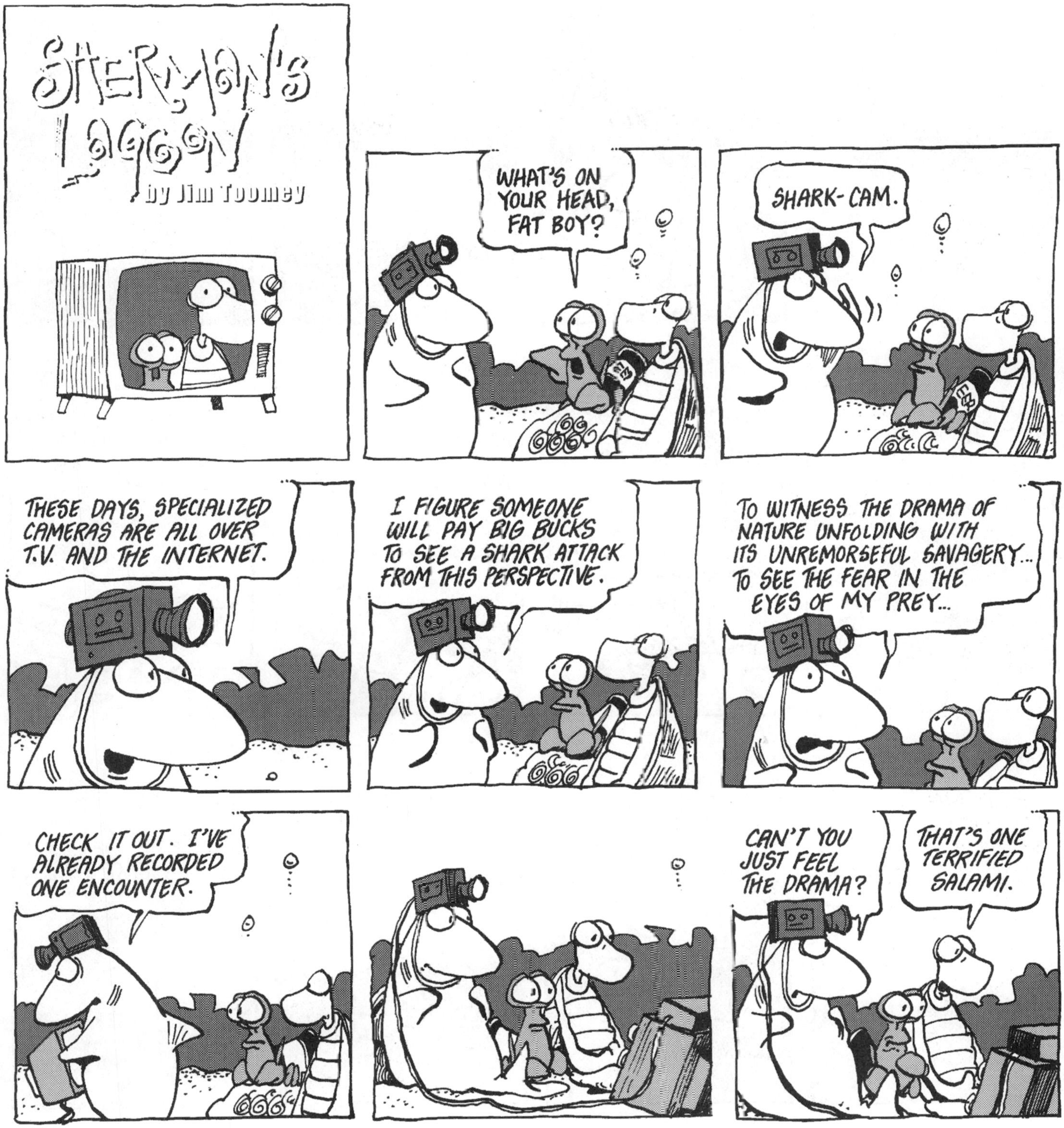
SHERMAN'S LAGOON
by Jim Toomey
WHAT'S ON YOUR HEAD, FAT BOY?
SHARK-CAM.
THESE DAYS, SPECIALIZED CAMERAS ARE ALL OVER T.V. AND THE INTERNET.
I FIGURE SOMEONE WILL PAY BIG BUCKS TO SEE A SHARK ATTACK FROM THIS PERSPECTIVE.
TO WITNESS THE DRAMA OF NATURE UNFOLDING WITH ITS UNREMORSEFUL SAVAGERY... TO SEE THE FEAR IN THE EYES OF MY PREY...
CHECK IT OUT. I'VE ALREADY RECORDED ONE ENCOUNTER.
CAN'T YOU JUST FEEL THE DRAMA?
THAT'S ONE TERRIFIED SALAMI.

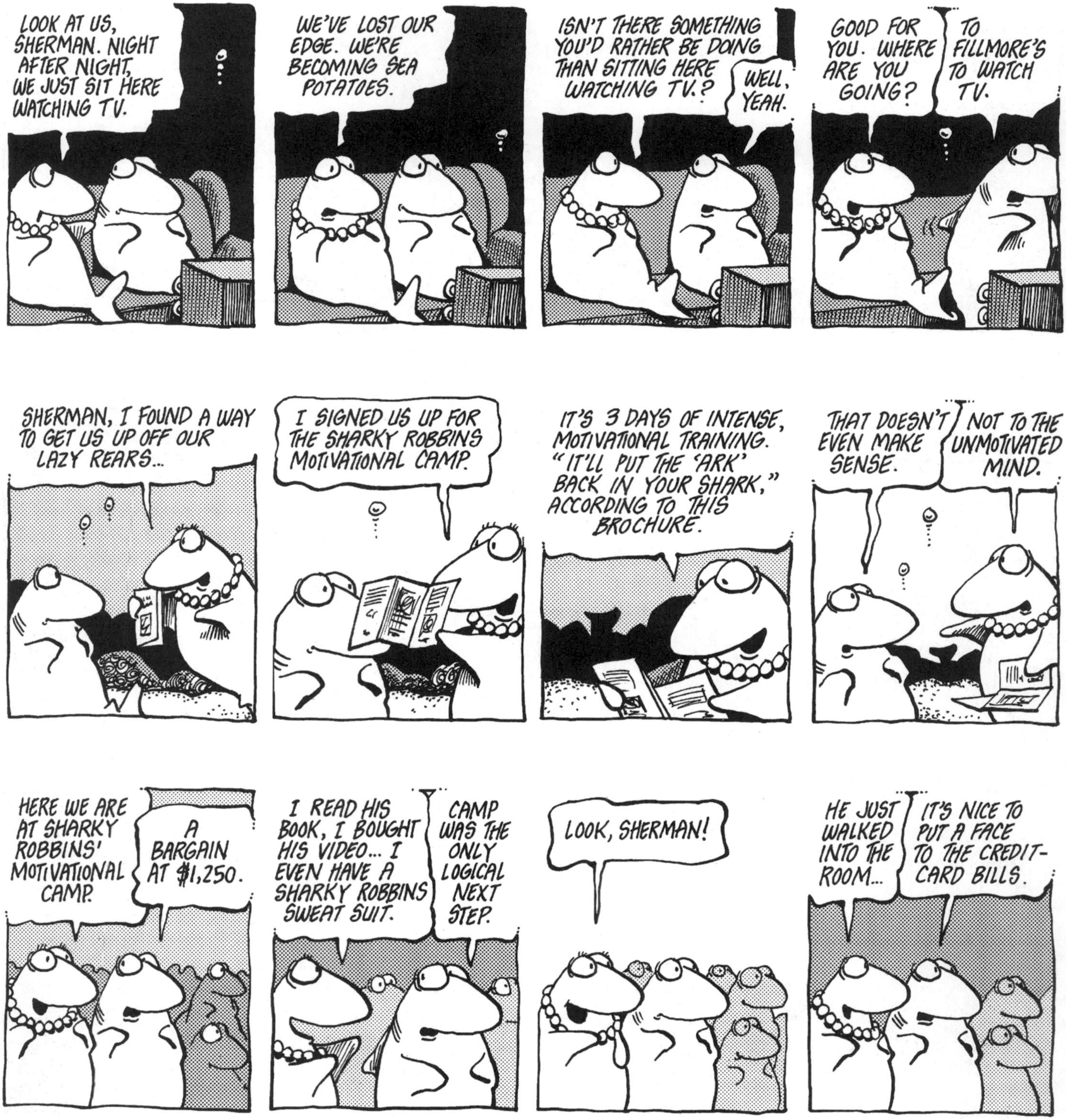
LOOK AT US, SHERMAN. NIGHT AFTER NIGHT, WE JUST SIT HERE WATCHING TV.
WE'VE LOST OUR EDGE. WE'RE BECOMING SEA POTATOES.
ISN'T THERE SOMETHING YOU'D RATHER BE DOING THAN SITTING HERE WATCHING TV.?
WELL, YEAH.
GOOD FOR YOU. WHERE ARE YOU GOING?
TO FILLMORE'S TO WATCH TV.
SHERMAN, I FOUND A WAY TO GET US UP OFF OUR LAZY REARS...
I SIGNED US UP FOR THE SHARKY ROBBINS MOTIVATIONAL CAMP.
IT'S 3 DAYS OF INTENSE, MOTIVATIONAL TRAINING. "IT'LL PUT THE 'ARK' BACK IN YOUR SHARK," ACCORDING TO THIS BROCHURE.
THAT DOESN'T EVEN MAKE SENSE.
NOT TO THE UNMOTIVATED MIND.
HERE WE ARE AT SHARKY ROBBINS' MOTIVATIONAL CAMP.
A BARGAIN AT $1,250.
I READ HIS BOOK, I BOUGHT HIS VIDEO... I EVEN HAVE A SHARKY ROBBINS SWEAT SUIT.
CAMP WAS THE ONLY LOGICAL NEXT STEP.
LOOK, SHERMAN!
HE JUST WALKED INTO THE ROOM...
IT'S NICE TO PUT A FACE TO THE CREDIT-CARD BILLS.

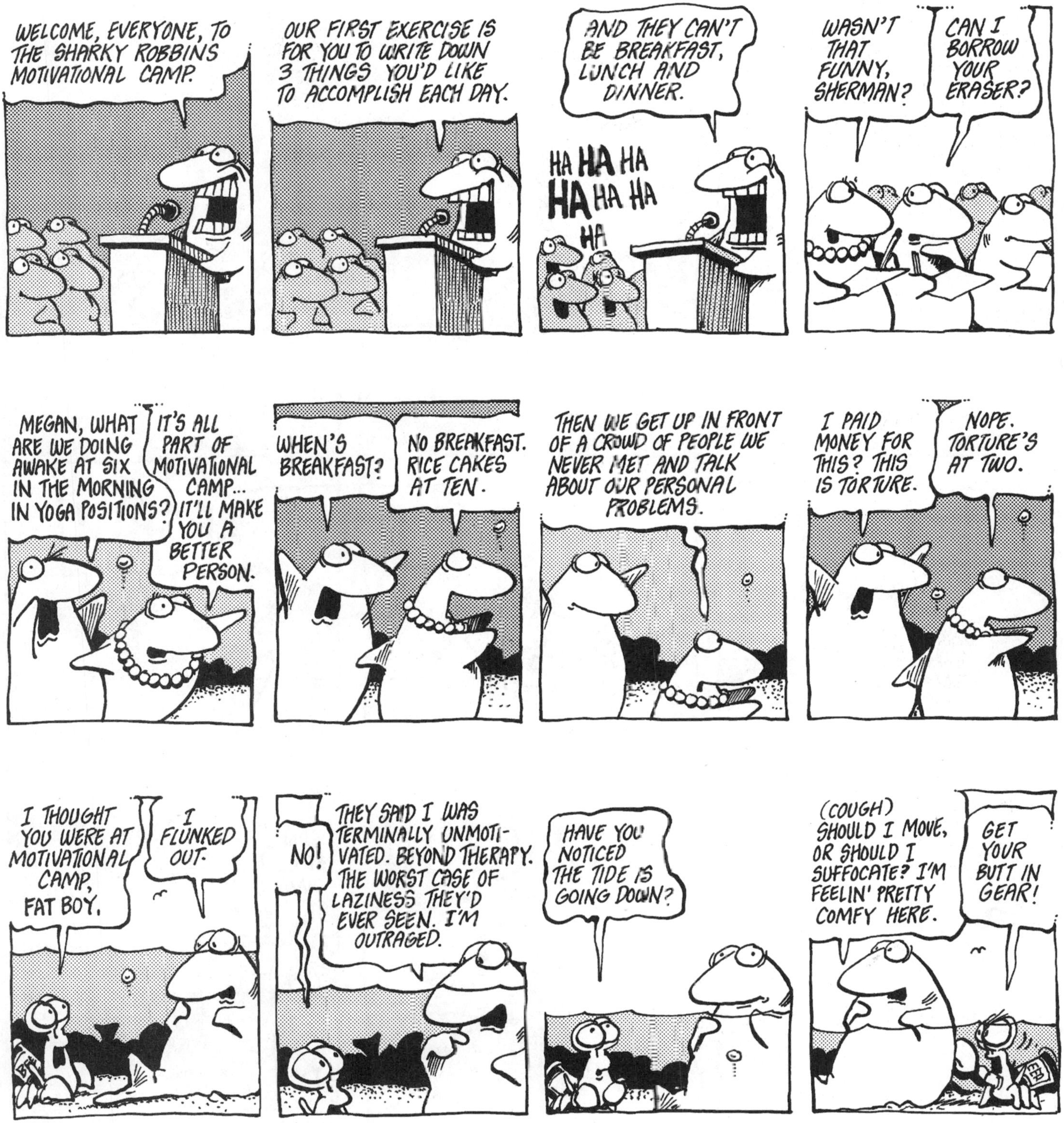

WELCOME, EVERYONE, TO THE SHARKY ROBBINS MOTIVATIONAL CAMP.
OUR FIRST EXERCISE IS FOR YOU TO WRITE DOWN 3 THINGS YOU'D LIKE TO ACCOMPLISH EACH DAY.
AND THEY CAN'T BE BREAKFAST, LUNCH AND DINNER.
HA HA HA HA HA HA HA
WASN'T THAT FUNNY, SHERMAN?
CAN I BORROW YOUR ERASER?
MEGAN, WHAT ARE WE DOING AWAKE AT SIX IN THE MORNING IN YOGA POSITIONS?
IT'S ALL PART OF MOTIVATIONAL CAMP... IT'LL MAKE YOU A BETTER PERSON.
WHEN'S BREAKFAST?
NO BREAKFAST. RICE CAKES AT TEN.
THEN WE GET UP IN FRONT OF A CROWD OF PEOPLE WE NEVER MET AND TALK ABOUT OUR PERSONAL PROBLEMS.
I PAID MONEY FOR THIS? THIS IS TORTURE.
NOPE. TORTURE'S AT TWO.
I THOUGHT YOU WERE AT MOTIVATIONAL CAMP, FAT BOY.
I FLUNKED OUT.
NO!
THEY SAID I WAS TERMINALLY UNMOTI-VATED. BEYOND THERAPY. THE WORST CASE OF LAZINESS THEY'D EVER SEEN. I'M OUTRAGED.
HAVE YOU NOTICED THE TIDE IS GOING DOWN?
(COUGH) SHOULD I MOVE, OR SHOULD I SUFFOCATE? I'M FEELIN' PRETTY COMFY HERE.
GET YOUR BUTT IN GEAR!

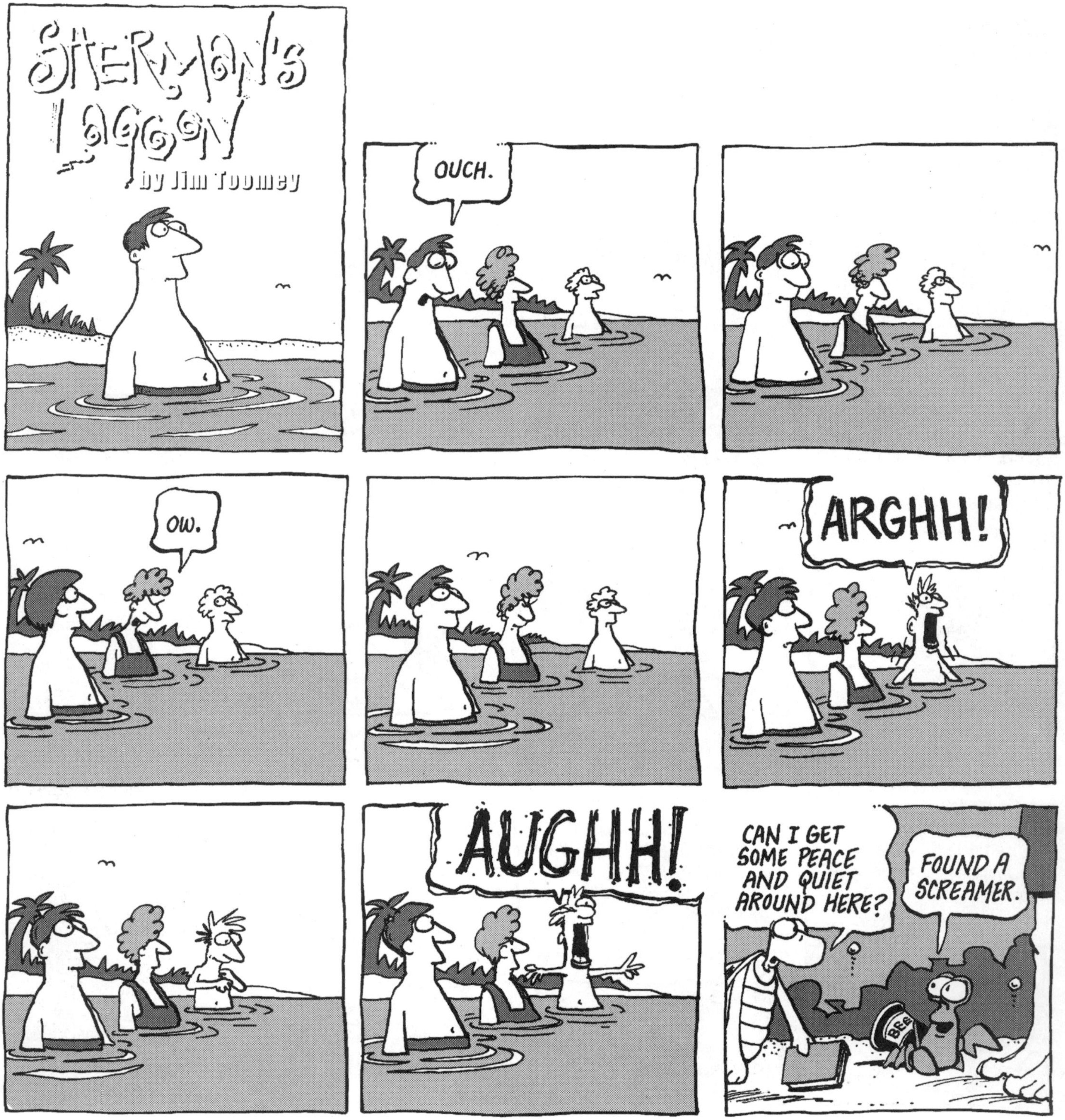
SHERMAN'S LAGOON
by Jim Toomey
OUCH.
OW.
ARGHH!
AUGHH!
CAN I GET SOME PEACE AND QUIET AROUND HERE?
FOUND A SCREAMER.
BEE

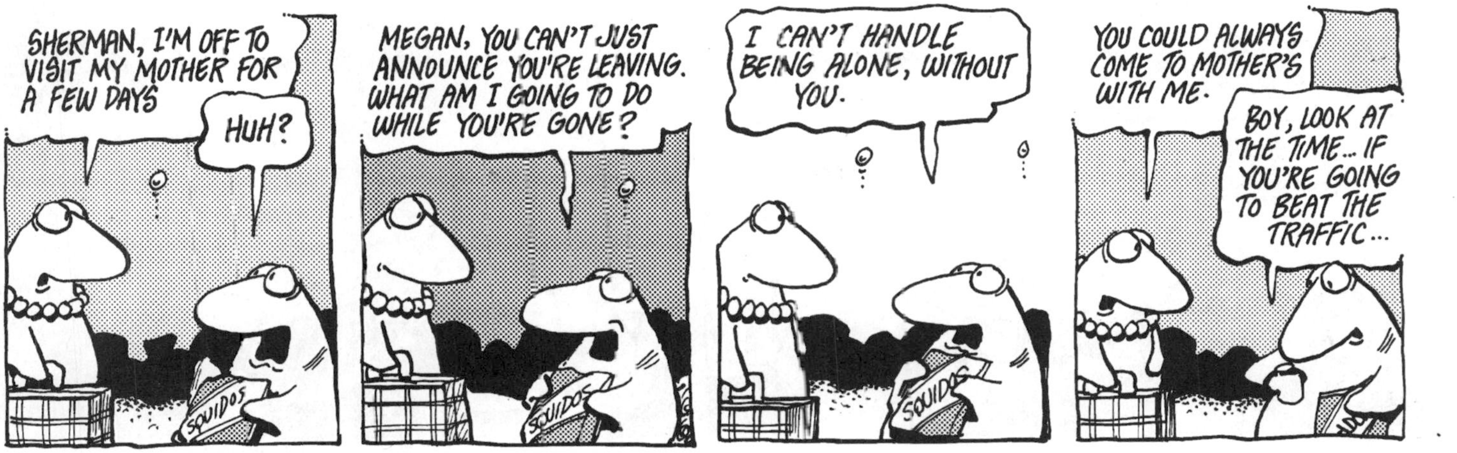
SHERMAN, I'M OFF TO VISIT MY MOTHER FOR A FEW DAYS
HUH?
MEGAN, YOU CAN'T JUST ANNOUNCE YOU'RE LEAVING. WHAT AM I GOING TO DO WHILE YOU'RE GONE?
SQUIDOS
I CAN'T HANDLE BEING ALONE, WITHOUT YOU.
YOU COULD ALWAYS COME TO MOTHER'S WITH ME.
BOY, LOOK AT THE TIME... IF YOU'RE GOING TO BEAT THE TRAFFIC...

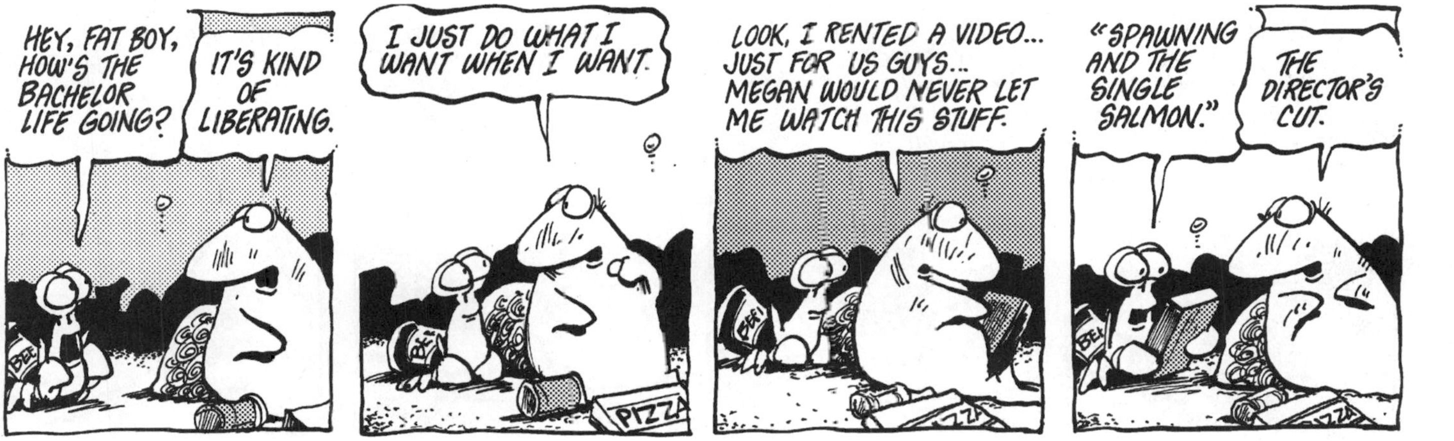
HEY, FAT BOY, HOW'S THE BACHELOR LIFE GOING?
IT'S KIND OF LIBERATING.
I JUST DO WHAT I WANT WHEN I WANT.
PIZZA
LOOK, I RENTED A VIDEO... JUST FOR US GUYS... MEGAN WOULD NEVER LET ME WATCH THIS STUFF.
"SPAWNING AND THE SINGLE SALMON."
THE DIRECTOR'S CUT.

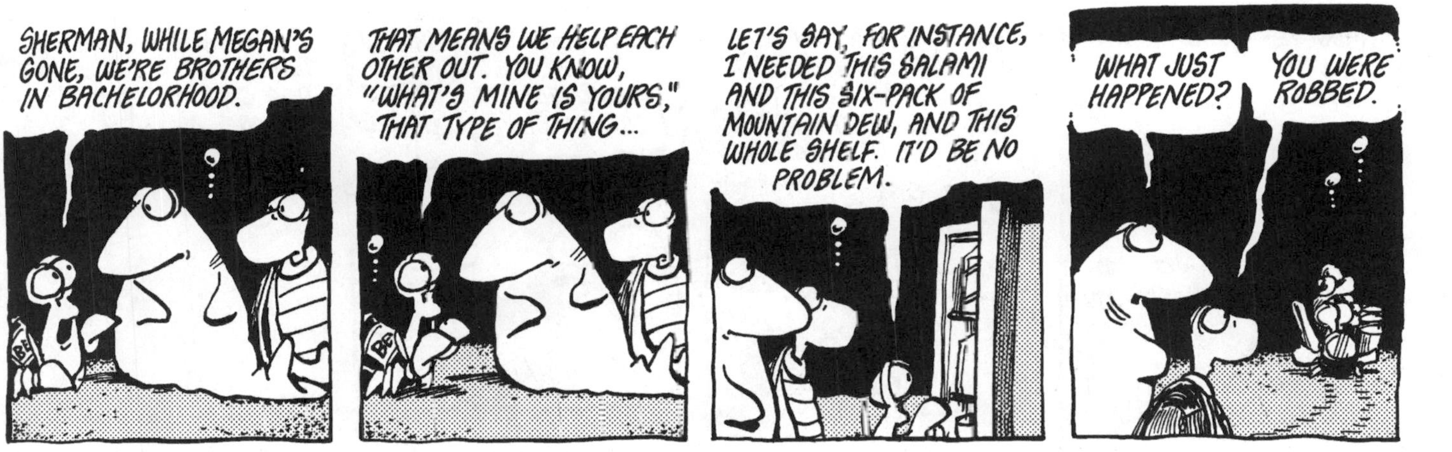
SHERMAN, WHILE MEGAN'S GONE, WE'RE BROTHERS IN BACHELORHOOD.
THAT MEANS WE HELP EACH OTHER OUT. YOU KNOW, "WHAT'S MINE IS YOURS," THAT TYPE OF THING...
LET'S SAY, FOR INSTANCE, I NEEDED THIS SALAMI AND THIS SIX-PACK OF MOUNTAIN DEW, AND THIS WHOLE SHELF. IT'D BE NO PROBLEM.
WHAT JUST HAPPENED?
YOU WERE ROBBED.

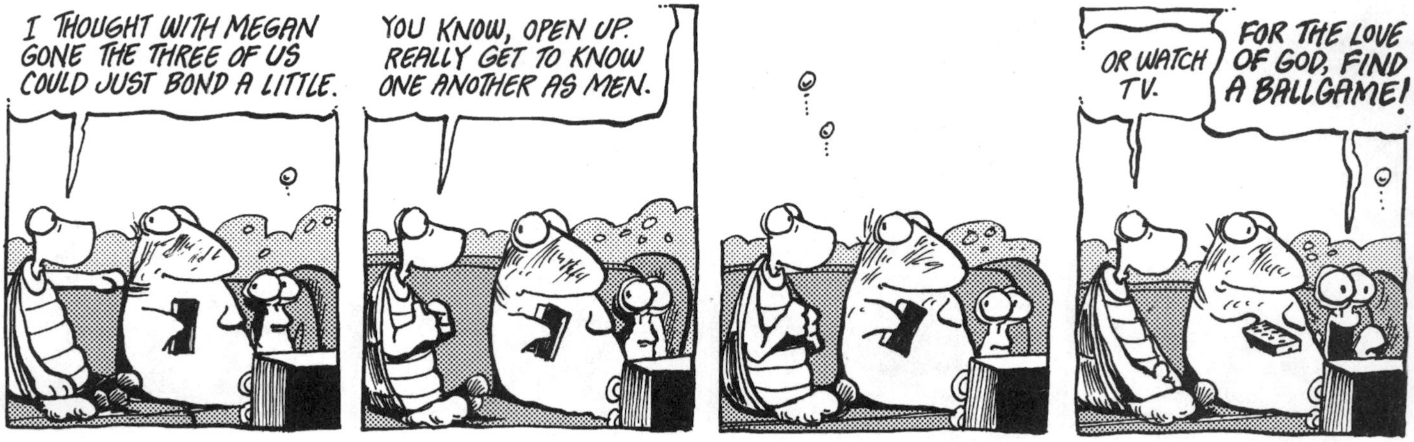
I THOUGHT WITH MEGAN GONE THE THREE OF US COULD JUST BOND A LITTLE.
YOU KNOW, OPEN UP. REALLY GET TO KNOW ONE ANOTHER AS MEN.
OR WATCH TV.
FOR THE LOVE OF GOD, FIND A BALLGAME!

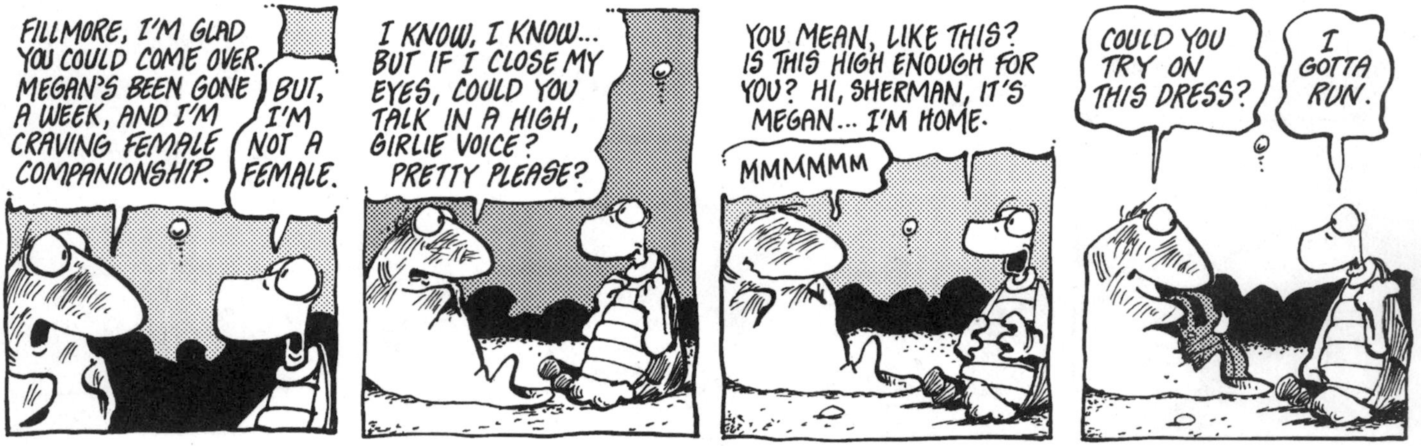
FILLMORE, I'M GLAD YOU COULD COME OVER. MEGAN'S BEEN GONE A WEEK, AND I'M CRAVING FEMALE COMPANIONSHIP.
BUT, I'M NOT A FEMALE.
I KNOW, I KNOW... BUT IF I CLOSE MY EYES, COULD YOU TALK IN A HIGH, GIRLIE VOICE? PRETTY PLEASE?
MMMMMM
YOU MEAN, LIKE THIS? IS THIS HIGH ENOUGH FOR YOU? HI, SHERMAN, IT'S MEGAN... I'M HOME.
COULD YOU TRY ON THIS DRESS?
I GOTTA RUN.

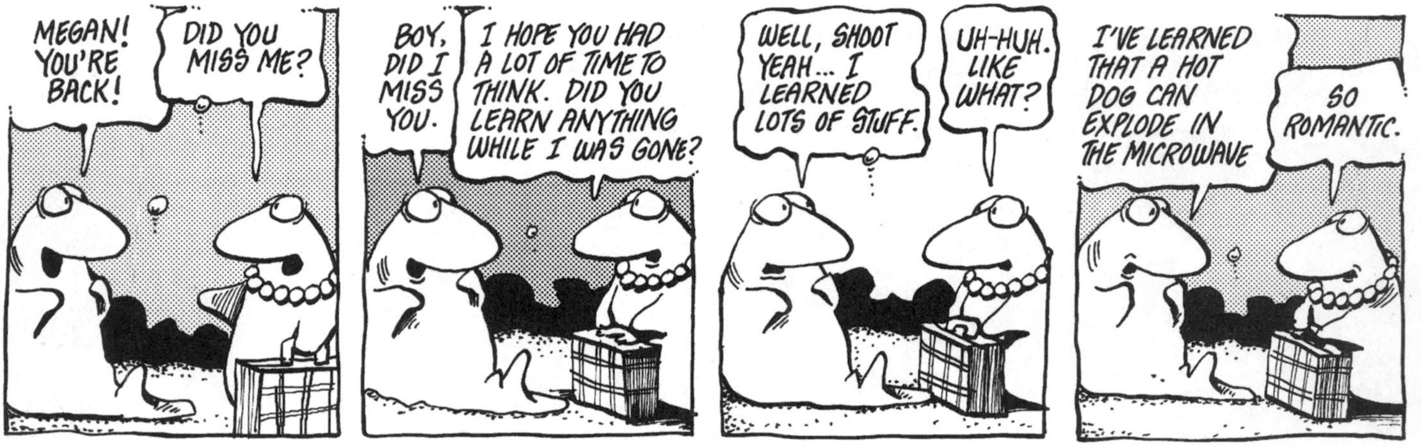
MEGAN! YOU'RE BACK!
DID YOU MISS ME?
BOY, DID I MISS YOU.
I HOPE YOU HAD A LOT OF TIME TO THINK. DID YOU LEARN ANYTHING WHILE I WAS GONE?
WELL, SHOOT YEAH... I LEARNED LOTS OF STUFF.
UH-HUH. LIKE WHAT?
I'VE LEARNED THAT A HOT DOG CAN EXPLODE IN THE MICROWAVE
SO ROMANTIC.

**SHERMAN'S LAGOON**
by Jim Toomey

LOOK AT THOSE TWO ON VACATION HAVING FUN, SHERMAN.

NOW THEY'RE HOLDING HANDS. ISN'T THAT SWEET?

WHY CAN'T WE BE LIKE THAT?

YOU'RE ALWAYS OFF IN YOUR PART OF THE LAGOON AND I'M ALWAYS SOMEWHERE ELSE...

WHY DON'T WE DO SOMETHING TOGETHER FOR A CHANGE?

I'LL TAKE THE ONE ON THE RIGHT.

LET'S HOLD HANDS.

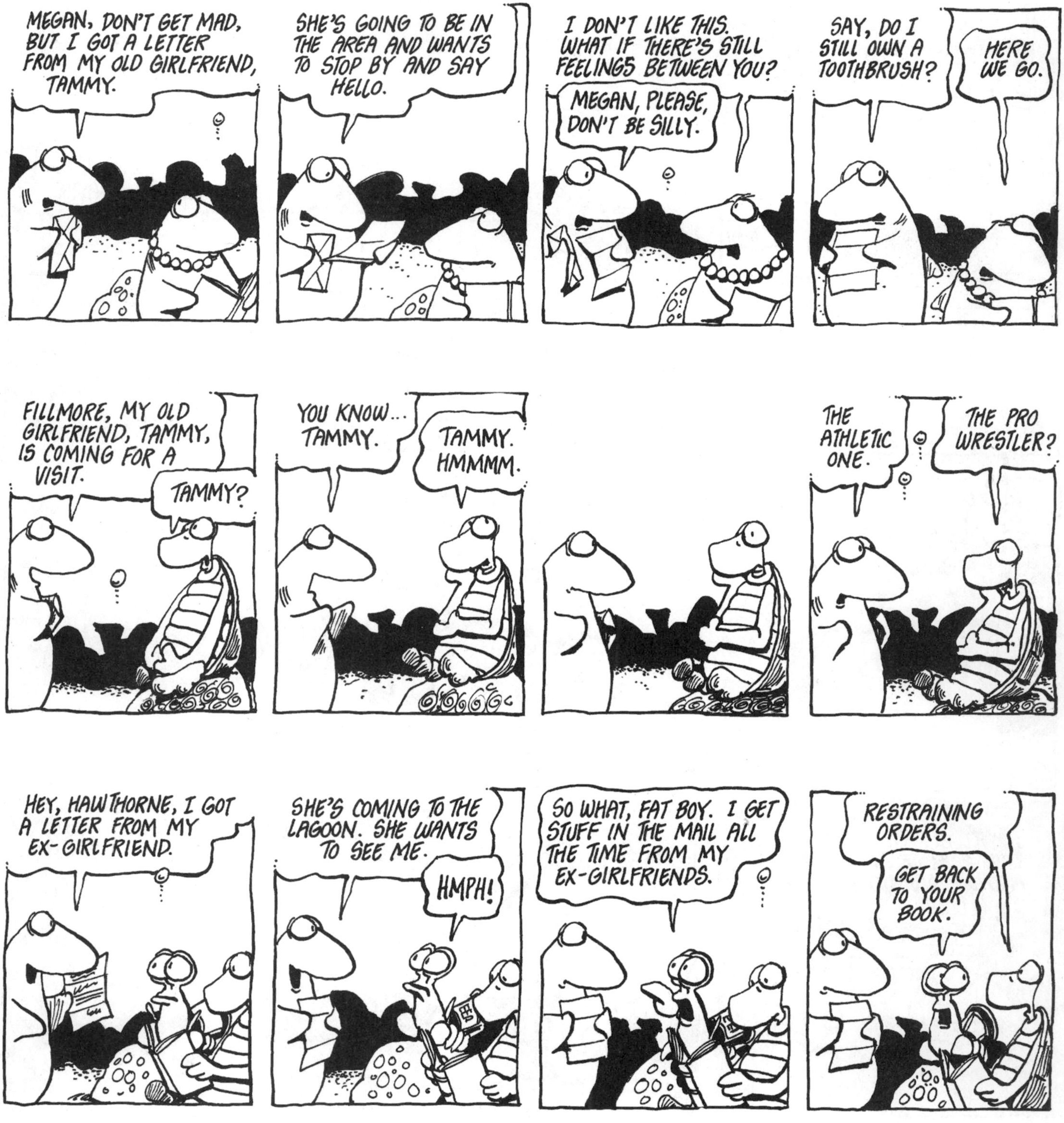
MEGAN, DON'T GET MAD, BUT I GOT A LETTER FROM MY OLD GIRLFRIEND, TAMMY.
SHE'S GOING TO BE IN THE AREA AND WANTS TO STOP BY AND SAY HELLO.
I DON'T LIKE THIS. WHAT IF THERE'S STILL FEELINGS BETWEEN YOU?
MEGAN, PLEASE, DON'T BE SILLY.
SAY, DO I STILL OWN A TOOTHBRUSH?
HERE WE GO.
FILLMORE, MY OLD GIRLFRIEND, TAMMY, IS COMING FOR A VISIT.
TAMMY?
YOU KNOW... TAMMY.
TAMMY. HMMMM.
THE ATHLETIC ONE.
THE PRO WRESTLER?
HEY, HAWTHORNE, I GOT A LETTER FROM MY EX-GIRLFRIEND.
SHE'S COMING TO THE LAGOON. SHE WANTS TO SEE ME.
HMPH!
SO WHAT, FAT BOY. I GET STUFF IN THE MAIL ALL THE TIME FROM MY EX-GIRLFRIENDS.
RESTRAINING ORDERS.
GET BACK TO YOUR BOOK.

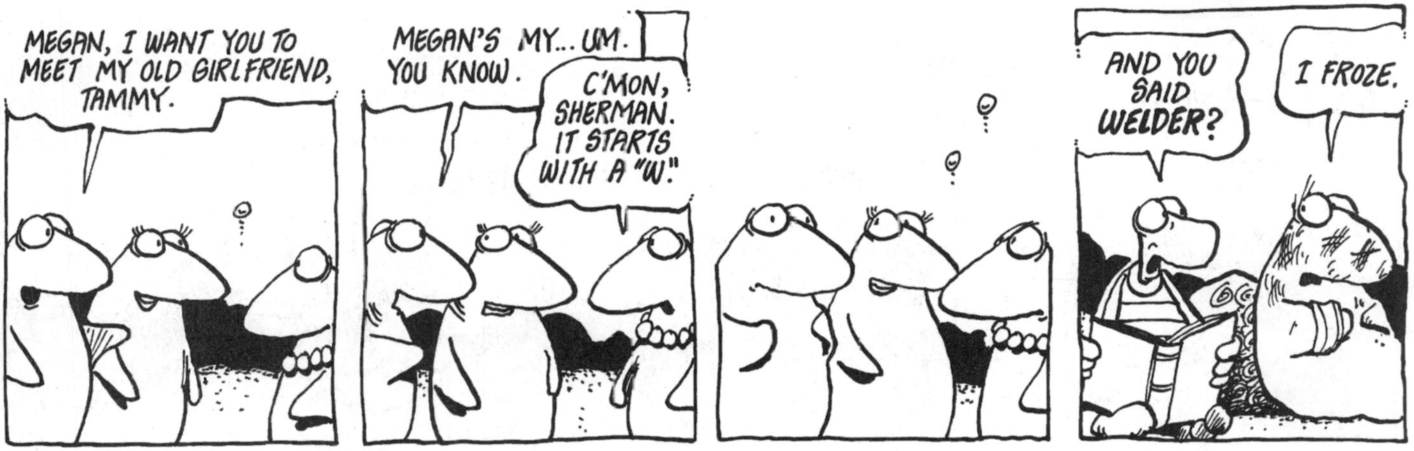
MEGAN, I WANT YOU TO MEET MY OLD GIRLFRIEND, TAMMY.
MEGAN'S MY... UM. YOU KNOW.
C'MON, SHERMAN. IT STARTS WITH A "W."
AND YOU SAID WELDER?
I FROZE.

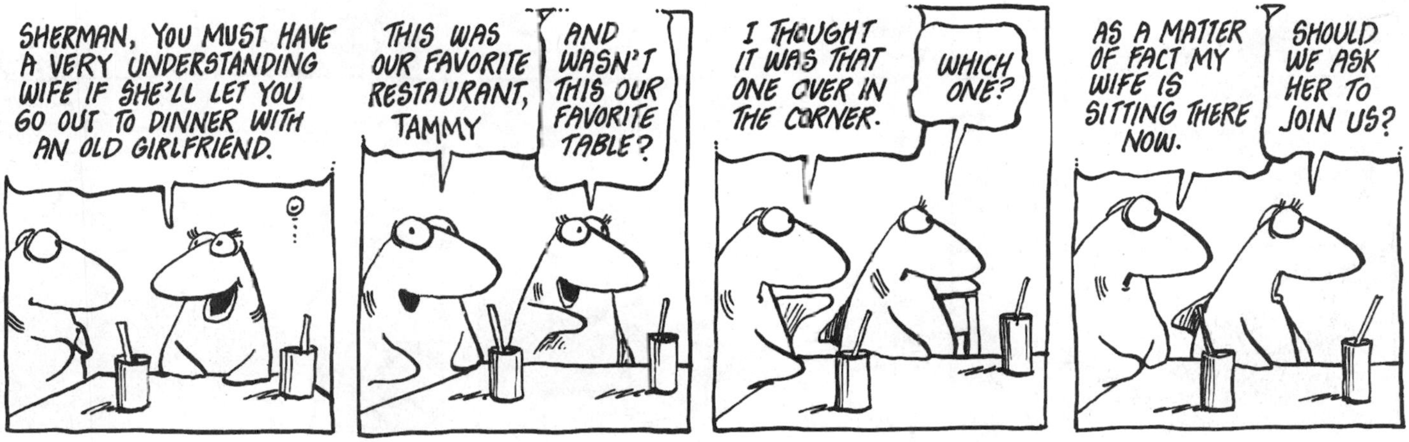
SHERMAN, YOU MUST HAVE A VERY UNDERSTANDING WIFE IF SHE'LL LET YOU GO OUT TO DINNER WITH AN OLD GIRLFRIEND.
THIS WAS OUR FAVORITE RESTAURANT, TAMMY
AND WASN'T THIS OUR FAVORITE TABLE?
I THOUGHT IT WAS THAT ONE OVER IN THE CORNER.
WHICH ONE?
AS A MATTER OF FACT MY WIFE IS SITTING THERE NOW.
SHOULD WE ASK HER TO JOIN US?

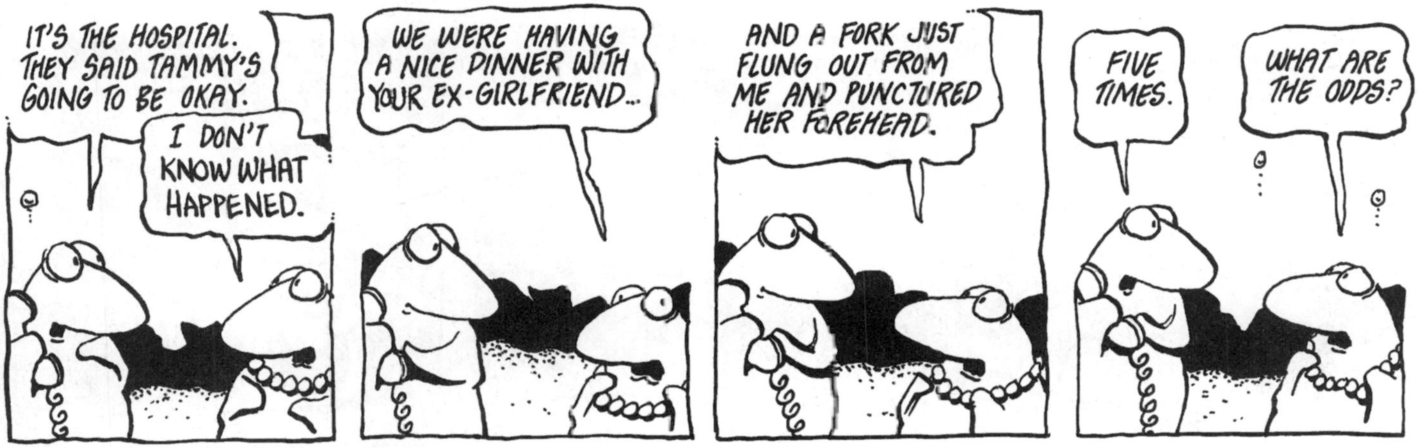
IT'S THE HOSPITAL. THEY SAID TAMMY'S GOING TO BE OKAY.
I DON'T KNOW WHAT HAPPENED.
WE WERE HAVING A NICE DINNER WITH YOUR EX-GIRLFRIEND...
AND A FORK JUST FLUNG OUT FROM ME AND PUNCTURED HER FOREHEAD.
FIVE TIMES.
WHAT ARE THE ODDS?

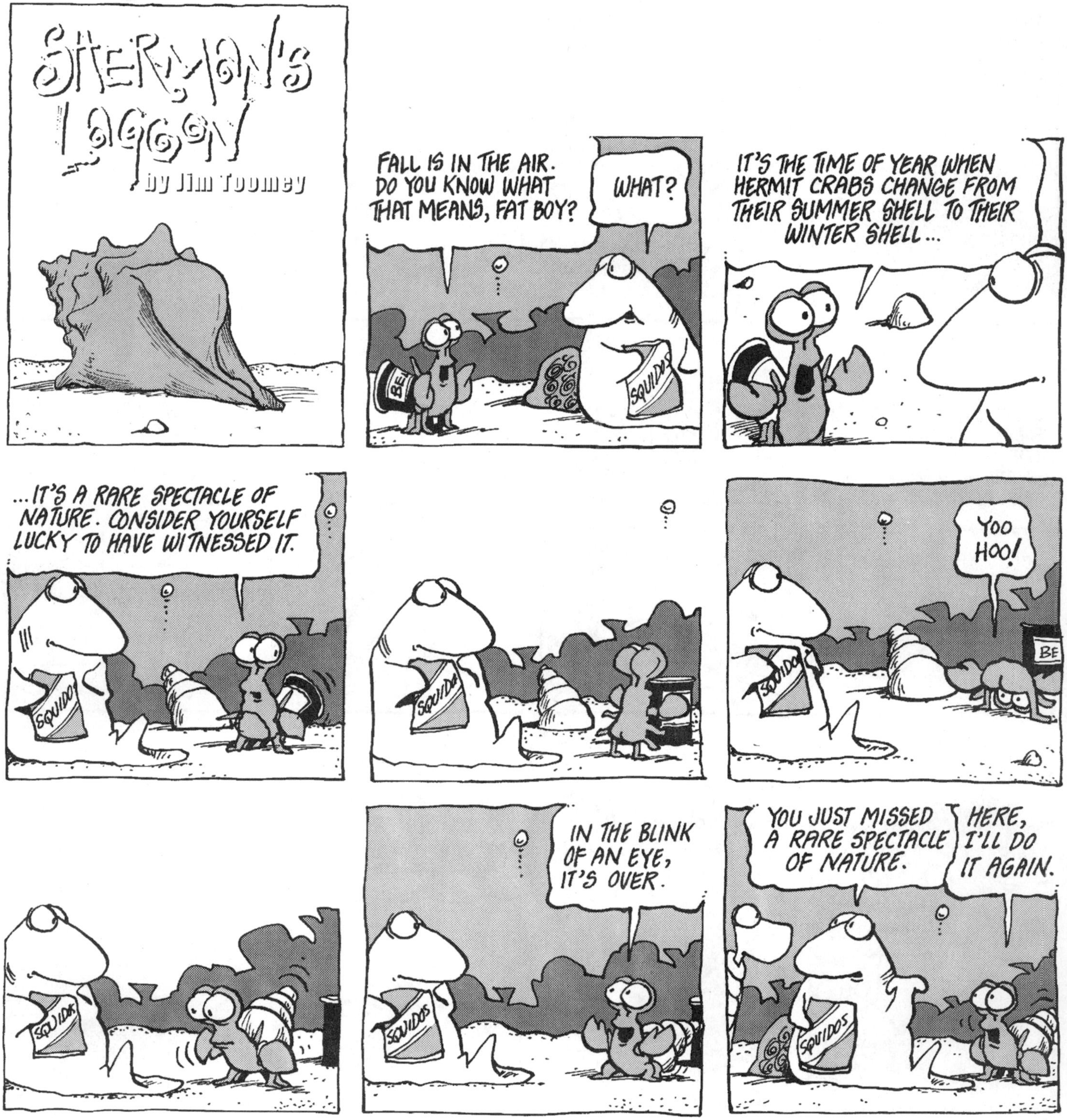
SHERMAN'S LAGOON
by Jim Toomey
FALL IS IN THE AIR. DO YOU KNOW WHAT THAT MEANS, FAT BOY?
WHAT?
IT'S THE TIME OF YEAR WHEN HERMIT CRABS CHANGE FROM THEIR SUMMER SHELL TO THEIR WINTER SHELL...
...IT'S A RARE SPECTACLE OF NATURE. CONSIDER YOURSELF LUCKY TO HAVE WITNESSED IT.
SQUIDOS
YOO HOO!
BE
IN THE BLINK OF AN EYE, IT'S OVER.
YOU JUST MISSED A RARE SPECTACLE OF NATURE.
HERE, I'LL DO IT AGAIN.

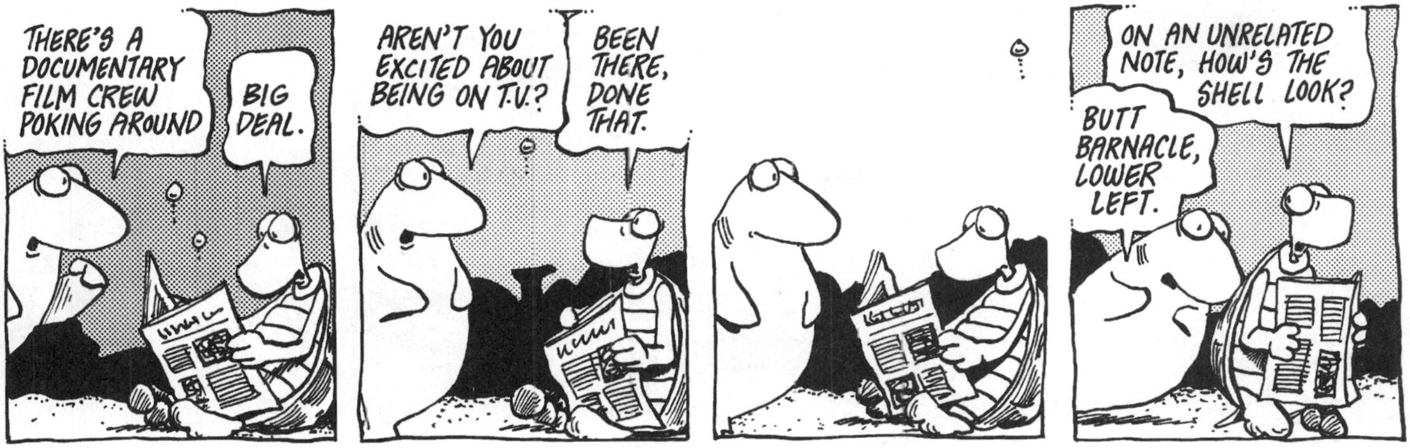
THERE'S A DOCUMENTARY FILM CREW POKING AROUND
BIG DEAL.
AREN'T YOU EXCITED ABOUT BEING ON T.V.?
BEEN THERE, DONE THAT.
ON AN UNRELATED NOTE, HOW'S THE SHELL LOOK?
BUTT BARNACLE, LOWER LEFT.

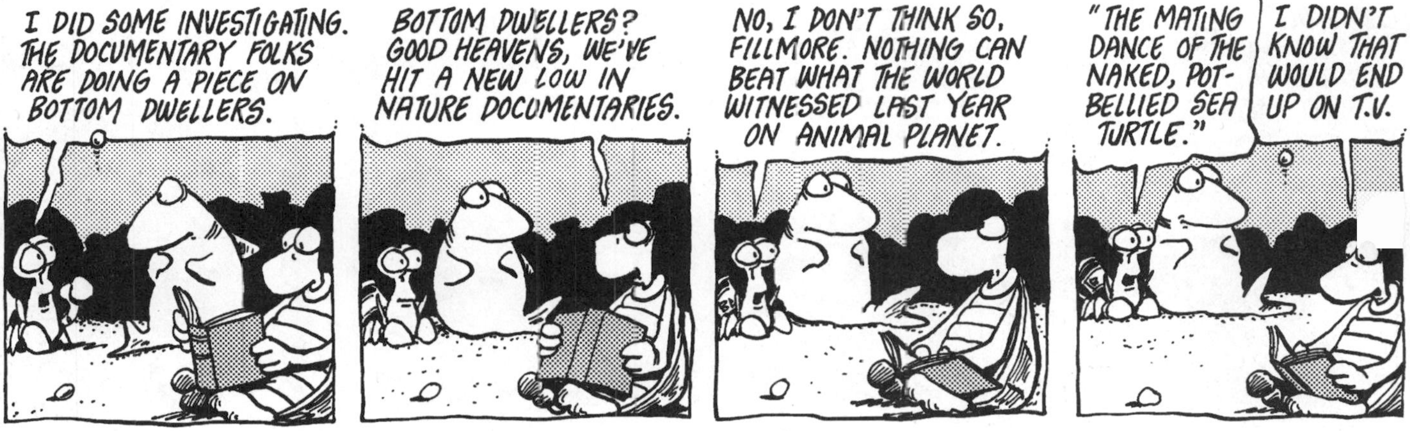
I DID SOME INVESTIGATING. THE DOCUMENTARY FOLKS ARE DOING A PIECE ON BOTTOM DWELLERS.
BOTTOM DWELLERS? GOOD HEAVENS, WE'VE HIT A NEW LOW IN NATURE DOCUMENTARIES.
NO, I DON'T THINK SO, FILLMORE. NOTHING CAN BEAT WHAT THE WORLD WITNESSED LAST YEAR ON ANIMAL PLANET.
"THE MATING DANCE OF THE NAKED, POT-BELLIED SEA TURTLE."
I DIDN'T KNOW THAT WOULD END UP ON T.V.

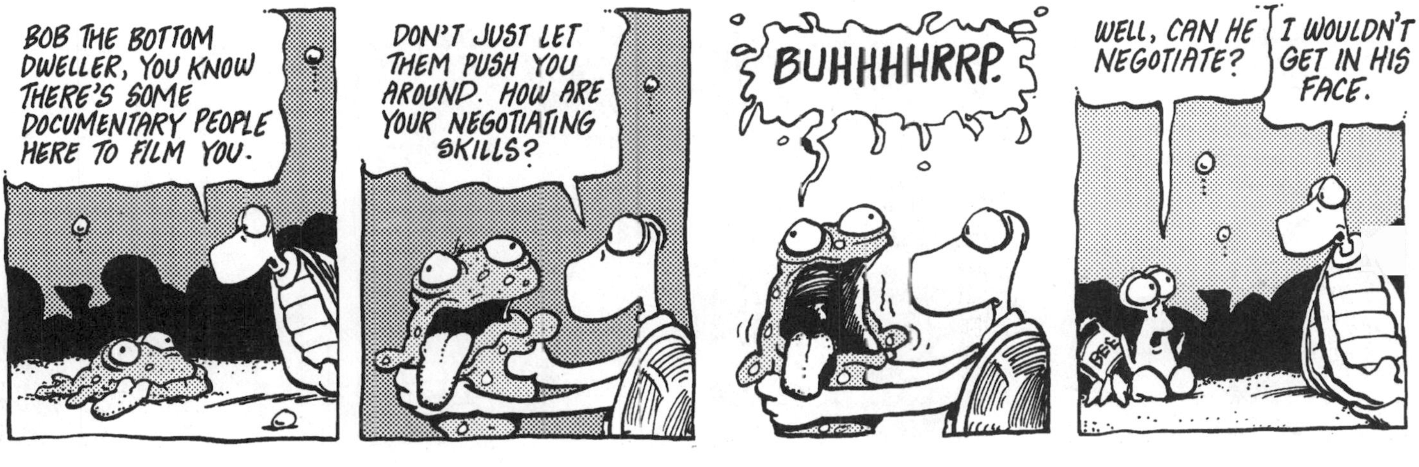
BOB THE BOTTOM DWELLER, YOU KNOW THERE'S SOME DOCUMENTARY PEOPLE HERE TO FILM YOU.
DON'T JUST LET THEM PUSH YOU AROUND. HOW ARE YOUR NEGOTIATING SKILLS?
BUHHHHRRP.
WELL, CAN HE NEGOTIATE?
I WOULDN'T GET IN HIS FACE.

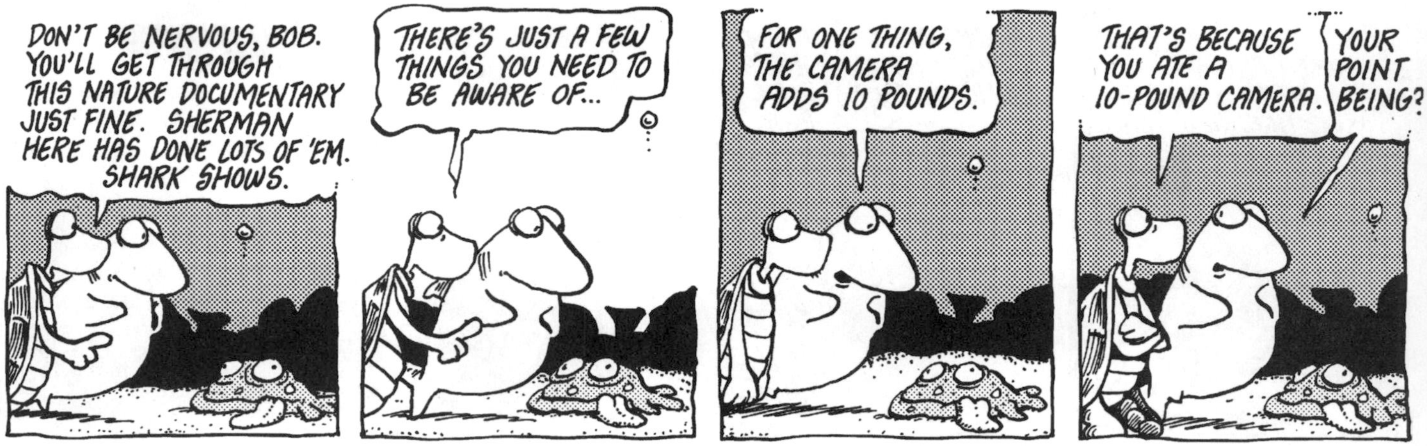
DON'T BE NERVOUS, BOB. YOU'LL GET THROUGH THIS NATURE DOCUMENTARY JUST FINE. SHERMAN HERE HAS DONE LOTS OF 'EM. SHARK SHOWS.
THERE'S JUST A FEW THINGS YOU NEED TO BE AWARE OF...
FOR ONE THING, THE CAMERA ADDS 10 POUNDS.
THAT'S BECAUSE YOU ATE A 10-POUND CAMERA.
YOUR POINT BEING?

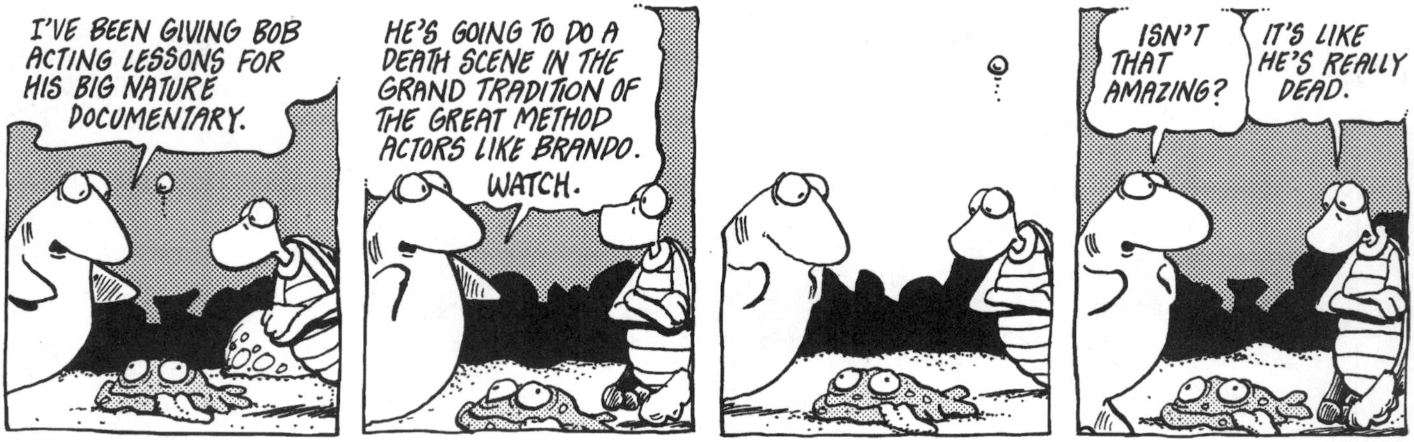
I'VE BEEN GIVING BOB ACTING LESSONS FOR HIS BIG NATURE DOCUMENTARY.
HE'S GOING TO DO A DEATH SCENE IN THE GRAND TRADITION OF THE GREAT METHOD ACTORS LIKE BRANDO.
WATCH.
ISN'T THAT AMAZING?
IT'S LIKE HE'S REALLY DEAD.

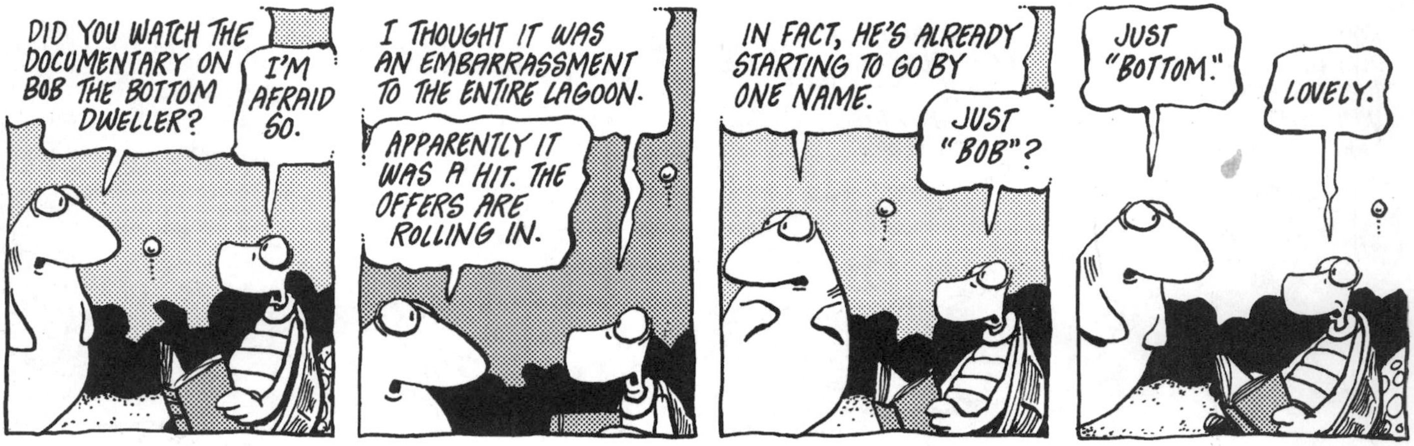
DID YOU WATCH THE DOCUMENTARY ON BOB THE BOTTOM DWELLER?
I'M AFRAID SO.
I THOUGHT IT WAS AN EMBARRASSMENT TO THE ENTIRE LAGOON.
APPARENTLY IT WAS A HIT. THE OFFERS ARE ROLLING IN.
IN FACT, HE'S ALREADY STARTING TO GO BY ONE NAME.
JUST "BOB"?
JUST "BOTTOM."
LOVELY.